9/3/08

To Helmut & Rose,

Wishing you   the

future.

Hope you will come back for an odd

game of Bridge, Helmut.

Kindest regards

John (Donnella

Lough Ree
And
Its Islands

By

Sean Cahill, Gearoid O'Brien
& Jimmy Casey

Three Counties Press
Athlone

This publication has received support from the Heritage Council
under the 2006 Publications Grant Scheme.

We also wish to acknowledge the generous support
of the following:

Longford
County Council

Roscommon
County Council

Westmeath
County Council

ISBN: 0 9554120 0 5
First published 2006
Reprinted 2007

Published by:
Three Counties Press
13 Beech Park
Athlone, Co Westmeath

Printed by:
Temple Printing Co. Ltd, Athlone.

Contents

Part II: The Islands

List of Illustrations

INTRODUCTION

Lough Ree is a storied lake. These stories come to us from all ages. From the realm of mythology we have lore about Queen Maeve and her sister Clothra. When the great antiquarian John O'Donovan visited the area during his research for the Ordnance Survey in the 1830s he was amazed to find a local who could point out the exact spot Maeve's assassin was standing on when he fired his fatal slingshot from the mainland. His informant could also identify the spot on the island where the unsuspecting victim was as she took her daily bath. That the distances between both places was greater than the trajectory of any slingshot was irrelevant – here we had history and mythology mingling together to give the perfect story.

In early Christian times the islands of Lough Ree were inhabited by saints and scholars seeking peace and quiet. All too often this peace was spoiled by marauding hoards of thieves and vandals. Quite often these were Irish but occasionally they were Vikings or Normans who came to take the spoils of the monasteries.

In more modern times, in the seventeenth century, the islands came into their own again when families dispossessed of their lands in the counties bordering the lake sought refuge on them. Here thriving communities lived in harmony as they eked out a living through farming and fishing. In the nineteenth century some of these islanders found their space invaded as the idle rich saw the possibilities offered by island hideaways. The native Irish had then to get used to sharing their space with the landlords and were not surprised on occasions when the bailiffs arrived to carry out evictions.

Census reports for 1901 and 1911 show still thriving island communities – the islanders of Inchmore and its neighbouring islands were so self-sufficient that for many years they had their own National School. During the War of Independence the islands were once again a place of refuge – this time for Irishmen on the run. Today the islanders have all but abandoned their island homes, some still farm the islands from a base on the mainland and others continue to fish but apart from occasional summer visitors the islands are largely uninhabited.

In this book, the first new book in fifty years to deal with Lough Ree and its islands, we have tried to bring together as much knowledge as possible and to record the social history of the many saints and sinners who have lived on the islands of Lough Ree or in the areas surrounding Lough Ree from time immemorial. The more we learned and wrote about these people the more we marvelled at them. We have not tried to produce a guide-book to Lough Ree – that has been more than adequately provided for by the *Shell Guide to the Shannon;* and we certainly haven't tried to depose Harry Rice's book *Thanks for the memory* which has been a firm favourite for over fifty years. Long may these books continue to take pride of place on bookshelves – if ours is deemed worthy to join them in the libraries of Shannon lovers then we would feel truly justified in our endeavours.

We are extremely grateful to the Heritage Council for a generous grant towards the publication of this book – this grant has helped in no small measure to make this book a quality publication allowing us to include a great many more illustrations and to subsidise the cost of production.

Lough Ree is bordered by three counties – Longford, Westmeath and Roscommon – the County Councils of all three counties have made very significant contributions to the development of the lake's natural amenities – they have also contributed handsomely to the production costs of this book and for all of this we are most grateful.

In undertaking this book we had to keep reminding ourselves that 'fools rush in where angels fear to tread'. The writing of it has been a labour of love for all of us, cementing the bonds of friendship and learning from each other and has been a hugely rewarding experience. When we started out we visualised a book of some 200 pages but as we progressed we realised that we could write several volumes without ever exhausting the great richness of the subject matter. Hopefully our enthusiasm for Lough Ree will be obvious to the reader. In presenting this book to you, our reader, we do not claim that it is either exhaustive or definitive – we just hope that it helps to record for future generations some of the wonderful history and lore of this truly remarkable lake.

Sean Cahill
Gearoid O'Brien
Jimmy Casey

October 2006.

ACKNOWLEDGEMENTS

In undertaking the research and writing of a book such as this authors invariably have to confer with various authorities on aspects of their work. All three of us have, at different times, depended on family, friends and acquaintances for support, knowledge and inspiration and for that which we have received we are, indeed, all most grateful.

We have carried out our research in various institutions and we are extremely grateful to the following: Mary Reynolds and staff Longford County Library; Richie Farrell and staff Roscommon County Library; Mary Farrell and staff Westmeath County Library, the staff of the Aidan Heavey Library, Athlone; the Director and staff of the National Archives of Ireland; the Director and staff of the National Library of Ireland; the Director and staff of the National Museum of Ireland; the Librarian and staff of the Royal Irish Academy and the Director and staff of the Irish Architectural Archives – in all of these valued institutions we have been met with warmth, efficiency and great co-operation.

In trying to put together a useful body of illustrative material to complement the text the following have rendered invaluable assistance: Aidan Heavey, Dublin for permission to reproduce illustrations from some of the many fine gems in his collection; to the Irish Architectural Archives and Lord Rossmore for permission to reproduce illustrations by Daniel Grose; to photographers Ann Hennessy who made her files of Lough Ree material available to us; Pat Halton, Garnafailagh who provided us with some wonderful pictures for the flora and fauna chapter from his own invaluable photographic archive; Michael Farrell who read and corrected the manuscript; Angela Hanley who helped to proof read the final text and in the process spared us considerable embarrassment; P.J. Murray who accompanied one of the authors on an island odyssey on Lough Ree in the 1980s and Catriona Casey for her evocative cover photograph which helps to convey something of the rugged strength and tranquillity of Lough Ree. We also wish to thank two artists for permission to reproduce their work: Lorraine Francis for her drawing of Rindoon Castle and Kevin McNamara who produced three drawings (to our specifications) at short notice. We also wish to thank Eddie Geraghty and staff, National Monuments Division,

Athenry, for allowing access to the island monuments.

Over the years so many individuals have helped us in one way or another, these include:

P. Brennan; Vincent Brennan; Rosarii Beirne; Aidan Carley; Michael Casey; Finian Corley; Tony Claffey; Joan & P.J. Donnellan; Mrs Bridie Donoghue and her daughter Ann; Bill Dooley; Noel Duffy; Maureen Egan; Owen Egan; Sean Fitzsimons; Jimmy Furey; Brian Ganly; Declan Gilmore; John Gilmore; Kathleen Glennon; Paddy Hanly; Angela Hanley; Johnny Harte; Lt. Cdr. Charles Lawn; Pat Hopkins; Sean Kelly; Kate Quigley; Fr Seamus Mulvany; Tommy Murray; Harman Murtagh; Ann Naughton; Brigid Rollins; Kate Shanley; Sid Shine; Albert Siggins; Kerry Sloan; James Skelly and Josie Warde. To these, and indeed to all who helped in any way a thousand thanks.

Having expressed our thanks to so many people and institutions we are aware that the buck stops here. We have tried to bring together as much of the history and lore of the lake as we could but for any errors in facts, or omissions which may have occurred, we alone are responsible and we will endeavour to remedy these in any subsequent edition.

Sean Cahill, Gearoid O'Brien & Jimmy Casey.

Loch Rí

Ar chiumhais Locha Rí
Ar spaisteoireacht Fómhair
Do ligeas lem smaointe
Ag lapadaíl leo.

M. F. Ó Conchúir

Faoi ghaetha na gréine
Ba léir dom trí cheo
Inis Cloithrín na séipéal
Mar bhí sí fadó.

Síorurnaí ag éalú
Ó mhanaigh nár bheo
Mar thonnta ag géimnigh
Ar chladach na Sló.

Uainín lem thaobhsa
Dhein méileach mhaith mhór;
D'altóraíos im smaointe é
I bPort Runn' in ómós.

Na ndíthreabhach a thuill leoithne
Leanúnach is cóir
Dá dturas chun na bhFlaitheas
Ó oileán seo na ndeor.

Na healaí go maorga
Ag seoladh le bród;
Mo smaointe ina scuaine
Im bhreith leo go seoigh.

An loch ina léinseach
Luite chun suain.
Oileainín geal Mhéabha
Mar chloch i mbéal cuain.

Mar chloch ar mo phaidrín
Go dté liom in úir
Ceartchreideamh an dísirt
Mar fhocal sa Chúirt.

CHAPTER 1

Beginnings

As the last Ice Age began to recede some ten thousand years ago and the glacier inched its way slowly southwards, the configuration of the Central Plain of Ireland gradually took shape. The dominant feature emerging on the flat landscape was the River Shannon, with its abundant lakes and tributaries. Situated near the half way point on the river's course and close to the geographical centre of the island is Lough Ree, surrounded by the glacial drift – the earth and stone deposits left behind by the retreating ice. The same deposits inhibited drainage across the low-lying plains, giving rise to the vast tracts of bogland that spread across the midlands.

The great river, some three hundred and sixty five kilometres in length, originates in the Shannon Pot, Log na Sionna, in the Cuilcagh mountains in Co. Cavan and flows southwards from Lough Allen, skirting the drumlins of Co. Leitrim and the eskers of Co. Roscommon. Near Rooskey, the Shannon makes contact with the extensive raised bogland plain, which adjoins it as it passes Tarmonbarry, and meanders along on its way to Lough Ree.

Gateway to the great lake is the arched bridge that joins the villages of Lanesborough and Ballyleague. Historic meeting point of east and west, this ancient crossing saw many attempts at primitive bridges in earlier centuries, before parliament erected a permanent stone structure in 1706, aided by a contribution of £100 from James Lane, Lord of Lanesborough.

South of the bridge, a picturesque lagoon, with a curvilinear shoreline some one thousand metres in width, offers a gentle introduction to the wider lake. Where the river bed silted up as it left the lagoon, the Shannon Navigation Works, in 1846, re-directed it straight through the low-lying Curreen promontory, creating the piece of water known ever since as the Cut.

Lough Ree, because of its situation in the central plain, has no mountain as such within sixty kilometres. Slieve Bawn to the northwest, with an elevation of some two hundred and ninety metres, dominates the flat landscape. By the lake shore the terrain is low lying, sloping down to marsh and callow, occasionally showing rocks and patches of gravel with some good strips of arable land interspersed. In bays and sheltered areas, where mud deposits had accumulated, extensive dark green reed beds give an added dimension to the scenery. The highest point on the western shore is at St John's, near Lecarrow, where the hill of Knockskehaun overlooks Rindoon from a height of some fifty metres, while the hills from Knockcroghery to Rahara rise inland to one hundred and fifty metres. On the eastern side of the lake there are some elevations along the shorelines of Rathcline and Cashel and inland in Kilkenny West, with small hills at Killinure and Ballykeeran.

Inner Lakes

Lough Ree lies north-south from the point where the river enters it at Lanesborough to the White Buoy on its southern shore, reaching to within three kilometres of the town of Athlone. Its maximum length is twenty eight kilometres while its maximum width, from the mouth of the river Inny to Carrownure Bay, is eleven kilometres. The average width of the upper section is three kilometres while that of the lower or southern section is six kilometres. As regards depth the variation follows a somewhat similar pattern with the northern portion rarely exceeding six metres, while the southern expanse reaches depths of thirty five metres in parts.

Close to Athlone, the lake branches to the east into what has become known as the Inner Lakes, namely, Killinure Lough, Coosan Lough and Ballykeeran Lough where Friars' Island lies in seclusion well away from the main waterway.

The Inny is by far the largest tributary river, starting out from the most southerly point of Co. Cavan and reaching Lough Ree a few miles to the south of Ballymahon. It is joined by the Tang River a short distance before entering the lake. To the south, the Doonis and Tonagh streams drain the Creggan Lough while further south the Breensford River flows into Ballykeeran Bay. On the western shore the Clooneigh River rises in the foothills of Slieve Bawn making its way into the lake to the west of Inchenagh. Further south, the Hind River drains the lowlands east of Roscommon town, before it enters the lake at Rinnany.

The absence of rivers of any considerable extent, excepting the Inny, is due to the carboniferous limestone which is the bedrock of all this area. The porous nature of the rock allows the water to seep through, and facilitates underground rivers that channel it into the lake below the surface. The same rock has given rise to several quarries by the lake, the most noteworthy being at Cashel in Co. Longford, Lecarrow in Co. Roscommon and Killinure in Co. Westmeath. The Lecarrow canal was made in 1842 for the purpose of transporting the local rock for the construction of the bridge and lock at Athlone.

The rock also gives name to several places around the lake from the flagstones of Ballyleague and Portlick to Lacken, Creggan and many more. Other placenames on these shores remind us of the great woods of former days that provided a substantial backdrop to the shimmering beauty of the lake. Names such as Portanure, Youghal and Killinure on the east and Carrownure and Yew Point on the west reflect the great forests of yew that once flourished here, while Derrydarragh, Dernagolia and Daroge remind us of the mighty oaks that stood here for centuries.

Necklace of Pearls

Visitors to Lough Ree over the years were captivated by the charm of its scenery. One such was the writer, Mary Banim, who visited the lake towards the end of the nineteenth century and expressed her fascination:

As we sail northwards from Rinn Duin we have perhaps the finest view of all to be had upon the lake. Below, to the south, is the wide sheet of water, alike beautiful, whether it glistens, blue and still, under a cloudless sky, or is created with the innumerable wavelets that a breeze quickly calls into motion. It is full of variety in the character of its banks, of the distant hills, of the many islands, described in such poetic words by St Ambrose: "Those islands which, as a necklace of pearls,

God has set upon the bosom of the waters." Just below, where the lake
is widest and then forks upwards into Westmeath and Longford, we
see groups of these lovely gems - emeralds rather than pearls - some of
them famed as the dwelling places of holy saints of long ago.
Northwards the water flows on by callow and wood and island, its
expanse now narrowing, now widening, now forming bays and quiet
inlets, until it seems to lave the very feet of Slieve Bawn and to catch
its own silvery hue in the distance.[1]

The Islands

There are fifty two named islands in Lough Ree, ranging from
Inchmore, the largest, with over two hundred acres, to others with
one acre or less. These islands have been the homes and habitations
of people since the dawn of history, and probably for a much longer
period in pre-history. Little more than a century ago, they housed
some one hundred and eighty people. A thousand years earlier,
they had many times that number. Today, there is but one
permanent resident on Lough Ree, who lives on Inchbofin. The
islands are well distributed, and if we set out at the northern
entrance to the lake, we can begin our tour and locate and introduce
the largest and most important of them and establish their names.

On our way southwards, from Lanesborough, we will follow
the navigation channels as indicated by the marker buoys on the
lake. Almost immediately, the channel is directed west of south, for
the upper regions of the lake are shallow and difficult to navigate.
To the east lie Rathcline and the ruined pile of Lord Lane's castle,
the stronghold of the O'Quinns in pre-plantation days. A cluster of
tiny islands in mid-water is covered with low bushes but they
scarcely qualify as islands for in high water only the bushes are
visible. They are known locally as the Gormauns. Leaving them to
the left, the channel points directly towards Ferrinch, an island of
some ten acres near to the western shore and completely covered in
trees and shrubbery.

The channel now turns abruptly to the east, a full ninety degrees
along the northern shore of Inse island, which contains about
twelve acres of reasonably good pasture-land. At the eastern

4

extremity of Inse the course changes again and we are now proceeding southwards picking up the first large island, Inchenagh, ahead and to the west, with its three small satellites, Lanagower, Lanasky and Lanagesh. Farther west from Inchenagh is the expanse of Clooneigh Bay dipping well into the Roscommon shoreline.

We keep to our southern course, passing by Inchenagh, and soon we see Clawinch, an island of some thirty seven acres to our right, lying close to the western shore, while straight ahead in mid-water is Inchcleraun, radiant as a jewel in this magnificent scenery - the Uisce Álainn[2] as it was identified in olden times. The Priest's Island, a small piece of ground, lies so close to the Longford shore on our left, as to be scarcely distinguishable from the land behind it. We proceed by the red marker buoys of the channel along the eastern shore of Inchcleraun, glimpsing the ruins of its "seven churches" on our way. Elfeet Bay and Barley Harbour can be seen to the east while St John's Wood comes into view on the western shore. As we pass the wood, famous for its flora, the promontory of Rindoon points above it like a giant's finger out into the lake.

We are now at the halfway stage on the north-south axis of Lough Ree, and here the lake opens out dramatically to the east, more than doubling its width. We depart the main channel, taking a secondary course to the east, leaving the Black Islands on our left and observing the abandoned dwelling houses that were the homes of the last full-time residents of these islands. We continue to travel due east until we reach the red marker buoy at the southern tip of another island, Inchbofin, some sixty acres in extent, and lying north/south. From here to the north we can see Saints' Island and a large expanse of water stretching along by the Longford shore and further east to the mouth of the river Inny, where it enters the lake, close to the Longford-Westmeath border. This completes our diversion east and north and we now retrace our course in the general direction of Athlone.

The Southern Lake

Going southwards we find, first, Inchturk and then Inchmore, the biggest island in the lake and indeed the biggest in the entire

Shannon system. West of here, towards the centre in open water, is the diminutive Nuns' Island, whose name calls up echoes of earlier ages. The marked channel keeps us on the western side of the lake as we continue southwards, past the Cribby Islands and Yew Point on the Roscommon shore. Opposite, towards the east, is the lake's last big island, Inis Aingin or Hare Island, site of Ciaran's first monastic foundation, situated at the entrance to the Inner Lakes and Ballykeeran. We look in briefly on those lakes and see Friars' Island, well-camouflaged among reeds and bulrushes. Returning past Coosan Point we are now nearing the southern shore of this great stretch of water, as we see Hodson Bay to the west, with the smaller Beam Island in mid-water. Carberry Island and the two Yellow Islands, Little and Great, mark the approaches to the extremity of Lough Ree where it narrows and reverts to becoming a river again on its way into Athlone.

We have now concluded our introductory overview of the largest of the islands that have adorned Lough Ree through the ages. To get to know their names and to place their locations may be sufficient for the observer who is satisfied to enjoy the visual beauty of the surroundings. Most, however, will want to go below the surface, to rediscover the stories of the people who were born and lived their lives in these isolated places. Others will be interested in going back to distant ages, when the lake and its islands played an important role in the historic development of the country, politically, socially and culturally. And the story does not begin even there but goes back to pre-historic times before ever saint or scholar set up house on Lough Ree.

Early lake dwellers

From ever the first inhabitants settled in its environs, the lake became a vital influence on their lives. An unfailing source of fresh water, it ensured a healthy supply for humans and animals alike. Abundantly stocked with fish and wild fowl it could make a basic contribution to the food supply, especially when bad harvests affected the land-based crops, causing severe shortages. Boat building and sailing were among the primary skills of the lake dwellers, and the water was their "high road". It also had an important social dimension in that it put people in touch with each other and made possible the exchange of information and the interchange of goods, initiating early patterns of trade and commerce. From a very early stage, people were able to take heavy loads, including live cattle, in boats, and the water facilitated the carrying of such loads over distances, with a minimum expenditure of energy.

In the inland waters, the dugout canoe (coite), of all sizes and dimensions, was in general use from the earliest period to modern times, both for purposes of war and for thieving and trade... However, large timber-built boats, equipped with a helm, were also in use in inland waters and details of the construction are given in the law tracts. The annals record the use of these boats only for raiding and for warfare, but there can be no doubt that they were equally used for ordinary purposes of transport and trade. The fact that so many of the monastic foundations cluster about waterways, both inland and sea-coast, equally indicates that intercourse between them must usually have been by boat.[3]

A good example of the use of the dugout canoes (cots) comes from the middle 12th century when some of the people on the eastern Lough Ree shore set out to steal the pigs of the Clonmacnois monks. A battle resulted which probably caused some loss of life. The entry in the annals runs as follows:

A battle was gained by Imhar Mac Carghamhna and Gillachrist, his son, and by Muintir-Maelshinna, over the Breaghmhaini, Muintir-Thadhgain, and Muintir-Tlamain, in which fell the chief of Muintir-Tlamain and his son. It was Ciaran that turned this battle against the Breagh Maini,[4] for they had gone to Cluain, bringing with them cots, in which they carried off all they could find of the pigs of Ciaran's clergy. The clergy went after them with their shrine, as far as Lis-an-tSoiscela, but they were not obeyed. On the following day they sustained a defeat in consequence of disobeying Ciaran's clergy.[5]

Stealing the monks' pigs.　　　　　　　　　　　*Drawing by Kevin McNamara.*

The number and variety of lake-craft was especially important in the geographical context of Lough Ree, because so much of the surrounding country consisted of impassable bog-land. The numerous efforts of early peoples to construct trackways over the bogs make the point. One such track-way, dating from the second century B.C. has been excavated and is on display at Kenagh, Co. Longford, a few miles from the shores of Lough Ree. Here it is easy to see the immense labour and hardship such projects involved, while the waters of the lake provided ready-made access to all places within their reach. In times of fear and danger the lake offered its own measure of protection. While the land dwellers built ditches and palisades around their ring forts, the lake man had his crannog on an offshore island, where he reckoned the strip of water, between him and the mainland, was a better defence than either walls or ditches. But the lake was not without its own risks and dangers. Storms on the water posed a bigger threat than on the land. Lough Ree's propensity for sudden squalls has caused innumerable drownings and continues to be a hazard right down to the present time.

Trade and Commerce

Sale and exchange of goods within the country was in progress from an early date. Manufactured articles, as well as iron and stone for the making of implements and weapons, were available in some areas and on demand in others. There was also a regular foreign trade exporting wool and hides, and importing goods, such as wine and salt. The importing of wine dates back to early times and the Irish, it seems, were good wine drinkers. In early Christian Ireland the monasteries were good customers and they often acted as distribution centres for wines and other imported goods. This is particularly relevant to Lough Ree which boasts the place-name *Portaneena*[6] on the deep water stretch of its eastern shore near Ballykeeran.

If Lough Ree played a part in enabling people to come together, it also had a role in keeping them apart. Early Irish society developed around the extended family, the *derbfine*, as it was known. This was the basic unit of the *tuath* or tribe, which varied in size and influence, according as its fortunes waxed and waned. It had a petty chieftain who usually gave allegiance to a local king or magnate. In the absence of a more orderly structure, these local kingdoms promoted their own advancement by preying on each other, whether as individuals or in planned alliances. Thus, the lake, from time immemorial, separated such warring powers, and when hostilities did break out, the lake was the scene of many fierce naval engagements.

Clan Divisions

Territories and kingdoms, bordering the lake, varied in size and importance over the centuries. Lough Ree, with its highly indented shoreline and its many sheltered bays, was inhabited from the earliest times. The heavily wooded terrain on the western side abounded in natural food and wildlife, while the somewhat more fertile eastern shore attracted the earliest farmers. Slieve Bawn, which overlooks the landscape to the northwest, was often called Slieve Bawn na dTuath in the old Irish sagas. The *tuatha* [tribes] in question were the O'Beirnes of Roscommon/south Leitrim, the MacBrennans and the O'Hanlys. The O'Hanlys were also known as Cinél Dofa from their eponymous ancestor. The plain of Maigh Ai, O'Hanly country, stretches from Boyle to Strokestown to Castlerea and is bordered by the Shannon on the east. This was their territory from time immemorial. They survived the Norman invaders but were ultimately dispossessed in the Cromwellian plantation to make room for the "transplanted" on their way "to Hell or to Connaught."

To the south of Maigh Ai was the territory of Uí Máine, patrimony of the O'Kellys, bordering Lough Ree, and stretching far to the south of it below Athlone. Uí Máine was a powerful kingdom, sometimes strong enough to be a king-maker in Connaught and at times entering alliances with surrounding kingdoms. Several smaller people-groups occupied Uí Máine, notably the O'Neachtains and O'Fallúins towards the south western shore of the lake.

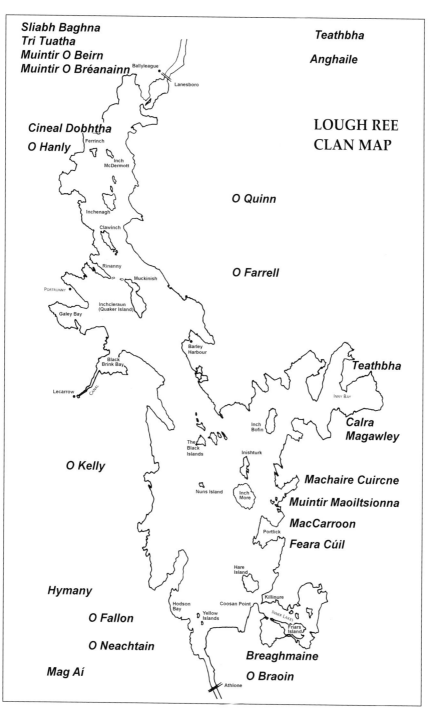

Sliabh Baghna
Tri Tuatha
Muintir O Beirn
Muintir O Bréanainn

Ballyleague

Lanesboro

Teathbha

Anghaile

Cineal Dobhtha

O Hanly

Ferrinch

Inch
McDermott

LOUGH REE
CLAN MAP

Inchenagh

Clawinch

O Quinn

Rinanny

Muckinish

PORTRUNNY

Inchcleraun
(Quaker Island)

Galey Bay

O Farrell

Barley
Harbour

Black
Brink Bay

Lecarrow

CANAL

INNY BAY

Teathbha

Inch
Bofin

The
Black
Islands

Inishturk

Calra
Magawley

O Kelly

Nuns Island

Inch
More

Portlick

Machaire Cuircne

Muintir Maoiltsionna

MacCarroon

Feara Cúil

Hare
Island

Hymany

Hodson
Bay

Coosan Point

Killinure

INNER LAKES

O Fallon

Yellow
Islands

Friars
Island

O Neachtain

Breaghmaine

Mag Aí

Athlone

O Braoin

11

To the north of the lake and the east of the Shannon lay the kingdom of Teabhtha, once ruled over by the sons of Niall the Great. In the Middle Ages the advancing Conmaicne forced the inhabitants south and east of the Inny into southern Teathbha. The new overlords changed the name from Teathbha to Anghaile, their dynastic family being the O'Farrells. That part of Anghaile along the north shore of Lough Ree became known as Caladh na hAnghaile. From the mouth of the Inny southwards was the kingdom of Cuircne, roughly corresponding to the barony of Kilkenny West today. Machaire Cuircne was the territory of the Cuircne people for many centuries before the coming of the Normans. It stretched along the lakeshore with southern Teabhtha on its east side. Its people were known as the Muintir Mael tSionna and its ruling family were the MacCarrghamhna [MacCarroon], mentioned in the Annals. In 1185 the lands of Cuircne were "granted" to the Dillons by Prince John. The Muintir Mael tSionna ultimately lost their territory as Machaire Cuircne became Dillon Country.

With the weakening of Norman power in the fourteenth century the Irish were able to reclaim some of the lost ground. The O'Farrells of Annaly, advancing across the Inny, defeated the Dillons and captured the areas of Forgney and portions of Noughaval in northern Cuircne. Also bordering Cuircne in southern Teabhtha was Magawley's country of Calraidhe near Moate. To the south and adjacent to the Inner Lakes was the chieftaincy of Breaghmuine (Brawney), extending around Athlone, patrimony of the O'Braoins. These small units and others were grouped around the Clan Colmáin territories of the Maelseachlainns, the dynastic family of Midhe, which stretched from the Shannon to the Liffey and the east coast, the most powerful kingdom in Ireland which frequently supplied the *ard rí* (high king).

Attaining and retaining the high kingship was generally a matter of defeating in battle all who staked rival claims to it, and to this end armies were raised and equipped to fight perceived enemies. In the case of Midhe its shoreline with Lough Ree was regarded as a weakness in its line of defence and a good opening for attack. Thus it was that over the centuries many fleets sailed into Lough Ree for this purpose. The Vikings in their time, expert sailors that they were, came here frequently on their plundering raids, and so the lake saw an impressive amount of naval action, especially between the eighth and the thirteenth centuries.

Legends

Lough Ree, in Irish *Loch Rí*, previous spelling *Ríbh*, is taken to mean the Lake of the King. John O'Donovan, the great nineteenth century antiquarian, didn't have much respect for some of the local stories he heard about the origin of the name. However, the Egyptian astronomer and geographer Ptolemy is believed to have marked it on his map in the second century. An expert, who visited the lake and wrote about its islands in 1907 has this to say:

> *Ptolemy's atlas, some of the material of which went back to Tyrian sources, several centuries before our era, marks, not far from the position of Lough Ree, a place called Rheba. This is almost certainly the ancient Irish name Rib or Ribh which the lake still bears.*[7]

Other sources - if one can so describe them - of information on Lough Ree also go back to very early times. The legend of Queen Maeve has the warrior queen at the conclusion of the *Táin Bó Cuailne* retiring to her sister's island retreat on the lake and her subsequent assassination which will be dealt with in a later chapter.

Lough Ree: Lake of the King

Another legend comes from Portlick on the eastern shore, and if the name Lough Ree means the lake of the king this legend may have some bearing on how that name came to be. It was collected by Richard Hayward in the 1930s and this is how he ran it:

> *And it was the way the daughter of Donal Dubh fell asleep one sunny evening on the shore of Loch Ree near the Harbour of the Flagstones, (Portlick) and she resting herself. And in that sleep a*

dream came to her, and it was the way she was told in that dream
that if she rubbed salmon gall on her eyes the sight would be brought
back to her and herself no more to be picking her steps in darkness.
And when she tells her father, Donal Dubh, of this dream, he goes to
his boat, as you might expect, with nothing in his mind but the
catching of a salmon to bring light to his daughter's darkness. But a
storm rises and, the boat destroyed, Donal Dubh sinks to the bottom
of Loch Ree, though not, as you might expect, to his death, but to the
castle of the King of Loch Ree, and him under a spell in that place at
the bottom of the great lake. And it isn't long before Donal Dubh
hears from the King how all around where the castle stands was once
green fields, and how his wicked stepmother, who is a witch, caused
the lake to overflow into that place and to keep himself captive ever
since.

"Tis long I have waited for you, Donal Dubh," says the King, "and
with your coming 'tis myself is thinking that my deliverance is not
far away. So haste you now to the big tree and it growing beside the
big flag beyond the Harbour of the Flagstones, and in under that
same big flag you'll find a sleeping cat. And all you have to do is
bring that cat to me, which is easy if you'll carry it by the tail. Only
carry it no other way, for it will make pretence of great friendliness
and try to wheedle itself into your arms, and that would be the end
of yourself and, what is more important, the end of me." And at this
the King puffed out his cheeks.

"I'm glad you think so well of yourself," said Donal Dubh, but,
being a wise man, he did the King's bidding, and was soon back at
the castle in under the waves, with the cat in his left hand and it
hanging by its tail and yammerin' to wake the dead.

"Good man yourself," says the King, and with the quick turn of a
knife he had the cat's belly open and the heart of the beast lying on
the ground before him.

"Well, that's the end of the poor cat," says Donal Dubh. "It is," says
the King, "and the end of my stepmother too, for 'twas herself was
the cat, and nothing else in it at all. `Poor cat,' says you! Moryah!"

"And what will we do with the cat and it dead?" says Donal Dubh.
"I'll throw it over my left shoulder for the Little Folk," says the
King, "the way they'll be using it to make strings for their wee fairy

fiddles to bring music to their gatherings and luck to ourselves."

"And will you throw the heart over your shoulder too?" says Donal Dubh.

"I would if I had no sense," says the King, "for that is the bait with which you'll catch the salmon, and when you have that caught it's not long your daughter will walk in darkness. And it's little wish I have to be married to a woman and her not able to see."

"And there I lave you," says Donal Dubh, "for it's often enough 'twould be a great comfort to myself and my own wife the least wee notion obscured in her sight, if you know what I mean. But what's this about my daughter and yourself to be married to her? It's the first I've heard of it, and being her father I'm what you might say interested!

"Ah, sure that's all part of the plan," says the King, "and this whole scheme concocted hundreds of years ago, the way I was sick, sore and tired waiting for you to turn up and start the ball rolling. I don't know what kept you at all."

And so it all turned out, for the salmon was caught with the cat's heart for bait, and Donal Dubh's daughter got her eyesight back, and she and the King of Loch Ree got married and lived happy from that time out.[8]

More legends

There are several legends of the Shannon and its lakes. One of them has to do with the origin of the name of the river. Sinann was the daughter of Lodan and the granddaughter of Lear, the great sea-king of the Tuatha de Danann in Erin. Their successor was Manannan, from whom the Isle of Man derives its name. There was a mystical fountain in Lower Ormond which was called Connla's well. Nine hazel trees grew over this well. The nuts, fruit of these trees, were crimson in colour and had the power to impart knowledge of all that was refined in literature, poetry and art. Those beautiful nuts, as soon as they were produced on the trees, dropped into the well creating shining red bubbles. The well was full of salmon that dashed to the surface and swallowed the nuts before they made their way up the river. As a result brilliant crimson spots appeared on these salmon and whoever ate one of them became learned in the arts and literature. Women were forbidden to come near Connla's Well. However the Lady Sinann, anxious to further her knowledge and refinement and be the equal of her male contemporaries travelled in secret to the well. As soon as she placed her feet on the brink the waters rose violently, bursting out and rushing towards the great river. The Lady Sinann was engulfed in the torrent and her dead body was washed up on the land at the confluence of the two streams. From then on the great river became known as the Shannon.[9]

Pre-Christian Cults

Another ancient story, the legend of the "Monster," takes us back to the first arrival of Christianity on the lake. The holy monk Diarmaid laboured all day to build his monastery while the destroyer attacked by night and broke down what had been built. Saint and monster jousted and skirmished but ultimately the saint prevailed and drove his adversary down into the depths of the lake. Nor was this fantastic occurrence unique to Lough Ree.

St. Senan, life-long friend of Diarmaid, had a similar experience when building his monastery on Scattery Island in the Shannon estuary, and St. Ruan, on his way to found the great monastery of Lorrha, was confronted by a savage boar, while upriver from Lough Ree, at Tarmon, St. Barry had to use his famous crozier the *Gearr Beraigh* against the predatory "*ollphiast.*"

Commentators see these legends as typifying the confrontation between the old Celtic religious practice and the new faith. Celtic rituals centred on the "elements" of earth, fire, wind and water and it is suggested that these rituals were enacted especially on islands where the "elements" were most in evidence. This was the primitive religious practice of the ordinary people handed down to them through the centuries. They were nature worshippers and islands would have had a special attraction for them, as would mountains, rivers and springs. They were immersed in a spirituality that sought to find the hidden presences behind the visible realities. They had a deep ingrained commitment to their beliefs and the new evangelists would have great difficulty converting them.

This ancient religious cult was established on the islands of Lough Ree long before Christianity and the new evangelists found it necessary to go out and confront it in its primal setting. This they did and did successfully, but the ancient spirituality continued to re-emerge in the new generation of Christians despite the best efforts of their mentors to fight it off. Such then was the monster, defeated but not destroyed by the saint, and living on, somewhere out there in the depth of the Irish psyche. Ultimately the survival of the old pre-Christian cults and rituals and the talismanic objects associated with them were realities the new church had to learn to accept. No attempt was made to force the new gospel on its hearers. Equally, the society of that time did not engage in any form of violent hostility, for it is well known that there were no martyrs in the early Irish church. Instead the new preachers took the pagan practices on board and attempted to Christianise them. Not a few have survived the centuries, even into our own time. The

The altar on Inchbofin with Early Christian graveslabs and round cursing stones.

17

celebration of Halloween, as it is still enacted in some places, is an excellent example.

Inchbofin, another monastery on Lough Ree, has its own relics from those early times of the ongoing struggle between the old and the new. Here are preserved some of the "cursing stones," recalling elements of the occult that, in effect, became part of the Christian practice and were never finally expurgated from it. The ruined monastery of Inismurray off the Sligo coast still exhibits its "cursing altar" and some of its cursing stones have the Christian cross carved on them. Inismurray is unique in that it was not colonised by the later religious orders when it ceased to be active in the Middle Ages, with the result that it still retains its original Celtic layout. It has a very old church with a stone roof called Teach Molaise. It also has a stone beehive hut and a wide perimeter stone ditch, within which the monks had their cells. It is reasonable to assume that similar or comparable features pertained on the Lough Ree sites but they were updated or replaced in the twelfth century or afterwards. When Francis Joseph Biggar,[10] the archaeologist, visited Inchcleraun in 1899 he found traces of a "druidic cult" on the island, though he didn't specify what these traces were. A stone from the same island, which has not been previously recorded, may reinforce Biggar's assertion. This is a small slab bearing an early Christian cross, incised and with fish finials. Below the right arm of the cross is a double spiral of the type seen on some early megalithic tombs. Further consideration of this point will ensue when the islands of Lough Ree are being treated individually in later chapters.

Cross and spiral stone.

CHAPTER 2

Christianity

The arrival of Christianity on the lake profoundly and radically altered the way of life of the people of the islands. Socially, politically and culturally their lives would never be the same again. A whole new system of living, with new outlooks and understandings came into being and continued to influence the ethos of the island peoples for more than a thousand years. Their history is thus inextricably bound up with the wider parameters of Christian history.

The success of the Christian mission on the lake is beyond question, and it is most likely that each of the larger islands housed a monastic foundation. The church established by Patrick and the early missionaries in the fifth century was not monastic in character, even though Patrick did found monasteries for men and women. He was himself a bishop and his church was basically an episcopal church with its infant dioceses based on tribal boundaries. Scholars today are uncertain as to how much of the island had been converted to Christianity in St. Patrick's time. Some incline to the view that the majority of the population was untouched by the new faith at the close of the fifth century. The monastic upheaval which swept the country in the sixth century may well have been a process of primary evangelisation, carried out by leaders, who had the benefit of training and formation, in institutions that followed on Patrick's mission, such as the monastery of St. Finian of Clonard.

St. Diarmaid is usually given primacy among the founders on Lough Ree. He was himself of royal lineage, being descended in the fourth generation from a former king of Tara. He was, according to tradition, the tutor of Ciaran, who went on to found the monastery of Clonmacnois. It has to be borne in mind that Ireland, unlike the continent, had no towns, and the entire population was agrarian. In the circumstances it is not difficult to see how this rural landscape facilitated a monastic rather than an episcopal church. There was need for a centre where the bishop would be visible and where the infant church might look for support and direction. The monastery supplied that need.

The Monastery

A monastic settlement of this period in Ireland requires some clarification. It bears little if any resemblance to what we understand as a monastery today. All that the two have in common is that they were a coming together of people living their lives for the glory of God. In every other respect the Celtic monastery was different. The Brehon Laws of ancient Ireland decreed that an individual could not own land. Property and land were

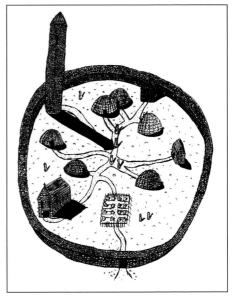

Typical layout of an Early Christian monastery. Drawing by Kevin McNamara.

held by the family group and only they could dispose of them. While a monastery might be called into being by a holy man or woman, it could not be established by that person. The extended families were the monastic founders and also the first members of the new community.

The Celtic monastery contained ordained priests and celibate monks who lived their lives according to the monastic rule. They worshipped God, prayed frequently and rose during the night to chant the sacred office in the monastery chapel. There were anchorites also, who lived lives of solitude. There were the lay *manaigh* (lay monks), married men, who lived on the monastic lands, rearing their families, doing the farming and the fishing, and generally providing for the temporal needs of the brethren.

The abbot was the head of the monastery. The *sechnab* was his deputy. The abbot was sometimes an ordained minister but occasionally a married layman. The monastery had a bishop, and large monasteries frequently had more than one bishop, with no diocesan jurisdiction, but providing a sacramental service for the community. The prayer and penitential exercises of the monks were reflected in the kindness and hospitality which were part of the monastic ethos. The monk in charge of the house was known as the *fertigis* and it was his responsibility to give proper welcome to visitors and to ensure that they were well looked after. The *arcinneach* (sometimes called the *erenach)* was the land steward whose duty it was to see that the farming was well done. It was he who decided how much of the crop would go to the central monastic compound and how much would be retained by the lay *manaigh* for themselves and their families. No doubt he had difficult and, sometimes, unpopular decisions to make, especially in times of bad harvests and lean years.

Places of Learning

The life of the monastery revolved around the gospel. Preaching and teaching were the central activities. All communication was necessarily oral at first, for spoken Irish had no literature except the few unwieldy words that were cut in *ogham* on timber and stone. In order to access the word of God in the gospels or the writings of the great teachers, such as Augustine or Martin of Tours, the early Irish evangelists had to learn Latin. In turn they had to teach it to their clerical pupils. Latin was undoubtedly one of the subjects taught in the early monasteries of Lough Ree. Knowledge of Latin, then the foremost language in the world, opened up new horizons, both secular and religious, for the Irish of that time. It also had a huge influence on the Irish language, propelling it into a literature of its own and enriching it with a plethora of new words and phrases. For instance *Natalis* the Latin word for a birth came into Irish as *Nodalaig* and ultimately shortened to *Nollaig*, the Irish word for Christmas today. Hundreds of such new words came into Irish at that time by a similar route.

New religious schools were established. Initially, they co-existed with the traditional secular schools, each maintaining its separate identity. The education imparted in the monastic schools was church oriented, but with the passage of time secular learning became part of the curriculum, resulting in a fruitful amalgam which equipped students to reach the frontiers of intellectual excellence in Ireland and overseas. There is the well known record of Alcuin, who wrote to his former teacher, Colgu, at Clonmacnois from the court of the Emperor Charlemagne in the early ninth century, sending gifts of silver, oil and wine from the Emperor and himself. Canon John Corkery comments:

Modern reproduction of 8th century crucifixion plaque from Rinnagan, Rindoon, Co. Roscommon.

> *Alcuin's letter speaks of the author as ego filius tuus and continues et tui amici toti, qui apud nos sunt in prosperitate Dei serviunt. This would seem to imply that Alcuin had been a pupil of Colgu and that several other students of his were in the Palatine school also. Charlemagne's school was the precursor of the universities of Europe, so that the claim of Clonmacnois to have been a university, not only of ecclesiastical learning, but of secular education also, is no idle one.*[1]

Clonmacnois is but two hours distance downstream from Lough Ree. There were schools and scholars on the Lough Ree islands also. The Annals have several references to them and to their *alumni*, who achieved fame for their learning farther afield. There is a tradition which points to the schools of Inchbofin as the university of the lake to which students came from other schools - a special academy for advanced studies!

Prayer and Penance

Ideally the Irish monastery was a Christian community where all shared in the fruits of their labour and no one was left in want. A Christian way of life was a basic requirement, comprising worship of God, love of neighbour, respect for authority, care of the earth and regard for all God's creatures whether wild or domesticated. Many of the saints had famous cows. This included Ciaran, who also had a pet fox. Mochua had a housefly and of course the anonymous monk had Pangur Bán, a cat. Marriage laws were strictly in line with the Christian ethic of one man one woman and the union was permanent. When people fell short of these standards, there was help and support in the monastic community and for those who felt that they could no longer live up to them there was the option of the secular world outside.

The epicentre of the community was within the monastic compound where many and varied buildings were grouped around the main church. The basic philosophy was lived out in the daily worship of God, and also in every good work that was undertaken by the brethren. They chanted the holy office, recited the psalms and spent time in silence and meditation before attending to their various avocations. Some were educators, their schools catering firstly for the children of their own community and expanding into wider fields as the monastery grew in size. Others were scribes who copied the gospels and psalms in Latin, composed prayerful tracts or wrote lives of the saints as on All Saints' Island in Lough Ree. In later centuries they recorded histories and wrote down the traditional lore and legend in the Irish language. In addition there were the artists and the metal workers and also the craftsmen, masons and builders. The new church's attempt to Christianise some of the early pagan practices was not always successful and there is evidence of a reform movement as early as the sixth century. The *Penitential of Vinnian* which introduced strict rules for both clerics and laymen comes down to us from this time. Vinnian directed:

Married persons to abstain from marital relations, not only every Saturday and Sunday, but also for three forty-day periods each year and from the time of conception of a child until after its birth. The married clergy were not to cohabit with their wives at all. Divorce and concubinage, which were prevalent, were forbidden. The penance for a married layman who had intercourse with a female slave was that she should be sold and that he should abstain from all intercourse with his own wife for one year. However, if the slave bore the man a child she was to be separated from him and freed, while he was sentenced to a year of strict penance on bread and water. The clergy were ordered not to practise magic or to prepare potions. (These obstinate practices had survived from pagan times). The punishment for a cleric who committed murder was ten years' exile, unless he could demonstrate that the victim had been his friend and that he had killed him, not in hatred, but in a sudden burst of anger. In such a case the penance was only six years in exile, three on bread and water and three without meat or wine.[2]

Céli Dé

As the monasteries grew in strength and influence they became victims of their own success as their wealth made them powerful. The established major dynasties courted this power. Since the head of the monastery was often a layman, and sometimes of royal blood, monasteries often found themselves in military alliances both with and against kings. Soon there were monastic armies fighting for secular magnates and monasteries were frequently attacked and plundered by warring forces. New levels of degeneration were reached when the armies of Clonmacnois and Durrow confronted each other in battle and left hundreds dead on the field. The Four Masters recount this latter event for 764 A.D.

In the second half of the eighth century a movement began to appear within the church aiming at an ascetic revival and reorganisation of its mission. The reformers called themselves *céli dé*, anglicised today as culdees (*Céli* came from the Irish word for a client or dependent). The movement originated with Mael Ruain, the great abbot of Tallaght. It achieved much as a leaven for the worldly ways into which the monasteries had slipped, but it did not succeed in eradicating the abuses. The renewed ascetic tradition also stimulated an important body of literature, especially the beautiful hermit poetry. The movement reached Lough Ree and several communities there had their culdees, but already there were other developments, more startling and menacing, that would have the gravest consequences for the Irish church, and Lough Ree was destined to be in the eye of the storm.

CHAPTER 3

Vikings

The adage that tells us that "eternal vigilance is the price of freedom" was never more appropriate than in the case of Celtic Ireland at the time of the first invasions of the Vikings. The country as a whole had come a long way since the early days of Christianity three centuries before. Economically, socially and culturally the people were well advanced and compared very favourably with the rest of the world at that time. However the age-old predilection with internal feuding and civil strife had impeded progress. The secular lust for power had infiltrated the monastic system and what should have been an alert and self-confident society was dragged inward on itself by individual greed and internecine rivalry. The energy that might have convinced the early Viking raiders that Ireland was no soft target was being dissipated in local inter-tribal squabbles. This is not to say that the social fabric had collapsed in any sense. It was still a vibrant society and it was called upon to prove itself many times in the next two centuries. That it took two whole centuries and thousands of Irish lives to quell the Viking menace bears witness to its lack of cohesion and sense of purpose at this time. Equally, it must be borne in mind that it was Ireland, alone in Europe that eventually inflicted a decisive military defeat on the invaders.

Before the appearance of the Vikings, Ireland had not suffered an invasion for more than a thousand years. In this it differed widely from the rest of Europe where, following the collapse of the Roman Empire, the peoples of that continent suffered wave after wave of invasions. Britain had experienced attack and conquest at the hands of the Angles, Saxons and Jutes in the sixth century. Those barbarous tribes who had over-run Britain in those years had long ago settled down and become civilised. They had been converted to Christianity - to a great extent through the labour of Irish missionaries in the previous two hundred years. Colmcille had founded Iona in the sixth century and the influence of this great monastery would spread to every corner of Britain especially through the work of his protégé, Aidan, whose influence radiated from his famous monastery of Lindisfarne, off the Northumberland coast.

As continental Europe gradually disintegrated under the attacks of the marauding tribes the Roman institutions collapsed and the society descended into barbarism. Men like Columbanus led the Irish mission to the continent in the seventh, eighth and ninth centuries, and their zeal was fundamental to the restructuring of the new Europe under Charlemagne.

No doubt, men and women from Lough Ree had a part in this historic achievement. Their names have long been lost in the shadows of the past but their bones lie somewhere in European earth between the Black Sea and the Atlantic. Long before the Vikings had set foot in Ireland, Irish anchorites and hermits had made their acquaintance in the Faroes and Iceland. These Irish monks had set off to lead lives of poverty and solitude on those faraway islands, which were now being invaded by the Norsemen, Nordmen or Normanni, as they were variously called. They came from the regions known to us today as Scandinavia. They were a

Viking raid on an island monastery.   *Drawing by Kevin McNamara.*

people whose numbers were increasing; their country was poor; and driven by want and hunger they set out to ravish neighbouring lands.

In an agrarian world they needed land for their children and grass for their stock; in an era of opening trade-routes they craved silver and the chattels silver could provide; in a hierarchical, warlike and still part-tribal society their leaders sought fame, power, wealth and sustenance through action. Thus it was chiefly land-hunger which led them to the windy sheep-runs of the Faroes, the butter-laden grass of habitable Iceland and the good and fragrant pasture of the west Greenland fjords. It was an ambition to distinguish themselves, win land and wealth to reward and enlarge their armed following, which impelled generation after generation of northern kings, jarls and sea-captains to assault the territories of their southern and south-western neighbours. It was a desire for profit and material goods which encouraged the Vikings to trade and carry in the Baltic and North Seas, the Black Sea and Caspian, across the Atlantic Ocean and along the great Russian rivers. They were particularly well placed to meet the inexhaustible European and Muslim demand for furs and slaves, but turned their hand to any saleable commodity: grain, fish, timber, hides, salt, wine, glass, glue, horses and cattle, white bears and falcons, walrus ivory and seal oil, honey, wax, malt, silks and woollens, amber and hazel nuts, soapstone dishes and basalt millstones, wrought weapons, ornaments and silver. For this alone the Viking peoples would be worthy of fame, for to this end they built ships and established market towns, developed trade routes and maintained spheres of influence, and fortified mercantile practice with piracy and conquest abroad.[1]

Viking Ships

The Vikings were maritime dwellers who inherited the expertise of the seafarer. They were skilled shipbuilders who came from a region where good timber was plentiful. Boats from the period have been recovered and studied by underwater archaeology and show impressive levels of technique and engineering. A Viking boat of this era could be over eighty feet in length from stem to stern, having a beam measuring from eighteen to twenty feet. The oak keel was fashioned from a single tree and iron plates and rivets were used on some of the main joints. Such was the skill of construction that despite the weight of the keel the boat was highly manoeuvrable and durable in all kinds of weather. It was equally adept on inshore waters where its shallow draft - a mere three to three and a half

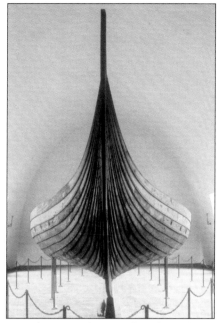

Modern reproduction of a Viking ship.

feet - enabled it to navigate most inland waterways and shallow harbours. Mast and sail mountings were of pine as were the sixteen to twenty pairs of oars with which the boat was equipped. Such a vessel was well suited to seafaring and to plundering, carrying as it did, from sixty to eighty armed men.

With shipping of this calibre, the Vikings were not afraid to face the dangers of the western seas. From the Shetlands they reached the Faroe Islands, as noted above, where they had their first encounter with the Irish monks, the *Peregrini pro Christo*, those who had sought the green martyrdom by leaving their native land. The monks scarcely impeded the onward march of the invading parties, who consolidated their possession of the Faroes having taken over the land for farming, and later using these islands as a base to strike for Iceland and farther afield in the next century. Meanwhile raiding parties were coming south along the east and west shores of Britain and Ireland. Lindisfarne of St. Aidan in Northumbria suffered a savage attack in 793 as did Iona two years later.

Monasteries Raided

The first Viking raid on Ireland, as every school pupil knows, took place in 795, with an attack on the island of *Reachra* or Lambay outside of Dublin and in the same year the monasteries of Inismurray off the Sligo coast and Inchbofin off the Mayo coast were plundered. For the next forty years the raids followed a pattern. The Vikings attacked targets on the coast or close to it; they grabbed the spoils and moved on. The north east of Ireland suffered most in the early years while the raiders continued coming gradually southwards until they eventually reached the coasts of Kerry and Cork.

Many of the great schools and monasteries were sacked during this period. Lough Ree and its monasteries, however, were well removed from these terrible scenes of slaughter and destruction - but not for much longer. The Vikings now appear to change their policy and they begin to occupy and consolidate what they have captured. In 842 Turgesius one of their leaders led a great fleet up the Shannon and into Lough Ree. He plundered Clonmacnois on his way and set up his wife, Ota, as a goddess on the high altar of the cathedral from which she gave oracles. He sacked the island monasteries on Lough Ree and many monks and nuns were put to the sword.

It is believed that Turgesius made a settlement on Lough Ree at this time as the lake provided a strategic base from which he might dominate the whole of the central plain of Ireland. His stronghold is said to have been Rindoon the present St. John's Point on the western shore of the lake. From here he launched forays both to the west into Connaught and to the east into the kingdom of Midhe, as well as further attacks on the Shannon monasteries of Clonfert and Clonmacnois. In one of his raids to the east however he was confronted by Maelsheachlainn, king of Midhe and later to be high king of Ireland, who overpowered him and drowned him in Lough Owel. Malachy's victory was celebrated throughout Ireland and a thousand years later the poet could recall that he wore -

"… the collar of gold
Which he won from her proud invader".[2]

The loss of their leader seems to have had a profound effect on Viking morale. Their depredations came to an end and their longboats were withdrawn from Lough Ree soon after 845.

No contemporary account has survived as to how the island monasteries fared during the occupation of the lake by Turgesius, but it is possible they may have been abandoned for a period. We would certainly have reason to be apprehensive if we were to go by the *Annals of Clonmacnoise.* Here the anonymous author makes his own comment on the invaders and their behaviour. He is referring to the period after 830. The following is an extract:

There was noe creature Living from the smallest chicken to the Greatest and full growen beast, but paid a yearly Tribute to theire Kinge, noe not soe much as the youngest infant newly borne, but paid a noble in gold or silver or the nose from the bare bone. If the owner of the house where a Dane would lodge, had noe more in the world to live upon but one milch cowe for the maintenance of himselfe and his familie, he was compelled presently to kill her to make the Dane good cheere, if it were not otherwise Redeemed with money or some other good Thing to his Likeing. The howses of religion generally throughout the whole Kingdome were by them turned to be Brothell houses, stables, & houses of easment. Yea, the sacred alters of God, that saints had in great Reverence were broken, abused and cast down by them most scornfully, Pagan like and wickedly, to the great Grief of all Christian people. The great Tamberlane, called the scorge of God, could not be compared to them for Cruelty, Covetousness & Insolency. As many women as they coud Lay hands upon, noble or ignoble, young or ould, married or unmarried, whatsoever birth or adge they were of, were by them abused most beastly, and filthily, and such of them as they liked best, were by them sent over seas into their own countryes there to be kept by them to use theire unlawfull lusts. [3]

Monasteries Recover

However, the island monasteries survived Turgesius. The monks returned and the old houses were renewed. We read in the annals of a celebrated abbot of Inchcleraun who died in 870 and was noted far and wide for his wisdom and scholastic achievements, which would indicate a prosperous monastery equipped with a library and scriptorium. Abbots of Inchbofin and Inis Aingin are also recorded in the half-century following Turgesius. The only disruption of this peaceful interlude resulted from a raid on the monasteries in 907 by no less a figure than the bishop of Cashel, Cormac Mac Cuileannáin, who became embroiled in a bitter dispute with the high king, Flann Sionna. Cormac put a fleet on the Shannon and sailed to Lough Ree to attack the kingdom of Midhe. This is another example of the divisive, wasteful fighting of the Irish and the debilitating involvement of the church. Flann defeated and killed the archbishop and destroyed the forces of Munster in the following year, with the result that the Vikings were subsequently able to re-establish themselves strongly in the south of the country. Flann himself was a great patron of the church; it was he who commissioned the celebrated Cross of the Scriptures, which stands to this day at Clonmacnois and asks in stone for "a prayer for Flann."

Renewed Strife

The period after 840 saw the Vikings tending to occupy the places they had taken over. These were mainly the *longforts* they had established along the coast, chief among which were Dublin, Annagasson, Waterford and Limerick, and these would continue to be strongholds of Viking power in the centuries ahead. In the latter decades of the ninth century in Ireland, the power of the invaders had waned considerably. They were busy with the colonisation of Iceland. The flow of hungry warriors in search of plunder, which had become such a chilling reality of Irish life, was now diverted. In addition, Viking armies in the west had suffered serious reverses which had curtailed their power in Brittany and Northern England.

The Dublin Vikings were weakened from supporting their overseas colleagues and when Cearbhall, king of Leinster, attacked in 902, he captured Dublin.

These years were the low point of Viking power in the country but it was not destined to remain at this level for very long. As Iceland became saturated with its new colonists, another Viking generation began pushing south in search of land and piracy. Neither France nor Britain was an inviting proposition for them. The Vikings in Normandy under Rollo had settled down as law abiding citizens and they fought off the new raiders. England had witnessed a resurgence of Angles and Saxons that had made it less hospitable to plundering visitors. Ireland, however, still had an abundance of wealth and was vulnerable to well equipped and determined attackers. Dublin was overrun by them and they defeated the Leinster men in 916 and made Sitric their king. Niall Glundubh, the Irish High King, marched on Dublin but he was heavily defeated and slain by the Vikings near Islandbridge in 919. This was the signal for a vigorous new Viking campaign with conquest as its primary objective.

Sitric, King of Dublin, left in 920 to become king of Scandinavian York. When his kinsman Godfrith succeeded him in Dublin in 921 he considered himself the strongest power in the land. In this year a new wave of Vikings, led by their king, Tamar Mac Ailche descended on Limerick and established their fortress there. They immediately made an expedition up the Shannon, plundering Clonmacnois and reaching Lough Ree in 921, when they despoiled the monasteries of the lake and "carried off a great booty of gold, silver and all manner of riches from the Lough."[4] In 922 we read that the foreigners were back on Lough Ree again, under a new leader, Colla, son of Berach, lord of Limerick, and it was by them Eachtighearn, Irish king of *Breagh Maine*,[5] was slain.

The *Annals of Clonmacnoise* under the year 926 inform us that "the Danes of Lymbrick resided on Loghrie." In 927 "a new fleet was launched upon Lough Ree between Conmaicne and Tuath nElla where Cathal Ua Maele and Flaithbheartach ... were slain." In 929, we are told, "the Vikings of Limerick took up their station" on Lough Ree. This period up to 937 is one of continuous occupation of Lough Ree by the Vikings and it includes a deadly power struggle between the Vikings of Dublin and of Limerick. It is well summed up by Alfred P. Smyth:

> From 931 to 937, it is possible to speak of continuous Scandinavian occupation on the lake which must have resulted in the temporary abandonment of the island monasteries and the occupation of the islands by Viking war bands. The Annals of Ulster note the presence of a `fleet on Lough Ree' in 932, while the Four Masters claim it sailed from Limerick and that it took up its position in 931. The Limerick origin of this fleet is confirmed by the Four Masters in 933 when they note that Olafr Cenncairech of Limerick slew Ui Maine leaders at Duibhthir, a region bordering on the south-western Connaught side of Lough Ree. In the following year (934) the Limerick Vikings were rampaging across the Plains of Connaught, a campaign which must have been launched from Lough Ree, and two years later (936), we hear of the Limerick Olafr taking his ships overland from the Erne back to Lough Ree after a campaign in the north. The annals specifically mention Olafr's continuous occupation of Lough Ree from Christmas night 936 to Lammas, or August, 937, when he was captured by Olafr Gothfrithsson of Dublin and had his Limerick long-ships broken up in the lake.[6]

Battle of Lough Ree

The battle on Lough Ree in August 937 was the culmination of a power struggle between the two strongest Viking forces in the country, those of Dublin and Limerick. It was a huge hosting and may have been the biggest military engagement ever seen on the lake up to that time. No record survives of the strength of the forces on either side, but, given that these two powers had opposed each other with might and main for nearly twenty years, it is certain that each side was at maximum strength. When the Dublin Vikings prevailed and captured the ships of their enemies, the annals tell us that they broke them, a very rare occurrence among Vikings, who knew the value of ships and had a special regard for them. The inference is that they captured so many ships that they did not have sufficient crew to take them away in safety, so they smashed them rather than run the risk of their falling into the hands of their former owners.

During this period of Viking supremacy on Lough Ree, the Limerick Vikings used the lake as a base for raiding parties, plundering the whole countryside within their reach over a period of years. For this they needed a fortified stronghold on the lake. An archaeological dig in the inner lakes near Ballykeeran has revealed that some work had been done there by the Vikings preparing a site for such a stronghold, but it was the opinion of the archaeological team that it had not been completed and had never been used, indicating perhaps that it may have been abandoned in favour of a different location. In this context it is worth recalling that in the centuries of Viking campaigns on the lake it was always from the eastern side they encountered most serious opposition. Here was the territory of the southern Uí Neill and the clan Colmain was powerful enough to claim the high kingship many times. It was here too that Turgesius came to a sudden end.

Now, a century later, the annals are recording that the *Fer Cúl*, a staunch petty kingdom on the eastern shore of Lough Ree, has established a fortress beside them on Inchmore. We do not hear of this Irish fortress until it figures in a dispute between the *Fer Cúl* and the king of Ui Maine on the Connaught side of the lake in 962, but thirty years earlier it may well have been the reason the Vikings abandoned their position in the south of the lake. Since the eastern shore was always so well defended by the Irish, it offered no advantages as a Viking base. The question is, then, where did the Vikings go for an alternative base? Not to Rindoon, if our hypothesis is correct, for that would have brought them right opposite Inchmore. The obvious way to go was north and west to Inchenagh and Clooneigh Bay on the Connaught shore. This links with the campaigns of the Limerick Vikings, which were directed mainly at Connaught between Lough Ree and Lough Corrib, and which campaigns would have profited from a base located to the west of the lake. A Viking hoard discovered in modern times near Strokestown is a further pointer in this direction.

Hoards

Further evidence of the size and scope of Viking activity on Lough Ree in this period comes from the discovery of two very valuable collections of treasure on Inis Aingin (Hare Island). Some one hundred and twenty Viking hoards, whether of coin, silver or gold, have been discovered in Ireland, the greatest concentration being in the midlands, especially in Co. Westmeath. Most of them were found in the nineteenth century, or earlier, when facilities for recording and preserving them were inadequate or non-existent. They are indicators of the great wealth of the country in Viking times, as compared with Scotland in the same period, where some thirty hoards have been discovered. Of the two Viking hoards found buried on Inis Aingin on Lough Ree, the first, discovered in 1802, contained ten gold arm rings, many of them richly ornamented, in all about eleven pounds in weight. The second contained a quantity of silver arm rings and silver ingots. It is believed that both hoards are associated with the occupation of Lough Ree by the Limerick Vikings in the 930s and in particular with the fierce naval battle on the lake in August 937 in which they were defeated by Olafr Gothfrithsson and his Dublin followers.

Part of a Viking gold hoard from Hare Island.

About eighty of the recorded hoards in Ireland are coin hoards. There was no native coinage in Ireland before the twelfth century and the Vikings did not commence minting here until the year 1000. Therefore, all coins prior to this date came from elsewhere; the majority from Britain — but others from France, Germany, Western Asia, the Caspian Sea and the Middle East, indicating the far-flung range of Viking activity whether as raiders or traders in these centuries. A further pair of silver arm rings, of a similar style to the first hoard, was found in the river Shannon at Athlone. These hoards bear witness to the success of the plundering invaders. Eleven pounds weight of solid gold is certainly impressive. The presence of such wealth is also linked with the affluence of the Lough Ree monasteries which must have compared well with the best in Ireland at that time.

The plundered monasteries of the lake were abandoned during the occupation. Their communities were scattered or killed and they lost everything. Some may never have regained their former status, a fact which must be borne in mind when examining individual island histories and features later on, as in the case of Inchenagh and perhaps Inchturk and Inchmore. The defeat of the Limerick Vikings in the battle of Lough Ree did not herald a period of domination by Godfraidh and his Dublin warriors. The men of Midhe were still a major stumbling block to Viking ambitions, a fact well evidenced by their fortifying Inchmore island. The advent of Malachy II as king of Midhe stiffened the Irish resistance from Lough Ree through Midhe and Leinster.

However, in the second half of the tenth century, the political centre of gravity began to move very slowly southwards. The rather small kingdom of *Dal gCais*, in present day Clare, was beginning to assert itself and the repercussions of its activities would eventually echo and re-echo across the land. These events would also have a profound effect on Lough Ree, its islands and shore dwellers, and the lake and its environs would be at the heart of some of the major political moves that were destined to shape the history of Ireland for succeeding centuries.

Dal gCais

Cinnétig, petty king of *Dal gCais*, was down the pecking order of royalty in Munster, where the *Eoghanacht* were traditional kings, commanding obedience from their palace in Cashel. The tenth century, however, had seen the former superiority of this dynasty come under serious challenge. Not only had they suffered at the hands of the invading Vikings, disaster had struck from within, when their king, the warrior bishop, Cormac Mac Cuileannáin went to war with the high king and was defeated and killed by him. As a result, the Vikings had taken a firm grip on Munster by mid-century. In the local power vacuum the *Dal gCais* began to emerge as the principal source of opposition to the foreigners. The sons of Cinnétig, and, in common with the kings of his time he had many of them, fought campaigns against the Vikings, albeit with limited success, one of them, at least, having given his life on the battlefield. Another son, Marcán, was abbot of the monastery of *Imlech Ibiur* (Emly) and later of *Tír Dá Glas* (Terryglass). The next son, Mathún by name, continued the struggle, encouraged and supported by the younger brother, Brian, who trained an army in the Slieve Aughty mountains, thus enabling Mathún to score a decisive victory over the Vikings at the battle of Sulcóid in 967.

The *Dal gCais* were now the strongest power in Munster. The *Eoghanacht* were incensed and plotted against Mathún. They had him assassinated in 976. Brian rose in anger to avenge his brother, decimated the *Eoghanacht* and became king of Munster in 978. Having firmly established his authority in the southern province, Brian set his sights on the high kingship. Malachy the second of Midhe had become the lawful *ard rí* in 980, and over the next fifteen years the two kings fought and skirmished for the throne.

Malachy's native territory bordered the eastern shore of Lough Ree. In 988, Brian arrived on the lake with a great fleet and attacked Midhe with apparent success. When part of Brian's fleet diverted to raid Connaught, he was defeated with heavy casualties. The annals record these events:

> *A fleet, viz. three hundred boats, was put on Lough Ree by Brian, and they harried Midhe and went to Uisneach. And twenty five boats of these went into Connachta and a great slaughter of their crews was inflicted there.*[7]

Five years later Brian was back on Lough Ree, this time to attack the men of Breifne, who had allied themselves with Malachy. The annals record briefly:

A naval raid by Brian and he reached Breifne from Lough Ree by way of Ath Liag[8] northwards.[9]

The pattern of attack and counter attack continued. Malachy raided the territory of the Dal gCais and felled the sacred tree on the coronation mound at Magh Aidhir. In 997, at the behest of Malachy, a deal was worked out between the two kings and Brian was back again on Lough Ree, this time for peace. This is how it is described in the Irish tract Cogadh Gaedhel re Gallaibh:

Brian, now made a great expedition to Plein Pattoici where Maelsechlainn came to meet him and they concluded a mutual peace there, viz,, such hostages of the Leth Mogha as Maelsechlainn had i.e. hostages of the foreigners and of the Laighin... to be ceded to Brian; and the sole sovereignty of Leth Cuinn, from thenceforth to belong to Maelsechlainn without war or trespass from Brian.[10]

Leth Moga (Leath Mhogha) was the southern half of Ireland which was now conceded to Brian, a move which provoked an immediate revolt by the Leinster men who hated the Munster king and resented his new found sovereignty over Leinster. Brian, however, mustered his troops and marched into Leinster where he inflicted a crushing defeat on his foes at Gleann Máma in Wicklow in 999. The victory increased his powers and enhanced his prospects of becoming *ard rí*, so that he reneged on his treaty with Malachy and once again in 1001 he is coming up the Shannon, at the head of an armed force, to renew hostilities with his erstwhile allies. However, Malachy and the men of Connaught placed a "great obstruction" on the river at Athlone to block his way forward. Shortly after this Malachy made one of the great gestures of Irish history when he abdicated his throne and handed the high kingship to Brian, in order that there might be a unified power in the country to confront the Viking threat. In the words of a latter day poet

"He laid down his crown for his country's sake
He served a rival and he saved the land"

With matters thus resolved it might have been thought that Lough Ree had seen the last of Brian Boru, but not so. Ulster now revolted and had to be subdued. Brian brought strong forces by land and water to the northern province in the years following. In this he was assisted by Malachy, the men of Connaught and even by the Vikings of Dublin, so that by 1006 he was able to make the "Circuit of Ireland," the traditional victory celebration of an Irish high king. The annalist records:

> *Brian, together with the men of Mumu, the Laigin, the men of Mide, Maelsechnaill, the Connachta, the foreigners of Ath Cliath and the men of the whole of Ireland south of Slieve Fuait to Ath Luain, went to Es Ruaid, proceeded across it northwards and made a circuit of the north of Ireland including Cenél Conaill, Cinél Eogain, Ulaid and Airgialla.*[11]

Brian was now undisputed *ard rí* and in the Book of Armagh he named himself "Imperator Scotorum," Emperor of the Irish.

Battle of Clontarf

As Brian's power reached its zenith, the inevitable confrontation with the Vikings loomed. A series of events brought matters to a head and the battle was fought at Clontarf outside Dublin on Good Friday 1014. Much has been written of this watershed of Irish history. Here a modern author sums it up well:

> *Between Liffey and Tolka, within a mile or two of Dublin Bay, there gathered on behalf of Ireland in April 1014 the high king, Brian with his son Murchad and grandson Tordelhach, Maelseachlainn and the southern O'Neill, and Ospak of Man. Opposing them, with their backs to the sea, stood jarl Sigurd the Stout of Orkney, Brodir of*

Man, Maelmordha with his Leinstermen, and the Dublin Vikings under the command of Dubhgall, brother of Sigtrygg Silk-beard. It was an alignment which set brother against brother, father-in-law against son-in-law, Irishman against Irishman, Viking against Viking and the skalds and sagamen did it justice, weaving many remarkable personalities, motives and incidents into their tragic tapestries. There was Gormflaith, (Kormlod) mother of Sigtrygg Silk-beard, sister of Maelmordha, widow of Olaf Kvaran, divorced consort of Maelsheachlainn, deserting wife of Brian, impossibly promised as a prize of victory to both Sigurd of Orkney and Brodir of Man, with the Dublin kingdom for dowry. On the Irish side Brian was cut down as he prayed for victory in "Tomar's Wood," his son Murchad was killed even as victory came in sight, and his grandson Tordelbach, hunting victims by the river-mouth as a seal hunts salmon, was drowned near the Weir of Clontarf. Along with their leaders died 4,000 Irishmen. Of Vikings and Leinstermen the slaughter was worse, for when they fled it was to the hardly attainable refuge of their ships or the Viking stronghold over the Liffey. Sigurd died bravely, Brodir gruesomely (if we may trust to Njals Saga 157), and with them 7,000 men. Thereafter it was clear that Ireland would never fall under a Norse yoke but it also happened that the Norsemen were neither now nor later expelled from Ireland. They remained important to the country's trade and the development of its towns, had kings here and princes there, survived the military disasters of 1052, and were still royally led at the coming of the English in the 1160s and 70s. [12]

CHAPTER 4

Post Viking Era

The two centuries which had elapsed from the first appearance of the Vikings had seen many changes. The establishment of towns such as Wexford, Waterford and Limerick was a new development. There was a rapid expansion in trade and commerce. The Vikings were talented as business people and Dublin became an important trading port. They were the first to mint coinage in Ireland. Another legacy was a huge increase in the use of ships for warfare in Ireland. When Turlough O'Connor brought a fleet of ships on to Lough Ree in 1137, the annalist comments that it was a "brave expedition" because Turlough had but twenty ships and his adversaries had two hundred vessels. A century later, the O'Connors established their supremacy by taking large fleets on the sea to places as far distant as Lough Swilly thus promoting themselves as chief contenders for the high-kingship.

In the field of literature and art the Viking period marked a shift in the literary centre of the country, away from Armagh and the

north, to Clonmacnois and the Shannon basin. In metalwork several Viking motifs were adapted. The artists practised an elegant and sophisticated animal art form, subsequently apparent in Irish masterpieces from the eleventh and twelfth centuries. One instance is the Cross of Cong, from the workshops of Clonmacnois. This priceless treasure was completed by the metal artists of the Roscommon monastery close to the shores of Lough Ree.[1] Thousands of lines of the

Cross of Cong as depicted by Margaret Stokes.

poetry of Giolla-na-naomh O Duind[2] [O Duinn] from Inchcleraun still survive[3]. Edward O'Reilly lists six poems ascribed to O Duind, the shortest of which contains 128 verses and the longest of which runs to 392 verses[4]. All six poems are to be found in manuscripts held in the Royal Irish Academy[5]. There is nothing from elsewhere in Lough Ree out of all that period despite the fame of some of the island monasteries for achievement and scholarship. Since so little has survived, it is tempting to think that much may have been plundered or destroyed,

Copy of poem by Giolla na Naomh O Duind.
Courtesy of the Royal Irish Academy.

and that the insular locations of the monasteries made safeguarding or concealing their valuables difficult if not impossible.

Reform

In the aftermath of Clontarf both church and state were in some disarray. Contention for the high-kingship intensified. Dynastic struggles, plunderings, burnings and open warfare characterised the next century and a half of Irish life. Lough Ree was no exception as civil strife erupted all along its eastern shore. Several of the petty kingdoms revolted against the house of Maelsheachlainn, resulting in conflict that cost many lives:

A great number of the people of West Meath, Dealbhna and Cuircne was slain on Lough Ree by Donal, son of Flann Ua Maelseachlann and the battle in which they were defeated was called the 'Breach of the Boats'.[6]

At a higher level the different kingdoms vied with each other for supremacy, as the rulers of the different provinces sought the high kingship, *na hArd Rithe co freasabhra*, the high kings with opposition as they were called. Modern historians, however, see a political progression at work and suggest that the country was in process of reaching new levels of unity and peace before the Norman invasion. The church, too, was in need of reorganisation. The Irish church from the time of St Patrick had developed in isolation and was in some important organisational areas quite different from the church in Europe. Monasteries had become secularised and prolonged exploitation by warring powers, both native and foreign, had weakened their essential fabric and lessened their moral impact. Unordained men held rights of succession to monasteries. Monastic boundaries were ill-defined or not defined at all. It is quite remarkable that the early Irish church had not extended its remit outside the immediate religious sphere and something as important as the marriages of the faithful belonged in the secular domain. Lanfranc, archbishop of Canterbury, when he wrote to the high king, Turlough O'Brien in 1074 was unhappy with moral standards in Ireland. He said among other things:

A man will abandon his lawfully wedded wife ... and take to himself some other wife ... Bishops are consecrated by one bishop only ... Many bishops are ordained in towns and cities ... Children are baptised without consecrated chrism ... Holy Orders are conferred by bishops for money.[7]

All, or nearly all, of the abuses would come under the heading of church structure and discipline. First, Ceallach (Celsus), and then Malachy of Armagh spearheaded the reform. The dioceses were constituted and their territorial boundaries delineated. A parochial system of organisation was put in place. Each diocese would be ruled by a bishop who would also be in charge of monastic properties, and all bishops would be appointed by Rome. The religious orders from the continent were invited to Ireland to build new monasteries and to colonise and reorganise old ones. The reform movement of St. Malachy signalled the end of the ancient Gaelic monastic system. Some of the reforms were far-reaching in their implications. Malachy himself was instrumental in introducing the Cistercians from Clairvaux in France and for them he founded the first Cistercian house at Mellifont in 1142.

Augustinian Canons

The Lough Ree monasteries, growing tired after five centuries, were about to experience a new lease of life. Between 1015 and 1193, they, at least according to the annalists, suffered no more than three serious incursions. This must rank as very exceptional. It had the merit of providing a much-needed breathing space for them as they were now entering a transition stage. The major reforms of the Irish church, mentioned above, were being put into operation.

The biggest change for the Lough Ree monasteries was the adoption of the rule of the Augustinian Canons. By far the most widespread of the new orders in Ireland were the monks who followed this rule. Malachy visited the Augustinian community in Arrouais in France in 1100 and took back with him the rules and documents governing them. Soon after, the first house of the order was established in Ireland. This order became known as the Canons

Augustinian Canon as depicted by Archdall in 1786.

Regular of St. Augustine. Very many of the existing monasteries now invited the new monks and adapted their rule and life-style. By the time of the Norman invasion (1169) there were more than sixty foundations of the order in Ireland, and at the height of its numerical strength it is calculated that it had 233 monasteries in Ireland for men and 33 for women.[8] Not infrequently nuns and monks of the order belonged to the same monastery, living in different areas of the grounds but worshipping in the same church.

The monastery of Inchcleraun adopted the rule about the year 1160 and became a priory dedicated to St. Mary. The order takes its name from St. Augustine, one of the great fathers of the church who was born in 354 A.D. and was bishop of Hippo, a town in North Africa on the Mediterranean coast. Augustine wrote extensively and one of his works *De Operibus Monicharum* treats of the religious life. Centuries later this work was receiving the attention of churchmen and scholars. The Lateran Council, in the year 1059, addressed itself to clergy attached to cathedral and collegiate churches exhorting them to lead a community life in accordance with some form of religious rule. The guidelines indicated by Augustine were adopted for the new order which now emerged.

The members of the new order had much of the life-style of monks. They lived in community, practised the vows of poverty, chastity and obedience and chanted the divine office. They also functioned as secular clergy, with full parish responsibilities and the pastoral care of their congregations. In addition, they set up almshouses where the poor and needy were provided for. They also undertook the care of the sick and many priories had hospitals attached.

Whether new personnel from France and Italy arrived on the lake we have no way of knowing, but it is quite certain that canons trained in the new system took charge of the monasteries sometime in the period 1135-1155. French, German and Italian clergy officiated in the Irish church in subsequent centuries. New stone buildings were erected in architectural styles other than the vernacular. The traditional flat lintelled doorways and antae projections of the Irish gave way to the new Hiberno-Romanesque styles, with windows splayed inwards to admit the maximum of light and the minimum of cold and wet. This style in its later development became very ornate and one of its most singular expressions is the beautiful window that still adorns the gable of the ruined church on Inchbofin. The Lough Ree institutions forfeited their appellation as monasteries and from now on are described as priories under the care of a prior.

Further Conflict

On the political scene, this period saw the Lough Ree priories coming more and more under the patronage of Connaught and the O'Connors rather than the families of the Meath dynasty. The two big raids of 1087 and 1089 are classic examples of the political turmoil that the country was experiencing at this time. Turlough O'Brien, king of Munster and *Rí Érenn* according to the annals of Ulster, died in 1086, his son Muircheartach having assumed the royal mantle. This was the signal for the other provinces, most of which had pretensions to the high kingship, to shake off the yoke of Munster. Connaught revolted. Maelsheachlann of Meath invaded north Leinster and Dublin. Muircheartach responded by moving against Connaught. He sent a great fleet up the Shannon to Lough Ree and plundered the churches of the lake. And so the conflict continued. A few years later he again found it necessary to subdue the Connaught men and another great fleet was sent to Lough Ree with similar devastating results for the monasteries. However, the primacy of the Munster kings was soon to wane. The advent of Turlough O'Connor in Connaught heralded the ascendancy of the western dynasty. Turlough became the strongest high king in Ireland since the time of Brian Boru. On his death in 1156 he was succeeded by his son Rory. The winter of that year turned out to be one of the coldest ever recorded in Ireland and Rory found it necessary to move his Lough Ree fleet to Rindoon.

There was great snow and intense frost in the winter of this year so that the lakes and rivers of Ireland were frozen over. Such was the greatness of the frost that Rory O'Connor drew his ships and boats on the ice from Bléan-Gaille to Rindoon. The most of the birds of

Ireland perished on account of the greatness of the snow and the frost.[9]

Prayer and Pilgrimage.

The supremacy of the Connaught kings brought an era of peace to Lough Ree and facilitated a new flourishing among the religious communities of the lake. Kings and chieftains came bearing gifts. There were pilgrimages which attracted people from near and far and the great and famous sought the monastic cemeteries as their last resting place. The buildings of the religious houses expanded too as the Romanesque architectural styles gave way to the Gothic, and later, as the centuries moved on, the beautiful tracery windows. Some of the priories had the care of churches on the mainland and supplied them with vicars from their own communities.

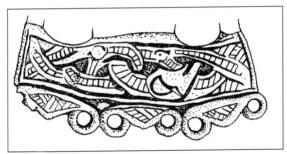

Detail of the decoration on a small bronze Viking fragment discovered on Inchbofin, circa 1911.

CHAPTER 5

The Normans

The Normans invaded Ireland in 1169 and their arrival was destined to have profound consequences for Lough Ree and its environs, as indeed it would have for the rest of the country in the centuries following. A hundred years earlier, the same Normans - descendants of the Viking conquerors of Normandy in France - had overrun England, taken its land and crushed its inhabitants without mercy. They were professional soldiers who fought for conquest and their own enrichment. They had applied new levels of expertise to the practice of warfare. Their arms were of the very best and they wore armour. Their knights fought on horseback while the foot

Anglo-Norman castle at Athlone, built 1210.

soldiers were the archers using the longbow and they boasted advanced military skills. The Normans were expert builders and they defended their conquered territories by erecting stone castles as fortifications around them. Avaricious adventurers, they cared little for anyone but themselves and frequently fought each other in bitter disputes. Their king, Henry of Anjou, who had his own reasons for sending his barons to Ireland, viewed them with the greatest suspicion, knowing that they would revolt against him as soon as it suited their interests.

Although the Normans overran England rapidly after the Battle of Hastings (1066), the conquest of Wales proved more difficult and, a century later, the Welsh were still keeping them at bay. The king, needing to keep a tight leash on his barons, had sent the most troublesome ones to the Welsh marches to grapple with the natives for land. It was to these same barons that he directed Dermot McMurrough, king of Leinster, when approached by that gentleman for help against his Irish enemies. In addition Henry needed a "moral" justification for his campaign of plunder and this he had got from the papal bull, *Laudibiliter*, of Pope Adrian, which in 1155 authorised him to take over Ireland for the purpose of reforming a dissipated and decadent Irish church.

Thus he was able to "bestow" the clan lands of Ireland on his barons as soon as they had gained a foothold on Irish soil. Hugh de Lacy, the most formidable of all the invaders, was given the wealthy kingdom of Meath stretching from the east coast to the shores of Lough Ree. The glory days of this kingdom, when it had frequently and regularly supplied the *ard rí*, were long ended. The dynastic house of Maelsheachlainn had been torn apart by dissensions and bitter internal feuding and in more recent times the western part of the kingdom had been weakened when the O'Farrell clan of northern Teathbha broke away, renaming their territory Anghaile (Annaly). De Lacy lost no time in capitalising on those weaknesses. As lord of Meath he was opposed by the aged chieftain of Breifne, Tighearnan O'Rourke, who had claims to sovereignty over Meath. A meeting between the two was arranged in 1172 at which O'Rourke was treacherously slain, *and they conveyed his head and body ignominiously to Dublin. The head was placed over the gate of the fortress as a spectacle of intense pity to the Irish, and the body was jibbeted with feet upwards, on the northern side of Dublin.*[1]

In the same year as de Lacy was consolidating his gains on the plains of Meath he was also pushing westward towards the Shannon and Lough Ree. Taking advantage of a feud among the O'Rourkes he linked up with one of the dissidents and

plundered Anghaile and Muintir Giollagain, carrying off many cows and prisoners. He afterwards made another incursion into Ardagh of Bishop Mel and ... slew Donnell O'Farrell, chief of Anghaile [2]

By 1177 an advance raiding party had arrived at Lough Ree and crossed the Shannon into Connaught. The entry in the annals for this year reflects something of the state of Ireland socially and politically at this time:

Milo de Cogan with his knights (Normans) was brought by Muircheartach, son of Rory O'Connor (the high king), to Roscommon to spoil Connaught, through hatred towards his father. Connaught truly was thereupon burned ... Rory O'Connor and the men of Connaught along with him gained a victory over the foreigners and drove them by force out of the country. Rory, moreover, blinded his son afterwards in revenge for this expedition.[3]

Strife and sedition

Not only were rival kingdoms and clans prepared to seek the help of the foreigners but even members of families, as in the case cited above, would join with them to despite their own kin. Lough Ree bears ample testimony to the fragmented state of Ireland at this time. An entry in the annals for 1174 states that Rory O'Carroll, Lord of Ely:

was slain in the middle of the island of Inis Clothrann (Inchcleraun in Lough Ree)[4]

Another Irish chieftain, Caroon O'Gilla Ultain, was killed by some of his own people on Inchenagh in Lough Ree in 1180 A.D.[5] while Sitric O'Cuinn, chieftain of Muintir Giollagain (present Co. Longford) was slain by the son of Aedh O'Farrell in 1181.[6] The Normans were faring no better in their own relationships. Strongman de Lacy was appointed the king's justiciar in Ireland but was soon relieved of his post as the king distrusted him deeply.

Rivalries and animosities between the barons were connived to prevent any one individual from becoming too powerful. Strongbow succeeded de Lacy as justiciar only for de Lacy to be re-appointed from 1179-1184. However, his days were numbered and it was a young man from the shores of Lough Ree who brought the career of the robber baron to a sudden and fateful conclusion. All the major annals record the event with undisguised satisfaction,

Hugh de Lacy, the profaner and destroyer of many churches, lord of the English of Meath, Breifne and Oriel, he to whom the tribute of Connaught was paid, he who had conquered the greater part of Ireland for the English, and of whose English castles, all Meath from the Shannon to the sea was full. After having finished the castle of Durrow, he set out, accompanied by three Englishmen, to view it. One of the men of Teathbha, a youth named Gilla-gan-athair O'Meyey approached him, and drawing out an axe, which he had kept concealed, he, with one blow of it, severed his head from his body and both head and trunk fell into the ditch of the castle. This was in revenge of Colmcille. Gilla-gan-athair fled and, by his fleetness of foot, made his escape from the English and Irish to the wood of Kilclare. He afterwards went to the Sinnach (Fox) and O'Breen, at whose instigation he had killed the earl.[7]

The Annals of Ulster record the incident and add that the youth was from Bregh Maine, a territory situated on the southern shore of Lough Ree.

O'Connor Dynasty

The royal house of Connaught which had become so united and powerful in the reign of Turlough Mór O'Connor was shaking in its foundations. Rory, who had succeeded his father, Turlough, as *ard rí*, had seen his country torn apart and his own authority flouted by the invaders. His son Murrough had betrayed him as already described in detail above. His other son Conor Maenmaigh revolted against him and expelled him in 1186, making himself king of Connaught. Three years later, Conor Maenmaigh was killed by his own kin. They then sent messengers to Rory to inform him of the death of his son and to invite him to return as king of Connaught. On his return he took the hostages of all Connaught - hostages that had already been delivered to Conor Maenmaigh, and the annals tell us that these hostages "had been kept on Inis Clothrann, an island in Lough Ree."[8] Fighting now broke out between Cathal Crovderg, youngest son of Turlough Mór O'Connor, and Cathal Carragh, son of Conor Maenmaigh.

A meeting between the followers of these princes was held at the monastery of Clonfert in 1190 with a view to reconciliation, but it broke up in failure. The annals tell us that

> *O'Connor (Crovderg) and his followers went to Clonmacnois on that night and early next morning embarked in their fleet and sailed up the Shannon until they came to Lough Ree. A violent storm arose on the lake by which their vessels were separated from each other and the storm so agitated the vessel in which O'Connor was that it could not be piloted. Such was the fury of the storm it foundered and all the crew perished, except O'Connor himself and six others.* [9]

The entry goes on to name several of those who were lost. Both the *Annals of Loch Cé* and the *Annals of Ulster* record this event and state that thirty-six men were lost on O'Connor's boat alone, an indication of the sudden and devastating storms associated with this lake right down to the present day.

Despite the lamentable disarray of the O'Connor dynasty the Normans had not so far succeeded in erecting a single castle in

Connaught. There had been a number of isolated raids, including a particularly vicious attack on the monastery of Inchcleraun, by the Norman Gilbert Mac Coisdealbha, aided and abetted by the sons of Conor Maenmaigh O'Connor in 1193. In another development in the O'Connor blood feud the Normans took sides with one of the protagonists in 1199.

> *John de Courcy, with the English of Ulidia, and the son of Hugh de Lacy, with the English of Meath, marched to Kilmacduagh to assist Cathal Crovderg O'Connor. Cathal Carragh, accompanied by the Connacians, came and gave them battle; and the English of Ulidia and Meath were defeated with such slaughter that of their five battalions only two survived; and these were pursued from the field of battle to Rindown on Lough Ree, in which place John was completely hemmed in. Many of his English were killed and others were drowned; for they found no passage by which to escape, except by crossing the lake in boats.[10]*

Rory O'Connor, last high king of Ireland died in 1198 and Cathal Crovderg became undisputed king of Connaught in 1201. De Burgh had been "granted" Connaught by King John, except five cantreds which the king retained for himself, and he now set about making settlements in the province and erecting castles but the move failed due to the power of Cathal Crovderg which continued up to his death in 1224.

The Annals of Loch Cé inform us of the "Foreign bishop" (de Grey) in Athlone who was appointed justiciar and ordered by the king to erect three castles in Connaught. The bishop, however, was recalled to England and Richard Tuite, one time underling to de Lacy in Meath, was appointed lord chief justice. Whereupon he:

> *went to Athlone that he himself might reside in Dublin and Athlone alternately, but it happened that some of the stones of the castle at Athlone fell upon his head and killed on the spot Richard Tuite with his priest and some of his people.[11]*

Connaught under new attack

Another attempt to gain a foothold in Connaught and erect castles there took place at the northern extremity of Lough Ree in 1220.

> *The castle of Áth Liag was attempted to be made by Walter de Lacy and all the forces of Midhe. When the Connaughtmen heard this they came across from the west and proceeded through the middle of Muintir Anghaile and into Magh-Breghmhuidhe, where they burned Daingen-Uí-Chuinn and went through it westwards into the Caladh; and the castle was abandoned to them, through force and on conditions of peace.*[12]

Walter de Lacy was the son of Hugh, first Lord of Meath. Again it was the strength and vigilance of Cathal Crovderg, king of Connaught, that prevented their incursion from being successful. *Caladh* was the name of the territory along Lough Ree roughly comprising the parishes of Rathcline and Cashel. This event is also chronicled for the year 1220 as follows:

> *An army was led by Walter de Lacy and the English of Meath to Athliag, where they erected the greater part of a castle. Another army was led by Cathal Crovderg eastwards across the Shannon into the territory of Caladh and the English, being stricken with fear, made peace with him and the Connaughtmen destroyed the castle. (Note: The site of this castle was on the west bank of the river at Ballyleague)*[13]

The death of Cathal Crovderg in 1224 marked the end of strong central government in Connaught. The kingship was assumed by Cathal's son, Hugh, but immediately contested by other branches of the family, and for the next twenty five years Connaught was in the grip of violence and anarchy. Hugh, opposed by the sons of Rory O'Connor, sought help from the Anglo Normans in Athlone who were happy to keep the blood feud going and thus advance their own ambitions of conquest. Dynastic struggles were often largely

Rindoon Castle. *Drawn by Lorraine Francis from an old engraving.*

contained within the ambit of the upper classes, but on this occasion there was a deliberate campaign of plundering the inhabitants, who fled before them in terror, as the scale of violence and devastation descended into barbarism. While some of the fugitives escaped, "the greater part...were drowned and the baskets of the fishing weirs were found full of drowned children ..."[14]

Despite the serious debility induced by internal strife in Connaught, the Normans failed to take full advantage of their opportunity. This was largely because of the rivalries and dissensions in their own camp. Their alliance with Hugh O'Connor was short-lived and he attacked them in Athlone and "plundered the market of Athlone and burned the whole town in 1227."[15] The same year Geoffrey de Marisco (Meares), aided by a dissident O'Connor prince erected a castle at Rindoon on the western shore of Lough Ree. Rindoon, it will be recalled, was the site of the fortress of the Viking Turgesius four centuries before and because of its natural advantages for strategic defence the place was probably used as a stronghold from the earliest times. The following year, the same de Marisco, who was the king's justiciar in Ireland, erected a castle at Ath Liag. This was on the east bank of the Shannon in present-day Lanesborough where the river enters Lough Ree. It was known through subsequent centuries as Meare's Fort commanding the river-crossing at this point. Having figured in many notable campaigns it finally came to an end when its masonry was used to build the first stone bridge at Lanesborough in 1706.

Rindoon

The de Burghs were gaining ground in Connaught and the year 1230 saw a great hosting by William de Burgh "so that much of Connaught was destroyed by him."[16] The Norman Mac Costelloes and their allies, having plundered east Connaught were guarding their prey of cows on Rindoon in Lough Ree. Felim O'Connor, the king, mustered a raiding party and marched to Rindoon.

> *And they advanced to Rindoon and went furiously across the bádhun and over the ditch of the island (peninsula) in which all the cows of the country were and every captain of a company and every chief of a host went after the cows and they took the cows away with them as they met them*[17]

However the king was forced to stand and fight. This he did and many of the enemy's forces were killed in this encounter by Felim upon the peninsula and outside it. The *Annals of Clonmacnoise* add some interesting detail to this account of the battle of Rindoon.

> *Felim O'Connor with an army came to Connaught again and marched on until he came to John's-house, took all the spoils of the town and lands thereof, and left nothing that they could take or see, from the door of the castle forth. Felim's camp lay at the market cross of the town; many of the meaner sort of Felim's army were drowned in the puddle of that town; he left much of the small cattle of the said prey.*[18]

This account goes on to say that the justiciar Macmorish at that time lived on Rindoon otherwise known as John's-house. It is evident that Rindoon was an important centre in the social and political life of those times. The puddle in which so many were drowned may

Remains of windmill at Rindoon.

have been the moat around the castle which is still quite visible or it may have been the swamp that lay to the south east. The Norman justiciar continued the policy of strengthening the fortifications on Rindoon, which was seen increasingly as an important post for the defence of Athlone and the consolidation of the Norman advance into Connaught. Robert De Ufford was justiciar in the year 1277 and he was actively maintaining the castle and repairing the wooden towers of the windmill, as appears from this contemporary document:

Expenditure of Robert, aforesaid, in bread, wine, beer, meat, fish, fees of castles, a mill lately constructed at Rendon, wooden towers newly constructed there, repairing and improving a fosse there, repairing houses of the castle of Athlone, purchase of cloth, furs, and horses, wages of crossbowmen, Welshmen, and other vassals, and other necessary expenses, both great and small, incurred by Adam aforesaid in Ireland, as appears by Robert's roll of expenditure delivered into the Exchequer by Adam - £2,136 9s 0d. 27th September 1277.[19]

Another occurrence at this time was the drowning of Rory O'Connor, grandson of Cathal Crovderg "in Curreen Connachtach at Ath Liag-na-Sinna on the ninth day of March 1244 and (he) was interred in the monastery of Cluain-tuaiscirt with great veneration."[20]

By this time the de Burgh power in Connaught had grown considerably and the Normans had made some inroads on the plains, stretching from the Shannon River to the western lakes of Corrib and Conn, where they were busily engaged in erecting castles on their frontiers. The O'Connor influence had diminished due largely to the bitter feuds that had raged throughout this dynastic family, following the death of Cathal Crovderg in 1224, and their dominance was now largely confined to counties Leitrim and Roscommon. As things turned out these gains were to mark the zenith of Norman achievement.

Rindoon: the extant remains

For a full description of the extant remains on the peninsula of Rindoon the reader is referred to Avril Thomas's *The walled towns of Ireland*[21]. Apart from the very considerable ruins of the Royal castle at Rindoon there are extensive stretches of the medieval town wall still standing. This wall enclosed an area of c25 hectares. The sheer size of the enclosure indicates that it was, in medieval times, a considerably larger town than its neighbour Athlone. The town wall at Rindoon has three squared towers and one surviving gateway. Other interesting structures include a windmill, the parish church and the friary church of the Fratres Cruciferi – the town has been deserted since the 13th century – sadly this site is not in state care. Rindoon is a storybook in stone just waiting to be discovered. From its origins possibly as a Celtic fort, to becoming a Viking base, a ferry route joining the ancient kingdoms of Meath and Connaught and finally a medieval castle and walled-town – the site is steeped in history and lore and surely deserves to be preserved and interpreted for future generations. The site is private property.

CHAPTER 6

Gaelicisation

The advent of Felim O'Connor as king of Connaught in 1249 signalled a campaign to restore stability to the province with the result that by the end of the thirteenth century the conquest had lost much of its original momentum. The king of England appointed a new justiciar, Alan La Zouche, who arrived in Ireland in 1256 and held a conference with Felim O'Connor at Rindoon where they made peace on condition that "the territory and lands of O'Connor should not be circumscribed"[1] as long as the justiciar held office. From now on the invaders acquired little in the way of new territory but rather concentrated on defending what they had.

The Irish made a determined effort to unite in a common cause at the conference of Caol Uisce in 1258, but they soon lapsed back into tribal conflict. Despite that, however, a new and better spirit seemed to prevail as the Gaelic chieftains began to regain lost ground. Lough Ree, which had been ringed by Norman fortifications, began to witness a change in fortune. The castle of Rindoon was burnt by Hugh O'Connor, the new king of Connaught, in 1270, while in the following year he demolished the castles at Ath Liag (Ballyleague) and Roscommon. In 1272 "Athlone was burned by him (Hugh) and its bridge broken down."[2]

On the eastern reaches of the lake also there was regrouping and reorganising on the part of the native clans. When Richard Tuite returned with an army of the foreigners of Meath in 1285, he was heavily defeated by Maelsheachlainn and the Irish, and he himself was killed in Athlone. He was a descendant of that Richard Tuite who also died in Athlone seventy five years earlier, when the newly built castle tower collapsed on him. The O'Farrells captured and demolished the castles of Baile Nui, Magh Dumha and Delamere's castle at Magh Breacruighe in 1295. The annals record these events and add "Sir John Delamere, knight, the best, worthyest, powerfullest knight of all Meath, was killed by Geoffrey O'Farrell in pursuit and defence of his own prey."[3] To the west and south of Lough Ree the O'Kellys of Uí Maine lost territory to the new

Augustinian Nun from Lough Ree.

occupiers, but their ongoing, staunch resistance prevented a wholesale conquest and confined the Norman settlement to the districts immediately around Athlone.

Two Nations

Slowly and painfully a pattern of land ownership was emerging and, however volatile the situation, it became increasingly evident that the two nations, each with its own language and culture, were fated to live together check by jowl. The Norman baron ruled from his castle under the provisions of the feudal statutes while the Irish chieftain dealt with his clans in accordance with traditional Brehon laws. Each feuded and fought among themselves and often against each other while on occasion elements from one camp joined with factions from the other, generally in pursuit of some local short term objective. The English crown, busy with other matters, took but occasional interest in the proceedings.

The Bruce invasion provided an opportunity for some of the Irish, especially in Leinster, to attempt reoccupation of their former lands. Their success however was but temporary. The nearest Bruce came to Lough Ree was when he spent Christmas of 1315 in the monastery of Loughsewdy in Ballymore, which is about twelve kilometres from the eastern shore.

A Gathering of the Bards of Ireland

The *Annals of Clonmacnoise* records a great cultural festival which was held on the shores of Lough Ree in 1351. It was hosted by William Boy O'Kelly and is recorded in the annals thus:

> "*A.D. 1351 – William Mac Donnough Moyneagh O'Kelly, invited all the Irish poets, brehons, bardes, harpers, gamesters, or common kearroghs, jesters, and others of their kind, of Ireland, to his house, upon Christmas, this year, where every one was well used during Christmas holydays, and gave contentment to each of them at the time of their departure, so as every one was well pleased, and extolled William for his bounty; one of which assembled composed certain verses in commendation of William and his house, which beginneth thus:*

> "*Filidh Eirionn go haointeach anocht…* " [*The poets of Erin to one house tonight]*".[4]

William O'Kelly, built the castle of Gaillie now known as Galey castle, on the banks of Lough Ree, near Knockcroghery, in County Roscommon. Among the many poets and bards who attended the festivities was Gofraidh Fionn Ó Dálaigh[5].

Gofraidh Fionn Ó Dálaigh

The Ó Dálaighs were one of the great Bardic families of Ireland. They had branches in various parts of Ireland particularly in Meath, Clare, Kerry and Cork but also in Westmeath and Offaly and other places. Many of the great poets of the Middle Ages were descended from Dalach, a pupil of St Colman's of Cork and Gofraidh Fionn Ó Dálaigh was described by the Irish annalists as 'chief professor of poetry in Munster'. A member of the Cork branch of the family, Gofraidh was born c1320 and died in 1387. He was the author of several poems which survived as part of the oral tradition.

Fáilte Uí Cheallaigh

This custom of extending a welcome to the poets and entertainers of Ireland to gather together in one place seems to have started with William O'Kelly's welcome – *Fáilte Uí Cheallaigh* – to a gairm-sgoile at his home Galey Castle. This gathering was obviously both spectacular and lavish – it is recorded in no fewer than four sets of annals: the *Annals of Clonmacnoise*, the *Annals of the Four Masters*, the *Annals of Ulster* and the *Annals of Lough Cé*.

However the greatest description we have of the occasion comes from the pen of Gofraidh Fionn Ó Dálaigh. His poem opens with four lines which could be paraphrased in English as:

> *"All the poets of Ireland assemble in one house tonight,*
> *Where the fare to be had will be rich and plentiful*
> *Which (poet) amongst us hasn't been snatched from sorrow,*
> *By the master of the house to which we have come..."* [6]

The poet describes the numerous guests who have gathered and for awhile he fears that the occasion and hospitality might not live up to expectations but gradually he is won over by the sheer scale of both the event itself and of the welcome and hospitality provided by their host.

He tells of the temporary 'wattle and daub' village built around the Castle of Galey to house the many guests. The assembled company included bards from Ireland and Scotland, and representatives of the 'seven true orders of poets'. There were jurists and wizards as well as authors and musicians and those dedicated to the various crafts.

As the guests arrived and approached the house they were faced with an 'avenue of peaked hostels'

The ivy-clad ruins of Galey Castle.

in readiness for them. There were special 'streets' dedicated to each class of performer with 'sleeping booths' wrought of woven branches on the hillsides. The feasting itself went on for a month and when it concluded we are told that the host gave "contentment to each one on his departure" in the form of generous gifts.

The Castle of Galey

Writing in the *Proceedings of the Royal Irish Academy* in 1857 Mr D. H. Kelly identified the scene of this great feasting as the Castle of Gallach, Castle Blakeney, Co Galway but it was John O'Donovan in *The Tribes and customs of Hy-Many*[7] that identified it as Galey Castle on the shores of Lough Ree. Later scholars, including Eleanor Knott, agreed with O'Donovan's findings.

A number of lines from the poem itself would seem to strengthen O'Donovan's claim that Galey was the site of this great gathering, see for example lines 109-112:

> Cinnlitir chloiche aille
> Duna [dh] flatha Fionnghaille;
> Daingean cloch an dunaidh dhe
> Loch ar culaibh na cloiche [8]

These lines have been translated by Eleanor Knott as: "The fortress of fair Gaille's chieftain is a capital letter of beauteous stone; the fortress is strengthened by the lake which lies behind it". Later in the poem three lines (lines 182-84) would seem to confirm the location. "Loch Riogh na riasg dtaobhuaine, / cuain ghorma bha ngealann grian / 'na gcolba dfearann Uilliam". (Knott's translation of these lines reads: "Loch Ree with its green marshes, these blue bays on which the sun shines brightly are the boundaries of William's land")[9].

In the course of the poem Ó Dálaigh seems to be impressed with O'Kelly's organisational skills. While he had the benefit of the company of all the great bards throughout the Christmas season all the other royal houses of Ireland were deprived of their services.

The great gathering at Galey castle on the shores of Lough Ree was probably the first of its type. Although similar gatherings were held at other places it is that great 'Failte Ui Cheallaigh' of 1351 which has given us an expression which is still used six centuries later to describe the 'welcome of all welcomes'.

In 1900 a poet from the Longford shore, Ned "the poet" Farrell from the Callows in Cashel parish, visited Galey Bay and found the same 'fáilte' was being extended to all visitors

One morning in summer, in spirits we went
Away to the Shannon on merriment bent
Where we launched a small boat and paddled our way
Across its clear waters to sweet Galey Bay.

The sail we enjoyed, as the day was so kind –
The green woods of Cashel we left far behind;
And just as we landed beyond on the quay
We got a reception at sweet Galey Bay.

We scarcely had been a full hour ashore –
We had at "the Castle" refreshments galore:
That ivied old pile I can honestly say
Was really our Mecca in sweet Galey Bay.

The place though being ancient, to us it was new
And yet of strange faces we saw but a few:
For there the young maids, fascinating and gay,
Showed friendship and 'fáilte' at sweet Galey Bay.

So when we get old, and grown worn with time,
In fancy we'll turn to the years of our prime;
And with pleasure and pride we'll think on the day
We spent on the Shannon at sweet Galey Bay.

Séan Mór Ó Dubhagáin

One of the great literary figures of this era died at Rindoon in 1372 having spent the last seven years of his life there. He was Seán Ó Dubhagáin (John O'Dugan), outstanding Gaelic poet and eminent man of letters. His epic topographical poem, consisting in all of 1660 stanzas contains the most comprehensive account that survives of the old Irish clans. Like most of the poets of ancient Ireland, Ó Dubhagáin was also an accomplished historian and antiquarian.

This famous poem commences with the lines "Triallom timcheall na Fódla". Two verses which are relevant to the hinterland of Lough Ree read:

> Clann Branáin, bríoghach a mbrígh,
> Is Uí Mhaoil mhaordha Míchíl,
> Cúis molta feadhna nach fann
> Ar Corca shealbhda Sheachlann
>
> Dúthaigh don fheadhain airmghéir
> Ceinél Dobhtha dlúthaimhréidh,
> Bídh a ccoimshearc in chridhe
> Díbh oireacht Ó nAinlidhe[10]

These verses have been translated by John O'Donovan[11] as follows:

> The Clann-Branain, powerful their vigour,
> And the majestic O'Maoilmhichils,
> The sway of the tribe, not feeble
> Extends over the wealthy Corca Sheachlann[12]
>
> Hereditary to the keen-armed tribe of O hAinlighe
> Is Cinel-Dobhtha[13], the fast rugged
> I have affection in my heart
> For the sept of the O hAinlighes.

Ó Dubhagáin has been described by Edward O'Reilly in his *Catalogue of Irish writers* as the "chief poet of the O'Kellys of Ibh Maine" a territory which lies close to the south west of Lough Ree. His poem was unfinished in his lifetime and was completed after his death by another noted literary figure of the time, Giolla-na-Naomh Ó Huidhrin (O'Heeran). The annals record Ó Dubhagáin's death: "John Ua Dubhagain, archhistorian of Ireland abandoned the delights of the world for the space of seven years and died with the community of John the Baptist in Rindoon".[14] O Huidhrin's *obit* is given for 1420 when he died at an advanced age.

Black Death

The prevalence of disease and plague is mentioned by the annalists throughout the Middle Ages. Smallpox, the *galar breac*, continued to kill and maim its victims for centuries. The Black Death, most fearful of all the plagues, arrived in Ireland from Europe, where it had annihilated one third of the population in the middle of the fourteenth century. In the course of the next hundred years or so it is recorded again and again wiping out whole sections of the Irish population. It raged through the monasteries also. There is an entry under the year 1447, "some say that seven hundred priests died of this plague."[15] In the following year is recorded the deaths of three friars of Longphort-uí-Fheargail, namely O'Farrell, Maconmaighe and Mactechedain, victims of the same plague. Very likely these were members of the newly founded Dominican priory, the site of which is in Church St. in Longford town.

Statutes of Kilkenny

The process of gaelicisation whereby the Norman English became more Irish than the Irish themselves was well under way at the start of the fourteenth century. One of the best examples was the Delamers already mentioned, located by the banks of the Inny river.[16] So Irish had they become that as well as adopting the Gaelic speech and customs of the Irish they even changed their name to

Mac hOireabhaird (Mac Herbert) and in the fifteenth century they were treated by the English as the king's rebels. All over Ireland this trend continued, with these descendants of the original settlers being known as the *Sean Gaill*, as distinct from later arrivals to be known as the New English.

Within England itself a comparable development was taking place as the French possessions were being lost and French, as the official language, was abandoned in favour of English. London was now looking with concern on the *Sean Gaill*, their colony in Ireland, which was becoming less English with every passing year. In 1367, the Duke of Clarence, son of the English king Edward III, came to Ireland and enacted the Statutes of Kilkenny in an effort to curtail this trend, and prevent the two races from intermingling socially, economically, culturally and religiously. The language of the enactments was strong and the penalties severe, but few, on either side in Ireland, took much heed of them.

Local Strife

Whatever the degree of rapprochement between the two nations, it did not signal the end of local or tribal strife. The English of Meath raided Annaly in 1373 and slew two O'Farrell chieftains. A second such attack occurred in 1376. This time O'Farrell retaliated with ferocity "so that he burned their farmhouses and towns, and plundered their territories and returned home in victory and triumph and loaded with immense spoils."[17] The annals record tersely that the castle of Athlone was taken by the English and the son of O'Fox was killed there. The Fox or O'Sinnigh was the name given to the O'Ceithearnaigs, lords of Muintir

All that remains of the Dillon castle at Ballinacliffy.

Tadhgain, by Lough Ree, and chieftains of southern Teathbha. In the year 1455 the castle changed hands again when it "was taken from the English having been betrayed by a woman who was in it."[18]

The skirmishing and plundering continued. A few more annalistic entries help to give a flavour of the times by the shores of Lough Ree. O'Farrell was defeated by the son of Conn O'Maelsheachlainn, the Dillons and Laoighseach the son of Ross at Nuachongbhail (Noughaval, a district at the mouth of the river Inny). He (O'Farrell) lost seventy men including the prisoners and the slain. Thomas O'Farrell, tanist of Annaly, was slain at Beal Atha-na-Pailise (Pallas) at night while in pursuit of a prey that the party of the Dillons, the clan-Connor were carrying off. "They bore away his head and his spoil having found him with merely a few troops, a circumstance of rare occurrence with him."[19]

To the south of Lough Ree by its eastern shore lay the territory of Brawney (Bragh Maine) where the O'Breen family provided civil and ecclesiastical leadership for centuries. Now Brian O'Breen conspired with Colla the prior of Teach Eoin (i.e. a religious community at Rindoon) to launch a predatory attack on Calry (Caladh), the patrimony of Magawley, situated between the present Mount Temple and the Lough Ree shore. Prior Colla was an O'Kelly from Uí Maine and had the support of his people in this enterprise as well as that of some of the O'Farrells. Their plans however went badly awry and Magawly routed them. "Brian O'Breen with ten of his people and ten others of the inhabitants of Caladh under the conduct of William son of Donough, son of prior O'Farrell, were slain by Magawly."[20]

A similar raid took place eight years later which is described as "a great attack" made by O'Kelly on the Tuites, Petitts, Tyrells and Daltons. This would have involved a fleet of boats crossing from Rindoon by Nuns' Island, Black Islands and Inchmore to the eastern shore. This raid was no more successful than the previous one. "O'Kelly was defeated; Donough O'Kelly and many others were taken prisoners, and a party of their foot soldiers and kerns were slain."[21]

At this time O'Donnell, chieftain of Cinél Conaill (Donegal) went on a circuit of the midlands with his army, plundering his enemies, making treaties and supporting his friends. He camped for one night in Cuircne (Kilkenny West) "and the Dillons and Daltons came into his house and made peace with him."[22]

O'Farrells

On the northern tip of the lake the O'Farrells burned Cluain Tuaiscirt na Sinna (i.e. the monastery) in revenge for which the O'Hanlys triumphantly plundered Tir Licin. The O'Farrells were back on Lough Ree in 1490 and an attack was made by Fergus, son of Edmond O'Farrell, on the sons of Gilla-na-Naomh at Cureen Connachtach. Despite that, one of the sons of Gilla-na-Naomh became chieftain of Caladh na hAnghaile that same year. Every shore of the lake from present day Lanesborough to Athlone was seeing its share of activity. Most of what is recorded is unedifying, to say the least, and often comes across to us today as harsh and cruel, even brutal.

Much of it, however, took place among the "upper" classes. The ordinary folk who sowed and reaped and tended their flocks were by no means immune to the strife, but neither were they overcome by it, except in particularly bloody confrontations. Local feuds and wars weren't waged to annihilate the enemy. They were generally to secure succession to a lordship or to avenge an old score or simply to plunder for personal gain. This was ongoing both with the *Sean Gaill*, later known as the Anglo-Irish, as well as with the native Irish. England showed little interest. Indeed, English power and influence in Ireland had been waning all through the fifteenth century, as English armies fought campaigns to further their king's claim to the throne of France, but the French finally expelled them and Joan of Arc wrote her name into the pages of history.

In England a long drawn out civil war raged between the king and the nobles. This was the War of the Roses and was eventually decided in favour of the Tudor kings. The loyal English colony in Ireland known as the Pale had by 1494 diminished to a small area stretching for some miles around the city of Dublin. The Kildare

Geraldines - old Norman stock settled here since the time of the invasion - were the most powerful family in Ireland. They were Gaelicised and spoke the Irish language. The reigning Lord generally held the post of king's deputy but he was strong enough to govern without reference to the king, and the Geraldines, had they wished, could have constituted a new monarchy in an independent Ireland and severed the connection with England. That they didn't so wish became a matter of history and so the century came to an end with the Geraldine earl, Gearóid Mór, as lord deputy and Henry VII, as king of England.

CHAPTER 7

Darker Days

The island monasteries did not escape the strife that plagued the country on every side of Lough Ree. In some cases they were party to it. Despite that, however, the records of the twelfth, thirteenth and fourteenth centuries leave no doubt as to the levels of excellence in prayer, scholarship and learning achieved in this era and detailed elsewhere in this work.

The sixteenth century was about to unfold, hiding in its misty future the dark and tragic times that lay ahead. It was to be the century of the new conquest of Ireland, when the old nation, of two thousand years and more, would be faced with ultimate extinction. It was the century of the Reformation, the century of Henry VIII and Elizabeth, all of which would have the most profound consequences for Lough Ree and its environs. The next hundred years would see the power of the lords and chieftains, Irish and Anglo-Irish alike, reduced beyond recognition while the clans were harassed, dispossessed and scattered in every direction. The monasteries would be suppressed and confiscated before being handed over to ambitious speculators, so that the whole way of life would collapse and the holy men and women, poets, artists, musicians and historians would no longer have anywhere to lay their heads. The end of that hundred years would witness the final overthrow of the native leadership of Ireland, as a ship sailed out of Lough Swilly taking the last survivors, the beaten chieftains of Ulster, into exile in Europe, destined never to return.

Dillons

Back at Lough Ree the annals are telling us of the death of "The Dillon" i.e. James Dillon, lord of Machaire Cuircne (Kilkenny West). His castle was at Ballinacliffy and he was held in highest esteem throughout his territory. He had lived to a good age and died in his bed, a somewhat unusual circumstance given the amount of strife and violence prevalent in those times among lords and chieftains alike. On the other side of the lake there was feuding among the O'Kellys, the dynastic family of Uí Maine and two leading members of the O'Kellys were "treacherously" killed by other members of the family at the Faes, a wooded district to the west of Athlone. In 1542 we find Mageoghegan from a native Irish family to the east of the lake teaming up with Edward Roe Dillon and killing O'Maelaghlin, the lawful heir to the chieftainship at Baile Sgrigin. The same Mageoghegan turned against O'Connor of Offaly - a good man who had been proclaimed a traitor by the English, which caused the annalist to comment:

> *At this time the power of the English was great and immense in Ireland, so that the bondage, in which the people of Leath-Mhogha were, had scarcely ever been equalled before that time. The power and jurisdiction of the English prevailed so much that, through terror, no one dared to give food or protection to O'Connor.*[1]

Athlone Castle

Athlone castle, which had been in the hands of the Irish, was taken over by the king's vice-treasurer in Ireland, William Brabazon, and repaired in 1547, an indication of the strategic importance that would be attached to Athlone in the changing times ahead.[2] The first stone castle had been built here by the justiciar, Bishop John de Grey, in 1210 to promote the Norman expansion into Connaught. It had changed hands many times over the subsequent three and a half centuries. The O'Kellys of Uí Maine wrested it from the Anglo-Irish Dillons and Daltons, to the east of the lake, and held it for varying periods before losing it again. At this time government agencies were working on new plans for it. In 1551 a great court was convened here where Irish chieftains could come in and make their obeisance to the king. Athlone was considered as a residence for the lord deputy and also as a centre for parliamentary sessions.

It was from here also that the final destruction of Clonmacnois was accomplished in 1552. Whether this was the implementation of the new edicts on confiscation of monastic property on behalf of the

Clonmacnois from an old engraving.

sovereign, or just one last predatory attack on the defenceless building, makes little difference. The annals record it with intense sadness:

> *Clonmacnois was plundered and devastated by the English of Athlone and the large bells were taken from the cloigtheach. There was not, moreover, a bell, small or large, an image or an altar, or a book or a gem, or even glass in a window, from the wall of the church out, which was not carried off. Lamentable was this deed, the plundering of the city of Ciaran, the holy patron.*[3]

That Athlone was favoured as a depot and launching pad for the new English conquest was borne out by the lord justice when he set out to defeat the O'Connors of Offaly and drive them out of Meelick,

> *for he conveyed and carried great guns to Athlone and from thence in boats to Meelick, while he himself marched his army through Bealach-an-Fhothair and by Lurgan-Lusmaighe.*[4]

Ten years later, in 1566, Sir Henry Sidney, the lord deputy, built the new bridge of Athlone. Another occurrence around this time had implications for Lough Ree and its environs even though it began far away in the west of Ireland. The English president of Connaught, Sir Edward Fitton, held a court in Galway at which the chieftains were bidden to pledge their loyalty to the crown. When the earl of Clanrickard attended he was arrested and taken to Dublin. The earl's sons Ulick and John Burke were indignant at their father's incarceration and called on the clans to rise against the English. They succeeded in assembling an army and proceeded to demolish the English castles and lay waste the country. They moved eastward, plundering the lands lying between the rivers Suck and Shannon and also the Faes of Athlone. They pillaged every person who was on friendly terms or in league with the English as far as the gates of Athlone. They afterwards continued, keeping the Shannon on the right, directly to Sliabh Bana-na-dTuath, crossed over to Caladh na hAnghaile and burned Ath Liag. They proceeded to burn every town including Mullingar until they arrived again at Athlone where they burned that part of the town from the bridge outwards. By that stage they had done a full circuit of Lough Ree. Sliabh Baghna (or Slieve Bawn) is the hill to the north of the lake in Co. Roscommon while Ath Liag is the modern Lanesborough/Ballyleague. Caladh na hAnghaile was the ancient name for the shoreline stretching eastward from Lanesborough by the parish of Cashel almost as far as the mouth of the Inny. Such was the ferocity of this campaign that the English, at length, were forced to set the earl at liberty and restore him as lord of his territory and lands.

CHAPTER 8

The Reformation

The annals record the Reformation under the year 1537 in the following lines:

A heresy and a new error sprang up in England, through pride, vainglory, avarice and lust, and through many strange sciences, so that the men of England went into opposition to the pope and to Rome. They, at the same time, adopted various opinions, and among others, the old law of Moses, in imitation of the Jewish people; and they styled the king the chief head of the church of God in his own kingdom. New laws and statutes were enacted by the king and council according to their own will. They destroyed the orders to whom worldly possessions were allowed, namely, the monks, canons, nuns, brethren of the cross, and the four poor orders, i.e. the orders of the Minors, Preachers, Carmelites, and Augustinians; and the lordships and livings of all these were taken up for the king. They broke down the monasteries, and sold their roofs and bells, so that from Aran of the Saints to the Iccian Sea there was not one monastery that was not broken and shattered, with the exception of a few in Ireland, of which the English took no notice or heed. They afterwards burned the images, shrines and relics of the saints of Ireland and England; they likewise burned the celebrated image of the Blessed Virgin Mary at Trim, which used to perform wonders and miracles, which used to heal the blind, the deaf and the crippled, and persons affected with all kinds of diseases, and they also burned the staff of Jesus, which was in Dublin, performing miracles, from the time of St. Patrick down to that time, and had been in the hands of Christ while he was among men. They also appointed archbishops and sub-bishops for themselves; and, though great was the persecution of the Roman emperors against the church, scarcely had there ever come so great a persecution from Rome as this; so that it is impossible to narrate or tell its description, unless it should be narrated by one who saw it.[1]

Henry VIII

Henry the VIII's quarrel with the pope came to a head in 1532 when the English monarch declared himself "Supreme Head of the Church in England" and renounced all allegiance to the Holy See. Thus the Reformation had reached England and Henry implemented it with fire and sword.

He extended it to Ireland in 1535 and in the following year the Irish Parliament enacted legislation for the dissolution of the monasteries, accusing them of engaging in idolatry and superstition. These laws commanded abbots and priors to surrender all their monastic properties to the king's officers who were embarked on a programme of inspection and discovery, compiling an inventory of each monastery, its lands, buildings and effects. Bells, crosses and chalices were seized, the latter generally sent to London to be melted down for the making of coinage in the mint. Lands and buildings were leased or sold to individuals or corporations.

The implementation of the king's policy moved at a much slower rate in Ireland than the king would have wished. The Irish did not take kindly to the new arrangement and wherever the clans

Saints Island monastic site from an old engraving.

held influence the old religion was still secure - for the time being at least. Monasteries on the east shore of Lough Ree were being assessed and inspected in 1540. That however was as far west as the king's agents could proceed in safety. A mere few miles away the accounting officer investigating Monasteryk (Abbeyderg) and Templenesgart (Teampall na sagart, Edgeworthstown) recorded as follows:

All the possessions are in the Annale among the Irish for fear of whom it is not safe to approach thither for the purpose of making extents.[2]

An act of parliament passed in 1543 declared that

the west part of the shire of Meath is laid about and beset with divers of the king's rebels and in several parts thereof the king's writs, for lack of ministration of justice have not of late been obeyed, nor his grace's laws put in due exercise.[3]

Monastic Lands

How, then, fared the monasteries of Lough Ree? Few records survive. These monasteries are not mentioned in the catalogue of Irish monastic possessions of that period. Both All Saints' Island and Inchcleraun were governed by recent priors bearing the name

O'Farrell and it is not unreasonable to assume that those who were afraid to consult them on land would be even more fearful of approaching them on water. We may take it then that the island monasteries survived at least for

Romanesque windows, Saints' Island.

the time being. At a later date, however, the king's agents could resort to more devious methods towards furthering their policy. Sometimes they assigned the monastic lands to an avaricious layman in the hope that he would do the dirty work of expelling the monks. He might even be a petty chieftain of native stock. On the other hand a sympathetic Anglo-Irish lord might apply for and secure the lease, in which case he offered a measure of protection to the monastic community. The Lough Ree islands were granted to one Thomas Philips in 1567 as appears from the following:

> *Lease under commission, 26th September IX of Elizabeth, to Thos. Philips, gent., of the islands of Inishmore in Loughry, in part of the flood of the Shynnen, Inshelyggen, Inshcloghrene, with four messuages and the stone walls of a monastery, Calanishe, alias Inshcalla, Inshenenagh and Inshekanbegdermuid, all in Loughry, with their tithes, to hold for 21 years at a rent of 25s.2d. Not to alien with licence. Not to let except to English by both parents, and not to charge coyn/fine, 20s.[4]*

Less than four years later, another fiant of Elizabeth may well raise questions about the feasibility of Thomas Philips farming the island lands. Obviously there were "marauders" on the lake and the queen appointed a chief sergeant and water bailiff to supervise the water traffic because the islands had been taken over by Irish rebels as appears from the following:

> *3641(2867) Grant (under queen's letter, 31 March xxii) to Edward Waterhouse, esq., one of the privy council; of the office of overseer and keeper of the river Shenan from the town of Letrym in the country of Barnard O'Rwark, chief of his nation, to the great rock near the castle (of Downeasse) in the tenure of George Fannynge, of the city of Limerick, merchant. To hold for ever. With power to make ordinances for matters concerning the river, and to fine and punish offenders. He is to be provided with two galleys, for the transport of men, and victuals in all places between Athlone and Killalowe, and also between Athlone and the upper parts of Loghrie, and is to maintain or replace them. He may receive fees from the owners of*

boats for their registration in books; may hold a court for the hearing
of controversies arising upon the river, and may retain the half of
forfeited recognizances. He shall have the fishing and fowling of the
river (the weirs of the manor and abbeys of Athlone excepted); also
the swans on the river, in like manner, as the overseer of the swans
on the Thames; and may take timber from the banks for repair of the
galleys. He shall have 2s. English a day for two masters of the
galleys, and 8d. a day each for 30 other men. He is to make Athlone
his head quarters, and to receive there ground for a house and
garden. Weirs being impediments to navigation and destructive to
fish, he may destroy them, those of the manor and abbeys of Athlone
excepted. The islands being usurped by rebels, the government of
these islands is given to him as sole justice of the peace there,
that he may endeavour to have them occupied by boatmen who may
assist the navigation of the river. - 17 June, xxii.[5]

Persecution

A determined effort to implant the Reformation in Ireland was made in the reign of Elizabeth and it took the form of a particularly brutal persecution in the late 1570s and 1580s. The barbarity of the official "execution" of Dermot O Hurley, Archbishop of Cashel, is beyond comment. Again in 1593, contemporary accounts speak of "the fierce persecution."

The death of Elizabeth and the accession of James Stuart, the son of the catholic Mary, Queen of Scots, in 1603, brought a sense of euphoria to Ireland, and even if the high hopes were not to be realised, there was considerable relief from the hardships of previous decades with only the occasional outburst of severity. The *Visitatio Regalis*, as its name implies, was a royal survey of the Protestant church to find out what progress it had made in establishing itself in Ireland. Its report for the year 1615, as well as listing reformed parishes, also named churches that still had papist clergy and those that were vacant as far as the inquisitors could ascertain. In it the churches of Inchcleraun and Saints' Island are listed as follows: Ecclesiae impropriatae - *Destitute propter defectum ministrorum et situatae sunt in locis remotioribus ubi nullus curatus audet in servire*.[6] This is saying that these churches are poor due to the failure of ministers and are situated in places so remote that no minister (Protestant) risks serving in them. Whether a catholic minister serves in them we are not told, but it is evident from the document that the protestant church authorities would wish to have a minister of their persuasion there. This implies that these churches had not been finally thrown down or rendered ruinous at the time of the confiscations.

In the 1620s the king's overtures to the catholic royal family of Spain in the hope of arranging a marriage with his son Charles caused him to soft-pedal on the enforcement of penal legislation in Ireland. As a result monks and friars became active again in many areas. They did not re-occupy the monasteries but here and there they re-roofed the chapel and in areas out of sight of the crown they lived in some of the old buildings on the site. We know that the friars of Saints' Island on Lough Ree were occupying at least part of their priory in 1627 because Br. Michael O'Clery, who was at that time working on the compilation of the *Annals of the Four Masters*, visited Saints' Island in that year and spent a considerable time with the friars there, consulting the histories and other books which had been written in the priory in the previous centuries.

CHAPTER 9

Confiscations around the lake

The end of an era had come for the Lough Ree islands. Their Christian foundations had survived in good times and bad for a thousand years. From now on there would be different owners and it would be a different life. With the dissolution of the monasteries a silence descends on the lake. That silence was affecting the whole country, for the annalists who had been recording the country's history over many centuries were no more. These were the monks who were heirs to a tradition of learning and scholarship and who had the advantages of a library and a scriptorium in their monasteries. The implications of their demise went beyond the mere recording of history. The disappearance of the monastic schools was a body blow to the wellbeing and prospects of Irish society at that time. A good example is the Franciscan monastery of Limerick, which had a school of six hundred pupils in the mid-fourteenth century. Such schools were widespread at that time. Their disappearance did not augur well for later generations. There still remained, however, the bardic schools, patronised by the Irish and Anglo-Irish chieftains and earls, but their days, too, were numbered. The confiscations and plantations of the century immediately following put an end to them as well and the old nation with its ancient culture was forced into rapid decline.

Franciscans

At the southern extremity of Lough Ree the Franciscans were driven out of their friary in Athlone. The Anglo-Irish Dillons who had ever been their friends and mentors provided them with a safe haven on Friars' Island on the inner lakes at Killinure. They even returned to Athlone in 1642 when for a few years the Confederation flew a banner of independence over Ireland. The arrival of Cromwell's puritan army in 1651 put an end to tolerance and a price on the heads of the Franciscans. While many went into exile there were many who stayed on and went into hiding around the southern shores of Lough Ree.

Surviving from this period of religious persecution is the old Mass Path or Sli an Aifrinn which linked the penal church of St. Mary's in Chapel Lane with Friars' Island. The late Fr. Quinn traced the mass path at a time when it was still possible to do so. Today the railway, several housing estates and extensive road works have altered the profile of the area, and indeed one of the few reminders of this ancient route is the housing estate known as Sli an Aifrinn.[1]

On the western bank of the river at Athlone close to Lough Ree the Cluniac monastery founded by Turlough O'Connor in 1150 was suppressed in the middle of the sixteenth century. Its lands were confiscated and added to the estate of Athlone castle, all of which lands had formerly belonged to the monastery. The church was turned over to secular ownership and for some years was used as a grain store. It was burned to the ground following an attack by the Irish on Athlone in 1572.

Knights Hospitallers

There were two religious houses on the Rindoon promontory. The site close to the castle and to the south west of it contains the ruins of a nave and chancel church, and is believed to be all that remains of the buildings of the Fratres Cruciferi, otherwise the Knights Hospitallers, which were founded here and dedicated to St. John the Baptist soon after the coming of the Normans. In 1312 after the suppression of the Knights Templars, the house of that order in Co. Sligo, Temple House, was placed under the control of the Rindoon

Archdall's depiction of a knight of St. John as would have lived in Rindoon.

community. The second house of Rindoon was founded for Premonstratensian Canons by the celebrated Clarus Mac Mailin,

archdeacon of Elphin and a monk of Trinity Island in Lough Key. His *obit* in 1251 states inter alia: "Clarus Mac Mailin …ecclesiam de Rinn-duin …aedificavit".[2] John A. Claffey in his paper to the Old Athlone Society reasons that this house was located where "the graveyard and church

Ruins of Church of Naomh Eoin, Rindoon.

ruin at the neck of the peninsula in Rinnagan townland"[3] can be seen today at the north west corner of the promontory. He goes on to quote O'Donovan to the effect that this site housed an early Celtic church dedicated to St. Eoin and that it is he, the native saint, who gives the name St John's to this parish. Nothing is known about the relationship between the two communities who lived within five hundred metres of each other and were both under the aegis of the Canons of St. Augustine. They may have complemented each other and shared responsibilities and resources. However, in company with all such religious establishments, Rindoon surrendered its property to the crown at the time of the suppression of the monasteries. The first leasing of the lands took place in 1567 in the ninth year of the reign of Elizabeth as follows:

1483 (1246). Lease, under commission, 26 September; ix, to Christopher Davers and Charles Egingham; of the site of the monastery of "Croched" friars of S. John Baptist by the Loghry in Omany in Connaght, cottages in the towns of S. John's, one quarter of land called Knockeaghane, Inwyre alias Nwyre, one quarter, Nemaddry, one, Ruynekane, one, in Glany, one, Gaylebeg and Leighcarro, one, and one half-quarter in Clogh alias Kylcloghagh, all in S. John's, lands of Skeghen and Krevyquyne near it, in Omany, and

Taghtample and other waste towns in O'Conor Slygagh's country, a third of the tithes of the vicarage of S. John extending to the said quarters and the rectory of Taghtample. To hold for 21 years, at a rent of £6 1s 8d. Maintaining one English archer. Not to alien without license, nor to charge coyn. Fine £3.[4]

Eleven years later the lease was re-established. In 1596 William Taffe gent., of Boneneddan, Co. Sligo, became the lessee.

Lough Ree was unusual in that it could boast two foundations for Cruciferi on its shores. The second was on the opposite or eastern side of the lake in the parish of Kilkenny West where an early Celtic monastery once stood which was founded by Saint Canice in the sixth century and gave the name Kilkenny (Cill Cainneich) to this district. The Cruciferi priory was established here at the behest of Rev. Thomas Dillon, son of Henry, Lord of Drumraney, in the thirteenth century under the protection of St. John the Baptist. It was patronised by the Dillon family in the centuries following and it contained a well-known hospital. It seems to have been active at the time of the suppression. Its lands and tithes were granted to Robert Dillon at an annual rent of £22-0s-10d on May the second, 1569. This monastery is famous for the *Liber Kilkenniensis*,[5] a manuscript compiled there, containing a collection of Latin *Lives of the saints*. It is now catalogued as Rawlinson B. 485 of the Bodleian collection in Oxford.

Within the barony of Kilkenny West in the old parish of Noughaval was situated another monastery, founded in the fourteenth century for Carmelites or White Friars, at Ardnacranny. Again the Dillons of Drumraney were the patrons. At the Dissolution the

Ruins of the Church of St. John, Rindoon.

buildings and lands were granted on temporary lease to James Dillon of Donimoney, who protected the abbey and enabled the clergy to continue in possession. So caring was James that he was nicknamed "The Prior." However, his reign was brief and in 1546 Henry VIII granted the property to Sir Robert Dillon, the chief justice, for a fine of £33-13s-4d.

Clonsellan and Clooncraff

The ancient abbey of Roscommon was founded by St. Coman in 742.[6] Like Ciaran of Clonmacnois, Coman had died before the abbey was a year old. It was located where the town of Roscommon now stands, on the site of

Clonsellan near Roscommon.

the present day Church of Ireland, beside the small car park off Church Street. Like most of the old Gaelic foundations it was renewed by the European orders in the course of the twelfth century reform movement. Around the year 1150 it adopted the rule of the Canons Regular of St. Augustine. There are a number of references to this monastery in the Annals and they indicate a very close connection between it and the monastery of Clonmacnois. In an entry in 979 A.D. Murcadh, son of Riada, is described as "abbot of Ros Chomáin and prior of Cluain-Mic-Nóis."[7] In 1052 "Eachthighern Ua Eaghrain, successor of Ciaran of Cluain-Mic-Nóis and of Coman, died on his pilgrimage at Cluain Iraird."[8] It would appear from this that the two monasteries were at this time under the same authority. This changed in time for we read in 1266: "Maelisa O Hainainn, Prior of Roscommon and Athleague, died."[9]

Apparently the Roscommon abbey had two dependent houses, one at Clonsellan and the other at Clooncraff. O'Donovan, writing of the Cloigtheach on Inchcleraun in 1837, tells us that "Tradition says that the bell in the belfry (i.e. on the island) was so loud sounding as to be heard at Roscommon, a distance of seven miles. At certain times the monks of this island used to meet those of Roscommon at a river called, from the circumstances, the Bannow River (Beannughadh) which is as much as to say in English, the River of Salutation."[10]

The clogas tower on Inchcleraun.

There is still a folk memory of this tradition in the locality and the Hind River is identified as the Bannow of olden times. Since this river passes close to the ruined church of Clonsellan before entering Lough Ree at Rinnany it is probable that here was the meeting place of the monks.

Roscommon had a high reputation for its artists and craftsmen and many of the celebrated artefacts from Clonmacnois were completed here. As indicated above, the two institutions worked in tandem over a considerable period. Tradition says that the monastic workshop was at the Clooncraff house. Its most famous product is undoubtedly the Cross of Cong which was completed here in the twelfth century.

Dominican Priory

The Dominicans in Roscommon were founded by Felim O'Connor king of Connaught and son of Cathal Crovderg in 1253. At the time of the Reformation the powerful local influence of the O'Connors prevented any serious interference with the priory until its lands were leased in 1573. Even this failed to interrupt the life of the friars and a new lease was made to Sir Nicholas Malby in 1577.

This ruthless English soldier was no lover of the Irish. "The friars were turned out and disbanded. Those who could not go into hiding were ruthlessly murdered. One of the last of them died in 1590. (He was) Diarmaid O'Connor, vicar of Temple an Aidhnein, formerly prior of the friars of Roscommon."[11]

Later on, some youthful friars came from the Irish colleges in Spain and Portugal to live in hiding in the houses of friends. By 1630 Roscommon had a small Dominican community again. Bearing testimony to this is a silver chalice - a gift from Conal Farrell and his wife Rose Garmley. It is inscribed "For the use of the friars and preachers of the convent of Roscommon"[12] and is dated 1636.

Bethlehem

Of all the religious foundations on the islands and shores of Lough Ree none presents such an enigma as that of Bethlehem whose ruins still survive on a little promontory in the barony of Kilkenny West in Co. Westmeath. One of the "youngest" of the lake's religious houses - a mere four centuries old - its short life has become so encrusted with story and folklore as to obscure its real history. This, despite its

Bethlehem - house of Poor Clares. Courtesy of the Irish Architectural Archives and Lord Rossmore.

having had several biographers, the first a mere forty years after its demise. There is a local or folk version of its story which has been told again and again around the lake and its environs. Inevitably its accuracy has suffered. It goes like this:

The nuns were in their convent in Bethlehem preparing for Christmas when word reached them that a company of Roundheads (soldiers) from Athlone were already on their way to plunder them. Locals hurried to bring their small boats, and the nuns barely escaped, leaving everything behind them. They were rowed to Nuns' Island in the middle of the lake where they spent the night before Christmas Eve in the open without shelter. On the day following, help arrived from the western shore where some of the nuns had family friends and they found place to lay their heads for Christmas. Meanwhile, back at the nunnery, the plundering hordes were looting the house, eating and drinking what they could find. Then they fired the building and withdrew to the old castle of Ballinacliffy having first procured a large quantity of liquor. While all this was happening messengers had been sent for help to Sir James Dillon, lord of the area and brother of Mother Cecily Dillon. He immediately despatched a troup of horse who arrived too late to save the convent but in time to surround Ballinacliffy castle and put everyone of the miscreant soldiers to the sword. After which the nuns continued through Roscommon travelling westward 'til they reached Galway where the Mayor of that city granted them a small piece of land where the River Corrib divides and which would be known ever afterwards as Nuns' Island.

Such is the story. We now turn to look at what has been written over the years about this foundation. Sir Henry Piers, a local landed gentleman, recorded his history in 1682. He informs us that "The Mother Abbess… was a lady of good extraction, the daughter of Sir Edward Tuit who sometime lived in this county at Tuitstown."
And he continues:

On the firing of their nunnery towards the end of the first year of the war; not long after the lord president had received the English forces, whither they retreated is not certain, I rather think they dispersed and scattered; but are of late united again at Athlone, and under the same mother abbess, a lady now of great years.

But the firing of their nunnery was a piece of service, if I may so call the burning of a house wherein none but women dwell, that was attended with a very sad circumstance for two foot companies of English forces, before mentioned, were commanded to quarter at

Ballinecloffy, a strong castle and dwelling house of a gentleman of an antient family and good estate, situate in the promontory before mentioned; these were commanded by a gentleman of a very noble extraction, captain Bertie or Bartue, brother to the lord chamberlain of England, the earl of Lindsey, who was general for the king at the battle of Edgehil. These men hearing of the nunnery hard by, immediately marched thither, whether with or without command of their officer I have not learned, and plundered the same; I do not hear of any force there to resist them, nor that any violence was offered to any of the virgins; however, after rifling of the place they burnt it, and leaving the house in flames they returned to their quarters at Ballinecloffy aforesaid,

Our Lady of "Bethlehem"

which had been deserted by the inhabitants on their appearance, but left well stored with excellent strong beer and aquavitae, and all sorts of provisions for food, and to it the whole party fell, officers and soldiers, without fear or wit, not fearing or suspecting any enemy, who yet was too near unto them. Ballinecloffy is seated in the mentioned promontory, which juts out into the lake or Shannon, nearer to the main land than Bethlem, and hath over against it on the other side of the Inny, which here falls into Lough-Ree in the Shannon, a place called Portenure, where a certain young gentleman lay; I do not hear that he was then in arms for the Irish, however, being informed at what rate the English at Ballinecloffy then drank, and knowing the house to be sufficiently stored to disorder them all, resolved to try if he could advantageously fall on them; immediately he gets together about six score men, who to be the more expedite stripped themselves to their shirts, and with such weapons as they had in readiness, hasted to the slaughter, having wafted themselves over the Annagh, as they call the water passage, they haste immediately to Ballinecloffy, where they find our English by this time of day neither men nor soldiers, but mere brutes, neither capable to make defence, or so much as to apprehend their danger, most of them being asleep or so disabled with drink, as not to be in a condition to put themselves in a posture of defence. Never was the poet's

> *Invadunt urbem somno vinoque sepultam*
> *Buried in wine and sleep the Trojans lay,*
> *The wily Greeks surprised their heedless prey.*

more true of Troy, than at this time at Ballinecloffy; the issue was, the captain, with some of the officers and soldiers were, to the number of sixty, miserably butchered; nevertheless, some who had not so miserably besotted themselves as the rest, escaped to bring the sad tidings to the next garrison, Connorstown; nor did these inhuman butchers satisfy their cruelty in the slaughter of the men only, (for some of the soldiers had wives) the women also must die, and the carcasses of both men and women be stripped and exposed naked; neither did their inhumanity end here but modesty and shame here arrest my pen, and suffer me not to write, what they barbarously acted; they dragged the dead bodies of the men; and covered these of the women with them, and exposing them in such a posture as I leave to the reader's imagination to make out.[13]

In the *Annals of Westmeath* James Wood writing in 1907 treats of the same subject in this way:

The following account of the plunder and burning of Bethlehem Convent is compiled from the History of Public Affairs in Ireland, 1641 to 1652. The Roundheads who were stationed in Athlone were ordered to garrison in the Dillon country, barony of Kilkenny West. There was a picturesque nook on the bank of Lough Ree. There was a nunnery belonging to the nuns of the Order of St. Clare. On the news spreading that the Roundheads were going to quarter themselves in the fair barony above-named, the inhabitants, knowing well from past experience that their object was robbery and murder, sought safety by transporting themselves and their property to an island in Lough Ree, where they would be out of the reach of the plunderers and assassins. The flight of the nuns and inhabitants was so sudden that many of them left valuable property after them. The Roundheads, to the number of eighty, paid a visit to the convent which was deserted by its occupants, and after plundering it set it on fire. Not content with robbery of the place, some of the scoundrels donned the habit of the nuns, and mockingly solicited alms of each other, that they were poor nuns of the Order of St. Clare. In fancied security the pillagers started for Athlone with their booty, but fate, or rather God's providence ordered it otherwise. The news of the flight of the nuns and the inhabitants of Bethlehem reached the castle of Sir James Dillon and two of his adherents, Captain Charles McLoughlin and Oliver Buoy Fitzgerald, with eighty men, started to intercept the robbers with their plunder. The little force under McLoughlin and Fitzgerald took up a position in a narrow defile through which the Cromwellians were to pass, carefully ambushed from view. When the robbers entered the gorge they were surrounded on all sides by the followers of Dillon, who despatched every one of them in a few minutes. There was only one casualty on the Irish side and he was shot in mistake for a Roundhead.[14]

Harman Murtagh in his history of Athlone refers to Bethlehem in the context of the 1641 rising. He is discussing an expedition by the Dublin Government in 1642 for the purpose of re-enforcing the garrison at Athlone and he continues:

There was a severe shortage of food with no more than five pounds of bread for each man in a fortnight and no salt. The result was widespread sickness, rendering many of the soldiers unfit for service. Two companies were sent forward to the Poor Clare Convent at Bethlehem. The nuns, who included two of Sir James Dillon's sisters, had withdrawn with his forces into Longford, and the abandoned building was wrecked and looted by the soldiers. But the expedition was ambushed by Dillon's men on the return journey and suffered many casualties, with the result that all the troops billeted in the locality burned the castles they occupied and retired to Athlone.[15]

Later in the same chapter he adds:

> *Another community of catholic regulars to take refuge in Athlone were some of the Poor Clare nuns whose convent at Bethlehem had been destroyed in 1642. In a petition to the supreme council in 1647 they related that after being driven from their convent, twenty-four of the Bethlehem nuns had taken refuge in 'islands, woods and bogs', before coming together to form a new community in Athlone shortly after the first cessation in autumn 1643. The new house was also called Bethlehem.*[16]

The most recent writer on this subject, Fr. Patrick Conlon, O.F.M., sets out to give an account of this Poor Clare community from its beginnings. He states that a small group led by an English lady founded a house for Poor Clares at Gravelines in northern France. They called the house Nazareth. Two young Irish women who entered this community in 1622 were Eleanor and Cecily Dillon, daughters of Sir Theobald Dillon, 1st Viscount Dillon of Costello-Gallen and his wife Eleanor, daughter of Sir Edward Tuite of Tuitestown in Co. Westmeath. With the arrival of more postulants from Ireland the Irish nuns set up their own house and soon began to think of establishing a house in Ireland. On arrival in Dublin in 1629 they found a hostile, intolerant government and they quickly realised that their only hope of surviving in Ireland was to find a remote and distant location far away from the eyes and ears of the authorities. Dillon provided them with such a place on a sodden water-logged promontory in Tubberclare on the eastern shore of Lough Ree where he built them a plain low limestone house. It was completed in 1631 and they called it Bethlehem.

For the next ten years the Bethlehem community flourished and rose to a numerical strength of sixty nuns. They observed the strict rule of the Poor Clares and recited the divine office daily and nightly. The rule of silence was observed and there was perpetual adoration of the Blessed Sacrament. Despite the remoteness of their convent and the difficulty of getting to it, they had many distinguished visitors both lay and clerical. One such was Lady Wentworth, wife of Thomas Wentworth, earl of Strafford and lord deputy of the king, Charles I. Another was the great scholar and historian, Br. Micheal O'Clery, who visited in 1636 following the completion of the *Annals of the Four Masters*. In 1641 seventeen nuns left Bethlehem to set up a new foundation in Drogheda while in the following year fourteen others led by Mother Gabriel Martin went to Galway and there established the Poor Clare house which flourishes to this day on Nuns' Island in that city. After the destruction of their convent and the dispersal of their community the Bethlehem nuns managed to come together again in Athlone. The respite was short however.

Monument to the Four Masters over the Drowes River.

The arrival of Cromwell and the destruction and desecration of all things Irish and Catholic followed rapidly. Fr. Conlon concludes:

> *While a small group did manage to continue in hiding, the bulk of the Irish Poor Clares went into exile, mainly to Spain. Of the Dillon sisters, Mother Cecily died on board a boat bound for Spain in 1653, while Sister Eleanor seems to have returned to Flanders to a rather enigmatic Irish Poor Clare convent in Dieppe. Several Galway girls who had joined the order in Bethlehem, including the first, Sr. Catherine Francis Browne, died in Spain. With the coming of peace, some of the sisters drifted back from Spain to Galway. The last mention of Bethlehem comes in 1696 when at least two sisters who had lived there were alive in Ireland. One of these was Sister Cecily Fitzgerald, a niece of Sisters Cecily and Eleanor Dillon. She had been professed here in that remote spot nearly sixty years previously.*[17]

A tangible link with the Bethlehem nunnery is a wooden statue of the Virgin and Child that once stood in the oratory by Lough Ree, and may be seen today in the Poor Clare convent in Nuns' Island in Galway. According to the folk memory around the lake the statue was found in the ruins of the nunnery after it had been burned by the attackers. Its preservation from the flames was attributed to miraculous intervention. However that may be, this statue has a more ancient provenance. It is apparently the product of a religious wood carving tradition in the country between Athlone and Portumna to the west of the Shannon from the twelfth to the fourteenth century. At least three such statues have survived from this area, including that of Our Lady of Clonfert, all carved from trees in the round, and similar in style.[18] It is not possible to say how the statue came into the possession of the Bethlehem nuns, but it is revered today by the Galway Poor Clares as a precious relic of those "dark and evil days."

CHAPTER 10

Cromwell and the Plantation

The Cromwellian campaign in the midlands was giving cause for official concern. More troops were dying from cold and hunger than from enemy engagements. In 1651 the Cromwellian commissioners wrote to General Reynolds, advising him "to make timely provision of what corn can be gotten out of Roscommon or the islands (of Lough Ree) or other parts in Connaught side and that a fit person of trust be appointed to take care of the corn and hay …"[1] It would seem that the amount of supplies obtained as a result of this directive was negligible for a year later we find a letter addressed to the Council of State as follows:

> We have taken … the boldness to inform your Lordships that there is no provision of corn, oatmeal, or cheese to be had in Ireland for the supplying of your forces in Connaught …[2]

The country about Athlone was so wasted that the commissioners were sending whatever food they could to keep the army "from perishing from want of bread." The capture of the fort of Ballyleague, on the northern extremity of the lake in Co. Longford, some months later, was a major achievement for General John Reynolds and the Cromwellians. Here they gained 400 barrels of corn, which must have been very welcome to their half-starved army. General Reynolds was the officer commanding Cromwellian forces in the midlands, stationed at Athlone.

Throughout the campaign the area of south Longford bordering on Lough Ree was successfully defended by Irish forces with headquarters at the fort of Ballyleague in Co. Longford. This territory acted as a conduit for Irish troops and supplies moving from Ulster to Connaught and inhibited the advance of Cromwellian forces. Richard O'Farrell, celebrated soldier on the continent, who came to Ireland with Owen Roe, had been commander at Ballyleague but was needed elsewhere following the death of Owen Roe and the military victories of Cromwell.

Lottery Castle, Westmeath, by Daniel Grose.
Courtesy of the Irish Architectural Archives and Lord Rossmore.

Defences in south Longford were therefore in some disarray when Reynolds' army advanced from the east over the Inny.

Commissary-General Reynolds, according to the contemporary account of this event,

> *marched into the Callough (being an island bordering on the west, upon the Shannon, and environed on the other side with bogs), where the enemy had three garrisons, the country wholly under their command. Upon his first entrance the enemy quitted two of their garrisons, and the next day surrendered the third, being the fort of Ballyleague, a place of much importance, indifferent strong and capacious, and the only pass for horses over the Shannon between Athlone and Jamestown. The articles of surrender we send enclosed. In the gaining of this place, there is gained 400 barrels of corn for your forces at Athlone, which we look upon as a very seasonable mercy, and likewise forage for some troops, which were in great necessity for want of quarters. It likewise interrupts the frequent conjunction of the Ulster and Connaught forces, and gives you good footing in the county of Longford, which hitherto hath been wholly possessed by the enemy... Sir Theophilus Jones' horse forced a castle upon the Inny, being a pass out of Westmeath into*

Longford, put some found there to the sword; and there being in the castle thirteen priests and friars, they leaped into the river (having about them £2000 in money and plate) and there perished.[3]

The Callough referred to above is the ancient territory of Caladh na h-Anghaile. The castle in which the priests and friars were hiding was Lottery Castle, situated on the Westmeath bank of the Inny, near to where the Red Bridge now stands. There was an ancient ford at this point on the river. The ruins of Lottery Castle were demolished and removed from the site in the course of drainage work carried out by the Board of Works in the 1960s. We are fortunate in that the castle was sketched and recorded by Daniel Grose at the end of the eighteenth century.[4]

The presence of the priests and friars in the castle raises several questions. It would appear that they had fled before the advance of the Cromwellian army. Like other clergy at this time, they had maintained a clandestine ministry, making the Mass and the sacraments available to the people in the more remote parts of the country. We do not know why they assembled at Lottery Castle. The probabilities are, however, that they were expecting a boat to take them to some of the Lough Ree islands, which, as pointed out elsewhere were outside the control of government forces at this time. The two thousand pounds in "money and plate" which they carried would have comprised the sacred vessels, the chalices and patens, which they had brought with them for safe keeping.

When next we return to the Lough Ree islands in the wake of Cromwell's plantation, all we can find are the ruined monastic sites and the names of the landlords who had taken them over as they appear in the records of the time.

Inchbofin	Now owned by the Earl of Roscommon.
Inchturk	Ditto
Inchmore	Ditto
Inis Aingin	Ditto
Inchcleraun	Now owned by Lord Barnewall
Clawinch	Ditto
Inchena	Ditto

The other little island*   Ditto
All Saints' Island   Now owned by Henry Sankey
Inishcorbettdermott (sic)** [Inch]
                              Now owned by Sir George Lane.

- * Probably Nuns' Island.
- ** Anglicisation of Inis Dhearmaid Diarmada

The list above is compiled from information gleaned from the books of survey and distribution of counties Westmeath, Roscommon and Longford. It shows that most of the proprietors had held possession through the Cromwellian plantation. The exceptions are Saints' Island which was formerly held by Gerald Fitzgerald and had now become the property of Henry Sankey, and Inch which had a new owner in the person of Sir George Lane. Sankey had been a soldier in the Cromwellian army and was already the recipient of the lands and castle of O'Farrell in Tenelick. Lane had been a royalist and owed his good fortune to the restoration of Charles II, who rewarded him with estates at Rathcline in Co. Longford and Tulsk in Co. Roscommon and raised him to the peerage in 1666. These monastery lands in the century since the confiscations had been leased to different people, usually

Rathcline Castle, Co. Longford, from Anthologia Hibernica, 1793.

for periods of twenty one years and some had been assigned to permanent owners in the early years of the seventeenth century. The above allocations remained constant, with the exception of the Saints' Island and Inishcorbettdermott lands, which reverted to the Barnewall family.

Nicholas Dowdall, believed to be of old Norman stock and a resident of Co. Longford compiled a fascinating description of the county in 1682. It covered many aspects of life in the late seventeenth century and refers specifically to the islands of Lough Ree:

> *in which there are many old churches and chappells. Some of these islands contain 100 acres very profitable both for tillage and pasture. The largest island is called Insula Sanctorum or the Saints' Island wherein is a very great old ruined monastery and is the chief of the Augustinian order, or the Canons Regular of St. Augustin's order, and governed by a Prior. This river runneth to Athlone and is there very rapid. It is well replenished with fish viz. pike, salmon, trout, eel, bream, roach, etc. The pikes are of an incredible bigness being some above four foot in length. It is navigable for boats of about 10 or 12 tuns, but the vessels most made use of for fishing, portage of goods, etc., are made of one tree like a trough, flatbottomed and some of them so large that they will carry 60 or 80 men, and are called cotts. They usually carry horses and other cattle in them, besides they make great use of them for carrying of timber from the adjacent woods and by laying of long poles over across the said cotts and fastening great beams of timber across the said cotts they will carry twenty tun of timber or more.*[5]

Lough Ree Resistance

A feature of this time was the continued widespread lawlessness on the lake and its islands. George Story in his history of the Williamite wars in Ireland informs us that in 1690 the lord justice

*ordered four longboats, like men-of-war's pinnaces, to be fitted up
with patteros and little small guns … for there are several islands on
the Shannon, wherein the Irish have very considerable riches.*[6]

These boats were to carry one hundred trained soldiers
commanded by one Captain Hoord. His strategy was

*to make incursions into the enemies' country, and to burn and
destroy all before them; if a small party appeared, then they would
fight them, but if a great body, then they could retreat to their fleet,
and go away to another place.*[7]

The boats were built apparently but the project was dropped
before they were launched. It appears from this development that
the English had not yet succeeded in subduing the Lough Ree
islands. The Act of Parliament of 1543, quoted in chapter 8 above,
describes the whole area to the west of Meath as "beset with divers
of the King's rebels", and while the territory around the lake had
been subdued in the meantime, the lake itself and its islands
remained outside the king's writ. Such is the state of the Lough Ree
islands more than a century after the confiscations.

This account of the state of the Shannon at the time of the
Williamite and Jacobite wars leaves little doubt that the lake was a
no-go area for outsiders. The capability of the natives, as Story saw
it, to repel intruders is impressive. The implication is that there
were such numbers of island dwellers as to make it very
inadvisable to confront them head-on and Hoord's plan was to wait
for opportunities to single out and attack small parties. It is not
unlikely that the numbers dwelling on the islands peaked in the
wake of the Cromwellian campaign since many of those who had
fought to reclaim their patrimony during the years of the
confederacy became fugitives at the end of the war. Under the new
regime they carried a price on their heads. Life on the lake therefore
was a measure of safety for those who might otherwise have faced
hanging on the nearest tree. Now they were enjoying "considerable
riches", whatever the source of those riches might be. One wonders,
then, how those who had leased the islands from the crown were

able to continue farming them in safety, or is the concept of "protection money" much older than we think? Many of the lessors themselves were not beloved of the new authorities either and would be unlikely to find much sympathy in official circles. Little wonder, then, that, after a promising start, Hoord's plan was dropped and we hear no more of it.

Throughout the country in general the scene was very different. The eighteenth century was the period of the "Hidden Ireland" when the "mere Irish" suffered under the penal code and an unjust landlord system. It was the determined aim of the Ascendancy, that is the new English, who were now in control, to hold firmly to the wealth and privilege which they had taken from the Irish. The economic and social milieu in which the native population was cast was inhuman, engendering in the words of Jonathan Swift "that poverty and lowness of spirit to which a kingdom may be subject as well as a particular person." Swift, although born into the ascendancy class, railed against the policies of the government and championed the cause of the underdog. One of his contemporaries was the poet, Oliver Goldsmith, born in Pallas and brought up at Lissoy, little more than a stone's throw from the shore of Lough Ree. Goldsmith's poem *The Deserted Village* laments the passing of a simple, happy way of life and condemns an overbearing, greedy aristocracy that tramples the spirit out of a vital peasant society.

> Princes and lords may flourish or may fade,
> A breath can make them as a breath has made,
> But a bold peasantry, their country's pride,
> When once destroyed, can never be supplied.

Thus did the country remain in stagnation and depression through the first three quarters of the eighteenth century, and the establishment paid little attention to the lake or its islands.

CHAPTER 11

Independence on the wane

Over the centuries a constant feature of Lough Ree was the interaction between the island dwellers and those on the lakeshore. In early times people went out to island sanctuaries on pilgrimage to reflect and pray. At other times island monks had to flee and seek safety on the mainland. Foreign fleets and local fleets terrorised the lake at intervals. By 1690, as we have seen, many Irish inhabited the islands which they successfully defended against English attacks. This was possible because pockets of Irish resistance remained intact in the woods and fens close to the shore.

As the eighteenth century developed and the power of the English big houses was secured, such pockets were finally suppressed. There was always a strong and necessary interdependence between the island communities and their counterparts on the shore. Now, with the changed conditions, a well policed mainland meant that the islanders also had to be amenable to the law. Otherwise they could be arrested if they came in from the lake in their boats to obtain supplies or to sell fish or farm products. Thus the attitude of defiant independence, manifested in Elizabeth's time and reflected in Hoord's proposals of the late 1600s, was gradually broken down and the large numbers of island dwellers, implied in these proposals, eventually drained away.

Quaker Meeting House, Ballymurray.

The last quarter of the eighteenth century witnessed a steady improvement in the Irish economy. The rapid industrialisation of England opened up ready markets for Irish foodstuffs especially grain and meat. Semi-dormant holdings such as the Lough Ree islands were gaining a new economic potential and it was at this point in 1780 that Lord Kingsland's (Barnewall) island holdings were put on the market. The Featherstone family, Robert and Francis, were the principal purchasers and they bought Saints' Island, Inchcleraun, Inchenagh, Inch and Clawinch.[1] The Delamers were already settled on Clawinch and no doubt paying rent for it. Saints' Island had also settled down to a fairly stable landlord-tenant arrangement. Inchcleraun was proving to be attractive pastureland for the Quaker settlement on the Connaught side at Ballymurray.

Close on the heels of this trend were the landlords pushing to get some income from their island properties - particularly the new landlords, when many of the islands changed ownership, in the third quarter of the eighteenth century. It was soon after this that Edward Fairbrother from Ballymurray leased the lands of Inchcleraun.

The ruins of the house of Mr. Fairbrother, the Quaker, on Inchcleraun.

Obviously some of the old Irish spirit was still alive as the islanders conspired to drive his cattle into the lake and then pin the blame on St. Diarmaid! But Fairbrother persevered and built a house on the island, partly for the purpose of protecting his stock. Other islands were leased in small holdings to resident tenants in the usual way, but there is reason to believe that rents were not always forthcoming and it was more difficult to enforce payment here than on the mainland, as will be seen later in the case of the landlord attempting evictions on Inchturk.

Thus the story of Lough Ree and its environs takes on new and different dimensions in its history since 1700. Old feudal lords like Dillons, Delamers, Nugents, Barnewalls, O'Kellys, O'Farrells and O'Fallons have lost all influence and are replaced by Handcocks, Smyths, Lanes, Hodsons, Croftons, Dawsons and King Harmans. This era is marked by a policy of total domination by the new overlords ably assisted by police and militia. Initially the population was sparse. The total number of people in Ireland in

1700 was less than two million and it was the policy of the English Williamite regime to suppress the indigenous stock and replace them with English protestants. This new policy was established on the basis of the plantations of the seventeenth century.

However, a number of the planters who had got lands in this way had become absentees like the Lanes of Rathcline. Others, although resident, were reluctant to work the land. The Smyths of Portlick offered 340 acres and "a good dwelling house well wainscotted and slated" for letting on 20th April 1742.[2] The following year John Stoyte is offering 150 acres, part of "the lands of Ballykeeran."[3] John Dawson of Tubberclare seems to be going broke. His notice in Faulkner's Dublin Journal in 1747 is offering for sale 1300 sheep, 20 rams, 100 bullocks, 20 heifers and horses for draught and saddle.[4] Robert Handcock is also broke and his lands are to be sold for the payment of his debts as follows - Tully, Tisarane, Estermore, Kiltoyle, in Co Roscommon and Loughily in Co. Westmeath.[5] In 1761 there is an application to parliament "to vest the lands of Ballykeeran and Friars' Island (700 acres) in trustees to be sold for the payment of debts."[6] A notice from 1768 offers "the lands of Kilteevan, Cloonclogher ... with three islands on the banks of the Shannon having remarkably good fisheries."[7]

The upturn in the economy in the last quarter of the century is reflected in the rapid rise in the Ballymurray linen and woollen industries. Lord Crofton, the landlord of Mote Park, was promoting local industry in the area of his estate, which bordered Lough Ree, and published an advertisement as follows:

Ballymurray is situate within six miles of the great Yarn Fair of Lanesborough and four from Roscommon. A river nearly navigable to the Shannon runs through the town. A mill at present obstructs it but it will be removed. Good encouragement will be given to any person who settles a manufactory and brings protestant workmen to said town. A stipulated sum will be given for every house built to a given plan. When the second house is built the first will be paid for and so continued until the last house is built. For further particulars apply Edward Crofton, Mote.[8]

Obviously the improvement in the economy was meant to benefit one section of the population only. The remainder was the underprivileged who resented their menial status. It galled them to watch the militia recruiting young men who would be used to keep their own people in bondage. They showed their resentment by protesting in public near the lakeshore in Co. Roscommon:

> *25th May 1793: A large and riotous mob assembled at Lacken and Turrough Co. Roscommon with intent to commit violence on those enrolling names of persons for the militia. Sir Edward Crofton and a party of twelve cavalry went out to quell and disperse them. The mob, composed of men and women, opposed the military and threw stones at them. Sir Edward, through humanity, rather than fire on them, retreated. They pursued Sir Edward closely and in their own defence (the military) were obliged to fire on the mob, killing seven and wounding sixteen. Eleven were made prisoners and lodged in Roscommon gaol.*[9]

This cruel incident at Lacken may be taken as typical of the mentality of the Ascendancy towards the native poor at this time. Even the chronicler of the event found it necessary to allude to Crofton's "humanity" despite his having the protection of trained, well-armed soldiers in the face of a ragged bunch of men and women who could do no better than throw stones at them to express their frustration. Grief and heartbreak would now be the lot of the survivors as they buried their dead and nursed their wounded, some of whom were maimed for life. Next would come the prosecutions of those who had been arrested, and as none of His Majesty's forces had been injured the lesser penalty would apply - transportation for life. Thousands would turn out to see their young men, chained together, and loaded on drays drawn up outside the gaol door. Gentry would go to the top windows of their houses to witness the spectacle of the prisoners taking a last look on the land of their birth. A vast concourse of people wailing piteously would follow them for a few miles as they started the long journey to reach their convict ship. Armed soldiers were ever present to ensure that the queen's writ was obeyed and the people were powerless. It is difficult to imagine how things could have got much worse. That however is precisely what happened. Five years later, the '98 Rebellion, with all its attendant horrors, stalked the land and the people's masters had new and more savage inventions like the pitch cap and the walking gallows.

Barbarity, once unleashed, is difficult to confine again and the naturally mild disposition of the Irish temperament became brutalised under the weight of oppression. Secret societies had sprung up around the country and they frequently perpetrated deeds of savage revenge on those identified as their tormentors. These in turn were punished by hangings and floggings followed by further reprisals until life at local level sometimes degenerated into warfare. This was the context for survival in rural Ireland in the eighteenth century and it set the agenda for the century ahead at a time when the native population was increasing in unprecedented numbers.

Despite the hard times and the pressures under which the people lived, this era witnessed the emergence of a new sense of identity among the local communities. A strong motivation to improve the lot of the children induced a new interest in education which ultimately had its sequel in the establishment of the national schools. The penal laws had been bitterly resented and the government, under pressure in the last quarter of the century had relaxed some of them. The drive for Catholic Emancipation also bore fruit in the early decades of the new century. Agricultural produce which had become more plentiful was mainly for export. Far too many of the rising population were dependent on potatoes for their staple food. The following are the prices realised at Athlone market on 18th October 1819.

Oats 7s 6d per barrel or 6d per stone
Oatmeal 1s 3d per stone
Potatoes 2d / 3d per stone
Mutton 5d-7d per lb.
Fresh butter 10d per lb.[10]

A report of 23rd December 1800 informs us that David Powell, pro-collector (revenue) of Athlone, went with a party of Captain Pennyfather's yeomen infantry to Muckenagh, Co. Westmeath, and, in a peninsula formed by a winding of the Shannon, they seized a 200-gallon still at full work which they conveyed to Athlone. They also seized a boat, the property of the owner of the still. They claim that this boat constantly plied to Lanesborough and was in readiness at the time to take another cargo of spirits on board. It is not stated whether the illicit cargo was destined for wider distribution or if the citizenry of Lanesborough were capable of consuming it without further assistance.[11]

Here, and also by the shore, the old Irish way of life was still surviving. Old customs and manners were in vogue and the native language was spoken, though few, if any, of the ordinary people could read or write it. Despite the havoc visited on the learned and on the places of learning, the western lake shore could produce poets of the calibre of Seán O'Neachtain and his son Tadhg from the parish of Drum who founded the Irish Folk School in Meath St. in Dublin which was run by them from 1690 to 1750. Another poet of this period is Brian O'Fearghail, author and collector, born at Knockskehan in the parish of Tigh Eoin (St. John's) overlooking Rindoon in 1715.[12] There was in addition O'Fearghail's contemporary, Mícheál Ó Braonáin, born at Lisgobbin between Roscommon and Ballyleague who wrote the poem *Príomh Shruth Éireann*.

Príomh Shruth Éireann[13]

Towards the end of the eighteenth century Lough Ree and its environs became the subject of part of an epic poem in the Irish language. This is a major literary work encompassing the entire Shannon River. Ó Braonáin's knowledge of his subject from source to estuary is little short of astonishing. However it is his peregrinations in and around Lough Ree that particularly call for our attention. He came from Lisgobbin, a small rural locality about three miles north east of Roscommon town and near to the western shore of Lough Ree. His poem was discovered in Ms. No.23 B.27 in the Royal Irish Academy. There is no record of who placed it there, or when, and nothing else is known of the poet other than that which was contained in the manuscript package.

The poem itself gives the author's name and the year of its composition, 1794. A number of accompanying documents, mainly letters, cast some tiny chinks of light on the man and his times. He was a hedge schoolmaster eking out a meagre and precarious existence. He had the classical European learning of those times, and knew Latin and French as well as being able to express himself fluently in English. His Irish is rich in imagery, fluent in style and there is impressive literary merit in his poem, but the trail ends there. Nothing else has survived concerning the life of Mícheál Ó Braonáin. He fits well into the old bardic tradition that suffered a lingering death following the dispossession of the chieftains and the destruction of the great houses of hospitality. As "patronage failed more and more the poet professor had often to learn a new trade if he were to live" and often "earned his living in the day-time by ploughing in his own or another's fields, by schoolmastering, or by keeping a tavern."[14] The poem, throughout its three hundred and thirty nine verses takes the reader on a tour of the river Shannon and includes, *inter alia*, more than three hundred place names. Ó Braonáin shows an intimate knowledge of Lough Ree and its islands: *Cláinse na náirní dubha (Clawinch of the black sloes)* and again: *Dairinis na ndruid is na gcorra (Dairinis of the starlings and the herons).*

He named twenty seven islands on Lough Ree calling them by their traditional Irish names. Most of them can be identified today, but regrettably a few identities are lost beyond recovery and it is no longer possible to say which islands are being named. He had the traditional lore of the lake that lived on in the folk memory of the local people and from this he has left us valuable information.

The names of the islands in Ó Braonáin's poem in the order in which they appear are as follows: Inis Cloithrinn, Inis Bófinne, Inis Mór, Oileán na Naomh, Inis Torc, Inis Éan na Caillí Duibhe, An Inis, Féarinse, Inis an Ghabhair, Inis Éanach, Cláinsí, Inis Uí Ruairc, Muicinis, Inis Rinn Éanaigh, Dairinis, Inis Ríóige, Na Trí Inse Dubha, Inis Shúil Daimh, Inis an Adhmaid, Na Trí Choirib, Inis Aínín, An t-Oileán Buí and Inis Chairbre.

CHAPTER 12

Social Tensions around the lake

The priests were a powerful influence for good on the people at this time. They had stood by their flocks in bloody persecutions a century earlier and many of them had paid the ultimate price. They had earned the trust and respect of their communities and they used it to the utmost to lead the people out of the morass of poverty and ignorance into which a greedy and heartless Ascendancy had plunged them. They led from the front, often publicly castigating the harshness and severity of the authorities, while counselling tolerance and restraint among the victims of injustice. Churches were generally in poor condition and in some parishes non-existent.

Public worship often took place in the open, especially on pattern days, which commemorated a local saint of earlier times and usually centred round a holy well. Patterns were generally lively affairs where the people began by praying with great sincerity and devotion and then went on to enjoy the occasion with equal enthusiasm and flair. All of which was a wonderful experience provided it didn't get out of hand. However, given the human condition and the perennial possibility of a surreptitious gallon or two of poteen for the afters, it did happen very occasionally that things went wrong. Some such took place at the pattern of St. John's on the 29th October 1819, and trouble developed. The local magistrate Oliver Hodson arrived with his men to quell what he termed a riot. Two locals named Devilly resented Hodson's interference and emphasised their indignation by landing a few punches on his person. They were arrested and duly prosecuted and sentenced to be flogged on the high road, the scene of their offence, "for the space of a mile and back again."[1]

Pattern celebrations were not the only hazards faced by priests in those years. Rev. Charles McDermott was the parish priest of Knockcroghery in 1811. He presided at the marriage of a couple who, it would appear, were already living together in the vicinity. The woman subsequently complained that she had been married against her will and the parish priest was lodged in gaol on May 11th at the instance of Sir Edward Crofton, the local landlord.[2]

Directly across the lake, in the parish of Cashel the local priest was having a similar experience having been let down by his own. James Moffett, faithful servant of the crown, wrote to Dublin Castle as follows:

Ballymahon
31st March 1815

Sir,

I find it necessary to acquaint you for the information of the government of the country, that, since the news of Buonaparte's arrival in France was made known here, the activity of the Threshers has increased very much, and few nights pass but we hear of some depredations committed by them and I fear they are but too successful in plundering the yeomen of their arms, the particulars of which I suppose have been reported by the proper channel, a business has occurred in the parish of Cashel which I regret very much to have to state the Rev. Mr. McGauran priest of that parish, by the most unwearied diligence and perseverance had induced the chief part of his flock to submit to his directions and surrender their arms to him and he had been busily employed for a month back in discovering and collecting what he could (sic). On Monday last he called on me to say he had recovered eleven and was promised two more either on that or the following night and would bring the whole to me on Thursday, together with the card which had been surrendered to him, but on the night of Tuesday the 20th, a party of armed men, for whom he opened his door, supposing them to be coming as friends, having gained admission immediately demanded his arms, searched his house, broke his parlour door which he refused to open, and also broke a closet door off the parlour where the arms were deposited and carried off the entire after breaking and damaging his house in other parts, such effect had the account of that man's arrival in Paris, on those deluded villains, that they at once violated the solemn promises they made so lately before, and outraged every feeling of the man and the Christian. Mr. McGauran

assures me they are determined to persevere and will shortly break
out into open rebellion.
Your obedient and very humble servant
Jas. Moffett[3]

The spirit of insurrection which had confronted Father McGauran was not confined to Cashel and was already spreading throughout Co. Westmeath. Secret societies such as the Threshers were operating under cover of darkness throughout large sections of the country. Of particular interest here were the Whitefeet and a faction known as the Shaskeens or Blackfeet. The latter took their name from the Shaskeen River, a tributary of the Inny, near to where it enters Lough Ree. The house of a man named Grennan at Cappabrack in Calry parish was maliciously set on fire and the inmates barely escaped. Eight sheep were shorn of their wool in the same parish and the fleeces carried away. The house of a gentleman in Shenglass was attacked by a body of men and two cases of pistols were taken.[4]

Next we learn that the parish of Drumraney is declared officially to be in a state of disturbance and was proclaimed under the Insurrection Act. On 27th October 1814 it was reported that "Threshers broke into the house of the herd to Charles Lennon, Drumraney, and with a pair of shears cut off both his ears."[5] This dreadful deed was done because he gave information to his master on the personnel associated with the secret society. A few nights later they "cut off one ear of a man who lives in Walderstown, two miles from Drumraney, a similar reason being given."[6]

However, those who had done most to lead the people in ways of peace continued to be outlawed. We read that on the 22nd March 1824 Thomas Doyle, a catholic clergyman, was indicted at Mullingar Assizes for marrying James Kelly, a protestant, to Mary Dolan, a papist. He was ordered to pay a fine of £500 and to be imprisoned until the fine was paid.[7] Thus, the lives of the ordinary people were often enmeshed in situations not of their own making, and poverty and fear played a big part in them. Their powerlessness and dependence were sometimes pathetic. A report of 15th July 1822 states that several men, women and children were busily employed at making a harbour in the river Shannon at Athlone at the Northgate side of the town. The persons thus employed "are compensated for their labour by a certain allowance of oaten meal, from which circumstances, the place has become known as Stirabout Harbour."[8]

A court case at Roscommon around this time brings us back to the Quakers at Ballymurray and the confusions and contradictions that were then part of everyday life. Edward Geraghty and Hugh Keaveney were indicted that on the night of 23rd May 1831, at Larkhill, they assaulted the habitation of James McClean. "They broke his delph and beat him. They also beat his cow that was in the house." McClean said he was not a Quaker but was apprenticed to a Quaker in Ballymurray named Simon Kellet. He was a protestant and went to church. He also went to Mass. His wife was a catholic. He was married by Fr Brown. Peggy McClean, his wife, swore she was married by Fr Brown at 11 o'clock at night in the presbytery of Athlone chapel. The clerk, John Forde, was present. The priest was concealed under the altar with a white gown on his shoulders. He had a light inside and they had a light outside. They gave a guinea to the priest. So much for the marriage - the outcome of the court case was predictable. Prisoners found guilty. They were later sentenced to transportation for life.[9]

On the northern shore of the lake a problem had developed around fishing rights. One man had secured a licence to fish while the others protested that the fishing belonged to everyone. The resultant friction is detailed in a letter from James Alworthy, chief constable, 1st class, Ballymahon, on 1st July 1834. He tells us that "on Monday night 27th ultimo the dwelling house of James Fox, Ballinahinch, in the parish of Cashel and barony of Rathcline was feloniously entered by four or five men who cut his fishing net and injured his boat by sinking it. The cause of this outrage is jealousy, Fox having obtained liberty to fish on a part of the Shannon, and others prevented. He says he suspects one of the party named Lan, a fisherman also."[10]

A year later in the same townland another outrage is reported by the same James Alworthy. He states that *on Sunday night the 3rd instant a threatening notice was posted on the door of the dwelling-house of Patt Skally of Ballinahinch in the parish of Cashel and Barony of Rathcline. On which notice was drawn the picture of a coffin, threatening his life if he worked for John Jordan, a freeholder, who resides in that neighbourhood and on the following night an armed party came to said dwelling-house and demanded said notice, which said Skally gave them. They then beat himself and his son severely and tore their flesh with a wool card. None of the offenders are, as yet, known, nor has any clue been obtained towards the discovery of any of the perpetrators.*

Recommended: The chief constable may offer from £20 to £30 for private information in these cases and will urge the police to make every exertion to put down these disgraceful proceedings.[11]

High over Lough Ree on the slopes of Slieve Bawn, six men were digging conacre potato land on the 9th April 1845. They had contracted to pay £3 per acre for this ground. The cost of conacre had become exorbitant at this time. Rates of £9 to £12 per acre were being charged, and landless men had become desperate for ground to grow potatoes. The comparatively low rent here was because it was on the side of the mountain and of poor quality. A body of police arrived while the men were working, and believing them to be persons engaged in unlawfully digging "feeding land" (such outrages having been committed in north Co. Roscommon recently) attempted to arrest these men. (In areas where conacre was denied to the labourers they sometimes went out at night and dug up the ground to prevent the landlord from using it as "feeding land" for cattle.) A man named Michael Horohoe had a blank cartridge discharged in his face and was stabbed in the arm. Also stabbed were two other men named Greene. At this time two countrymen who were well known to the police named McNally and Patrick Lyons interfered, and it was arranged that all would go before a magistrate voluntarily. The police then went some distance away, loaded their carbines and fired at the men, badly wounding a man named John Gavigan, who was merely a spectator. The police then took the wounded man with them across the mountain. The following day, Mr Rutherford, the local magistrate, visited the land and stated that the people were entitled to work there.[12]

11th April 1845: "John Gavigan the man wounded by the police has died and an inquest will be held".[13] We presume that the men continued their digging and that the potatoes were set on the mountainside. This was destined to be the crop that was destroyed by the blight, in the harvest of 1845, which marked the beginning of the Great Famine.

The same year saw a very serious boating accident on Lough Ree. It happened on 4th of March when nine men and two women were crossing to their homes in a boat, having worked all day in a local quarry, near the residence of Lord Castlemaine at Coosan Point. The boat sank without warning and only two men and one woman were saved.[14]

At the other end of the social spectrum the Smyths of Portlick Castle had acquired high levels of skill and expertise racing boats over the lake. They had a boat specially built for racing called the "Unique" and in July 1844 they took it to Kingstown Regatta where they engaged in competition with a similar entry from the

Portlick Castle, Athlone.

Pembroke club whose boat's name was the "Unknown." After several races the Pembroke boat was declared the winner. This had a sequel the following year when the Lough Ree Regatta took place on Monday 1st September. The Smyths challenged for a rematch, each side wagering 50 guineas. Excitement was high resulting in the Smyths winning the race by eleven seconds.[15]

Pattern days on the western side of the lake had problems of their own. We've already seen how at the Pattern of St. John's in 1818 an incident took place involving the local magistrate and resulting in penalties for two local men. At the Lecarrow Pattern Day in 1845 on 1st of July a soldier from Athlone barracks was drunk and disorderly. He was arrested by his own authorities and on the following day he received a hundred lashes as punishment on the barrack square.[16]

CHAPTER 13

The changing environment on Lough Ree

The first half of the nineteenth century was a time of unprecedented change for Lough Ree and the Shannon generally. The construction of The Grand Canal commenced in Dublin in 1756 and by 1804 it had reached the Shannon at Shannon Harbour. Expectations were high that the river would now become a major thoroughfare facilitating business and commerce from north to south. When, some fifteen years later, the Royal Canal joined the Shannon at Clondra a few miles north of Lough Ree it was felt by many that the lake was destined to be at the centre of the new economic expansion. Unfortunately, however, those expectations were not fulfilled, and Isaac Weld in 1832 bemoaned the lack of business and the total absence of berthing and harbour facilities for commercial boats:

Along the whole Roscommon shore, there is not a single public quay for boats of burthen, and but few places naturally favourable for loading or unloading… During different visits of several days each, to different parts of the lake, both along the shores and on the water, and invariably with fine weather, I never saw, except in one instance, a boat of burthen upon its waters. Pleasure boats, however, are numerous, little fleets of which occasionally start from Athlone, and sometimes coming from different quarters, they rendezvous at some agreeable spot on island or mainland, where the parties disembark for refreshment or amusement. Boating is indeed a very common pastime along the whole line of the lake, but by far more general at the lower end, where the shores are the best inhabited. The whole traffic of Lough Ree is confined, or very nearly so, to the intercourse between Lanesborough and Athlone, and vice versa. Manure, indeed, may be occasionally conveyed from Athlone, and a chance load of slates or foreign timber dropped along the shores; potatoes or corn may also be carried to or from one market or the other; but there can scarcely be said to exist any steady, regular traffic, except it be for the few cargoes of native coal brought down from Lough Allen; and this coal is neither in request for the distilleries and breweries of Athlone, nor for the steamboats on the lower lakes of the Shannon; the former chiefly consume turf, the latter, sea borne coal.[1]

Weld goes on to look at the natural advantages of Lough Ree and its surroundings, and he expresses some hopes for its development in the future:

No part, probably, of the whole course of the Shannon, most certainly no part of the upper Shannon, affords so many advantageous positions for towns and villages, as the shores of Lough Ree; and were the example followed of Holland or Switzerland, those two regions of industry and perseverance; where the population spreads down to the lakes, the rivers and canals, as affording the means of frequent and ready intercourse, the waters of Lough Ree might become enlightened with the sail and oar, and the cheerful notes of commerce be echoed from shore to shore. At present, except for the accidental appearance of the light skiff, wafted over the surface by the zephyr; the face of the lake is a scene of solitude, silence and melancholy.[2]

Richmond Harbour.

The Ordnance Survey took place in the 1830s and it must have created a stir among the island folk to see the army sappers arriving in their boats, complete with tripods and theodolites, to map the islands. Of greater interest perhaps was John O'Donovan who wanted to listen to the islanders and hear their stories and the seanchas (folklore) of the islands. In addition he examined the old ruins that remained from monastic times and succeeded in identifying the ancient names of the islands and their history. The great antiquarian opened up worlds of learning that might have been otherwise irrevocably lost. He gave a new incentive to the study of Irish topography and Irish literature, thus laying the foundations of the spirit that inspired the Celtic Revival towards the end of that century.

The improvement of the Shannon navigation occupied the minds of various companies and individuals from the earliest days of the eighteenth century. Several surveys and reports on the subject were commissioned and laid before parliament in the succeeding one hundred and fifty years. In 1835 yet another commission was set up and instructed to prepare plans for the development of the Shannon navigation. With the completion of the two canals the age of water transport had arrived and the river Shannon, running north-south for a distance equal to two thirds of the length of the entire island, was seen as a great prospect for the movement of both passengers and goods.

Several fords, many of which had figured prominently in the early history of the country, were proving obstacles to navigational progress. Makeshift solutions such as the building of lateral canals had been found to be inadequate, especially in times of low water. The Irish word for a ford is *Áth* and it is no coincidence that the Shannon enters Lough Ree at *Béal Átha Liag* and exits the lake at *Béal Átha Luain*. In each case a ridge of carboniferous limestone had impeded the flow of water from time immemorial. Since both crossings were in need of new bridges it was decided to dredge out the riverbeds and dispense with canals which had been, at best, a makeshift arrangement. Athlone had the problem of being downstream from Lough Ree so a decision was taken to divert the river and erect a dam to hold back the waters of the lake in order to remove the shoals. Fortunately most of the work of blasting and clearing the channel had been completed before the dam gave way releasing a torrent of water. Surprisingly there seem to have been no casualties. At Ballyleague the old canal wall ran adjacent to the west bank and parallel with it. This canal had a single set of gates at its downstream extremity, over which was constructed a lockhouse. All this was dredged out and became part of the new channel which effectively remains unchanged to the present day.

Similar excavation was done where the river enters the lake at Ballyclare Island and again where it exits on its way to Athlone. The Lecarrow canal from Blackbrink Bay was completed in 1842 to enable the transportation of stone from the quarry there for the completion of the bridge and docks of Athlone.

Lecarrow Canal.

CHAPTER 14

The Great Famine

The census of 1841 records that there were 272 people living on the Lough Ree islands. They were distributed over eleven islands, very unequally, with Inchmore having 29 people and King's island (Black Islands), less than one eighth of its size - having 22. This anomaly is explained by the fact that the lands on the larger fertile islands were rented to well off lessees such as Major Sandys on Inchmore and Edward Fairbrother (the Quaker) on Inchcleraun reflecting the land distribution pattern across the country as a whole at that time.

Despite that, however, the island people survived well and they fared much better in the Great Famine than their neighbours on the mainland. In the ten year period 1841-51 the population of the islands dropped just fifteen per cent while that of Rathcline parish dropped by twenty seven per cent and the population of Cashel parish by a searing thirty-five per cent. Various reasons are advanced as to why this was so, the most plausible being the availability of fish as a nutritious food and the relative isolation of the lake dwellers, which must have saved them from the contagious fever that swept the surrounding counties in 1847.

All around the shore the cold hand of famine and death had silenced the natural exuberance of the people. John Keegan, of Moate, was at this time working for the Ordnance Survey in the area around Lough Ree. He has left us this account of his observations:

> The failure of the potatoes has brought desolation over the whole
> land and deadened (I trust not destroyed) the nobler feelings of
> family and kindred. Even those who have means affect poverty and
> close their doors and hearts against their friends and relations and
> are not ashamed to take what is intended for the needy and destitute.
> Although I am lodging in a country place, and frequently walk out
> on a Sunday evening, I scarcely meet a soul on the roads, and as for
> a dance, hurling or football, the people appear to have forgotten there

were ever such amusements. How often have I seen poor John Dooley, the blind piper of Ballinderry, playing for a merry, light-footed group, not one of whom ever having heard of Indian meal. What if a few fought and got drunk? It was preferable to the present death-like stillness and apathy.[1]

The failure of the potato crop was the immediate cause of the famine. However, the land ownership system whereby those who lived by the land had no right of tenure was the long term cause. All around Lough Ree the small tenant farmers were at the mercy of the prevailing economic reality. They could be driven out of their cabins at will by the landlord. Such a scene was described at a meeting of the Athlone Board of Guardians in 1843, when a "boy" of about eighteen years of age and four sisters ranging from seven to fourteen, applied for admission to the workhouse. They had been evicted from their home near the lakeshore. The following verbatim account appeared in the Freeman's Journal. The Chairman, Mr Gerald Dillon is addressing the "boy", Michael Gosling:

Chairman: Are these girls your sisters?
Michael Gosling: Yes, yer honour, they are sure enough.
Chairman: Where is your father?
Michael Gosling: He is in America.
Chairman: Where is your mother?
Michael Gosling: Troth I don't know yer honour but I believe she wint to me father when we were turned out.
Chairman: Who turned you out?
Michael Gosling: Mr Hill did.
Chairman: Who is Mr Hill?
Michael Gosling: Divil a wan of meself knows. He only came there some years agone as agent, an ids the sore day to hus all. He's agent I hear to Mr Disney.
Chairman: Oh! you live on the Ballykeeran property?
Michael Gosling: Yes yer honour bud I was turned out three weeks since and I was trying to support myself and the childer here til I was ladin a horse that ran away wud me and hurt me leg an I was not able to work an I was forced to let

meself and the childer come here.

Chairman: You would not come in here only you hurt your leg?

Michael Gosling: No in troth yer honour bad manners to the bit o' me near you good or bad bud for the hurt an I'd get enough to help me. Mr Murtagh or any o'thim about Ballykeeran would be glad to have me and give me plenty to do.

Chairman: How much land had you?

Michael Gosling: Three rood or near and a schravogue of a garden.

Chairman: How many families were turned out?

Michael Gosling: Forty families with six or seven and sometimes eight or nine in every one of them.

Chairman: That is at the lowest calculation two hundred and eighty souls at one clearing. Well it was not a bad day's work certainly. Alas poor Ireland.

The Chairman later questioned the manner in which this land was divided.

Chairman: I should suppose those who got land gave something for it to the agent, did they?

Michael Gosling: Divil a one of meself can tell only as the neighbours say. I hard John Headen gave £7 or £8, an Larry Headen, everyone knows, gave a heifer and a pound note an he got nine acres, bud though John Kerney gave £3 he only got one acre. Captain Stubbs got the most entirely af anyone that's in id.

Chairman: Did Captain Stubbs give any money?

Michael Gosling: Don't you know well enough he did. I didn't see any of the money counted to be sure, but the divil a perch anyone got if he didn't give some, an that everyone knows, an anyone that didn't was turned out.

Chairman: Was it Mr Hill got all this money?

Michael Gosling: It was to be sure an he'd take more av he got it, but he's in a blue stew now himself for he's wrote against to the head man.

Chairman: Who wrote against him?

Michael Gosling: Troth wan that knew how to do it well, Mr Tom Gannon, sure yer reverence knows him well enough.

Chairman: Was there any money sent to be given to the poor people when they were turned out?

Michael Gosling: The neighbours say there was, an that he robbed the people an didn't give them the half.

Chairman: Who is the owner of the property?

Michael Gosling: Colonel Bligh yer honour.

Chairman: Does Colonel Bligh or Mr Disney know of this work at Ballykeeran?

Michael Gosling: Bad manners to me if I can well tell bud sure Mr Gannon wrote to some a them an tould them all. Some would say that the colonel is a good man an av he knew id he would put a stop to id and some say they'd be no use telling him about id, that his mind is poisoned with lies and stories; meself doesn't think he knows the half of id, for no Christian who thinks he has a sowl to be saved would do the like, more especially some a them that were a lyin or red hot out of the fever, the Lord save us, an they were all hurled out in the door just like pigs ye'd be drivin to a fair.[2]

As the waves of emigration took their toll on rural Ireland, those left behind had to concentrate more on survival. When a new political movement, the Fenians, emerged in the

John Keegan Casey, Fenian Poet.

late 1850s its aim was separation from Britain and it was committed to the use of force. The Fenian movement was active in the midlands and there were many arrests in Roscommon and Westmeath on the eve of the Fenian Rising in 1867. Of all the leaders the most colourful and appealing was undoubtedly the young poet, John Keegan Casey, who organised the movement in south Longford from his home in Gurteen by Lough Ree. Later he would move to Castlerea in Co. Roscommon where he was afterwards arrested and imprisoned in Mountjoy. Writing under the pen name "Leo" he became well known throughout Ireland for his songs and ballads including the popular *Maire My Girl* and *The Rising of the Moon*. He was a great lover of the lake and while still a teenager he had procured a small boat which enabled him to visit the families on the islands and to travel as far as the Connaught shore. He made songs to many girls in the environs of the lake including "his darling Mary." Here he is lamenting his separation from her and from Lough Ree.

The Inny's shore and tall Rathmore,
The sunlight on the trembling meadows,
The pastured lea by fair Lough Ree
Are now, to me, but fading shadows
Two eyes of blue still keep their hue –
Two lustrous eyes that never vary
And on me shine with love divine
Those eyes are thine, my darling Mary!

Shortly before Leo's release from Mountjoy he is on record as saying that he intended to write a great deal to make up for lost time. He fulfilled his promise with many new poems while at the same time he worked as a journalist for a number of newspapers. He also wrote prose and over a dozen stories of varying lengths which were published in the columns of weeklies and periodicals of that era. One such story *The Green Flag in France* opens on the island of Inchbofin in Lough Ree in the ruined walls of the ancient monastery there.[3]

CHAPTER 15

The Land Question and Emerging Nationalism

Many landlords in the nineteenth century were living beyond their means and they continued to raise the rent on the tenant farmers to subsidise their lifestyles. Others, finding that cattle-farming was more profitable, evicted the tenants regardless of rent and cleared them off their estates. Inevitably this led to confrontation between the landlords and the tenants, who were supported by a growing Land League organisation. The intimidating power of the landlords was well exemplified at Ballymurray, overlooking Lough Ree from the west, in 1882, where an evicting party arrived on 27th February. It consisted of

> *Mr Irwin the sheriff, four emergency-men with bedding etc on four Athlone cars, Mr Beckett R.M., Mr Dillon R.M., one hundred men of the 64th under Major Denniston, Captain Monco and Lieut Shanley, and sixty police under C.J. Carr, S.I. Waters and S.I. Jaques. There was also a doctor and an ambulance car fitted with lint and bandages.*[1]

Obviously the eviction party meant business.

As the Land League developed its twin weapons became "the plan of campaign" and the "boycott." Under the plan of campaign the tenants on an estate came together and offered the landlord what they considered to be a fair rent. If he refused to accept this they were to pay him no rent at all but to put their money in an estate fund to be used for the protection of those who would now be evicted as a result of not paying their rent. The "boycott" was to prevent the land grabbers from taking the farms of the unjustly evicted tenants. The tenants of the Naghton estate near Athlone operated the plan of campaign successfully in 1887. In the same year a great meeting was held on Carrick Hill, Auburn, to honour the men of the Auburn estate who had adopted the plan of campaign. Fr Carey addressed the crowd and Mr J.D. Keenan also spoke. A contingent from Noughaval, on the lakeshore, with the

First Blood Band, came to the Three Jolly Pigeons and were welcomed there by Mr Thomas Murray, the proprietor and his wife, who presented the band with a red rose. [2]

The collection of rates on the islands of Lough Ree was attempted, but owing to lack of boats, seizure could not be carried out. Boat owners refused to lend their boats. A contemporary report describes the "great excitement" in Athlone at the presence of a large police force to protect the sheriff who intended to carry out evictions at Inchturk on Lough Ree. The difficulty in obtaining suitable boats delayed action. In a later report, however, this difficulty had been rectified:

> *Police having got boats from Mr Michael Browne of the Strand, Inchturk was visited by the sheriff to carry out evictions. After a few evictions a settlement was come to and some of the tenants were returned as caretakers. It was considered an impossible matter to remove the people off the island, which would be necessary if the cases were proceeded with.* [3]

One man who lost his farm on the island was Daniel Hanly who then went to live with his nephew, James Cloonan, in Collum in Cashel parish. Subsequently in 1897 he was drowned in a boating accident at Brick Island when he and his nephew and Willie Ganly from Inchturk were returning from Athlone. Willie Ganly lost his

Eviction Stone 1814. Weekfield, Roscommon.

life also in the same accident, while James Cloonan managed to swim to the shore.[4]

The people of the islands had shown their determination to remain in their holdings. Up to 1871 there were still more than two hundred people living on Lough Ree, an indication of how well this population was holding up at a time when the rest of Ireland was being decimated by emigration. The campaign of the tenant farmers in the years that followed, under the banner of the Land League, brought about the various Land Acts which enabled the resident tenants to become the full owners of their island lands.

The campaign of land agitation was paralleled by an emerging nationalist spirit which inspired the founding of the Gaelic Athletic Association (G.A.A.) in 1884 and the Gaelic League some years later. The G.A.A. had a remarkable effect on the social lives of the people from the very beginning and the area around Lough Ree was no exception. A report from Athlone in 1887 laments the absence of a committee to cooperate with the central executive of the G.A.A. in promoting hurling and football in the town. It continues:

> we have no branch of the G.A.A. in this town and more is the pity. It is the one athletic association in Ireland that enjoys the approval and patronage of Archbishop Croke, Mr. Parnell and Mr. Davitt. Most of the other clubs have their rules to suit the effeminate spirit of the age. [5]

The strong link between the newly formed G.A.A. and the nationalist spirit of the time is made plain in a football match between Ballymahon and Glasson in Kilkenny West in June 1888. Play had proceeded for a time when it was ascertained that the team from Ballymahon came on "cars that had driven police to evictions" and the Glasson men refused to continue the play. However they entertained the Ballymahon team to refreshments and offered cars on which to return but they were not accepted. The owner of these cars, being a wealthy person, could afford to do without the custom of the police.[6] On Sunday 11th May 1890 Ballinahown Gaelic Club travelled to Glasson to play a return match with the local team. The Ballinahown ladies chartered a special wagonette to accompany the team and follow the fortunes of the white harp. (The Ballinahown colours were green with a white harp on left breast). The drive was through Ballykeeran and the view of the lake was enchanting. Glasson was reached at two o'clock and the team went to the field about a mile from the village. Glasson won the toss and there was a fine display of football. At half-time the Athlone national band arrived and played airs. Ballinahown won the match three points to nil. The team lists read as follows:

> Ballinahown: F. O'Donoghue, J. Heavy, Michael, Joseph and Kieran Rohan, K. and J. Hunt, K. and P. Rigney, D. Sweeney, J. Longworth, P. Kennedy, P. Egan and K. Horan
> Glasson: Farrell, Connaughton, Murray (2), Langley, McCormack, Mulhall, Maguire, Walker, Grennan (2) and four others. [7]

Gaeilge á labhairt

The nationalist character of the G.A.A. was mirrored in other movements which commenced around this time. A campaign to save the Irish language and restore it as the language of the people was launched with the founding of the Gaelic League in 1893. The erosion of Irish as the language of communication among the people had been happening from the eighteenth century onwards. The identification of the language with poverty and want induced people to look to English as a gateway to a better way of life. The population explosion of the early 1800s, followed by the famine, brought about emigration on a massive scale and the need for English became compelling.

Through the Gaelic League people were rediscovering the cultural richness and beauty of Irish and appreciating its great antiquity as a spoken language. In the 1901 census none of the islanders lays claim to an ability to speak Irish. The language however had been alive a mere twenty five years before that. The Irish scholar Donn Sigerson Piatt,[8] surveying the state of the Irish language in the 1930s, met Patrick Shea of Blenavoher on the Rathcline shore, who told him that as a young boy on Inchenagh sixty four years earlier he spoke Irish with his uncle Dan Shea from whom he also learned his prayers in Irish.

This is how Piatt describes the encounter:

Bhí na paidreacha Gaeilge ina óige ag seanduine eile, as an taobh thiar theas de'n chondae, i.e. Inis Éanach ar Loch Rí i. Pádraig Mac Síthigh (Shea), a bhfuil a áit cónaí i mBléan an Bhothair, in aice le Béal Ath Liag. Dúirt sé an tAve Maria i nGaeilg agus mé ag ligean cioth fearthaine tharam. D'inis sé dom i mBéarla nár mhaith leis féachaint le Gaeilge a labhairt mar nár chuala sé focal di le ceithre bliana is trí fichead roimhe sin. [1938] ...'oncal dom a raibh Dan Shea air as Inis Éanach, a fuair bás agus mé sé mbliana d'aois. I nGaeilge a bhí na paidreacha aige agus i nGaeilge a deireadh muid na paidreacha nó go bhfuair sé bás'.

(The prayers in Irish were also known to another old person born in the south west of the county on Inchenagh in Lough Ree. He was Patrick Shea who was residing in Blenavoher, near Lanesborough. He said the Hail Mary in Irish while I was sheltering from a shower. He told me in English that he wouldn't like to try speaking Irish as he hadn't heard a word of it for sixty three years previously (1938) ...an uncle of mine, by the name of Dan Shea, Inchenagh, who died when I was six years old. He had the prayers in Irish and it was in Irish we would say our prayers up until he died.)[9]

It would seem likely from the above that Irish continued to be the spoken language on the islands well after the middle of the nineteenth century.

Farming and fishing

Many of the Lough Ree islanders gained full possession of their lands under the Land Acts. The islands, in general, were very suitable for tillage crops. The light sandy texture of the soil was particularly suited for the growing of potatoes, which cropped well and were dry and appetising. Oats was the principal grain crop sown, and oatmeal was an important ingredient in the diet of the people, while the grain was also used for animal feed. Those on the Black Islands, Inchmore and Inchturk derived most of their livelihood from fishing. The commercial fishing consisted mainly of taking trout in nets and eels on long lines. The catch was marketed in Athlone and on the English fish market.

The Irish government decided to harness the river Shannon for the production of hydro-electric power in the late 1920s. The newly formed Electricity Supply Board (ESB) acquired the rights of all Shannon fisheries in 1938. Lough Ree fishermen were allowed to continue taking fish for the immediate future but in 1945 the ESB stepped in to limit their fishing activities. The next fifteen years are noteworthy for a campaign of agitation by the fishermen resulting in prosecutions and jail sentences. Boats, fish and fishing equipment were seized and heavy fines imposed, but the Lough Ree men continued to agitate. In 1968 an agreement was reached whereby the board would compensate the fishermen for the loss of their livelihood. By this time, however, the people had begun to abandon the islands and build new homes on the mainland. The Inchenagh families departed the island in July 1956. This process continued over the next fifty years until Paddy Hanly and Nancy Conroy finally left the Black Islands in 1986, which leaves just one surviving island inhabitant on Lough Ree in 2006.

Former family home, Inchenagh.

CHAPTER 16

Pastime and Pleasure

Over the centuries there were always those who were fascinated by the beauty of the lake and for whom water had a great attraction as a source of pastime and enjoyment. The first regatta on Lough Ree that can be documented was held from Monday 28th of July 1731 to Saturday 2nd August. Regattas were held at intervals on the lake through the centuries. There are several published, mid-nineteenth century accounts of regattas on Lough Ree to be found. One such is by W. F. Wakeman, who states:

In August of each year, for a considerable time past, a regatta has been held upon Lough Ree. Hither flock the fashion and beauty of the district for miles around; and once more a fleet enlivens the aspect of the usually deserted lake. Gay vessels decorated with many-coloured streamers, accompanied by bands of music, and laden with gentlest ladies and gallant gentlemen glide tranquilly over the scene of many a well-contested battle.[1]

Another rich source of information on regattas is the contemporary newspaper accounts which of course are quite numerous from Victorian times. These help to give us some idea of the atmosphere and sense of occasion which prevailed. The following account of a regatta was reported in The Freeman's Journal of 28th August, 1862:

Yesterday, Wednesday, Athlone Regatta was held amidst the greatest excitement. The day was exceptionally favourable and the locality selected was well adapted for the purpose. The gay bannerets of the various yachts, the boats that studded the bosom of the lake and the snow white tents and marquees along the shore while multitudes of both sexes arrived in holiday sheen, and music that burst on the ear added considerably to the minds of all, were due to the excellent arrangements of the stewards ... Events included a schooner race over six miles, with prize-money of £5 and £1; a sprit and foresail event over five miles, a two oared race and a single rowing match as well as a greasy-pole contest. [2]

The Victorian period witnessed a great surge in sailing on Lough Ree with personnel from the various British regiments then stationed in Athlone often to the fore. Apart from regattas there were other sailing contests and cruises organised on the lake and members from the Yacht Club participated in regattas on Lough Derg and elsewhere.

The Gailey Bay Regatta was held in "good weather" in August 1886 and lasted for a week. The winners' rostrum gives a flavour of the participants. Mr P. Kelly's "Snowdrop" sailed by P. Ward won the first race. The "Countess" owned by Captain Smithwick, Lough Derg, won the Cup race. The "Siren", owned by Mr Joseph Burke, Lough Ree, won an arranged match race. "Snowdrop" won again on Thursday and in a race for centreboard spritsail boats Mr R.D. Levinge's "Doras" won. [3]

The following year, 1887, in August there is a report on the Athlone Regatta which seems to have catered more for the common folk in small lake boats and lists among the winners, names such as Moran, O'Hara, Curley, Broderick and Mulvihill. No doubt both regattas were enjoyable events and the names of the winners in each case tell their own story. [4]

One of the greatest events in the history of pleasure boating on the lake was the founding of Lough Ree Yacht Club. This club has the distinction of being the second oldest yacht club in the world; its

---

Monday and Tuesday,
13th and 14th August.

1906.
Programme

GAILEY BAY REGATTA.

SAILING AND ROWING RACES.

MESSENGER PRINTING WORKS, ROSCOMMON.

Cover of Gailey Bay Regatta Programme, 1906.

Ballyglass Sailing Regatta, Athlone

foundation date is accepted by Lloyds Register of Yachts as 1770.

While little documentary evidence survives to record the early history of the club, 1770 was the foundation date put forward by Capt. A. Woulfe Smyth in an article published in the Athlone Civic Week brochure of 1950. It was the opinion of the late N.W. (Billy) English the historian of L.R.Y.C. that as Capt. Smyth's family had resided on or near the shores of Lough Ree from about 1700, and they were involved with yachting from its beginning, there may have been evidence available to Smyth in family papers which has since been lost.

The Split

However, the story is well documented from the 1830s, a time when, according to Smyth, the club was divided into "two political groups" one of which broke away to form the short-lived Killinure Yacht Club, with its club house on Temple Island in the inner lakes. Smyth records the clubhouse as being on Friars' Island but this appears to have been a mistake on his part. The Commodore of Killinure Yacht Club in 1831 was Robert H. Temple Esq. and a manuscript document recording the founding of the club in that year and addressed from Temple Island was reproduced as an appendix to "Lough Ree Yacht Club 1770-1970": a memoir by N.W.English.

By 1836 the Killinure Club had disbanded and the members were reunited with Athlone Yacht Club. While the Killinure club had their clubhouse on Temple Island in the 1830s the Athlone Yacht Club had theirs on Carberry Island.

Club Reformed

In 1895, Athlone Yacht Club was reformed. The first rule of the new club proclaims the change of name:

> *This club shall be called the Lough Ree Yacht Club and shall consist of gentlemen desirous of encouraging yachting, match sailing, and boating on Lough Ree.*

A brief report in The Westmeath Independent of 25th April, 1914 records the club's move to Ballyglass:

> *In the coming season the Lough Ree Yacht Club will have the advantage of a much-needed clubhouse, which has been erected on the shores of Ballyglass Bay. Ballyglass has been the venue of many enjoyable gatherings in the past, but the club was limited to the accommodation which a couple of temporary tents afforded them.*[5]

One of the problems which beset Lough Ree Yacht Club was that while sailing of centreboard craft grew in popularity there was no standard for sail size. While some specifications did exist there was room for manoeuvre and it was Mr R.D. Levinge who wrote to the secretary of the club suggesting the need for a standard because, as he said, "I see them building queer-shaped things here to win the centreboard race."

The Shannon One Design

In the aftermath of World War I, when things began to return to normal, the question of a standard design for a centreboard craft

Four Shannon One Designs under sail near Carberry Island, c. 1930.

once again exercised the minds of Shannon sailors. A meeting of the three yacht clubs Lough Ree, Lough Derg and the North Shannon Yacht Club from Lough Boderg, decided that "An open centreboard boat, to be known as the Shannon One Design Class, be established for all yacht clubs on the Shannon."
Delegates from Lough Ree Yacht Club who attended this meeting were: Major Handcock, R.D. Levinge, W. Levinge, D. Cameron, F. Coen, N. Lyster, M.J. Hogan, R.S. English and W.J. Bolton.

This meeting was to have an enormous and very positive impact on sailing on the Shannon in the twentieth century. It was later agreed to commission a design from Morgan Giles, one of the leading British yacht designers of the day. Giles also designed the Essex One Design which unlike the Shannon One Design was half-decked, the Essex was also sloop-rigged as against the cat-rigging of the Shannon craft. The Shannon One Design was introduced in 1922. Did it compete in the Lough Ree regatta that year? Unfortunately we don't know – the only press report which survives relates to the suspension of sailing on the last Wednesday of August as a mark of respect to General Michael Collins, who had been killed in action in Cork. But certainly the craft met with instant approval from Shannon sailors. Many of the Shannon One Design Class were built by local boat-builders, among them Walter Levinge, of Creaghduff, Patrick Keneavy of Brick Island, Patrick Ward of the Strand, Athlone, Peter Quigley of Killinure and Jimmy Furey of Lecarrow.

Lough Ree Yacht Club today is a thriving entity, participating in national and international competitions. It organises courses in sailing, aquatic expertise and boat management for a wide variety of people. It excels in providing training for large numbers of youthful enthusiasts who have their first taste of the delights and disciplines of water sport under its experienced eye.

A feature of boating in general in the last half century has been the steady increase in the popularity of the power-driven cruiser as compared with the sailing yacht. Large numbers of tourists of German, French, Swiss and English origin have been attracted to our inland waters and to the Shannon system in particular. A lucrative industry has grown up around the provision and hiring of holiday cruisers and Lough Ree, situated at the centre of the Shannon system, greatly benefited from this business. A visitor coming to Ireland to hire a cruiser contributes handsomely to the economy and the importance of this trade to the country has been recognised by further investment in our waterways. Lough Ree has harbours at Hodson Bay and Lecarrow[6] while a new marina has just been completed at Ballyleague. At the time of writing extensive operations are in progress at Portrunny which will include modern berthing facilities and ancillary services. Isaac Weld would have been very pleased! Longford Co. Council was ahead of its time in the 1960s when it developed the attractive Barley Harbour project on the Cashel shore. Muckenagh on the Westmeath side of the lake is another excellent development, while there is scope for further berthing facilities in the areas of the Inny estuary and Portlick. All this tourist activity might never have occurred were it not for the foresight of those who saw the impending danger to Shannon navigation in the early fifties and organised themselves to counter the threat.

The Inland-Waterways Association of Ireland

The catalyst for the formation of this group, which was to be called the Inland Waterways Association of Ireland (I.W.A.I.) came in 1953 when a headline proclaimed "Athlone Bridge to be fixed". The fixing did not refer to "fix" in the sense of repair but rather that Athlone was to get a fixed span in place of the swivel section of the town bridge which had served for over a century. At the time the Shannon navigation works of the 1840s were carried out, the new town bridge consisted of three stone arches to the east and a final swivel-span at

Col Harry Rice (1894-1964), author of the great Lough Ree classic "Thanks for the Memory".

the western end. This was constructed from seventy tons of metal castings which arrived in Athlone in 1843. After one hundred and ten years, this metal section had become dangerous and was in need of repair. The suggestion was that it would be replaced with a fixed span. This would mean in effect that boats above a certain air draught would be unable to pass under the bridge. At this time the writing was on the wall as regards water transport in Ireland, as the public attached little value to waterways. There had been a gradual changeover to both rail and road transportation and the odds against reviving a water-based transport system were becoming longer. Few could have predicted the rising importance to the Irish economy of tourist traffic on our waterways in the following half-century. Had the bridge been "fixed" it could have paralysed the navigational possibilities of the middle Shannon. Fortunately for everyone, there were far-seeing people in Athlone who loved the river and were prepared to make a stand on its behalf. Chief among those was Col Harry Rice, the author of *Thanks for the Memory*, a

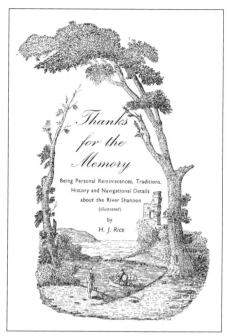

Harry Rice's original design of the title page for "Thanks for the Memory".

book that is still considered one of the great classics of Shannon literature and is sure of an enduring place in the hearts of all who love the Shannon.

Harry, with Vincent Delany, was instrumental in launching the Inland Waterways Association of Ireland in the Shelbourne Hotel on 7th January, 1954. Delany, too, was a lifelong devotee of the Shannon. His wife, Ruth Delany, is the author of among other works *Ireland's Inland Waterways* (1986) and *By Shannon Shores* (1987), two delightfully written books, that are required reading for all lovers of our inland waterways. Harry was elected the first president, with Vincent Delany and L.M. Goodbody elected as joint honorary secretaries.

The stated aims of the fledgling society were to:

(1) Encourage inland water transport on the lines of canal utilisation as found in Europe.

(2) Act as a tourist amenity and collaborate with tourist bodies in publishing guide-books, charts, maps, etc. for the use of persons travelling on the waterways for pleasure.

(3) Encourage the sport of yachting and cruising, whether sail or power, on our rivers.

(4) Compile historical records and data relative to the development of inland navigation in Ireland.

Shortly after the launch of the I.W.A.I. in Dublin, letters were issued by T.A. Marrinan, the acting honorary secretary, inviting interested parties to attend a meeting in the Crescent Ballroom, Athlone, on February 19th, 1954. One of the interesting and enlightened points about this letter, which was canvassing support for the founding of an Athlone branch of I.W.A.I. was the welcome extended not only to the men but to "the women of our district. We hope they may come and give us their counsel." They did and continue to do so to this day. The contribution of women to the I.W.A.I. has been immense over the course of the last fifty years.

The following were elected as the first officers of the Branch: Mr W.A. Tormey, chairman, Mr T.A. Marrinan, hon. secretary and Mrs Cynthia Rice, hon. treasurer. The first committee members were: Fr Moran, Miss D. Lyster, Mrs James Reid, Dr John O'Meara, Mr John Newell, Mr P.C. Molloy, Mr Tommy Gallagher, Mr Tom Hogan, Mr Arthur Fadden, Mr John Williams, Mr Joe Wheatley, Mr Harry Waters, Mr P. Hanly, Mr Kieran Kenny (Banagher) and Mr J. O'Callaghan (Boyle) who were elected as delegate members of the committee. A number of other locals, including Mr Walter Levinge, Mr Sid Shine, Mr Frank Waters and Mr Paddy Lenihan, were already serving the association at national level. Among those who attended that first meeting were Col Harry Rice, Vincent and Ruth Delany, Walter Levinge and Sean McBride.

It is not too much to claim that I.W.A.I. and its founders are largely responsible for the freedom of access enjoyed by all boats into Lough Ree at the present time. Having entered, the visitor becomes immediately aware of the magnificent scenery for which the lake has been renowned over the centuries. Writers and visitors have enthused over its beauty. Mary Banim, writer and journalist, visited here in the 1880s and was captivated by the magic of the setting sun. Describing the islands as "Pearls that the Almighty has sown upon the bosom of the lake," she continues:

> *we sail back upon Lough Ree, our eyes and hearts feasted by one of those glorious sunsets that are amongst its peculiar beauties. First, the waters glow a molten gold, while all the land around seems bathed in yellow light; then, between us and the distant mountain,*

a veil of purple slowly rises, leaving a shadow land behind it; near us a glistening mirror, here golden, there violet-red; again, lit by a pale rosy light; everywhere reflecting the sun that grows larger and more brilliant at every instant, until it disappears behind the distant mountain. And then - slowly, gently - the colours soften and fade; the shadows deepen, one by one; islands, mountains, the Lake of Kings, are but shadows in the evening twilight, and we have ended our sail upon Lough Ree.[7]

In the twentieth century there have been several major developments along the shores of Lough Ree to facilitate the use of the lake for pleasure and pastimes. Some of these already mentioned have been undertaken by the local authorities in the three counties which touch on Lough Ree. There have also been private developments which would include the new club-house and mooring facilities for Lough Ree Yacht Club as well as mooring facilities at the Wineport Restaurant and Hotel Complex in Ballykeeran, and the building of chalets at various points around the lake shore. Given the special importance of Lough Ree as an S.A.C. area all developments are carefully monitored by several bodies including the respective local authorities and Waterways Ireland.

Waterways Ireland is a North-South body, one of six implementation bodies set up under the terms of the British-Irish Agreement in 1999. It has the responsibility for the management, maintenance, development and restoration of our inland waterways principally for recreational purposes. The waterways which come under the remit of Waterways Ireland are the Shannon-Erne waterway, the rivers Shannon and Erne, the Barrow navigation, the Lower Bann and our two major canals: The Royal and The Grand.

All boats using the Shannon navigation, including, of course, Lough Ree must be registered with the Inspector of Navigation at The Docks in Athlone. The only exceptions are for those which are already registered with the Warden's Office in Enniskillen as a mutual recognition scheme operates on the Shannon, the Erne and the Shannon-Erne waterway.

Waterways Ireland has been responsible for some of the most tasteful and useful recreational developments on Lough Ree – in recent years they have greatly enhanced the facilities at Portrunny in Co. Roscommon and Coosan Point in Co. Westmeath. An obvious question might be what the future has in store for Lough Ree in terms of developments. There has been a proposal to link the village of Glassan to the lake by cutting a new length of canal and developing a harbour close to the village. If this proposal gets the go-ahead it will be a major development which will come under the remit of Waterways Ireland. A major concern at the time of going to press in autumn 2006 must be the proposal to pump enormous quantities of water to Dublin from Lough Ree to augment the present water supply. The impact of this draw-down of water, especially on the summer water levels of the lake, must pose considerable concerns for the authorities. Such a scheme if it goes ahead will also have consequences for the lakeshore habitats which are an integral part of this Special Area of Conservation and arguably deserve to be declared a National Park – further information on the importance of Lough Ree as a wildlife habit is contained in Chapter 17 on Flora and Fauna.

Cruising on Lough Ree.

CHAPTER 17

Flora and Fauna

L ough Ree has long been regarded as a haven for both flora and fauna. It has often been suggested that it should become a national park and indeed, at the time of writing, further research is being undertaken into the implications of such a move. It already enjoys particular status as a Special Area of Conservation (SAC), a Natural Heritage Area (NHA) and a Special Protection Area (SPA) under the EC directive on The Conservation of Wild Birds (1979). All of these designations are in place in an effort to protect the many sites of ecological interest on the islands, shores and hinterland of Lough Ree. The fish-life, bird-life and flora of Lough Ree and its islands, the butterflies, crustaceans and insects all deserve the attention of naturalists and scientists. While a detailed survey is beyond the scope of this work, a few remarks may help to stimulate the interest of the casual observer.

The flora of Lough Ree has been the subject of numerous studies over the years. One of the earliest was a "Report on the flora of the shores of Lough Ree", a paper written by Richard M. Barrington and Richard P. Vowell and read before the Royal Irish Academy in 1887. This paper was published in the proceedings of the Royal Irish Academy that year. Because of the range of exciting habitats afforded by Lough Ree, a number of doctoral students from the University of Utrecht came to this area in the late 1960s and early 1970s. Out of this programme came the most comprehensive report to date on the vegetation of Lough Ree. Published by the University of Utrecht in 1975, Johannes Klein's *An Irish landscape* is a major study of the natural and semi-natural vegetation in the Lough Ree area. This study is divided into four sections dealing with (i) woodlands, (ii) woodland margins and hedges, (iii) grasslands and (iv) bog formations.

In terms of the actual flora, a thesis by P. Hessel and W.V. Rubers presented to the same university in 1971 includes a floristical inventory of the Lough Ree area which yielded about 600 taxa. A comparison with Barrington & Vowell (1887) which listed 481 species shows that the majority of the species they listed are still present while about 40 were not located. Another major contributor to our knowledge of the flora and fauna of Lough Ree is Daphne Levinge, originally of Creaghduff, Coosan, who presented a thesis "Ecological studies on Green Island, Lough Ree" to the University of Dublin and who edited the findings of an Athlone field meeting in the Irish Biogeographical Society Bulletin, No 1, 1976.

Quite apart from the great biodiversity of this area, the botanist will be rewarded with opportunities to record a dozen or more species of flora which warrant protected status or which are considered to be endangered species[1]. These classifications are made in *The Irish Red Data Book I*, vascular plants (Curtis and McGough, 1988). They include bird cherry and alder buckthorn, which occur in bog-woodland habitats such as that of St. John's Wood and are considered "rare"; and the occasional occurrences of plants both here and at other sites in Lough Ree i.e. basil thyme; betony; blue fleabane; bird's nest orchid; fen violet; marsh pea; nettle-leaved bellflower; shepherd's needle; water germander and the rare round-fruited rush.

St. John's Wood and Rindoon Wood

In early times much of the area around Lough Ree would have been woodland. Eileen McCracken in *The Irish woods since Tudor times* states

> *From Athlone to the Shannon's source there was a great deal of woodland, particularly in the land adjoining Loughs Ree and Allen. On the westward side of Lough Ree lay the Fews, which stretched upwards to the 500ft. contour. Above this altitude the oak gave way to hazel scrub.*[2]

Much of this wood had disappeared by 1800. Isaac Weld, writing in 1832, was generous in his praise for the scenery around Lough Ree, but pointed out:

The greatest deficiency in the scene is the want of wood, and considering how many are the rugged headlands, where the ground in its natural and uncultivated state is of little or no value, except for rough pasturage, yet which if properly planted and fenced, would soon produce trees and yield considerable profit, it is lamentable to think that more attention should have been paid to a subject intimately connected with the national wealth and the consequent prosperity and improvement of the people. Timber likewise might be readily transported along the lake to a sure market.[3]

Today the most important woodland in the vicinity of Lough Ree is, without doubt, the 330 acres of St. John's Wood. It is a shining example of the richness which could adorn the shores of Lough Ree. The Woods of St. John's have long been famous and one local laureate writing towards the end of the nineteenth century commemorated them in verse:

Ye dark solemn woods by the Shannon's green shores,
What rapture I feel as I see ye once more,
And rest in your soul-soothing shadows today,
Where fleeted life's happiest moments away.[4]

The local bard was Ned Brennan. He emigrated from his native Kiltoom to America where he worked as a journalist on *The Boston Pilot*[5]. On returning to Ireland he obtained a post as workhouse master in Athlone but later lost his job due to his fondness for drink.

St. John's Wood was advertised for sale in 1806, consisting then of 153 acres of mature ash and oak. Today this wood is regarded as an area of national importance. Apart from oak and ash there are extensive stands of hazel, holly and wych elm. In midland terms it is an almost unique ecological heritage site hosting an extremely important flora and fauna. The late Harry Rice, writing in 1952, claimed of St. John's Wood that it is:

all that remains of what was once a great forest. Here, in olden days, packs of wolves hunted their prey, and herds of swine roamed, feeding on acorns and beech mast.[6]

St. John's Wood has been left relatively undisturbed for so long that a rich and varied plant-life has become established. Ireland has twenty-six native tree species and of these twenty-three can be found in St. John's. Much of this wood has developed over limestone bedrock but the edges of the woodland have a very different bog-land or swamp habitat that also sustains a rich and varied flora.

St. John's Wood is a favourite haunt of ornithologists as it hosts an abundance of woodland birds. Among the summer visitors are the chiffchaff, garden warbler, sedge warbler, spotted flycatcher and whitethroat. The woods also sustain a resident population of birds of prey including sparrow-hawks, barn owl and long-eared owl[7].

Other Woodlands of Lough Ree

While St. John's Wood and Rindoon Wood deserve special mention, there are several other important areas of woodland in and around Lough Ree. To the north, areas such as Barley Harbour and Culnagore Wood near Elfeet together with Lanesborough Commons, Annamore and White Sand Wood are all important woodlands. To the south Yew Point near Hodson Bay, Meehan Wood and Coosan Point near Athlone and the woodlands at Killinure Point, Killinure Bay and Portlick are all important habitats.

The amenity development at Portlick gives access to woodland which is rich in oak, ash, hawthorn, blackthorn, holly and hazel – the bluebells at Portlick are spectacular in season.

In terms of wooded islands, Hare Island and Carberry Island are perhaps the most spectacular. Hare Island has almost 30 hectares of oak-dominated woodland. The composition of the woods is broadly similar to that of St. John's with some more exotic species introduced by Lord Castlemaine[8]. The natural flora of the island includes four species which are listed in the *Red Data Book:* the narrow-leaved helleborine which is found here in abundance while betony, birds-nest orchid and bird cherry are also present. In the introduced flora the species of daffodil which flowers here in spring is unusual – it was obviously introduced by Lord

Castlemaine as it also occurs near the ruins of his family seat at Moydrum Castle.

Bird-life around Lough Ree

As already mentioned St. John's Wood is an area of particular interest to ornithologists. It sustains a large population of warblers as do many of the other woodland areas surrounding the lake. Other important areas in terms of wintering birdlife are at the mouth of the Inny on the Longford shore and Rinnany Point on the Roscommon shore.

In winter Lough Ree accommodates an estimated 25,000 wild-fowl including large numbers of waders and wildfowl arriving from Greenland and Siberia as well as birds from Britain and Northern Europe[9]. There are internationally important flocks of Greenland white-fronted geese, whooper swans, widgeon and black-tailed godwits. Lough Ree is one of the last surviving Irish breeding sites for the common scoter which despite its name is listed in the *Irish Red Data Book,* and the most important inland site for the common tern.

Lough Ree sustains a fine resident population of mute swans and ducks. Among the water-birds to be found are: coot, moorhen and water rail; goldeneye, mallard, pintail, pochard, red-breasted merganser, shelduck, shoveler, teal, tufted duck and widgeon. Lough Ree also has breeding pairs of the little grebe and great crested grebe as well as cormorants and the ubiquitous grey heron. The lake shore has important populations of waders such as curlew, golden plover, lapwing, redshank and snipe as well as gulls such as the black-headed gull, common gull and herring gull.

Anyone visiting Lough Ree who has even the most elementary interest in bird-watching would be well advised to come prepared with binoculars and one of the standard reference works on Irish birds. One can often be rewarded with a sighting of the courting rituals of the grebes or the spectacular action of one of the many birds of prey. These include kestrel, merlin and sparrow-hawks as well as the hen harrier. The woodlands around Lough Ree are a stronghold of the garden warbler, a bird which is now almost confined to the Shannon lakes.

Mammals, Amphibians and Invertebrates around Lough Ree

Just as it is an ideal habitat for unusual flora and a great variety of bird-life, Lough Ree and its hinterland is also home to a great many mammals. Among the most notable is the otter, which is to be found on the islands as well as in the feeder streams and along the lake-shore. The pine-marten has become more numerous on the Roscommon shore; the badger, rabbit and hedgehog are also widespread as is the Irish hare. The American mink which is an escaped species breeds around Lough Ree as does our native fox. The American grey squirrel is more often found on the Longford and Westmeath shores while the red squirrel is still common on the Roscommon shore. Field mice and pygmy shrews are to be found as of course is the ubiquitous rat. In terms of amphibians the common frog is still common while newts inhabit many of the feeder streams and ponds around the lake.

The butterflies recorded from around the lake include the brimstone, clouded yellow, common blue, green-veined white, large white, meadow brown, painted lady, peacock, red-admiral, ringlet, small copper, small tortoiseshell, small white and speckled wood varieties[10]. The most commonly recorded dragonfly species is the emperor dragonfly.

The Fish life[11]

Lough Ree abounds in fish; and the following is just a brief introduction to the varieties which occur.

Brown trout are widespread in the lake and the size and quality of the fish compare favourably with anything elsewhere in Ireland. The trout season lasts from March to the end of September. In the early season they are often taken on the worm, they are also caught either by trolling or fly-fishing and May-June is the "dapping" season when the mayfly is up. The brown trout, unlike the sea trout, spends all of its life in fresh water.

Above: Yellow loosestrife and purple loosestrife.
Below: Wild forget-me-not.
Both pictures courtesy of Pat Halton.

Above: Grey squirrel, photographed by Pat Halton.
Below: Family of mallard on Friars' Island, photograph by Ann Hennessy.

Above: Marsh Pea.
Below: Damsel Fly. Both photographs by Pat Halton.

Above: A Lough Ree perch, once considered a delicacy.
Below: Mute swan, photographed by Ann Hennessy.

Top left: Moorhen. Top right: Black Headed Gull. (Photographs: Ann Hennessy).
Middle: Pike – a great Lough Ree predator.
Bottom: Spotted Fly Catcher (Photograph: Pat Halton).

Two evening scenes on Lough Ree.
Photographs by Ann Hennessy.

Since the building of the Ardnacrusha power station, salmon have become scarce on the Shannon. Occasional fish do occur and it is still not unknown for a salmon to be taken on the lake. The salmon spends much of its adult life at sea but returns to rivers to breed. It moves upstream when the river is in full spate and spawns in shallow gravel beds. The young salmon migrate to the sea after two years or so in fresh water. At one time salmon were so plentiful in Lough Ree that it is said that families requested employers in Athlone and elsewhere to sign a clause in apprenticeship contracts stating that the young boy or girl would not be fed salmon more than twice a week!

Pike are widespread in Lough Ree ranging from small jack-pike (30cm) to massive pike of up to 120cm in length. The pike is a predator and is often caught by using dead-bait (small roach and rudd or bought bait such as herrings, mackerel or sprats). Fishing the margins of the lake with a trolled spoon or plug-bait can also be very rewarding. Small pike feed on invertebrates in the water and will be attracted by fry, while larger fish will also attack young waterfowl and other fish.

The eel is common on the Shannon and has been fished commercially at Athlone since 1215 at least[12]. One needs a special licence to net eels, but they will sometimes be caught on rod and line using worm as bait. They are often fished for at night during the summer. The eels spawn in the Sargasso Sea and arrive on our shores as tiny elvers. They make their way up the rivers and develop a yellow-brown hue. As mature adults they are sometimes called silver eels. It is at this point that they begin to migrate to the sea. The traditional method of eel fishing in the muddy bays of Lough Ree in the 19th century was the use of an eel-fork – a three or four pronged serrated fork cast into the muddy bottom to impale the eel. Fishing for eel and trout provided many of the Lough Ree islanders with a means of livelihood.

Perch, though once a widespread and common fish, seems less abundant where roach have taken over. The distinctive perch has a spiny dorsal fin and a bright red hue in its tail and lower fins. It is caught by spinning with small bright lure or by float-fishing using worm or maggot as bait. The perch taken in the lake tend to be larger than those caught in other parts of the river.

The rudd is a shy fish and a surface feeder. It prefers the weedy lakeside margins and the quiet backwaters and bays. In appearance it is a deep-bodied golden fish with red fins. It is usually fished for on summer evenings using bread or maggots as bait – a favourite haunt is near Charlie's Island at the lower end of Lough Ree as well as the "hot water stretch" at Lanesborough, where specimen fish can be found. Rudd-Bream hybrids are also to be found.

Today, bream is fished almost exclusively for sport and can be a most rewarding fish to catch. It enjoys a quiet existence in muddy sections of the lake. It can be attracted by baiting an area heavily with bread and maggots and sometimes will put up a fight which would put any trout to shame. Today it is seldom eaten but it once formed part of the staple diet of the poor in towns such as Athlone and Lanesborough. It is also to be found in the inner lakes at Ballykeeran.

The roach, which is a prolific breeder, is like a smaller and slimmer version of the rudd. It can be caught using maggot as bait. Frequently the two species are confused – roach were introduced into the Shannon in the 1970s.

Tench are most at home in the weedy sections of the lake. They are a greenish-brown fish with a distinctive barbell. The tench is loved by anglers because of the great fight it puts up. Lough Ree is well known for specimen tench.[13] Like the bream it responds to ground baiting – and will usually be caught when fishing worm, maggot or bread-bait.

The lamprey is a genus (petromyzon) of cyclostomes that fix themselves to stones by their mouths. The lamprey is seldom seen but does exist in Lough Ree and will sometimes affix itself to a boat. When the infamous Lough Ree Monster episode of 1960 occurred, one of the lighter moments was the discovery of a lamprey attached to a wooden boat. The fisherman who discovered it had never seen anything like it and believed that it could be the young of the monster he believed inhabited the depths of the lake.

Lough Ree contains one of only two Irish populations of pollan (an endangered fish species). They are sometimes described as fresh water herrings. They are seldom caught but have been recorded. The freshwater shrimp (mysis relicta) also occurs in Lough Ree and is a relic of the glacial period in Ireland[14].

The Future of Lough Ree

Today no prowling wolves lurk by its shores but a more insidious and sinister enemy lies hidden in the calm waters of the lake itself. The onset of more affluent times in Ireland has brought about new departures in industry and agriculture. A growing trend towards urbanisation has meant concentrations of people in the smaller and bigger towns around the country. All these developments had created large quantities of toxic waste before municipal authorities had taken adequate steps to dispose of them safely. The result has been the pollution of many of our fresh water streams, rivers and lakes.

Lough Ree has been no exception to this malaise as recent surveys have pointed out. The greatest danger to clean water is eutrophication which is the accumulation in it of excessive quantities of the nutrients, phosphorus and nitrogen. This results in the overproduction of cyanobacteria, recognisable as blue green algae, and planktonic algae. These over-stimulate plant growth, adversely affecting the quality of the water. In the case of Lough Ree the greatest inputs of phosphorus occur in summertime between May and October. The key to reducing this accumulation is to control discharges from municipal, industrial and agricultural sources. It has been estimated by J.J. Bowman, who investigated the eutrophication of Lough Ree for the Environmental Protection Agency in 1996 that the levels of phosphorus would need to reduce by 40 tonnes per annum to achieve a reversal of the decline in water quality.

A further concern for those interested in the future welfare of the lake is the damage being caused by the dreaded zebra mussel. This small mollusc which was introduced into the Shannon system accidentally c. 1995 has the potential to do untold damage to the lake. Its razor-sharp presence on stones and rocks is deterring regular swimmers from bathing in Lough Ree at some of the places which were recognised swimming spots for generations.

The zebra mussel is a filter-feeder and already it has altered the physical properties of the lake in terms of increasing water clarity. To the untrained eye this could seem like an improvement in the water quality but sadly that is not the case. There are concerns that the improvement in clarity could favour the feeding habits of predator fish species over other fish and that the lake will have less zooplankton reserves and thus deprive fish species which graze on this matter. There is also a major concern that improved water clarity will give rise to greater weed problems in certain shallower areas of the lake thus making pleasure boating more hazardous. In America the zebra mussel has caused major problems by clogging the mouths of intake and outlet pipes in lakes and water courses. It would seem that it is only a matter of time until this problem affects Lough Ree. The zebra mussel congregates in very large numbers: as many as 100,000 per square metre.[15]

In recent years improved wastewater treatment plants, built by the local authorities, have helped to reduce the amount of phosphates entering the waterways feeding into Lough Ree. It is hoped that the protective legislation which is now in place, combined with the status which areas of Lough Ree have by virtue of being a special area of conservation will help to put in place measures to improve the water quality of the lake and thus ensure that this great natural heritage area will be enjoyed by countless generations to come.

A great deal of research still needs to be done on the flora and fauna of Lough Ree. Almost everyone who has ever taken on a serious research project on any aspect of the area has ended up recording material which was not previously known.

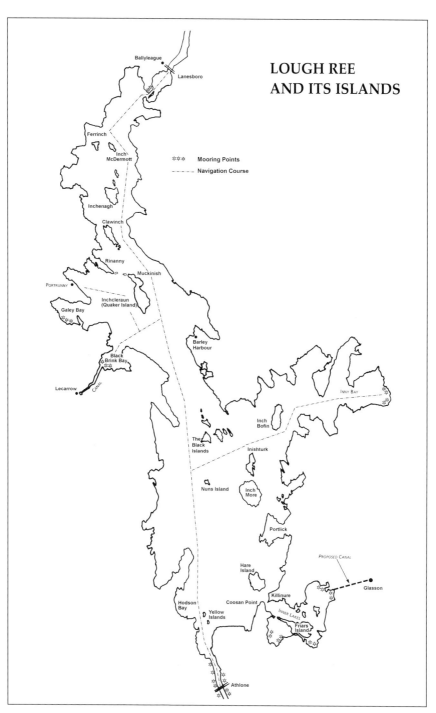

LOUGH REE
AND ITS ISLANDS

Ballyleague

Lanesboro

Ferrinch

Inch
McDermott

✳✳✳   Mooring Points
— · — · — Navigation Course

Inchenagh

Clawinch

Rinanny

Muckinish

PORTRUNNY

Inchcleraun
(Quaker Island)

Galey Bay

Barley
Harbour

Black
Brink Bay

Lecarrow   CANAL

INNY BAY

Inch
Bofin

The
Black
Islands   Inishturk

Nuns Island   Inch
More

Portlick

PROPOSED CANAL

Hare
Island

Killinure   Glasson

Hodson   Coosan Point
Bay
          Yellow   INNER LAKES
          Islands

                              Friars
                              Island

Athlone

159

CHAPTER 18

Inchenagh

According to John O'Donovan in his Longford letters dated 1837 from the Ordnance Survey, the ancient name Inis Éndaimh is the modern Inse Énach, an island near Lanesborough. Inchenagh presents something of an enigma to the historian. It is the only large island on Lough Ree that has no vestige of a monastic tradition. Over eighty acres in extent, it lies

Inchenagh Island.

in the northern half of the lake, opposite the county Longford shore at Blenavoher, and with Clooneigh Bay and Roscommon county to the west. The well-known small islands of Lanageish, Lanasky and Lanagower protrude from its northern tip and are accessible on foot from one to the other in low water. The land is level and for the most part good quality and well wooded at the present time. To the south east of the island is the ruin of a walled enclosure, similar to, but smaller than that on Inchcleraun. The wall, while dilapidated on its eastern or lakeshore side, has survived well on its western boundary, being up to twelve feet wide in places. It encloses a green area of some two and a half acres with a centrepiece containing interesting stones and earthworks. It is obviously of great antiquity and while observers have been aware of it for centuries few have attempted to explain its provenance.

There are few references to Inchenagh in the annals. The first for the year 898 AD reads as follows:

Caenchomrac of Inis-Endoimh, Bishop and Abbot of Lughmhadh, the tutor of Aenagan, son of Eigeartach and of Dunadhach, son of Eigeartach, from whom are descended the Uí Cuinn na mBocht, died on the 23rd day of July.[1]

From this we can deduce that Caenchomrac was a bishop in the second half of the ninth century, that he came from Inchenagh either as the place of his birth or having formerly been a cleric (possibly in a monastery there) and that he went on to be abbot of the monastery of Lughmhadh, the present day town of Louth in the county of that name. It is worth bearing in mind that, earlier in the same century, the abbot of Inchcleraun was also abbot of Caille Focladha, a monastery near Fore in County Westmeath, indicating that the Lough Ree community had close connections with their brethren a long way off. We learn more about Caenchomrac from the following:

> *Caenchomrac, Bishop, of Inis-Endoimh, in Loch Ribh, and he had been bishop at Cluain-mic-nois at first ... and he left Cluain in consequence of the veneration of which he was held there, for the neighbours worshipped him as a prophet so that he went to seek for solitude in Loch Ribh afterwards.[2]*

This reference also confirms that he came from Inchenagh. It would seem that much of his life was spent in Clonmacnois until he came home to "seek solitude in Lough Ree." Subsequently he joined the monastery in Lughmhadh, where he became abbot and where he died in 898.

On the question as to whether Inchenagh did, in fact, have an early monastery, the evidence is at best circumstantial. A stone found here some years ago is a fragment of a bullaun, the stone basin so often found on early Christian sites.The walled enclosure on the island with its similarity to that on Inchcleraun suggests some early settlement or foundation that may not have survived the Viking occupation of the second and third decades of the tenth century. It is generally accepted that the Vikings had a fortified base on Lough Ree at this time and it is

Bullaun fragment, Inchenagh.

possible that that base was the monastery of Inchenagh which they had converted to a fortress. Only an archaeological excavation will determine if this was so.

We hear nothing further of Inchenagh in the Middle Ages and can only speculate on whether its lands were taken over and farmed by the monks of Inchcleraun. In the aftermath of the suppression, the monastery lands of Lough Ree were leased for short periods to a variety of people - Cusacks, Dillons, Nugents, Newcomens et al. In the latter years of the sixteenth century the lands of Inchenagh, Inchcleraun, Clawinch and several smaller islands were granted to the Barnewall family of Grace Dieu, Co. Dublin, by a fiant (5426) of Elizabeth I dated 12th August 1590. Sir Patrick Barnewall had been master of the rolls for Henry VIII. His grandson, Sir Nicholas Barnewall, was raised to the peerage becoming Lord Kingsland in 1622. The lands continued in the ownership of the Barnewalls. As noted elsewhere they lost Saints' Island and Inch in the Cromwellian plantation but quickly regained them. Sir George Barnewall, fifth Viscount Kingsland, was the last to inherit them and when he died without leaving an heir most of the lands passed to the Bellew family who were connected by marriage. However a sale took place at this time of some portions of the Kingsland estate and the Lough Ree islands *inter alia* went on the market in 1778.

Inchenagh, Inchcleraun, Clawinch, Inch and the smaller islands were purchased by Robert Featherstone. It is also of some interest that another purchaser, one Robert Birch, bought the:

> *monastery, town and lands of Clontuskert ... Ballyleague, with their fairs and markets, the weir of Ballyleague and the fishings of Loghree in the river Shannon*[3]

The Featherstones held the island lands until the mid nineteenth century when they were divided between the younger Featherstone and his brother-in-law Charles O'Neill. In 1861 Featherstone sold his share, which included Inchenagh and Inch, to McGann of Killashee from whom it passed in 1900 to the resident tenants under the Ashbourne Land Act of 1885. O'Neill sold his part, which included the islands of Clawinch and Inchcleraun, to the O'Carroll family of Co. Kildare, who subsequently sold it to the resident tenants under the Wyndham Act of 1903. The price of the land to the tenants was fixed at eighteen and a half times the current rent. The tenants borrowed that amount from the government at three and a quarter per cent and undertook to pay off the debt in a period of sixty nine years.

Shortly after the change of ownership from Barnewall/Kingsland to Featherstone, we have our first confirmation of residents on Inchenagh from Micheál Ó Braonáin in 1792. There were six houses on the island at the time of the 1841 census and a total population of 43 persons. For some reason they fared badly during the Famine, losing 18 of their number - a massive drop of 41 per cent, very much at variance with the trend on the Lough Ree islands generally, and well above the average drop for the parish of Rathcline between 1841 and 1851. Numbers picked up again in the following years and the 1881 census shows a population of 38. Thirty years later, in 1901, the number of houses on Inchenagh was reduced to four and the population had dropped further to 19.

The 1901 census has recorded the names of all who lived on Inchenagh in that year as follows:

Name	Relation	Age
1st Family		
Michael Shea	Head	38
Patrick Shea	Brother	30
John Shea	Uncle	66
Eliza Shea	Sister	32
2nd Family.		
Michael Killian	Head	81
Patrick Killian	Son	40
Michael Killian	Son	37
3rd Family.		
Patrick Connaughton	Head	72
Patrick Connaughton	Son	40
Margaret Connaughton	Daughter	34
Mary Gillooly	G.Niece	6

4th Family.

Luke Killian	Head	44
Teresa Killian	Wife	42
Luke Killian	Son	14
John Killian	Son	12
Mary Ellen Killian	Daughter	9
Joseph Killian	Son	7
Thomas Killian	Son	5
William Killian	Son	4

The island lifestyle differed in many respects from that on the mainland. Surrounded by a body of water, access could be slow or irregular, sometimes risky or even impossible. Continuous windstorms or prolonged severe frost could leave the island dwellers marooned and they had to be ready for these emergencies. Stories abound of big freeze ups when the lake was a sheet of ice from shore to shore. One such story comes from the great frost and snow of 1947 when a tramp arrived at one of the Inchenagh houses and after getting his appetite satisfied he told his hosts that he had walked the length and breadth of Ireland but had never seen a field so big and he pointed backwards in the direction he had come over the snow. When they told him he had walked across Lough Ree on the ice he staggered into a seat and nothing would induce him to make the return journey until the ice melted and he was left out by boat.

In the follow-ing pages two local men, descendants of the Inchenagh families, write about the island from contrasting perspectives.

House ruins on Inchenagh.

Inchenagh Island and the Struggle for Independence.
By Tommy Murray

The islands of Lough Ree and their inhabitants were not
untouched by the hostilities of the War of Independence. The
people of Inchenagh Island played no small part in that struggle by
providing a place of refuge and succour for the Volunteers on both
sides of the lake, but particularly on the Roscommon side. My
paternal grandmother was a Connaughton from Inchenagh and
much of what I am about to recount was told to me by my late
father, Jim Murray, a native of Clooncraff, Kilteevan and a member,
with his brother Tom, of the Kilteevan Company, Third Battalion of
the Volunteers in Co. Roscommon. Both of them took refuge with
their mother's people on the island on more than one occasion
when things got too hot on the mainland. My father told me,
however, that they had an excellent hideout/dugout in Clooncraff
bog whenever "the Tans" raided the village. I also checked many of
the details of this story with relations of the main players involved.
I also consulted library sources.

By April 1919, Co. Roscommon was declared a "disturbed area"
by the British authorities and a reign of terror began. As the struggle
progressed the Third Battalion and its constituent companies was
active: drilling, raiding for firearms, carrying out ambushes and
disrupting transport and communications. Shootings, arrests,
beatings, interrogations and other acts of terror were carried out by
the military, Tans and Auxiliaries stationed in Roscommon town.
Many outlying barracks, such as Athleague, Fourmilehouse
and Beechwood were closed and forces withdrawn to Roscommon town.

One of the tactics of the Volunteers, to make travel, transport
and communications difficult for the forces of the Crown was to
block roads. In the spring of 1921 the Cloontuskert Company of the
Volunteers opened a trench on the Roscommon-Lanesborough road
at Cloontymullen. The Tans and Auxiliaries from the barracks in
Roscommon filled it in again but secretly placed a landmine in it. It
lay untouched for a while. Some time later, John Scally of Gallagh
and some of his comrades, including his namesake John Scally of

Portnahinch, Johnny Connor, Lisinaria, Peter Egan, Portnahinch, Johnny Kelly, Antrabeg and Jimmy Gannon, Weekfield, all from the Cloontuskert Company, had set about the task of reopening the trench, when an explosion occurred, injuring four of them. Peter Egan was unscathed. My father and others from the Kilteevan Company were on the hill of Ballinaboy, acting as scouts, on the lookout for British Forces, when they heard the explosion and knew immediately that it was a booby trap.

The injured were first brought to Portnahinch, where their wounds were bandaged, and from there by boat to Inchenagh island as a safe haven from British Forces, who, by now, were searching the countryside, knowing that serious injury or even death, had been inflicted by the detonation of their deadly landmine.

At this point in the story, I found a conflict of evidence with regard to the whereabouts of the safe haven to which the injured were taken. Micheál O'Callaghan, in his excellent account of the struggle in Co. Roscommon *For Ireland and freedom* states that the injured were brought to Inchcleraun or Quaker island as it is more popularly known. Bill Mulligan, in an informative article on the tragedy entitled, *Tragedy in Cloontymullen,* also stated that Quaker island was the one in question. However, local people, on either side of the lake, are in no doubt and the people of Inchenagh and their descendants have testified on many occasions to the fact that the island in question was Inchenagh. Perhaps the most telling testament to this effect came from my conversation with Danny Farrell of Elfeet, Newtowncashel, who was born and raised on the Quaker Island (Inchcleraun), who told me that he always understood that the island where John Scally died was Inchenagh. It is just possible, however, that some of the less badly wounded and their comrades who would have had to go "on the run" following the Cloontymullen explosion, did find sanctuary with the people of Quaker island.

As I was writing the final draft of this article, Kathleen Hegarty Thorne published her masterful tome on the role of the Roscommon Volunteers in the War of Independence. Entitled *They put the flag a-flying,* it is the result of years of research on her part. She states clearly that the injured men were first brought to Inchenagh island

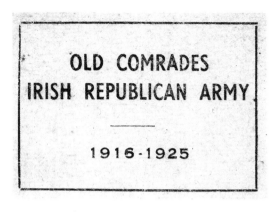

OLD COMRADES

IRISH REPUBLICAN ARMY

1916-1925

Bridget Farrell's membership card.

where their wounds were treated. She goes on to say that three of the men were later transferred to Quaker Island (Inchcleraun). In due course Johnny Connor and Jimmy Gannon returned home leaving Johnny Kelly to recuperate alone. She goes on to state that he was taken from Quaker Island "to a place called Rinnany". This in fact is Rinnany island where he spent some time with the Donoghue family, relations of his, before being removed to Jervis Street Hospital, Dublin, after the Truce.

O'Callaghan tells us that the first medical aid to reach the injured was administered by Dr C. Kelly of Abbey Street, Roscommon. According to O'Callaghan, in order to avoid detection by the police and military, who were watching the movements of all doctors in the region, Dr Kelly went to the railway station and bought a ticket to Dublin. He then travelled to Athlone and was taken by boat to the island to attend the wounded. According to Hegarty Thorne he was rowed to the island by Paddy McDermott of Annamore. Her version would seem more likely. Dr Kelly could easily have left the train at Knockcroghery Station. The journey by rowboat from Athlone would be long and difficult. O'Callaghan also mentions, as does Bill Mulligan, that Dr Dudley Forde from Strokestown was brought secretly to the island to tend to the injured on a number of occasions. The late Jimmy Shea from Blenavoher often told of seeing Dr O'Halloran and Nurse Donlon from Lanesborough being taken out to the island to give medical aid. It would, indeed, seem logical that different doctors would be used to throw the authorities off the scent and because of the need for great secrecy.

Of course, the injured men had to be nursed and looked after between the visits of the doctors. That was done by a rota of caring women from the *mainland*. This is where my second connection with this sad incident occurs. My grandmother, on my mother's side, was Bridget Farrell of Lisnacusha. Known throughout south Longford as "the Sinn Féin woman", she was a nurse and a member of Cumann na mBan. Like the rest of the people connected with this incident she is dead for many a year, but her son, Joe Farrell, resides in Lisnacusha and he is in no doubt that his mother was brought secretly to Inchenagh island, on several occasions, by the Volunteers from the Rathcline/Cashel area, to attend to the injured and clean their wounds. Joe states that she was assisted and relieved by two other women, Hannah Martin/Moran and Molly Bannon/Thompson, who later became a nurse. Joe tells that his mother (Bridget Farrell) lost a child as a result of one such visit on a very stormy night. On returning to the Longford shore she was disembarking when a fierce gust of wind thrust the boat against her with such force that she later lost the child she was expecting. The same Bridget Farrell was arrested by the Royal Irish Constabulary (R.I.C.) on two occasions during the "Troubles" and held at the barracks in Lanesboro. She also dressed the wounds of Ernie O'Malley as he was fleeing east, having been in an ambush by local police near Ballymoe. Micheál O'Callaghan pays tribute to two other nurses, a Miss Kenny and a Miss Fayne. Were they from the Longford side or Roscommon side of the lake? Families with these surnames still reside on both sides. The former may have been the Kathleen Kenny of Blenavoher referred to by John Casey in his *Stories of Inchenagh.* The latter, according to Hegarty Thorne, was Alice Fayne of Cloonmore, Co. Roscommon.

All these dedicated and loyal women and the people of Inchenagh and Inchcleraun should be remembered for the sacrifices they made for their comrades and their country. The families of the injured and the dead, who must have suffered great emotional pain, should not be forgotten, nor should the comrades of the injured who continued to put up stout resistance to the forces of the crown right down to the Truce.

Of the four injured men, John Kelly and John Connor were the most severely wounded. The former was subsequently brought to a

Dublin hospital where he had a plate inserted in his stomach, the latter had shrapnel in his hip and a piece of his ear blown off. John Scally was wounded in his legs, but was not considered in any danger until he developed lead poisoning caused by the lead eyelets of his boots which had penetrated his flesh with the force of the explosion. Alas, despite the best efforts of his carers, he died on 11th May 1921. My father and other volunteers from Kilteevan, under the command of Matt Davis, were involved with the secret removal of his body from the island to Kilteevan cemetery, where he was buried at night by his comrades from the local companies of the Volunteers. Great care was taken to leave no tell-tale signs of a burial, as the crown forces were still searching the graveyards of the region in the sure understanding that some of the men involved in the re-opening of the trench must have been severely or mortally wounded at the scene of the explosion. The Tans searched Kilteevan graveyard thoroughly a few days later but could find no trace of the newly-made grave. Some time after the Truce, John Scally's body was exhumed and re-interred with full military honours and in the presence of all his comrades in Cloontuskert cemetery. My father, who was in the guard of honour, told me it was a very warm summer's day and having stood for three hours in Kilteevan cemetery, the members of the guard of honour walked beside the cortege all the way to Cloontuskert cemetery and there stood to attention for another hour, for the re-interment.

So this extraordinary story of heroism, courage and disaster indirectly touched both sides of my family. I'm glad to have the opportunity to add these few personal anecdotes to the heroic and sad story that began in Cloontymullen and was played out on the island of Inchenagh and Quaker Island (Inchcleraun) in 1921.

Postscript: During the Civil War my father was among a number of Republicans or "irregulars" that held out for a while on Inchenagh, where they made occasional raids on passing barges to supplement their food supplies. They were eventually captured by Free State forces and taken to Athlone. In contrast, his brother Tom joined the Free State Army, was made captain and was based in Roscommon town. My aunt Mary told me that during the brief but tragic Civil

War she would always have to be sure that one was away when the other came home for a quick visit. Of course they became good friends again when hostilities ceased and some years later Tom left Ireland for the U.S. where he died in 1965, never having returned.[4]

Inchenagh and I
By   Michael J. Farrell.

My mother was born in Inchenagh on Lough Ree. One of a large family, she went off to America for several years, then returned and settled on the mainland. Thus I inherited a grandfather and grandmother, an uncle and bevy of aunts for whom "the island" was the ancestral home. From my early years I realized there was something out of the ordinary, poetic even, about the island, although the islanders themselves did not share this attitude most of the time.

As the Nile is to Egypt or the Mississippi to America, the Shannon is to Ireland more than a river: shaper of people's lives, source of songs and repository of folklore. So it's easy to get carried away as history and mythology do a dance where this exotic ribbon of water runs down the spine of Ireland. The plot gets thicker when my unreliable memory, corroded by the years, looks back nostalgically at the springtime of a life that was surely too good to be true.

I have no clear recollection when I first visited Inchenagh – can't be sure any more what is memory and what was told to me afterwards. I may have been six or eight when, along with my sister, I first went on my holidays there, an event my brothers and sisters were to repeat in the years that followed.

Just getting to the island was a major adventure. In those early years the typical road transport was horse and trap. The trap would be parked at John Shea's house in Blenavoher. Then we would walk along the shore to Patrick Shea's. The lake was usually serene because we would not even set out on such a journey unless the weather was favourable. Water behaves in approximately the same way everywhere, from raging against rocks to lapping at the shore. Yet there are memories I associate only with the Shannon, not just the river but its unique context: the reeds growing green out of the water, and the boat cutting through them; water hens darting for cover; dead reeds and occasional debris bobbing on the waves like corks; and seagulls forever soaring and diving.

At Patrick Shea's there was a quay, or several, where the islanders always landed; presumably there was some right of way involved. What happened next depended on whether or not we were expected on the island. If we were, all we had to do was wait. On the island, meanwhile, Uncle Jimmy would be on the lookout for us. This entailed crossing a couple of fields and standing on a wall to see the other side. It was like searching for flies on the moon. In later years binoculars were brought to bear, the technological age making inroads (the first radio I ever saw, or heard, was on the island).

Since we were approaching from the Longford shore, and the three Inchenagh houses were clustered closer to the Roscommon side, Jimmy then had to walk through several fields to get to the boat at "the point" - the islanders opted to stay on dry land as long as they could, and took the boats only from the farthest point of the island, in order to shorten the navigation part of their journey.

Then we on Patrick Shea's shore would see the boat coming, a speck in the distance at first, the oars lifting and falling in mesmerizing rhythm, water dripping from them when the boat got closer. There were special Shannon sounds as the boat touched the rocks of the quay, as the oars were deployed on the seats, then the grinding sound as it was dragged over sand. Embarking was always unsteady and inelegant, punctuated with warnings, as we unruly young landlubbers climbed awkwardly aboard.

If we were not expected there was a different ritual entirely. The problem then was to attract the attention of someone on the island, a matter of chance. My father would march along the shore in an effort to be conspicuous. Then he would wave a white handkerchief. As a last resort he would collect twigs and start a little fire, and the smoke usually did the trick.

The stretch of water was shorter in summer when the Shannon was low. There were times when the elements did not allow any crossing, for days if not weeks, supplies sometimes running low, not to mention the feeling of isolation that must have haunted the islanders at such times. Weather forecasts were rudimentary then, so they relied heavily on their own intuitions, always on the lookout for omens and always showing a high degree of respect for the elements. What James Joyce called the "dark mutinous Shannon," like any big body of water, can get angry and sinister. I remember well the white foam and the growl of it. Our imaginations were fed on the sad tales of people caught unawares and drowned, a litany of tragedies. Yet none of the islanders knew how to swim. The folklore said this was to avoid a slow death in case of accident, but the islanders insisted it was nothing so dramatic; they simply were not interested in swimming.

But what I remember best is the benign and beautiful Shannon on summer Sundays. The fascination was endless, especially for young imaginations. There were fish down there, including mythical big ones. The experience of a boat on water was so unlike anything else in life. While poets and painters have done their best, no one has yet captured the magic. The more our world is dominated by concrete and tarmac, the more do lakes and rivers respond to some yearning of the human psyche.

There was no road on the island, just a path through the fields, and stiles to get over the stone walls. In one field, off to the side, the stone remains of an ancient building had almost disappeared among the bushes, relic of an old church or monastery, the locals said. While many curious researchers, then as now, came in search of old secrets on the island, the locals had little interest in the history of the place, though they were always amazingly gracious about answering the questions of outsiders.

First on the right was Killians' house, then Sheas' on the left – one couldn't travel far without running into one or another family of Sheas. At that point the path gave way to a boreen paved with stones. Down the boreen, on the right, was Connaughtons'. This boreen continued, under overarching trees, down to the water's edge on the Roscommon side of the island. If I could visit only one more place before I died, I would want to walk that stretch of boreen again, down to the restless water. Maybe I would get lucky and an old steamer would come huffing and puffing. I'd scan the Connaught side for Clonmore and Annahona and other names that were mythical in my childhood. I would turn right for a hundred yards to where the well was. I would, if I could, walk all around the jagged shore where over centuries the water had won small victories over the land and left the patient rocks pockmarked forever.

Each of the three families had its own quays, one for the small boat and another for the big black boat that took heavy loads such as cattle. Each aspect of country life, taken for granted elsewhere, posed its own challenge on Inchenagh. Coaxing cattle or horses into a boat demanded a special talent. Rowing that boat with its nervous cargo was not for the faint of heart.

Once, when I must have been nine or ten, Uncle Jimmy took me with him to the Clonmore bog for turf. Filling the turf into bags and hauling them to the boat took longer than anticipated. Darkness had fallen by the time we set out for home. Worse, a storm had arisen. I, of course, was no help with the rowing. Rather than proceeding as the crow flies, Jimmy stayed close to shore on the Roscommon side. The point of this, as I recall it, was to row into the wind until we were above the island, then row down with the wind and waves. I remember a single point of light in a house in the distance otherwise there was only a vague luminescence from the water. Whether it's memory or imagination, I know that I was afraid. I remember my uncle looming ahead of me in the boat amid the bags of turf, brooding and intense, and no doubt sorry he hadn't left me at home.

Just as they had lived together in cooperation and harmony, the three families exited Inchenagh together as soon as an opportunity arose in the 1950s. They settled side by side again on the hill of Rathcline. They share a unique bond that has outlasted the years.

Forty years later, I revisited the island. The homesteads were in various stages of disintegration. A large tree grew in the kitchen of the house in which my mother was born, a kitchen that had seen so much life, so many tribulations and joys intensely lived. While I am pitifully unreliable about the details, I am certain of the big picture. There was love and courage and generosity and undying hope in Inchenagh. May time lap gently on its memory.

CHAPTER 19

Clawinch

No early records survive of Clawinch as it would appear there was no early Christian foundation there. There are, however, two ring forts on the island indicating human habitation some considerable time ago. Clawinch was confiscated under the act suppressing the monasteries, which is a good indication that it may have been owned and farmed by some of the monastic institutions. It was granted by Queen Elizabeth I to Thomas Philips on the 26th September 1567[1] and together with some of the other islands was transferred to Sir Patrick Barnewall of Grace Dieu, Dublin, on 12th August 1590[2]. It remained in the Barnewall family for almost two hundred years

Clawinch Island.

Clawinch Island and the Delameres[3]

In the year 1656 William Delamere was transplanted to Co. Roscommon and received grants of lands there under the provisions of the Cromwellian plantation and resettlement. The Delameres were a Norman French family who came to Ireland in the early waves of the Norman invasions following 1170. They established themselves with considerable holdings of prime Irish land in Meath and Westmeath under the lordship of de Lacy. Now, in 1656, being a catholic family, they were viewed by the Cromwellians as guilty of disloyalty and had their Westmeath holdings confiscated.

Shortly after their having been transplanted to Connaught (Roscommon), a branch of this family settled a short distance away in Cashel, Co. Longford. The first reference we have to them, in this location, comes in the year 1670 when John Delamere of Cashel was named as surety for the priest, Brian Muldoon of Claris. Family tradition states that they lived in Cashel House, a building adjacent

The Shannon Pot.

Saints Island today.

The Shannon at Lanesborough Bridge.

Lanesborough Harbour.

A brooding Lough Ree, captured by Caitriona Casey.

Above: Sailing on Lough Ree.
Below: The modern Viking Boat which plies the lake.
{Photographs: Ann Hennessy)

Two views capturing the atmosphere of Lough Ree.
Photographs by Pat Halton.

Boating to Mass on Inchturk.
Photograph: Ann Hennessy.

Mass in the Teampall Mór, Inchcleraun, with Bishop Colm O'Reilly, 1992.

to the old church of Cashel which stands in the townland of the same name.

In 1769, "Jeffrey Delamer" of Cashel died.[4] His widow is said "to have lost two hundred acres and a fine horse to a Protestant" and she went to live on Clawinch island in Lough Ree, with her young children, at least two sons named John and Jeffrey, and possibly other siblings. Jeffrey remained unmarried and died in 1845 aged 80 years. John married around the year 1800 and had two sons John and Martin and at least one daughter, Elizabeth. This family was now the third generation of Delameres on the island. Elizabeth married Patrick Noone and had at least three children, two boys and a girl. They may have emigrated during the famine years for the name is not to be found on the island subsequently. We have no information on John but Martin married Catherine Donlon, daughter of John Donlon of Derrygowna, Co. Longford, about the year 1825. Martin and Catherine had at least five children. There were three boys, Patrick, Martin and John Thomas in the family and two girls, Brigid and Mary. Patrick died at the age of fourteen while his brother, Martin, was said to have drowned in Lough Ree. The oldest, John Thomas, emigrated to Wisconsin and became the progenitor of an important overseas branch of the family, but it is with the two girls that we are mainly concerned here. Brigid, married Patrick Brennan of Clooncraff on 28th February 1850, while her sister Mary later married Patrick's brother, Luke.

Brigid and Patrick were the parents of Martin, baptised on 11 February 1851; John, baptised on 8 August 1852; Patrick, baptised on 11 June 1854; Luke, baptised on 21 October 1858; Anne, baptised on 11 May 1861; Michael, baptised on 4 April 1868; (Jeffrey? Michael was drowned in Lough Ree in March, 1882. He was taking a boat-load of potatoes to the Lanesborough market when the accident happened), and Thomas, baptised on 22 December 1871.

Thomas, the youngest, married Margaret Tracy (Later to become known as Maggie Clawinch). Their family consisted of six boys and two girls – Patrick, who never married; Tom, who died young; Luke and John who went to America; Michael who married Kathleen Gilleran and had three children Frances, Florrie and Vincent; Jim who married Tess Horan and became the father of

Seamus, the present Minister of Social and Family Affairs; Bridie who married Hubert O'Hara in America and May, who married Christopher Naughton/Norton. A branch of the family settled in Cullentra and their descendants include the Brennan family, Cullentra and the Kenny family, Ballinahinch.

Like the other islands that were once inhabited, Clawinch today lies peacefully in the waters of Lough Ree, unaware perhaps of all the people from near and far who have an affinity to it as illustrated by the above brief account of the Delamere family and their descendants.

In the Griffith's Valuation of 1854 the owners of Clawinch are given as Francis Featherstone and Charles O'Neill. In the same valuation list the occupier tenants are given as Martin Delamere and Patrick Brennan, indicating that Martin may have divided the property with his son-in-law, Patrick Brennan.

The following are the details of the 1901 Census:

Name	Relation	Age
Brigid Brennan	Head of family	72
Thomas Brennan	Son	27

The Brennan family home, Clawinch.

CHAPTER 20

Rinnany Island

R innany is a Gaelic name which means a marshy promontory. The island is situated close to the western shore of Lough Ree, roughly half way between the islands of Clawinch and Inchcleraun and in the parish of Kilteevan in Co. Roscommon. It is attached to the mainland by an isthmus which, when the water is low, forms a land entry to the island. It comprises some fifty acres of arable land together with shore and fen. The presence of a crannóg adjacent to the isthmus would indicate human habitation in this area from a very early date. The 1901 Census shows a dwelling-house on the island where Michael Donoghue is described as the head of the house. Here he lived with his wife Annie, baby son Patrick, and stepdaughter Mary Ann Brennan. Patrick grew up on Rinnany and got married in 1946 to Bridie. They continued to live on the island for the next sixteen years during which five children were born to them. This is Bridie's account of her experiences:

Rinnany Island.

> *I got married to my husband Pat in 1946; he lived on an island in the River Shannon. There were many more people living there. When I went to live there it was very strange to me, as there was no shop, school or church. We had to use a boat to get to and from the mainland. My father-in-law lived with us. He was a very good oarsman and went back and forth as if on the road. We had two mares and the old man was very fond of them. He groomed and fed them every day and they, in turn, were very attached to him. Then he fell ill and the doctor, who lived seven miles away, had to be rowed in to the island to attend to him. However he did not recover and the corpse had to be taken to the mainland on the boat and mourners as well. The two mares followed the funeral to the shore and remained there, until it reached the other side. We had the village stations*

every four years and the neighbouring villagers on the mainland had to be rowed in to the station house; ten people each round until all were in, then when Mass was over and breakfast was eaten, all had to be rowed back again. I often rowed the boat myself when my husband was very busy on the farm. We had forty-five acres of good land, but it sometimes flooded badly, if the winter was wet. We had five children, one died and the two boys and the two girls had to go to school by boat and then when they came back in the evening, I had to meet them before they reached the river. I was always afraid that they might go into the water and drown. Thank God that did not happen. It was terrible hardship in the cold of winter and I would not get across on time. They often had to stay from school for two months at a time in the wintertime.

The turf, too, had to be cut in the bog across from the island and when it was dry, it had to be taken in by boat. It was a rush every year to get it cut and dry early, so as to have it home before the river rose too high. Likewise when the cattle were ready for sale they were made to swim across. One day a farmer had two horses for the fair and they had to swim across after the boat. Unfortunately, when he arrived on the other side, the two horses were dead. All he could do was to take off the ropes and let them down to the bottom of the Shannon. It was a terrible risky life, especially for old people. I saw an old man call to our house one night; there was a terrible storm and he could not get home. He was soaked wet and he dried himself at the fire and a large roll of notes he had in his pocket dried out as well. He remained until morning and made his way home.

Life on the island was very hard for me with crops and fowl and animals to be looked after, as well as trips to the town and to visit my parents. All this had to be done while the children were at school and be back home to row them in again after school. Once we had to leave our home and go to live in Roscommon town with my parents; we spent two months there until the weather improved. My husband remained on the island to look after the farm animals. Then luck came our way; we got a letter from the Irish Land Commission, that we were being changed to a holding of land and a new house in Mount-Prospect, Fuerty. We were very pleased with the news, especially for the safety of the children so that they could get to school regularly. It was a new life for us. That was in 1962. We bid goodbye to Rinnany (that was the name of the island) and started all over again. My husband died three years ago, aged 94 years. He enjoyed every day he lived in Fuerty and took great pride in his home, which was a credit to him.[1]

In those words Bridie recorded some of her memories of Rinnany. Later on she and her daughter Ann amplified those and discussed other aspects of their lives on the island. Farming was of course their main preoccupation. The farm apparently consisted of four large fields, described by Ann as "The Four Green Fields" - the point field, two middle fields and the near field. Farming followed the usual pattern of the time. Livestock was kept. Ann remembers that the neighbours on the mainland had doubts if their cows gave much milk because of the speed at which the young ones used to rush them home for milking in the evenings!

She recalls making the belts and tying the sheaves of corn, the stooks in the field and the stacks in the haggard. One of the most exciting events of the year was the arrival of the thresher which was able to make a grand entry before the onset of the winter rains. One

House at Rinnany.

185

year when the young people were bringing out the sacks of corn with the ass and cart there was an upset at the kesh and the sacks ended up on the ground. Fortunately no great damage was done to either animal or human ego and most of the corn was saved.

Fish formed an important part of the diet but not the trout and eels so much associated with Lough Ree. These were perch waters and drum nets were used to catch the fish which are remembered as being particularly tasty. Wild fowl, too, were in abundance and Pat Donoghue, Bridie's husband, used his gun to provide many a wholesome meal. Ann remembers a frosty Sunday morning when a wild fowler with gun and two dogs called at the house on his way to the point of the island which was ringed with ice. She has a vivid recollection of seeing him return some two hours later with just one dog and tears streaming down his face. The other dog had gone out to retrieve a bird on the ice which broke under him and he drowned in full view of his master who was unable to save him. The lake iced up on a number of occasions with the ice sometimes several feet in thickness. Four young men from the mainland, Pat Glennon, Luke Kilcline, John Devanny and Andy Fayne proposed walking on the ice to the island but for safety they pushed a boat in front of them. The ice gave way and all four jumped into the boat. They then found that they had to break the ice ahead of the boat all the way to the island which took hours of hard work.

Bridie, in her article above, referred to having to leave their island home for two months. This was because the rising water had reached unprecedented levels and there were fears that the island might become inundated. Ann recalls the excitement of the ambulance arriving on the mainland to transport them and their vital necessities, hurriedly thrown together, into the town of Roscommon.

Perhaps the most bizarre event in the history of the island occurred in 1949 when a Piper Cub aeroplane landed on the sandy shore which had increased fourfold because of the prolonged drought. The pilot, Texas born Sam Pratt, was accompanied by an *Irish Press* reporter. One can only imagine the feelings of eighty-one year old Michael Donoghue, Pat's father, who told them that he often rowed his boat over the very spot where the plane had now landed!

Michael died in 1960. His wake is well remembered by his family. A ladder was laid on some porter barrels providing a form on which people could sit. When required each barrel was removed and replaced by an empty one. The funeral left the island with the coffin resting across the gunwale of the boat while the hearse waited to receive it in Glennon's street. Bridie has mentioned the poignant honour guard of the two white mares at the shore - shades of Colmcille's parting with his beloved grey.

Glennon's house was a rendezvous for island dwellers, especially those from Clawinch, Rinnany and Inchcleraun. Sr. Kathleen Glennon, whose vocation took her farther afield, has left us a precious memoir of times that will not come again.

Growing Up on the Shores of Lough Ree
By Sr. Kathleen Glennon

Memories of my childhood on the shores of Lough Ree are rich, colourful and abundant. Growing up beside a lake gives one a healthy respect for, and love of water. Water played many roles in our lives. One of these was recreation. We paddled, skinny dipped, swam, sailed imaginary galleons to strange and wonderful places, "saw" the magic city buried on the lake bed, played hide and seek among the rushes.

Summer Sundays were special. After dinner my grandfather, who was a skilled oarsman took us boating. Saturday afternoon was devoted to catching worms and preparing fishing rods. I have no memory of ever catching even a minnow. I am glad of that now with my heightened ecological awareness. But we learned much about the ways of water and the ecosystem it supports. We admired swans gliding gracefully with their cygnets; knew the habitats of water birds: mallards, bald coots, widgeons, water hens; learned the movements of fishes: bream, perch, pike, trout; were educated into the danger of rocks and eddies; were aware of algae on the lake bed. Most of all we enjoyed the magical flow of the water.

These boating trips were extra special when we visited one of the three inhabited islands – Inchcleraun (The Quaker), Clawinch, or Inchenagh. Our favourite island was what was colloquially known as the Quaker. On the way to its harbour my grandfather showed us the sunken stone which is purported to have acted as a funeral bier for coffins to the mainland at Portrunny. No matter how often we heard this story, we listened in awe and saw the stone skimming the two-mile journey to the shore. In my youth two families lived on the island - Farrells and Walshs. The Farrells were distant cousins and they always greeted us with homemade currant cake and gooseberry jam. While the adults entertained one another we, children, played in the ruins of six of the seven churches on the island. (One of the churches remains hidden to this day). The stone slabs of these churches were not protected then but we treated them with reverence. We came to know the intricacy of their designs, the skill of their etchers and the antiquity of their origin. Often we played monks chanting made-up Latin in the ruined cloisters.

No visit to the Quaker was complete without a pilgrimage to Fionn Mac Cumhail's boulder. He is alleged to have thrown this rock from the Giant's Causeway at Queen Maeve's sister, Clothra, when she distracted him by swimming naked. We were always intrigued by the traces of his fingers on the rock. That this piece of history was anachronistic, that it is impossible to see that distance, didn't seem to bother anyone.

I remember visiting Inchenagh Island only once, though my grandfather often went rambling there. Three families lived there and they had orchards of gooseberries, raspberries, currants - the fruits of Eden to a child.

Clawinch Island was different. The Brennans who lived on Clawinch were regarded as our nearest neighbours. "Maggie Clawinch" was my grandmother's best friend. My earliest memories revolve around going with my grandmother to the lakeshore where she talked across the water to Maggie while I played with dried rushes. My grandmother would inform Maggie of letters or parcels which the postman had delivered to our house. Later her son, Pat, would row across to collect them. Maggie came to our house once a week to the travelling shop where she bought groceries, like all the other women, with the money made by selling eggs. I was four when Maggie and Pat left the island. They went to live in Galway. It was a sad parting for two old friends. All of us missed the intercourse between the island and the shore.

The lake has a rich source of food. During the summer when our well ran dry we brought barrels of water from the lake. Fish was a constant part of our diet. In springtime we put down nets to catch perch. I have memories of scaling perch, of distributing perch among the neighbours, of sometimes having perch even for breakfast! In the summertime pike, bream and trout were on the menu. I remember my grandmother and my mother showing us the bones of the pike. They firmly believed that they were similar to the instruments used in the crucifixion of Jesus - the lance, the nails etc. My grandfather often caught eel with a sort of trident. Eels are oily fish which are regarded as a delicacy today. Eel, like worms, have the capacity to retain the life force in each section when cut. It always upset me to see sections of eel wriggle alive on the pan.

Among other memories are stories of the Big Freeze in 1947. My older brother and sisters tell the story of my father's and Pat Brennan's narrow escape. The lake was frozen over that winter for weeks. That was a rare phenomenon. At any rate the ice must have been rock solid because one evening my father and Pat cycled on it to Lanesborough to the pub. While they were gone the thaw set in. In our house the worry began and the rosary was started for their safe return. At the third decade my father's whistling wafted through the night air and the rosary was abandoned! That winter the men of our village brought supplies to the islanders. They filled a boat and walked beside it ready to jump in if the ice gave way.

Our house was the last house on the road but a family of Donoghues lived further in on Rinnany peninsula. They came to school by boat in bad weather. One winter of huge floods they had to be evacuated from their home. Shortly afterwards they moved to a house on the mainland. That same winter floods made our road impassable. I have vivid memories of my mother and father loading "Christmas" to be brought by boat to Bracknagh, and then transported by cart to the market in Roscommon. The sale of turkeys was vital to farming economy. The quality of Christmas celebrations depended on the price of turkeys. That year Santa travelled by boat to our home. I seem to recall that our celebrations were the best ever but then memory is selective and plays trick with the facts.

Life on the islands wasn't easy. I recall children rowing two miles across the lake, walking the fields to our house, and then walking a mile to school. Education came at a price. Fair days meant swimming or transporting cattle in large boats to and from the mainland. Bad weather meant that islanders needed to have stocked up on supplies or be without sugar or tea for weeks.

Life has changed. The islands are uninhabited by humans, the water shows traces of pollution, fish stocks are being depleted, wild fowl are getting scarcer, but for me the mystical water of my childhood is laced with the same allure!

CHAPTER 21

Saints' Island

The island of All Saints is situated in Lough Ree to the south and east of the parish of Cashel in Co. Longford and lies close to the shore. It is now accessible from the mainland by means of a road built on a former causeway. The island takes its name from a religious foundation established here in the early decades of the thirteenth century. This foundation is well

Saints' Island.

documented and was a priory for the Canons of St Augustine under the patronage of the Dillon family, Anglo-Irish lords of Westmeath. In the context of the monastic history of the lake the Saints' Island priory is a comparative "newcomer." Monasteries such as Inchbofin and Inchcleraun would have pre-dated it by more than seven centuries. However, there has been a strong belief in times past that

Ornate detail, Saints' Island.

a Celtic monastery did in fact flourish here in those early centuries. The great antiquarian and collector, Sir James Ware, who lived in the seventeenth century, believed it to be so and wrote that St. Ciaran founded the first monastery here in the sixth century. However, subsequent historians have discounted this claim, although admitting a strong connection between the thirteenth century priory on Saints' Island and the church of St. Ciaran on Inis Aingin in the south of the lake. That the older tradition was still part of the lore of the lake in later centuries is evidenced in the work of Ó Braonáin, the Gaelic poet of the Shannon in his poem of 1794:

In Oileán na Naomh i lúb den tSionainn
nach bfhuil i bhfad ó chíosa fearainn,
eang den Chaladh in iar bharr Chontae
an Longfoirt, triuch ba dhluth is b'aimhréidh.[1]

In Saints' Island in a bend of the Shannon,
Which is not far from the mainland,
An area of An Caladh, in the County of Longford,
A region which was dense and uneven.

The first written record from this foundation comes from the Register of Tristernagh,[2] an Augustinian monastery in Meath diocese. It names Clement, prior of the Island of All Saints, as witnessing a charter in 1259 A.D. The monastery at this time may have been anything up to fifty years old. There is reason to believe that many of the early community were transferred here from Inis Aingin. Archdall quotes from the Annals of All Saints recording the death of the prior Airectac Y Fin in 1272. We hear nothing further until the end of the next century when some of the canons took up appointments outside in the secular church, viz. Richard O Fergail, a priest of the priory was appointed vicar of Rath Claoin in 1397.[3] Paul McMurray, one of the great priors of Saints' Island, is recorded as undertaking extensive reconstruction of the monastic buildings. He died in 1394. This is how his death is recorded:

Pól Mac Muirith i.e. Pól an Oileáin, a man renowned for his charity, piety and good works - by him were cleared for the clergy Doire na gCailleach and Doire Meinci - died with repentance at a ripe old age.[4]

Varied Fortunes

A sudden rise in affluence follows soon after and this monastery with a valuation of 100 marks has become one of the richest houses in Ireland by 1410. In this year the priory was rendered vacant by the demise of prior William Magunbui (Mac Conbuidhe) and was conferred on Kiannane Ofergail (O'Ferral) who was then a monk of the Cistercian house of Kilbeggan. He was "to wear the habit of the canons of Oilean na Naomh and to conform to the laws of St. Augustine's Order."[5] However, the priory's good fortune was short lived and some years later its value has fallen again and it is impoverished. We have no evidence to indicate why this happened.

In 1425 the prior Donatus Mecongolan (Donnchadh Mac Conghalain) resigned, and the office was entrusted to Maolseachlainn Offergail / Malachy O'Ferrall, a priest of the community. A record in the Roman Registers refers to this resignation in what seemed to be unusual circumstances but it is not possible to say if this was connected with its decline in fortune. Pope Martin V by Bull dated IV Kal. Oct., ann.VIII., commissioned the prior of the St. John the Baptist foundation, Kilkenny West, and others: should they "find on diligent enquiry that the resignation of the priory of S. Mary's of All Saints' Island, in Lough Ree, by Donatus Mecongolan, has been made freely *sine labe seu vicio simonie, et absque fraude et dolo,* to approve and ratify it, by apostolic authority, and confer it on Malachy Offergail, priest and professed canon of the same name."[6] In 1442 it has become necessary for the priory to appeal for donations to reconstruct the church as appears from the following communication from Pope Eugenius IV:

> … *Relaxation, to be valid during twenty years only, of four years and four quarantines of enjoined penance to penitents who on each of the feasts of Whitsuntide and the Assumption of St Mary the Virgin, and on All Saints', visit and give alms for the repair etc of the church of the Augustinian priory of Saints' Island [Insula Omnium Sanctorum] in the diocese of Ardagh.*[7]

There is no ready explanation for this strange history of rags to riches and back to rags again. However, an entry in the annals for 1464 may cast some light on this puzzling development:

> *Brian O'Breen with ten of his people and ten others of the inhabitants of Caladh under the conduct of William, son of Donough, son of the Prior O'Farrell were slain by Magawley, chief of Calry in Teffia.*[8]

These disputes were usually about wealth and property and there are some indications that the Saints' Island community may have been involved here.

Augustin Magraidin

Of all the company of canons in this monastery the most celebrated was Augustine Magraidin. Ware-Harris[9] in *Writers of Ireland* speaks of him as follows:

> *Augustine Magraidin, a man of wisdom and learning, flourished in the 14th and beginning of the 15th century. He was an Augustinian canon in a monastery of the Island of Saints in the River Shannon, on the west bounds of the county of Longford. Among other fruits of his studies, he writ: 'Vitae Sanctorum Hiberniae, and continued a "Chronicle", which other canons of the same monastery had begun down to his own times, part of which Sir James Ware had in Ms. with some additions made after his death. He died on the Wednesday next after All Saints, A.D. 1405 and was buried in the said abbey.*[10]

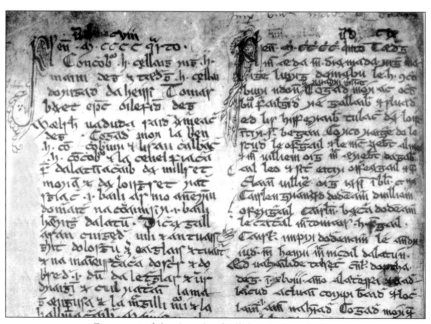

Fragment of the Annals of All Saints, Lough Ree.

As Ware-Harris remarks, Augustine Magraidin was one of a long line of scribes who kept records in the scriptorium of the Saints' Island priory. It is a tragic reality that most of the great works produced there were destroyed or lost in the later Cromwellian period and in the half century that followed it. Were it not for the foresight of the few who knew the value of these works and had the means to save them, it is possible that nothing at all of the rich scholarship of this island priory would have survived for posterity.

From the scattered remains that are still available it is possible to identify four distinct literary works wrought in this priory. The first is that usually known as Fragment III of the Miscellaneous Annals. As its name implies Fragment III is but a part of a larger document. It is preserved in the Bodleian Library in Oxford and is catalogued under Rawlinson B. 488. It is the work of Augustine Magraidin who is described in it as "compiler of this book and many other books."[11] It was continued by other monks of the order after the death of Magraidin in 1405. It consists, in the main, of a record of events in the general area of Lough Ree and in particular in the regions of south Longford and Westmeath.

The second work consists of lives of the saints and was also compiled by Magraidin who is recorded as the author of *Lives of the Saints and Histories.* A copy of this work is to be found in the Franciscan Archives, in University College Dublin. The original known as *Codex Insulae Sanctorum* is also preserved in the Bodleian Library, Oxford as Rawlinson B. 485.

Thirdly there was "Leabhar Oilein na Naomh for Loch Ribh", annals covering the centuries down to 1227 A.D. and now lost. Extracts from this book were used by the Four Masters in compiling the annals of the Kingdom of Ireland for the period commencing 1005 A.D. Micheal O'Clery visited the island in 1627 A.D. for the purpose of copying these excerpts from the original manuscript.

Lastly there is reference to *Leubar eris ann Oilean na Nam* or "a chronology of Saints' Island." This reference occurs in a marginal note dated 1232 A.D. in the *Annals of Boyle. Leubar eris ann Ollean na Nam,* in common with many works from these islands, is now lost[12].

These then are the literary works known to have been compiled in the monastery of Saints' Island. Some of them came into the possession of the collector and antiquarian, Sir James Ware, in the second half of the seventeenth century. In 1686 A.D. they passed from Ware-Harris to Hyde, Earl of Clarendon. On the latter's death they were acquired by James Bridges, Duke of Chandos and from his library they passed to Richard Rawlinson, who donated them to the Bodleian Library in Oxford.

The lives of the Irish saints are to be found in the Rawlinson Mss. in the Bodleian Library in Oxford. According to McNamee on one of those manuscripts is scribbled the *obit* of a prior of Saints' Island, Flaithbheartach Mac Conmidhe Ua Fearghail, who died in 1504.[13]

There is evidence that the priory of Saints' Island survived for almost a hundred years after the suppression of the monasteries. As already noted Br Michael O'Clery, one of the Four Masters, collected material there in the 1620s as did Colgan, a Franciscan monk and historian, in the 1630s.

Monastic Remains

What remains today of the Saints' Island monastery consists of a number of ruined buildings, wall footings and earthworks, on a site about an acre in extent, which is still used as a cemetery by the local community. By far the most imposing of these ruins is the church which is some 70 feet long by 20 feet broad and orientated east-west. It has a magnificent tracery window in its east gable dating from the fifteenth century. Most of the south wall is intact and it contains four round-headed splayed windows, three of which are in good condition. The north wall is less complete, its west end being the highest part of it and here a number of corbels are visible some twelve feet above ground level indicating either an adjoining building or perhaps this was the cloister and the corbels were carrying the cloister roof. The west gable has largely disappeared.

When Daniel Grose painted this building two hundred years ago the west gable stood high with a pointed gothic window towards its top.[14] Beneath this window was the doorway by which one entered the large chapel by a lofty arch. Projecting northwards from the gable was a range of apartments with vaulted stone roofs which are still in a fair state of preservation. Opposite to these and parallel to them is a range of oblong buildings projecting northwards from the east gable of the church. Adjoining the south wall is another building which probably was a chapel; its east gable contains the remains of an ornate tracery window with a hood moulding having decorated terminals. In Grose's time this part of the building was in much better condition. This is how he describes it at the end of the eighteenth century:

> *On the south side, is another adjoining smaller chapel, with a tracery window pretty entire. Near this and probably communicating with it, stood a lofty belfry, which fell about 13 years ago and greatly disfigured the surrounding remains. Its fall was occasioned by a quantity of stones being taken out of its foundation to build a Masshouse. The priory of All Saints when entire must have covered a great space of ground, and was surrounded by a lofty wall with a square and ample gate, near which, part of the porters lodge still remains, and facing, stood a stone cross, the stump yet standing in the pedestal.*[15]

Within the church much of the stone altar has survived. There is a piscina in the south wall with a cut stone basin and a small drain hole into the interior masonry of the wall. Near to it is an ornate double ambry of cut stone. There is also an ambry near the altar in the north wall. In the foreground of Grose's painting there are "fragments of an exquisite fifteenth-century cloister arcade." This is now no more but its beautifully worked stones are still visible on the site today and some of them are identifiable from the drawings in Grose's picture.

Some portions of the original enclosing

Corrahacapikeen.

wall of the monastery are still standing. To the north west of the site there is a length of some sixty feet of wall in reasonably good condition. It stands over sixteen feet high in places. Another stretch survives on the south-western boundary but here it is reduced to half its original height. At the west end of this wall there is a small stone building which is said to have been a latrine. This building according to local lore was known as Corrahacapikeen. It is believed to be the only original placename on the site that has come down to us through the local lore.[16] In the northeast corner of the cemetery, well away from the main ruins, is a small rectangular building, lying east-west with an opening in its east gable that once held a window. This is the porter's lodge identified by Grose above.

The stump of the stone cross is no longer to be seen. It is interesting that Ó Braonáin refers to a *clogas ard* on the island. An entry in the Moran Ms refers to one Edward Clarke from Saints' Island who had recently helped to save the lives of three people in a boating accident. The report continues:

Formerly on this little island there is said to have been a tower attached to one of the churches that answered for a belfry and at night as a sort of lighthouse. The people still tell that the monks used to place a light in one of the windows of the tower to guide boats on the lake at night. This ancient custom is remembered and practised.[17]

Tá clogas ard is díothú mórán
de theampaill fós i gcló ar an oileán,
ba tháschmhar tuairisc, céim is gairm,
in aimsir Chiaráin a bheith air marthain.[18]

There is a high bell-tower and many ruins
Of churches still on the island
That had great fame and reputation
In the days of St. Ciaran.

Folklore and story

This monastery played a large part in the lives of the people over a wide area. In the years since its suppression a significant body of folklore and story has built up around its memory and has been handed down through various channels. Grose, who visited in the 1790s, found that several relics were kept in the ambrys of the old church on Saints' Island, and he continues:

> *In one of these is carefully kept three pieces of rotten wood, called the blessed tree preserved here as tradition says, since the first foundation of the priory. Many miraculous qualities are ascribed to this blessed tree which are implicitly believed in, not only by the inhabitants of the island but by those on the mainland, for a great distance. Whoever takes an oath falsely, on any of these pieces of wood, the offender's mouth is immediately transferred to the back of his head, and he remains a conspicuous monument of the wonder-working powers of this miraculous tree. A few days before this drawing was taken, it made a considerable tour, and was soon again to go around, through three townlands, in search of stolen timber. It was once taken, we are told, for a similar purpose by a man, who having made successful use of it, carelessly threw it aside, and it was mislaid amongst some nettles at his door, but woeful consequences soon followed this culpable neglect, for in less than a month, the man and his whole family died. So firm a faith is placed in the powers of this tree, that many have been known to fly the country, rather than swear by it.*[19]

J.P. Farrell in his History of Co. Longford a hundred years later recounts more legends of Saints' Island.

> *One of the stories I have heard in connection with it is in relation to Saints' Island. In this island there is a graveyard where a large proportion of the inhabitants of Newtowncashel are interred. Up to about fifty or sixty years ago there was a remarkable flat stone in this island, which was said to be possessed of a very unwonted power. This was that when a funeral arrived at the shore of the lake, preparatory to being transmitted to its last resting-place, the stone*

was always standing still on the surface of the water, waiting to
carry across to the island the remains of the deceased. Incredible as
this may seem, it was, nevertheless, a fact. The coffin was placed on
the stone, which was elongated and slab-like, and, in the twinkling
of an eye, had cleft the waters and deposited its burden on the shore
of Saints' Island, whilst the friends followed in their boats, and the
stone returned to its resting-place. One day a certain family went to
bury a friend in the island, and, either on their return from or entry
to it, one of their number committed a nuisance on the stone, which
immediately sank to the bottom of the lake, nor could the person who
committed this sacrilege ever lift his eyes from the downward
position in which they were at the time he did the deed.

There was another tradition in reference to this island,
which shows the sacred feelings with which it was regarded by the
people. Men or women, when they wanted to protest the truth in a
very solemn manner, always swore "By the Crineeve" or called that
word to witness the truth of their assertion. Their reason for this
was, that there was a stone figure on this island representing a
man's head; and the people believed that if they took an oath in the
presence of this figure, and that the substance of their declaration
was untrue, the result would be that their own heads would be
turned on their bodies.[20]

Another tradition associated with this area had to do with a
designated bush under which was spilled the water that had
washed the corpse of a deceased person. Memories of this custom
still survive among the older generation in the locality.

Confiscation

The monastic lands of Saints' Island passed through many
hands after the suppression. Gerald Fitzgerald was the proprietor in
the first half of the seventeenth century and it was probably his
patronage that enabled the monastery to function right up to
Cromwell's time. Fitzgerald was dispossessed in the Cromwellian
plantation and in the Book of Survey and Distribution, Henry
Sankey, a Cromwellian soldier, is given as the proprietor in 1664.

Subsequently the lands went to the Barnewall family who later in 1778 sold them to Robert Featherstone.

Fifty years later, in the Tithe Applotment book, the owner of Saints' Island is given as William Lewis. Four families were tenants on the island at the time, Widow Mary Clarke, James Fagan, Thomas Mulvihill, Snr. and John and Widow Scally. The Tithes were a tax levied on all occupiers of land for the support and upkeep of the established church. They provoked fierce opposition among catholics, especially in the early decades of the nineteenth century and one result of this was that the government ordered a survey to be done throughout the country of all who were liable to pay tithes. Only the heads of households are listed so that the document gives little indication as to numbers of people, but it provides valuable information for historians and other interested parties from that period.

In the Griffith Valuation list of 1854 William Lewis is coupled with William Clarke as proprietors. There are now ten houses on the island, one of which is vacant. The others are occupied by the tenants as follows: Anne Clarke, William Clarke, James Kelly, Thomas Fagan, William Nally, Pat Scally, John Scally, John McGrath and Catherine Nally. The population of the island at the 1901 Census was forty four. They were made up of eight families.

1901 Census

1st Family

Name	Relation	Age
Thomas Fegan	Head	47
Bridget Fegan	Wife	34
Maryanne Fegan	Daughter	1

2nd Family

William Nally	Head	83
James Nally	Son	36
Patrick Nally	Son	34
Kate Nally	Daugh.-in-law	25
Thomas Nally	Grandson	5

Michael Nally	Grandson	4
Mary Nally	Granddaughter	1

3rd Family.

James Fegan	Head	37
Margaret Fegan	Wife	28

4th Family.

Thomas Kelly	Head	46
Anne Kelly	Wife	43

5th Family.

John Clarke	Head	60
Mary Clarke	Wife	50
Anne Clarke	Sister	50
Maryanne Clarke	Daughter	7
John Clarke	Son	6
William Clarke	Son	4
Timothy Clarke	Son	3
James Clarke	Son	8 mths.

6th Family

Patrick Skelly	Head	50
Anne Skelly	Wife	30

7th Family.

Edward Clarke	Head	60
Maggie Clarke	Wife	35
William Clarke	Son	8
Maria Clarke	Daughter	5
Anne Clarke	Daughter	3
John Clarke	Son	1

8th Family.

Patrick Skelly	Head	60
Catherine Skelly	Wife	30
John Skelly	Son	15

| Patrick Skelly | Son | 13 |
| Anne Skelly | Son | 8 |

William Bond had a house on the island but it was uninhabited.

Today there are no permanent dwellers on Saints' Island. There are five houses, some are empty and some are used as holiday homes.

Earlier reference has been made to the uncertainty surrounding the first establishment of a monastery on the island of All Saints and the question as to whether the first foundation dated back to St Ciaran in the sixth century. Long after monastic life had ceased on the island, a move was made which might have brought about the founding of a modern monastery on this site. A representative of the Redemptorist order wrote to the bishop of Ardagh and Clonmacnois, Dr. Hoare in 1896 seeking lands on which to establish a house of the order. This was the bishop's reply:

St Mels,
Longford.
March 22 1896.

V. Rev. M.Somers, C.S.S.R.

My dear Fr Somers,

The chapter was unanimously of opinion that, with the parochial clergy of both dioceses and the Franciscans already in Athlone, there was not room for another order, with or without a church.

But one of the Chapter, Canon Gilligan, offers to help to secure a site in his parish on a promontory commonly called Saints' Island where St. Ciaran lived, eight miles from Athlone by water (the Shannon), seven miles from Ballymahon by road. This is the most I can do for you. I hope it - site - will be found suitable.

I should recommend you to write to Very Rev. Canon Gilligan, P.P., Cashel, Lanesborough, Co. Longford asking him to appoint a day when you could see him. On whatever day you appoint, if the weather is fine, you could come to Athlone and take a boat from that to Cashel Lodge and thence to the P.P.s residence.

For my part I shall be delighted to see you come there, and have a church.

I am, Dear Fr Somers,
Faithfully yours,
+ J. Hoare.[21]

However these negotiations proved unfruitful and Saints' Island was not to see the beginnings of a new monastic era. The Redemptorists located instead in Esker, Co. Galway where a thriving community continues to the present day.

CHAPTER 22

Inchcleraun - Inis na Seacht dTeampall-(Quaker Island)

The volume and complexity of information on Inchcleraun is impressive. There is, to begin with, its heroic age when it is prominent at the dawn of our history in the days when myth and legend first held sway. Again at the outset of the Christian era it towers over surrounding monastic foundations and is the subject of frequent notices from the annalists for over seven hundred years. So much of the ruins of its former eminence have survived on the site that these remains constitute an important source of information on its life story. Finally the period since its demise as a monastery, some four and a half centuries ago, has its own unique colour and requires to be treated in its own right.

Inchcleraun

Maeve: the legendary Queen

We begin with the name of the island. Inchcleraun is an anglicisation of Inis Clothrann, the name by which the island has been known down through the centuries. Clothra was the legendary sister of Maeve, whose name hovers over this island out of the mists of prehistory. Maeve, like Brigid, has origins in the goddess culture of pre-Celtic Ireland. She is described as "the goddess of the land and of sovereignty."[1] She was also "the old cailleach" - the crone or hag - who guards the well. A religious cult flourished around her name and some of the old Irish writings have reference to the priestesses of the goddess Maeve. In the epic story of *An Táin* she seems to alternate between other world deity and warrior queen; between the divine and the human. Some scholars suggest that *An Táin* itself marks the transition from a matrifocal civilisation to a society dominated by the cult of the male warrior which finally triumphed and put an end to the priesthood of Maeve.

However subsequent tradition on the lake and on this island, has placed Maeve firmly in the human realm and she bears the hallmarks of mortality. She is the warrior queen of Connaught leading her armies in the Táin wars that constitute this ancient epic of heroic Ireland, centred round the brown bull of Cooley. When the war with the Ulstermen was ended and Cuchulainn was dead and the bulls had, in the modern idiom, sorted each other out, Maeve retired to Clothra's evening isle, for peace and tranquility in the twilight of her life.

But it was not to be. The Irish had long memories even then, and Ulstermen still seethed with anger at the humiliation they had endured at the hands of the queen. Forbuidhe, son of Conchobhar Mac Neasa, the Ulster king, laid his plans carefully. For a year and a day he practised with his *crann tabhaill* (or slingshot) until his aim was perfect. Then, concealed on the lakeshore, he waited patiently until the queen came down to bathe in the well whereupon he hurled the missile straight and true, killing her instantly.

There are different tellings but the story substantially remains the same. It can also be found in Céitinn's *Foras Feasa*, Vol 2. When John O'Donovan visited Inchcleraun in 1837 he was astonished to find how well the ancient lore had survived in the folk memory of the island. Not only did they know the legend but the very spot where the queen fell was marked and named Inidmarfameva (the place of the death of Maeve.) O'Donovan gave instructions that in exactly this manner it was to be entered on the new ordnance map. He quotes James Moran, the "oldest man on the Island" telling him of the Grianán Maedbha and the ruins of Maeve's dun or fort on the summit.[2] The survival of this ancient lore points to a well-knit community on the island and an unbroken link with monastic times when this *seanchus* and history would have been well preserved and copied in the scriptorium of the monastery. Elsewhere, however, and even on the lakeshore, that link had become tenuous. O'Donovan himself was puzzled when he set out from Cruit, with his boatman Brannan. He wanted, in his own words "To ascertain if I could prove it to be the Inis Clothrann of the annals."[3] and he was well rewarded by his contacts on the island.

Returning to its early history we find that Inchcleraun was a religious centre in the post-Maeve and pre-Christian era, with the probability of druidic rituals being practised there. Francis J. Biggar, historian and archaeologist, who visited the island in 1899, has this to say:

The family of Queen Maeva were great enchanters, and the pagan priests or druids may have held religious sway in Inis Chlothrann before Diarmaid's time; for there is a reference to a religious settlement on the island before the saint came, and we know that the church in Celtic lands succeeded the druids in their possessions, often assimilating customs with an easy transition that fitted in tranquilly with the feelings of the clans.[4]

Diarmaid Naofa

It is not possible to say for certain whether the presence of an earlier religious cult had any bearing on the foundation of a very early Christian monastery on Inchcleraun in the sixth century. Historians date this event at 540 A.D. The founder was the holy man Diarmaid, who was of royal descent and a native of Roscommon. We know little about the beginnings of the monastery - a wooden church perhaps with thatched roof and a cluster of beehive cells. Of the company who joined Diarmaid initially we know little.

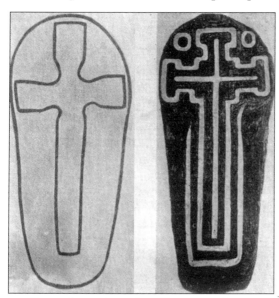

The clergy were of various origins; distinguishing themselves from the pagans by shaven heads and wearing tunics; some were of noble blood; some had been slaves; and they were permitted to remain married, but to one wife only.[5]

East and west faces of small cross standing at Teampul More., known as the Dermot Stone.

Its earliest years are highlighted by the memory of its most illustrious son Ciaran, Ciaran Mac an tSaoir, who studied under Diarmaid at Inchcleraun and went on to found the monastery of Inis Aingin (Hare Island) and in due course followed the river southwards to found the great monastery of Clonmacnois in 549 A.D. By the middle of that century a number of very important monastic foundations had been firmly established in Ireland, the most notable being Aran, founded by Enda; Clones, founded by Tighernach; Terryglass,

Ogee window, Inchcleraun.

founded by Colum; Clonard, founded by Finian and Clonmacnois, founded by Ciaran.

It would seem that they together formed the solid core on which Celtic Christianity was built. From these primary foundations other monasteries were established and we find in the succeeding century "clusters" [*paruchiae*] of monasteries having sprung up and having affiliations to one or other of the older establishments as from a "mother" house.

It is likely that a similar local *paruchia* of monasteries on Lough Ree had its origin in the monastery of Inchcleraun. We know that the foundation of Diarmaid flourished from the beginning. By the end of the sixth century its founder had died and later its first stone building was raised to commemorate his memory. A century afterwards we have the first of the written references to the importance of the place and to the famous and holy persons who lived there or who came to pray or to die in this hallowed sanctuary. Inchcleraun had its anchorites, its eremites and its *céli dé* (culdees). The way of life within the settlement would have been typical of the old Irish monastic system which was unique in the world. Canon John Corkery in his work "Cluain Chiarain" has this to say:

We know that the Irish monastery had not merely celibates as members. It also had married people. It was not a collection of individual anchorites, though they too could exist as eremites within the monastic compound. It was primarily a community with the ordinary Irish laws of inheritance governing its holding of land and property, while the emphasis was on individual sanctification with its three stages of - asceticism that strips one of self; the purging of vices; and the attainment of the most perfect and perpetual love of God. This is not achieved necessarily in isolation. The saint is compelled by Christ to urge and kindle men to serve the Lord. All aspire to the vision of God; but the presence of God may be found in the natural world, another form of contemplation; the waves breaking on the rocks, the gull's cry, the blackbird's song, the smooth strands, the pet animals - all may be vehicles of God's message. The old saints all seem to have been animal lovers and nature lovers.[6]

Lancet windows, Inchcleraun.

Written History

The first written reference to Inchcleraun is in the *Annals of the Four Masters* which records the death of St Sinneach on the island on April 20th 719 A.D. This is an early saint from south east Longford whose name is venerated in the parish of Tashinny (*Teach Sinigh*). The next two references record the deaths of two men who were abbots both of Inchcleraun and of *Caille Focladha* near Fore, Co. Westmeath. This is Faughalstown[7] a monastery said to be founded by St.

Diarmaid of Lough Ree. No further information has survived but the close link between the two monasteries - despite the distance that separated them - is beyond doubt. This seems to be an example of the type of monastic affiliation referred to above. The first of those two abbots, Eochaidh, is given in the *Four Masters* as having died in 780.[8] The *Annals of Ulster* record the death of the second, Curoi, "son of Aldnia of Inis Clothrann and of Fochla of Mide, a learned abbot and the most expert in the histories of the Irish fell asleep in Christ" in 870 A.D. Curoi is mentioned in glowing terms for his wisdom and learning. He is described as *sapientissimus* and *peritissimus* and when it is realised that these superlatives were still accorded to him many centuries after his death some glimpse may be gained of his standing as a scholar and of the fame which he enjoyed throughout the whole country.[9]

Tracery window, Inchcleraun.

Education

The education system in operation on Inchcleraun would have resembled that of other monasteries. There would have been an emphasis on religious learning especially in the earlier times. There was also a considerable input of "secular" learning. Relations with non-monastic learning were slow to develop in the early stages of Christianity, but when they did the amalgam bore fruit in abundance. Donncha Ó Corráin sums it up:

From the seventh century, relations between the monastic scholars and the native literati, though often uneasy, grew increasingly close. In the late eighth and early ninth centuries the important ascetic movement of the Céli Dé took place and this gave rise to the "hermit" poetry, nature poetry remarkable for its fine sensibility and delicacy of touch. The compromise between the two types of learning led not only to the preservation in writing of a great deal of secular material, but to the composition of an extensive body of religious and ecclesiastical literature in Irish. At the same time motifs and materials from Irish saga, folklore and popular belief began to penetrate into purely monastic literature. The annals, product of monastic learning which was originally a bare historical record, were interpolated and filled out from genealogy, saga and poetry. In the ninth century and earlier the synthesis between the two types of learning is complete and in the great unreformed monasteries of the later centuries the ecclesiastical poets and historians worked out most fully the "senchas" of Ireland, it's traditions, history and prehistory. These poets, historians and jurists, secular and ecclesiastical, left behind them the materials from which the early history of Ireland, must, in large measure, be reconstructed.[10]

Means of livelihood

The monastic community lived off the land in accordance with the farming patterns of their times. Corn and milk were the two primary products. The reliance of the people on corn is borne out by the fact that in the years when the corn crop failed due to adverse weather conditions the records show that a famine often followed. The annals have frequent references to corn-drying and corn-milling. Cultivation was done by spade and on more sophisticated farms by plough (often made of wood) drawn by oxen, as workhorses were hardly ever used in ancient Ireland.

Harvesting was done by sickle, threshing by flail, followed by winnowing and grinding in a water-mill - a process which continued in Ireland right into the last century. For the most part corn was eaten as porridge though various forms of bread were made from both oaten and wheaten meal. Milk and its derivative foods formed a very important part of the diet and people were well-versed in the making of butter, curds, cheeses and various milk dishes. Pig production formed a considerable part of the economy. Pork and bacon were highly rated and often featured on the menu for important guests. The northern portion of Inchcleraun is called Muckinish, indicating a long association with pig farming. Sheep which were generally black or brown in colour were kept for their wool. The use of sheeps milk for food was not uncommon. There was much emphasis on the vegetable garden or *Lubhgort*. Many of the common vegetables of today were grown and also wild garlic (*cremh*). Apples and nuts were widely grown and held in high esteem. Apples were a kind of currency and could be exchanged in barter for a variety of other requirements.

While timber was plentiful and widely used as fuel there were obvious limitations on a small island. It is now well established that turf was used as fuel from an early date. The proximity of extensive bogland on the western shore of Lough Ree most likely provided the community's sources of fuel. There was no transport problem as boats were in plentiful supply - even larger boats capable of taking a ton of turf or more. The pastoral life on an island such as this evokes a sense of peace and tranquillity. It would however be rash to presume that this was all an idyllic life. Early Ireland was ruled by petty kings and chieftains who were frequently in contention with each other and the monasteries did not escape the turmoil. However a greater menace was looming.

Viking Invasions

The Norsemen had found our shores in the early days of this ninth century. While local wars, between native chieftains, were not uncommon, the comparative peacefulness of the Irish society facilitated these plundering barbarian hordes, and since they were adept at travelling by water, our island monasteries did not for long escape their devastating fury. In the period from 843 to 987 A.D. Lough Ree and its environs came under Viking attack at least seven times. From the time of the notorious Turgesius and for a hundred and fifty years afterwards they continued to raid and plunder and "they plundered Inis Celtra and Muicinis and burned Cluain Moccu Nois and went on Loch Ri and plundered all its islands."[11]

Raiding Irish

One of the most bitter confrontations took place in 987 when the men of Munster and the Danes of Waterford attacked the settlements in Lough Ree.

> *The Connaught men assembled against them and a battle was fought between them. Great numbers of the Munster men and Danes were cut off with slaughter and amongst others, Dulaing, their heir apparent of the crown of Munster, and many others along with him.*[12]

So, as the first millennium A.D. draws to a close, we can but guess at the damage inflicted on the Inchcleraun foundation in the previous 150 years. We can imagine the ongoing agony of a monastic community subjected to the horrors of war, their repeated efforts to restore and rebuild and renew, all in vain, as fresh waves of barbarous men, native and foreign, plundered and rampaged again and again. Even some of the monastic community were caught up in the turmoil driven by greed, anger and revenge. As the century moves towards its last quarter, the whole country is changing in character and is now prepared to fight the foreigner in earnest. Lough Ree's story is but a microcosm of the history of Ireland at the time, as the men of Connaught inflict a memorable defeat on the marauders. To reverse the biblical quotation, the plough shares have been melted to make swords and the sons of the men of peace are ready to engage in bloody war.

The consequences of this upheaval were immediately evident in the century and a half which followed the defeat of the Vikings at Clontarf. The political life of the country frequently erupted in turmoil, and the monasteries did not escape the lawlessness and aggression which had been unloosed. The annalists tell us that Inchcleraun was plundered in 1010, and again in 1050. There is another account of a raid by the Munster men in 1087:

led by Murtagh O'Brien they sailed on the Shannon to Lough Ree
and plundered the islands on the lake, Inis Clothrann, Inis Bó Finne,
Inis Ainghin[13]

Whether this attack was for the enrichment of the raiders or part
of a struggle between the kings of Munster and Connaught in
which the monasteries were but pawns, is not clear, and indeed
mattered little to the unfortunate victims, whose way of life was
being disrupted. Already, however, these interruptions were
becoming less frequent and for the next two hundred years
comparative peace reigned in Inchcleraun.

Rebuilding from the ruins

One ventures to think that it was at the commencement of this
period that the Teampall Mór was built. Its original architectural
features date from about this time and the presence of "stray"
stones, referred to below, indicates earlier buildings that had been
perhaps levelled by the raiders. The annals are now telling a
different story, a story of an island that was once again a shrine of
holiness, a place of penance and pilgrimage and the final resting
place of the great. Aodh O'Finn, bishop of Breifne, died while on
pilgrimage in Inchcleraun in 1136.[14] Giolla Na Naomh O'Farrell,
the first recorded chieftain of Muintir Anghaile, was buried in the
cemetery of Inchcleraun in 1141.[15] His son Murchadh was interred
there nine years later. This Murchadh O'Farrell was the founder of
the Cistercian Abbey at Abbeyshrule, Co. Longford.

We read in Archdall for the year 1155: "The Abbey was burnt on
the feast of St. Peter and St. Paul." Under the year 1160, we read of
the death of Giolla na Naomh Ua Duinn, who is described as
"scholar and principal of the schools of Inis Clothrann"[16] - a tiny
glimpse for us, 800 years later, into the work, the teaching and the
learning that prospered on this island. O'Duinn was chief poet to
the king of Leinster and has left us a large collection of his verse.

Another entry in the annals for 1167 notes that Cinaeth Ua
Cethearnaigh, "priest of Inis Clothrann, died."[17] We read that in the
following year Dubhchobhlach,[18] the daughter of O'Quinn the
former chieftain of ancient Teabhtha, died on the island. It would

The Clogas Church, Inchcleraun.

seem that she had gone to spend her final days there. Diarmuid Ua Braein, a native of Breaghmáine in present day Co. Westmeath came from a family noted for ecclesiastical scholarship. He is described as "Coarb of Comman and chief senior of the East of Connacht."[19] He too would seem to have spent his last years here for he died on the island in 1170 "in the ninety-fifth year of his age."

Further Strife

A period of apparent unrest now followed. In 1174, Ruaidhri O'Carroll, chieftain of Ely, "was slain in the middle of the island."[20] In 1189, we are told, "it was at Inchcleraun in Lough Ree that the hostages of O'Connor Maenmaigh were kept at this time."[21] Both these entries would appear to signify an intervention by the monks to resolve local disputes. Maybe this had something to do with a fierce attack on the monastery by the Costelloes or De Nangles in 1193. Farrell in his *History of the County Longford* states:

> *After escaping the danger of the Danes and the Ostmen, it (Inchcleraun monastery) was finally razed to the ground, and its inhabitants murdered by Gilbert De Nangle, a Norman knight, who came over to Ireland in the train of Henry the Second. This tragic event took place in 1193, after which this island ceased to be the refuge of sanctity.[22]*

O'Farrell was of course, in error in his judgement regarding the demise of the monastery, as the *Annals of Loch Cé* tell us that in the year 1193, "Macbethaidh O'Dobhailen, airchinneach of Camach mortuus est in pilgrimage in Inis-Clothrann,"[23] indicating that the practice of pilgrimage was continuing on the island. The same annals go on to state that scholarship and sanctity continued to flourish when they record the death of Giollachriost Mac Gorman in the year 1220 "after a triumph of devotion and pilgrimage in the sanctuary of Inis Clothrann."[24] We learn also of the death in 1232 of Tipraide Ua Braein of the same race as Diarmaid, above mentioned, who also was "coarb of Saint Comman, an ecclesiastic learned in history and law, who died on his pilgrimage to Inis Clothrann."[25] In 1244 the bishop of Elphin, Donnchadh O'Connor, of royal lineage also died here on his pilgrimage and was buried in the monastery of Boyle.[26]

Roman Records

Reforms that had taken place in the Irish church in the 12th century had brought church organisation under Roman direction. One of the results of this change was that records were kept in Rome, which survived from this century onwards. Later they cover a period when Inchcleraun is no longer mentioned by the Irish annalists.

It is recorded in the Lateran registers that the prior of Inchcleraun, Dermot O'hUbagan died in 1424, and Pope Martin V appointed Giolla na Naomh Magraidin in his place. Eighteen years later, in 1442, Prior Magraidin was relieved of his post and Irial O'Farrell appointed in his place. Also from the same source we learn that in 1501 Prior Muiris O'Farrell was deposed by order of the Pope and Ruaidhri O'Farrell was appointed in his place. Ruaidhri was a member of the community of the monastery of All Saints' Island.[27]

No records survive to tell us anything about the pastoral work of the monks in the early centuries of the monastery. Did they have care of other communities on the mainland, east or west? There is some reason to believe that the site of the old church of Rathcline did in fact house a monastic cell in early medieval times.[28] In the Archaeological Survey of Ireland compiled by the Office of Public Works in 1988, Rathcline is marked as a "church and monastic site". It is possible that Rathcline at some stage was colonised by the Inchcleraun monks and became a daughter house. It is also of interest that the two sites were linked by Lough Ree and that Rathcline was quite visible from the clogas tower on the island. In the later Middle Ages Rathcline had become a parish church and all recorded associations are with the monastery of All Saints. There is also a tradition that the old medieval church of Cashel was served by priests from Inchcleraun and a suggestion that they resided for long periods on the Priests' Island, adjacent to the shore, which would account for the name of the island. A long-standing relationship between the monks of Inchcleraun and those of Roscommon monastery is mentioned by O'Donovan. Meetings were arranged by ringing the clogas bell on the island after which the Inchcleraun men crossed over in their boat and met their fellow monks at the Bannow river which got its name from 'Beannughadh' i.e. to greet or to salute as the monks used to chant together on its bank.

Inchcleraun today

The ruins of six churches can be clearly identified as follows:

1. Teampall Dhiarmada

We begin with the buildings in "The Moor". The "Moor" from the Latin word *murus* (a wall), consists of an area of six and a quarter acres by the lakeshore, on the eastern side of the island, enclosed by a retaining wall and containing four of the main buildings. First is Teampall Dhiarmada, which is the smallest of the churches and, incidentally, the smallest surviving church ruin in Ireland. The outside measurements are 14' 7" by 10' while the inside measurements are a mere 8' by 7'. It is oriented a few points south of east, from which some have deduced that its foundation may have been marked out towards the end of the year.

Only a little of the side-walls are left standing, but the west-end gable survives which incorporates a flat-headed doorway with a level horizontal lintel. Most of the doorways in early Irish buildings are of this kind. The altar, east gable and window have long disappeared. The likelihood is that this building had a stone roof and is very ancient. H.G. Leask, in *Irish Churches and Monastic*

Buildings, discusses at considerable length features common to churches like Teampall Dhiarmada. He implies that the ratio of breath to length is a significant factor in determining the antiquity of the building. Where the length is less than one and a half times the breadth, an early date is indicated. This would place Teampall Dhiarmada amongst the very earliest such buildings.

Teampall Dhiarmada.

Leask goes on to consider what purpose was served by buildings with so small a floor area:

> *Some of the single-chamber structures are so small that they could not have held more than two or three people in addition to priest and acolyte; it would be more accurate to call them oratories. Even in the larger of them the congregations cannot have been numerous. This diminutiveness puzzles the observer of today who often asks for an explanation. Perhaps this is to be found in the low-walled enclosure which survives in Duvillaun (Co. Mayo) and some other places where a sub-division of the enclosed space may have constituted an open-air church to which the little oratory itself served as both tabernacle and sacristy. At this and several similar sites a large upright carved slab stands beside the oratory and at the head of a tomb, presumably that of the saintly founder. Against this slab a wooden altar could be placed to become the focus of the open-air gathering.*
>
> *One is tempted to believe that such gatherings may have been less subject to hardship in the period when the very small*

churches were erected, and that it is significant that the climate of the sixth and seventh centuries, though deteriorating slowly during the latter, was much finer and warmer than it is today.[29]

In the light of Leask's observation it is of interest to recall that the ancient grave slab known as the Dermot stone was sited a mere few feet from the north wall of Teampall Dhiarmada.

Another feature of this little building is the presence of antae i.e. the projection of the side walls to east and west beyond the line of the gables, the length of the projections in this case being about 18 inches. It is believed that antae derive from the earlier timber buildings when construction began with the placing of four posts in the earth. These antae appeared as addenda to the side walls when the building was complete. The earliest stone buildings followed this style. However this may be, Leask has no doubt that antae had a practical purpose in the case of later buildings, inasmuch as they were used to support timbers that carried the roof forward on the gables. If, however, as has been suggested, Teampall Dhiarmada had a stone roof, its antae would not have been functional but would have derived from the style of an earlier timber structure.

The inference here is that this little church belongs to a very early period and possibly was built in honour of the founder and dedicated to his memory, and may have been the only stone building on the site for many generations.

2. Teampall Mór

Some twelve feet to the North of Teampall Dhiarmada stands the largest building on Inchcleraun - Teampall Mór. This is where O'Donovan thought he found two churches, but it is clearly the ruins of a church and community apartments, including a cloister. The standing buildings are in the shape of an inverted "L" with nothing remaining of the cloister except wall footings and outlines. Adjacent to this area, there would most likely have been kitchens and other domestic buildings, but no trace of them remains above the ground nor have they ever been recorded in any survey. The "foot" of the "L" is that part of the building nearest to Teampall Dhiarmada and parallel to it. It consists of a single-nave church

46' 9" long by 21' 6" wide, oriented almost perfectly east-west. The walls stand to about 12ft high with the east gable appearing to be in excellent condition. The north wall - particularly the portion of it which adjoins the western gable - is overhanging and in need of attention.

Teampall Mór, Inchcleraun.

This church presents a complex history of architectural design. The north wall just mentioned would appear to belong to a much earlier period and perhaps to have formed part of an earlier edifice. The lower portions of this wall resemble the building in Teampall Dhiarmada both in the size and shape of the stone and the manner of construction. It is as if the builder of the church decided to use this wall and built on to it and on top of it.

The stones high up on the wall are of a different shape and pattern and much larger than those nearer to the ground. Towards the eastern end there are carved stones revealed where the wall has fallen away showing the evidence of a window or perhaps a stairway which was built in and sealed up. The western doorway has completely disappeared as has a doorway in the north wall which opened on to the cloister. The south wall, which is in good condition, has two round-headed Romanesque windows. A later insertion of a gothic window, now in ruins, gives the wall an irregular and asymmetrical appearance. High in this wall on the interior there appears a carved arch-stone used in the building which obviously belonged to an earlier building and was moved from there.

The east gable is in an excellent state of preservation and has two framed lancet windows. On the interior the windows are similar, but on the outside one is elaborately and ornately moulded while the other is severe and plain. Both are, of course, later insertions but whether they were both made at the same time is difficult to say. Even if one was of more recent origin than the other, the striking contrast of pretty and plain is difficult to understand. Going back to the interior of these windows, another anomaly presents itself. To the right of the window, as one faces the east gable, there is an ambry and piscina and carved octagonal stone stand. The sill extends to the left under the window jamb, which clearly has been built on top of it, thereby covering part of the stand and the other half of what was a double piscina. The window which was placed in this incongruent setting is the plain window. It may have been moved to its present position by the builder to make place for the second and more ornate window. Whatever the purpose was, the end result is that the beautifully carved ambry has suffered and one looks in vain for some explanation. But on Inchcleraun, as on so many similar sites, answers and explanations are often in short supply, while questions and ambiguities abound.

Attached to this church on the north side is the range of community apartments. The sacristy next to the church is vaulted and has an exquisite 15th century ogee window in the east wall. There are several chambers on two floors. The upper chamber - perhaps the community room - has a beautiful tracery window recessed into the north gable and an attractive window seat in stone work in the recession. The "L" shape of the buildings obviously provided shelter for the two sides of the cloister and some of the corbels which supported the roof of the south cloister are still in evidence on the exterior of the north wall of the church. Two of the cloister-arches survive. It would seem that there were five arches on the east side. Of the north and west sides nothing remains.

3. Teampall Mhuire

To the north west of Teampall Mór stand the remains of the third church, Templemurry, Teampall Mhuire, sometimes referred to as the chancel church. This building consists of a nave and chancel. The nave is 29 ft. in length on the inside and the chancel a further 14 feet 10 inches. There were doorways in both the north and south walls of the nave, of which little or nothing remains. The entire chancel arch and dressings have disappeared but the window in the east gable is in good condition and is round-headed

Romanesque. Beneath this window are the ruins of the altar. The west window is almost as good as the day it was made and is a beautiful example of this architectural style. Biggar in 1899 found a "rough heap of broken masonry" to the east of the chancel wall. This he thought to be a "saint's bed."[30] He also comments on "the great Irish yew at the east end quite overshadowing the whole structure. It is one of the most venerable in Ireland." The heap of broken masonry can still be identified and some of the base and roots of the "venerable yew" can still be seen today. A legend associated with this church tells how women were forbidden to enter it on pain of death. The legend is mentioned by O'Donovan - there are various forms of it, one of which suggests that there was an underground tunnel leading from the church.

4. Teampall na Marbh

Teampall na Marbh, the church of the dead, is located to the west of Teampall Mhuire and is 23 feet 8 inches by 15 feet in dimension. There are but scanty remains of the sidewalls, west-gable and doorway. Much of the east gable survives and incorporates a most interesting window above where the altar stood. From the interior the window is regular Romanesque, arched with four well-cut sandstones and splayed. On the exterior the top two stones are cut and shaped to form a pointed Gothic arch. One can picture the mason who learned his trade in the older established Romanesque tradition being excited by the novelty and glamour of the new style but not yet prepared to abandon the old form. Combining both the old and new, he sculpted this precious little thing, quaint and beautiful. It must epitomise in its own simple way the transitional stage of Irish middle ages architectural development and can therefore be dated fairly accurately at 1175 - 1200 A.D. It would also indicate that Teampall na Marbh is posterior in time to the churches already dealt with above.

These four churches are surrounded by the wall or cashel mentioned above. There are considerable remains of the wall to the south and southwest, while to the east, by the lakeshore, not much is evident save the scattered stones. At this side a gate entrance has been identified. This was the main entrance to the monastery from the lake and consisted of a Romanesque archway where the keystone bore the effigy of a bishop's head carved in relief. The arch was in two orders but only a few ornate stones remain in situ and their design and ornament date them from the twelfth century. The north and northwest perimeters of the boundary wall have also fallen down. Within the enclosure, there is evidence of intermediary walls and cashels, perhaps the remains of earlier smaller enclosures or divisions between stockyards, apiaries, stone cutters' yards, vegetable gardens, and such. There are also traces of earthworks strewn over the site. These ruins provide the only clues extant of the layout of the monastery and the chronological progression of buildings down the centuries. Outside the enclosure, however, there are two further buildings to examine.

5. The Clogas

On the highest point towards the centre of the island stands the clogas or belfry tower and attached to it the ruins of a church. The church, rectangular in shape, is 34 feet by 16 feet 8 inches and has one surviving window in its east gable. This is Romanesque in form, the rounded top having been carved out of a single stone. O'Donovan seemed to think that this church was as old as Teampall Dhiarmada but it is generally agreed that it is not earlier than the eleventh century. He also found a lancet window, of which there is no trace today.

The clogas adjoins the west gable of the church and was a later addition to it. It is square in shape, roughly built and what remains of it is some 30 feet high. It had at least four floors which would have been made of timber, the emplacements of which are still in evidence in the masonry. The ground floor was entered through a flat-headed plain doorway from the church. The other floors were reached by means of a stone stairway built into the north steps and perhaps a ladder reached to the doorway of the upper floor.

The clogas or *cloightheach* was a feature common to many monastic sites, more usual as a round rather than a square tower. This one, built on the highest point on the island, within a few yards of the site of the *Grianán Meadhbha*, would seem to have had a function as a look-out post. A small island offered few possibilities

An old engraving of the Clogas Church at Inchcleraun.

for retreat or flight; therefore, advance warning of an enemy's approach was essential. As a place of safety while under attack, its upper floors offered a measure of security for the monks and their treasured possessions. But its primary use would seem be have been as a *cloightheach* or belfry.

6. Teampall na mBan

This church is situated a short distance outside the cashel to the south. Today it is called Teampall na mBan, the women's church, indicating perhaps a community of nuns at some stage. Since this church was built outside the enclosing walls of the monastery proper it was seen as a means of separating men and women religious on the site.

O'Donovan seemed to be frustrated by conflicting names and claims regarding the identity of the buildings. In his letter of July 9th 1837, setting out what had been finally agreed on the "seven" churches, he does not name this one but says no name is remembered.[31] The building itself is a plain featureless structure, rectangular in shape. The remains of its four walls vary in height from two to nine feet. Attached to this church at the northwest end is a smaller rectangular structure. There is nothing to indicate what its function was. There are no doorways or windows remaining. The altar is marked at the end gable by stones and rubble placed there by the Board of Works and also two beautifully worked stones which Biggar thought might have formed part of "thirteenth century clustered columns."

These are the monastic buildings as observed on the island today. They are almost identical with what O'Donovan described in 1837, what Mary Banim recorded in 1887 and what Biggar noted in 1899. There are but the remains of six churches. It is indeed quite possible that there were others that suffered total and final destruction. Were it not for the enlightened - though belated - intervention of the preservationists in the 19th century, even that which we have left today on this and similar sites would by now have faded into oblivion.

Grave Slabs

When Biggar visited the island in 1899, he found three grave slabs including the "Dermot Stone" which he describes as follows:

> *Between the walls of this church (Teampall Dhiarmada) and Teampall Mór stands a little stone with crosses on both sides of it rudely cut on a natural slab which must be of an early date. We heard of another stone cross with a head carved upon it which had been removed to the mainland by a peasant to make a gable block.*[32]

Near to the women's church he found another slab lying face-downward with a "Celtic interlaced cross incised on its surface". It measured 26 inches by 21 inches and had an inscription in Irish only part of which he could decipher. These letters appear on it: b, a, a, c, h. On the low wall in front of Farrells' cottage, he found another incised stone, very worn but apparently bearing a Celtic cross. In 1933 the top portion of a grave slab with cross decoration was found on this island by Rev. Campbell, Dean of Clonmacnois. His son, W.J. Verschoyle Campbell, had it deposited in the National Museum. We are fortunate that these four grave slabs are still to be had. Within the sacristy vault are preserved several stones from the monastery. They exhibit various styles of carved ornament from the chevron and beading of Romanesque days to the pointed Gothic of later centuries.

Placenames

For the few original placenames that we have on the island we are indebted to John O'Donovan. Not one survives in contemporary usage. The *Grianán* and *Inidmarfameva* have already been detailed. The latter is located in a field named Beor-Laighionn, which adjoins the eastern shore of the island and may mean "Leinster Water." On the ordnance map the southern point of the island is marked "*Cornahinch.*" The most easterly point is named "*Corraphortanarla.*" There are remains here of a man-made harbour of considerable size. This, no doubt, explains the "port". But what of "arla?" Niall Ó Domhnaill in his *Foclóir Gaeilge-Béarla* gives "airleach" as an archaic form of "eirleach" which would be translated as "wanton slaughter". There is a temptation to think that it may refer to a particular slaughter in a turbulent era of the monastery. On the other hand the word *arla* is identified as counselling, also very appropriate to the surroundings!

We do not have a firm date for the actual closing of the monastery. The parliament assembled on 1 May 1536 and the bill for suppression was introduced. Sir Patrick Barnewell of Fieldston, the Kings sergeant-at-law in Dublin gave it as his legal opinion that the king had no right in law to suppress the Irish monasteries. Owing to his efforts the bill was rejected by the Lower House. However, it was introduced again in 1537, passed and made law. Lord Cromwell wrote 3rd February 1539, to Archbishop Browne and William Brabazon, vice-treasurer, appointing them his deputies. On the same date, letters patent under the privy seal were issued to them and others, directing them to proceed with suppression of the monasteries. We know that suppression was activated immediately in the eastern parts of the country, but farther west it was more retarded. However, it was now the law, and in time it would be fully implemented.

Suppression and confiscation

The Act of Suppression brought to an end one thousand years of monastic life on Inchcleraun, years of peace and tranquillity, years of learned scholarship, years of struggle and sacrifice and of war and destruction. But despite all it suffered down through the centuries, the monastery could always rise phoenix-like from its ashes and build anew to become great once again. In this way it had survived Vikings and Normans as well as the marauding Irish. This time was different - it would never rise again.

The first record we have of a takeover of the lands comes from the Fiants of Elizabeth 1567 as quoted previously in Chapter 8, in which the beneficiary was Thomas Philips. There is another record which states that Inchcleraun and several other islands in the middle of the lake were granted to one Richard Power by Elizabeth I in 1590. However that may be, in the same year under Queen's letter dated 12th August these islands were granted to the Barnewall family.[33]

In 1622, the monastery lands are in possession of Sir Nicholas Barnewall, 1st Lord Kingsland, great grandson of Patrick Barnewall, above mentioned. They continued in the Barnewall family to Henry, son of Nicholas, and in 1688 to Nicholas 3rd Viscount Kingsland. Nicholas's son, Henry, was the next recipient and in 1744 George Barnewall 5th Viscount Kingsland, nephew of Henry, became the last of the family to own the Inchcleraun lands. He died without leaving an heir and the property was sold to Robert Featherstone in 1778. From him they passed to Lady Featherstone and from her to her son-in-law Charles O'Neill, who later sold them to John Walter O'Carroll of Moore Abbey in Co. Kildare, from whom they passed to Dr. Fred O'Carroll and then in due course to the resident tenants under the Wyndham Act of 1903.

The Quaker

It was during the proprietorship of Lady Featherstone in the early 1800s that the island was leased to a new tenant - a certain Edward Fairbrother, the Quaker who has become famous, inasmuch as the island has been named, ever since his time, Quaker

Island. And so it is known today to all the people in the vicinity of Lough Ree but few could tell you that the man's name was Edward Fairbrother. The stories about him live on. He is said to have taken the stones of the monastery to build a house, the ruins of which can still be seen. This deed brought down a predictable curse on him, which caused his cattle to go berserk, charging madly around the island until they plunged into the lake and were drowned! The Quaker must have been a colourful character who made a deep impression on the people of the area. Stories abound about the stir he would cause on his arrival at the fairs of Knockcroghery and Athlone to buy cattle and he was obviously looked upon as a good buyer by the local people.

He came from Ballymurray, close to the lakeshore, on the Roscommon side of Inchcleraun. A community of Quakers was living here in the early years of the nineteenth century as pointed out by Isaac Weld in his *Statistical Survey of Co. Roscommon* in 1832.

> *On the flat ground near the River Hind, on the road to Moate Park, the seat of Lord Crofton, which lies two or three miles from the town, a little district commands notice for the neatness of the cottages, and the excellent quickset hedges and enclosures. It was formerly inhabited almost exclusively by quakers, but the place has been latterly deserted by the greater part of the friends, a circumstance attributable, as I was given to understand, to the decline of the linen and yarn business in which many of them had been engaged. They have left behind them, however, memorials of their industry, and of their love of order and neatness.[34]*

The Quakers, properly called the Society of Friends, were founded by George Fox in 1648 in England. They were a Christian movement but at variance with the established church, a circumstance which frequently brought them into conflict with the authorities. Many of their followers were imprisoned, tortured or flogged. The movement spread to Ireland and took root especially in the south. They were a people noted for their industry, their honesty and their compassion. They had come initially to the shores of Lough Ree from Sligo where they had been suffering persecution from the established church early in the 1700s. Sir Edward Crofton, the landlord of Mote Park, welcomed them.

Albert Siggins, a local historian in Roscommon, has done extensive research on this topic and writes as follows concerning the early years of the Quakers in Ballymurray:

> *Some of the names of Friends known to come between 1717 and 1749 are Byrn (Byrne), Boate, Siggins, Alexander, McHutcheon, McLaughlin, Sinklar and probably Jackson. Later on in the century names like Nevitt and Robinson occur. Later still is found the name Fairbrother. This name occurs on a Crofton Estate map for 1829 in Corgarve, and O'Donovan in his Letters for the Ordnance Survey in 1837 mentions the Fairbrothers building a house on Inis Clothrann on Lough Ree and ever since it has been known as Quaker Island. These names come from both Friends archives and the Synge census of 1749 but in Synge there is some confusion as to which is Protestant or Quaker, and again with Synge some have servants listed, a rare event with the generality of neighbours around them.*[35]

There is a Quaker meeting house in ruins in the townland of Corgariff close to Ballymurray School. Opposite Ballymurray School is a farm occupied in 1829 by George Fairbrother, a member of the family that leased the Inchcleraun lands. To the back of the meeting house is a small Quaker cemetery, now sadly neglected. It contains three tombstones commemorating James Killroy of Churchpark, William Siggins and John Lewis and the Lewis family. Apparently it wasn't always politic among the Friends to erect monuments and it is believed that there were many other interments in this plot and that one of them was Edward Fairbrother the Quaker of Inchcleraun.

Holy Wells

The special connection between Ballymurray in County Roscommon and the Lough Ree islands is alluded to above in the story of the Bannow River and the Inchcleraun monks who came visiting there. There is a further connection in two holy wells in the same district. On the western shore of the lake an ancient holy well

Tobar Dhiarmada.

close to the shore at Portrunny bears the name St. Dermot's Well, after the founder of the Inchcleraun monastery and local tradition states that water from this well cured diseases of the eyes. Another well, not very far distant from this, bears the name Tobar Ríoch. Together they reflect the veneration attaching to those two names down through the centuries.

When the Tithe Applotment lists were made out in 1827, the owner of Inchcleraun was given as Lady Featherstone and the only tenant with a liability for tithes was Edward Fairbrother, the Quaker, despite the fact that it would seem there were other residents on the island at the time. Ten years later, O'Donovan could refer to James Moran as the oldest man on the island and consult him on events that happened years before that. Griffith's Valuation of 1854 also gives Lady Featherstone as the owner and St. George Johnston as the tenant farming 97 acres. It gives John Moran as farming three and a half acres. Curiously St. George Johnston is given as the owner of these three and a half acres.

We move now to the 1901 census which records two families resident on Inchcleraun. Michael Walsh and his wife Kate were a young couple with two children, Thomas aged 4 and Patrick aged 2. The Farrell family consisted of James and Maria, parents, and a daughter and son, Mary aged 18 and Daniel aged 16.

1901 Census

Name	Relation	Age
Michael Walsh	Head	30
Kate Walsh	Wife	32
Thomas Walsh	Son	4
Patrick Walsh	Son	2
James Farrell	Head	60
Maria Farrell	Wife	48
Mary Farrell *	Daughter	18
Daniel Farrell	Son	16

* In the register of Carrabeg female National School for June 1891, Mary Farrell, Church Island, is listed as a pupil.

CHAPTER 23

Inchbofin

Inchbofin (Inis Bó Finne, the island of the white cow) shares its name with several other islands and lakes in Ireland. Stories of the white cow have roots going deep into Irish mythology and may even date back to pre-Celtic origins, in the East, where the cow is still held in veneration. The milk of the white cow had special properties for healing in old Ireland and it was used at rituals and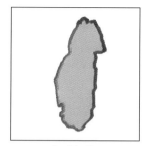

Inchbofin

for blessings. It is likely that such rituals were practised on this island in pre-Christian times, which may have accounted for the establishment of an early Christian monastery here. Tradition says that the founder, Rioch, was the son of Darerca, the sister of St. Patrick. The same tradition states that Rioch was the keeper of St. Patrick's books and that, as a consequence, the school on this island in later centuries became the "university of the lake." In line with the general policy of evangelisation in pre-Christian Ireland, the founders would have retained the established religious practices and "christianised" them. Thus the Bó Fionn, in her new state, would have maintained her status in the life of the island well into the early centuries of the Christian era.

> *In Ireland from earliest times down to and including the Christian period (c. seventh to eighth century) the holy women, nuns and midwives always had a sacred white cow whose milk was used to heal, and to baptise newborns, and whose butter was used for healing. This fat may have been used in keeping the eternal flame lit in St. Brigid's of Kildare (a custom that relates back to the goddess rituals.)* [1]

Brigid in her goddess manifestation is sometimes symbolised in the ancient sagas by a sacred cow. The milk of this cow was noted for its wholesome properties. It was believed to have various curative powers and to be an antidote to poisoned weapons.

While Eremon was king of Ireland, the king of Leinster and his people were sorely harassed by a neighbouring British people who used poisoned weapons, so that the least wound they inflicted was followed by certain death. At last, the king, by the advice of a druid, prepared a bath on the eve of the next battle, into which was poured the milk of one hundred and fifty white hornless cows. During the battle, as fast as the king's men were wounded they were plunged into this bath, which at once healed them and by this means the poison tribe were defeated and slaughtered.[2]

Rituals associated with the white cow extended throughout the country generally, and the Irish continued to baptise with milk until the twelfth century. In the older matricentred societies the notion of cow and goddess were closely aligned. The river Boyne for instance got its name from Bóand the cow goddess. "The association of goddesses with cows is widespread: the goddess is often imaged as the celestial cow that nourished the earth with her milk."[3] Many other pastoral peoples had a high regard for the cow. The Masai tribe of east Africa used cows' milk for ritual blessings on special occasions, such as rites of passage.[4]

Inchbofin monastic site.

The "Bó Fionn" that gave her name to this little island was no empty shibboleth and the breeding and raising of sacred white cows continued for centuries after the introduction of Christianity. People from the neighbouring islands and from the mainland would have come here, on occasions of special significance, to solicit some of the blessed milk to take back to their own communities.

According to Joseph McGivney's book on Longford placenames an ancient name given to this island was Inis Mhic

Carved head of bishop, Inchbofin.

Ualaing. It is not possible to say at what stage in history it bore this name. The first reference to it in the annals is under the name Inchbofin.[5] Under date 750 A.D. it is recorded:

Fionngalach, son of Anmchadh, son of Maelcuraich, abbot of Inis Bó Finne died.[6]

The next reference is to Blathmac,[7] also an abbot of Inchbofin and foster son of Colgan, who died in 809 A.D. The monastery suffered from the plunderings of Turgesius and the Vikings, towards the middle of the ninth century. The annalists tell us that in 916 Fearadach,[8] abbot of Inis Bó Finne, died. In the years following the death of this abbot the Vikings took possession of all the monasteries on the lake and Inchbofin suffered accordingly. However, the Inchbofin monastery recovered, for in 1015 and again in 1089 it was plundered by the Munstermen who brought fleets up the river into Lough Ree.

The monastery was occupied by the canons of St. Augustine in the twelfth century and continued in operation up to the suppression. There are substantial ruins of the monastic buildings still visible on the island. The larger ruin known as the "monastery" is located on the northeast shore of the island.

Henry S. Crawford of the Royal Irish Academy visited Inchbofin in 1916. The following is his description of the ruined "monastery":

> The larger, or monastic church, has no chancel but consists of a plain rectangular nave with a large transept, or chapel opening off it to the north. To the west of the transept is a vaulted sacristy, with a large chamber above. … The nave is 44 feet 8 inches in length and 18 feet in breadth internally; it is the oldest portion of the building. The doorway is in the south wall, the head was a pointed arch, the stones of which are preserved in the sacristy with other interesting remains.
>
> The east and west windows have been destroyed, but the lower portion of the altar still exists. It is 6 feet 2 inches in length and 3 feet 5 inches in breadth. The most interesting features are in the side-walls south and north of the altar; to the south is a small plain window of early type, the head of which is lost, and near it an ambry and piscina. The ambry is a recess, 14 inches wide and 15 inches deep, finishing above in a point formed of two stones inclined together.
>
> The piscina is unusual. A stone 7 inches in breadth and 5 inches in thickness, projects 7 inches from the wall, and is sloped away on the under side. In its upper surface is a circular basin 5$\frac{1}{2}$ inches in diameter and 1$\frac{1}{4}$ inches in depth; a small open channel cut in the stone runs from the basin into the centre of the wall. It is unusual to find a piscina projecting from the wall like a stoup, and having an open channel instead of a perforation through the base. Arrangements of this kind, however, exist at Ballinskelligs Abbey, County Kerry, and in St. Fechin's Church, at Fore, County Westmeath. In the latter instance there is a recess, and only a portion of the basin projects from the wall surface. Ullard Church, County Kilkenny, also possesses a piscina with an open channel, but it is placed in a recess in the ordinary way.

The north wall contains a fine Romanesque window, which is one of the best examples in Ireland. It is early in style, and decorated with carving of slight depth. The opening is 2 feet 8 inches in height and 6¹/₄ inches in width, splaying to 3 feet 3 inches at the interior face of the wall. Several stones of the outer face are missing, but their positions are quite clear.

The ornament is incised along a band round the interior arris; this band is 5¹/₂ inches wide on the face and the same on the soffit and reveals. The carving consists of a narrow chevron moulding between two wider ones, with a. straight row of pellets outside. The triangular spaces between the chevrons and pellets are filled in on the jambs by sets of four inclined lines, the inner pair of which meet in a point; on the arch the lines are replaced by simple fret patterns. The whole design is repeated symmetrically on the soffit and reveals, the chevrons interlocking along the arris.

The transept is of later date than the nave, and is itself of two periods, the northern portion being an extension. The internal

measurements are 27 feet 7 inches by 21 feet 6 inches; an arch, now defaced, opens into the nave. There are cusped and moulded windows of two lights in the east and north walls; that in the east wall has lost its mullion and tracery, but as the design is simple, it can be restored from the existing portions. This wall also contains the jamb of an earlier window to the south of the present one, as well as two small aumbries or recesses. Portion of the altar remains, and is larger than that in the nave, being 9 feet in length and 3 feet 6 inches in breadth.[9]

Beautiful Romanesque window, Inchbofin.

Crawford made a detailed study of the dilapidated buildings. He went on to examine the extension made to the monastery in the fifteenth century. Here the north gable of the "new" transept contains a fifteenth century tracery window with a bishop's head carved at the apex of the exterior hood moulding. The sacristy to the west had monastic chambers overhead. The site, which incorporates a graveyard, is surrounded by a low wall. Remains of other buildings and wall footings are close at hand.

About a hundred yards to the south is another ruined building known locally as the Church. This is a smaller structure consisting of a nave 23 feet long and 15 feet in breadth and a chancel 14 feet by 10 feet on the inside. Joining nave and chancel is a semi-circular arch of well-cut stone. There are two round- headed windows in the chancel in good condition and a third in the nave. The doorway is in the south wall. There seems to be a graveyard to the west of the building with a number of plain stones still standing.

Graveslabs[10]

Graveslab of Inchbofin.

Nine grave slabs or fragments have been found on Inchbofin together with certain other rounded stones regarded as cursing stones. Cursing stones have been found on several religious sites, most notably that of Inismurray, off the Sligo coast.

The Inchbofin grave slabs were also examined by Crawford who described them in detail. They have now been conveyed to a place of safe-keeping. Some are damaged and some are intact. The following is a brief synopsis:

1. A slab bearing a two-line incised cross one foot nine by one foot two, bearing the inscription: *MAEL MARTAIN*. Intact.

2. The second slab is one foot ten inches by one foot seven inches and bears a three line incised cross with a circular centre and semi-circular extremities. Intact.
3. A slab one foot nine by one foot eight, similar to No. 2 except that the centre is blank. Cracked across the centre.
4. A slab bearing a three-line cross two foot ten inches by two foot two with semi-circular ends. The word OR appears at the head of the stone. The centre is well-worn making it impossible to decipher the remainder of the inscription.
5. A smaller slab one foot two by one foot, bearing a plain incised single-line cross. Intact.
6. This slab broken in several pieces is three foot six by two foot one, on which a two-line ringed cross is incised. It bears the inscription (O)ROIT do (CH)ORMACAN. The fragments have been put together by the Board Of Works. Muireartach, High king of Ireland in the tenth century, did a famous march around Ireland which was immortalised in song by his chief bard Cormacan Éigeas. Some people have suggested that the bard is buried on Inchbofin and that this is his grave slab.
7. Two fragments one foot two by one foot, and five inches by four inches showing portions of a three-line cross.
8. A fragment eleven inches by six and a half inches, on which are incised the letters T,D and H.
All these graveslabs date from the tenth century or earlier.

The monastery, in common with the other monasteries on Lough Ree, was suppressed in the reign of Henry VIII and its lands became the property of the king. By fiant dated 4 July 1588 Inchbofin was granted by Elizabeth I to Tyrlagh O'Byrne to hold for ever in common socage. Rent £5 6s 9d. Following the Cromwellian plantation and the restoration of Charles II the island was the property of the Earl of Roscommon.

Daniel Grose did two paintings of the ruins in the 1790s and it would appear that there was more of the masonry extant at that time. We have no record of people living on the island in the time of Grose. However, the Tithes List of 1827 gives three families on the island: Patt Scally, Patt Heveran and Bryan Connell. Thirty years later the Griffith's Valuation list provides us with further information. The owner of the island in 1854 was Susan Galbraith and the tenants were James Heffernan, Bryan Connell and Patrick Skelly.

1901 Census Return

Name	Relation	Age
William Heffernan	Head	67
James Heffernan	Son	30
Margt Heffernan	D.in-law	29
Barney Heffernan	G.son	24
Willie Heffernan	G.son	17
Patrick Heffernan	G.son	15
Willie J. Heffernan	G.son	12
Ann Skelly	Head	60
Patrick Skelly	Son	32
James Skelly	Son	30
Katie Skelly	Daugh.	28
Maggie Skelly	Daugh.	26
Lizzie Skelly	Daugh.	24
John Connell	Head	60
Mary Connell	Wife	52
John Connell	Son	24
Bernard Connell	Son	22
Patrick Connell	Son	12
Maria Connell	Daugh.	12

CHAPTER 24

Hare Island (Inis Ainghin)

Hare Island or Inis Ainghin is located in the parish of St Mary's, Athlone, the barony of Brawney, the Catholic dioceses of Ardagh and Clonmacnois and the county of Westmeath. Its nearest landmark on the mainland is Coosan Point some 800 metres away.

Hare Island.

One of the great *eureka* moments in relation to the historiography of Lough Ree and its islands must surely have been the meeting between Rose Killen, a former inhabitant of Hare Island, and John O'Donovan in 1837[1]. Rose Killen, when asked by O'Donovan about the name of the holy well on the island, replied that she had never heard a name for it but had often seen people make "Stations" at it. When O'Donovan then asked her whether she ever heard an old name for the island it must have been music to his ears when she replied "Inis Ainin". It had long been a source of puzzlement to historians as to which island was referred to in the annals as "Inis Ainghin." Now O'Donovan had cracked it.

The name "Inis Ainghin" turns up in various annals (including the *Annals of the Four Masters* and the *Annals of Clonmacnoise*) as well as in the *Latin and Irish lives of St. Ciaran*.

St. Ciaran

Several chroniclers have left us lives of St. Ciaran but they contain various anomalies and variations in date and thus we cannot be categorical about his date or place of birth. It is generally agreed that he was born in Co. Roscommon – the son of Beoaidh and Darerca – and that his father was a chariot-maker or carpenter by trade. Whatever about his year of birth, his death is generally agreed to have taken place in the year 549. He studied under the two greatest church leaders of his day: St. Finian of Clonard and St. Enda of Aran. While studying under St. Enda on the largest of the

Aran Islands, Inishmore, Ciaran had a vision of a large tree planted in the centre of Ireland, its branches overspreading the land, with a myriad of birds alighting on it and carrying its fruits over land and sea. St. Enda interpreted this vision for him. "The tree is thyself," he said "and your work will bear fruit and spread throughout the world," and with these words he encouraged Ciaran to return to the midlands and start his own monastery.[2]

Ciaran left Aran and came first to Scattery Island on the Shannon estuary where he worked for a time with St. Senan. Then, making his way up-river, he came to the "great ford of antiquity" which was later to become Athlone. As he made his way northwards towards Lough Ree and his homeland, he was obviously greatly taken with the beauty of Inis Ainghin. As with many of the details of the saint's life, there are two different accounts of how St. Ciaran got Inis Ainghin. One version of the story, from the *Book of Navan*, claims he received the island from Diarmuid, king of Ireland, while another source (a life of Ciaran contained in the *Book of Lismore*) claims that "a priest named Daniel, filled with God's grace, presented Inis Ainghin, which he owned, in perpetuity to the Almighty and St. Ciaran."[3]

There is a piece of folklore relating to Ciaran's time on Hare Island which was still spoken about in nineteenth century Athlone. It is the story of "The Coosan robbers." Apparently, Ciaran's father gave him a cow to provide milk for the monastery. Ciaran walked the cow from Roscommon to Athlone but was then faced with the logistical nightmare of getting it to the island. He tethered the beast on the mainland at Coosan in order to get assistance, but by the time he returned to collect it the cow had been stolen by the Coosan robbers.

St. Ciaran on Inis Aingin

Two stories which come to us from the *Latin and Irish lives of St. Ciaran* have been re-told several times. The following version comes from Fr. John O'Hanlon's *Lives of the Irish Saints:*

> *While he dwelt in Inis-Aingin, Ciaran one day heard a noise in the harbour. He then said to the brethren there, "Go to meet*

Old Church in Inis-Aingen, Lough Ree.

your future abbot". When reaching the harbour, however, they only found a heathen youth, and this they reported to Ciaran. "Nevertheless," he replied, "go again for him, since it is manifest to me from his voice that he shall be your abbot after me". Then the youth was brought to Ciaran. His name was Enna Mac-Hui-Laigsi, and having received tonsure, he read under Ciaran. He was a holy man, admirable in the Lord's sight, and he succeeded Ciaran as abbot in Inis Aingin. [4]

The second story concerns the naming of Gospel-Book Harbour, a name which is recorded on the Ordnance Survey map. As with many other stories of Ciaran, the re-telling of this one causes further confusion, because in it a different successor to Ciaran as abbot of Inis Aingin is named:

It so happened that Ciaran's Book of Gospels was dropped into the lake by a careless brother. There it remained for a long time. On a certain day in summer, cows went into the water, and the strap of that Book stuck to the foot of one animal, that brought it quite dry to the landing place. When opened, not a single letter was defaced, and afterwards the landing place was called Port in Sosceoil, or Harbour of the Gospel. A certain man, named Donnan, came from Corco-Baiscin to St. Ciaran. He was son to a brother of Senan, son of Gergenn, while he and Senan had the same mother. Senan said to him "What dost thou wish or why dost thou come?" He replied "To seek a place wherein I may abide and serve God." When Ciaran had resolved on leaving Aingin, after a residence of three years and three months, he intended Donnan should succeed him. He also left with him as reliquaries, that Book of Gospels which had been recovered from the lake, his bell, and his bearer Mael Odran. [5]

St. Ciaran left Inis Aingin and went down river to found Clonmacnois, one of the great monasteries of Ireland which, with the charisma of Ciaran combined with the patronage of kings, soon flourished. Within a century of its foundation Clonmacnois had become internationally known as a university city which was greatly respected as a centre of art, learning and spirituality.

The Evidence of the Annals

The *Annals of the Four Masters,* under the year 894 A.D., state:

An army was led by the Connaughtmen into Westmeath. Inis Aingin was profaned and a man was mortally wounded in the middle of it, and the shrine of Ciaran there, and a synod of seniors, with Cairbre Crom, bishop of Cluain-Mic-Nois. A victory was gained on the same day over the Connaughtmen, at Ath-Luain (Athlone), by (the men of) Westmeath, and a slaughter of heads left behind with them. [6]

The island had long been in the *paruchia* of Clonmacnois, but the presence of the bishop of Clonmacnois on the island in 894 A.D. suggests that the monastery was still considered to be of great importance. A further entry for the following year: 895 states that Toichiuch of Inis Aingin died. Toichiuch was, presumably, the abbot of the monastery at that time. The island was repeatedly plundered. According to the annals raids took place in 843, 894, 1087 and 1089. For 1087 we find the following entry:

Munstermen brought a greater fleet on the river of Synann, and Loghrye & robbed and took spoyles of the churches upon the islands of the Lough. King of Connaught, seeing, hee caused to be stopped the foordes on the Synann called Adyrchreach and Rathkrae, to the end they should be at liberty to pass the said passages at their

Returnes, and were driven to the turne to Athlone where they were overtaken by Donell Mcfflynn O'Melaghlin, King of Meath, to whose protection they wholly committed themselves and yielded all their shippes, barkes, boates and coyttes alsoe to be disposed off at his pleasure, which hee received and sent safe conduct with them until they were left in their native place in Mounster" [7]

It would seem likely that the early monastery on the island continued on until the twelfth century. Gwynn and Hadcock are of the opinion that it may have come under Augustinian rule some time after 1140.

The Vikings

The history of Viking activity on Lough Ree has been described in chapter three above. However, based on the discovery of two major Viking hoards on Hare Island in 1802 we can safely assume that the island was among those occupied by the Vikings during either or both of their major periods of occupation on Lough Ree. Charles Vallancey, writing in 1804, records a hoard which contained "ten gold bracelets, a number of silver anklets, and some ingots of silver" which had been found on Hare Island two years previously. The pieces were then in the possession of "Mr Delandre, goldsmith, in Skinner-Row, Dublin" he having "purchased them for 700l. and upwards." According to Professor J.A. Graham-Campbell of London University, who estimates the gold hoard at c 5 kilos: this was "a hoard unique in the Western world, and one of exceptional size surpassing all previous gold finds of the period." [8]

Viking gold arm-ring from Hare Island.

The Marquis of Lansdowne purchased the gold antiquities in Dublin. In 1812, after his death, they were offered for sale again, this time by Messrs Rundel and Bridge, Silversmiths of Ludgate Street, London. Fortunately for us Vallancey had made drawings of four of the ten arm-rings because it seems that they were later consigned to the melting pot. This is not perhaps so surprising when one considers that the intrinsic value of the hoard was put at "nearly a thousand guineas." [9]

We can tell from the surviving descriptions that this was a hoard of great significance. A British antiquarian described the arm-rings: "some are sculptured with the heads of serpents, and others with fancy ornaments by no means devoid of elegance." [10]

The Island in Medieval Times

After 1185 the Dillons, a Norman family who occupied the nearby barony of Kilkenny West, are said to have built a monastery here. Perhaps they rebuilt the earlier monastery. It would seem that the church remains, which survive on the island today, may be a relic of this twelfth century development. The extant remains include a late Romanesque nave and chancel church surrounded by traces of a monastic enclosure and other earthworks. There is a suggestion that the monks from Hare Island may have transferred to the monastery at Saints' Island.

The Dillons would seem to have continued on as proprietors of Hare Island after the dissolution of the monastery. Sir James Dillon negotiated the surrender of Athlone to Sir Charles Coote, Lord President of Connacht, in 1651. He himself surrendered in May 1652 and retired with his family to Hare Island. The following year his estate was confiscated and he went into exile in Flanders in 1653 until the restoration. In the parliament of 1661 Athlone was represented by a Dublin merchant, Ridgely Hatfield, who was sheriff of Westmeath, and Lt. Arthur St. George, both of whom were ex-commonwealth supporters. In the Cromwellian settlements Hatfield was granted land including Hare Island. It passed from the Hatfield family to a family named Hackett in the eighteenth century. The Hackett family, in turn sold the island to the Handcock family, one of the two ruling families of Athlone, who had their seat at Moydrum Castle and a sporting lodge on Hare Island.

The Duffy Family

Today Hare Island is in the ownership of the Duffy family. This family has had a known connection with the island for over 200 years. They almost certainly descended from a Connacht sept of the Duffy clan which had its territory at Lissonuffy (or Lissyduffy) near Strokestown in County Roscommon. They were neighbours of the Hanlys some of whom settled on the Black Islands. The most valuable account we have of this island was written by John O'Donovan in his *Ordnance Survey Letters of County Westmeath* in 1837:

> *Yesterday being a glorious day, O'Conor and I hired a boat at Athlone and we were rowed down (rectus up) Lough Ree with considerable rapidity. The scenery is magical, but tame and tranquil, Slieve Baane being the only object which adds a little sublimity to the scenery.*

Landing-Place at Hare Island, Lough Ree.

Lough Ree is thick set with very beautiful islands sparsely scattered in it, here a cluster, there a solitary island. We landed on Carbry's Island to see if it contained anything of antiquarian interest and learn, if possible, who the Carbry was from whom it received its name, but it contains nothing but a cottage belonging to Mr. Naghtan.

From here we proceeded to the Hare Island, a large island (150 acres) wooded with native timber and containing a good house (a large cottage) belonging to Lord Castlemaine. This, said I to myself, was very imposing to an early Saint to settle upon it; let us try if we could discover any monument of its early inhabitation by God's blessed people. We landed and were struck forcibly with the civilisation of the place. Mrs Duffy, who, and whose husband, take care of the house and island, at once showed us a small church of the primitive age, but with its lancet windows very much injured. I asked her how long she was living on the island and she said forty years.

O'Donovan: "Did you ever hear any name on the church?"
Mrs. Duffy: "No."
O'Donovan: "Why was it called Hare Island?"
Mrs. Duffy: "From the number of hares and rabbits that used to be on it, but there is not one on it now."
O'Donovan: "When did it cease to be a burial place?"
Mrs. Duffy: "About 100 years ago, as the old people say".
O'Donovan: "Is there any holy well on the island?"
Mrs. Duffy: "There is". And she walked to the place and showed it. It lies near the shore and is now nearly choaked (sic) up with briars and rotten branches.
O'Donovan: "Has this well any name?"
Mrs. Duffy: "No".
O'Donovan: "How do you know then that it is a holy well?"
Mrs. Duffy: "When I came to live here about 40 years ago, I saw rags tied on the bushes which then grew over it, and the old woman who had care of the island before me told me not to use the water of it for washing or boiling potatoes, that it was a blessed well and that it might not be proper to use it."
O'Donovan: "Is that old woman still living?"
Mrs. Duffy: "She is. She lives in Cuarsen just opposite my finger on the other side of the water. Her name is Rose Killen".

O'Donovan: "Do you think she knows the old names of the island, the church and the well?
Mrs. Duffy: "It is very likely she does, because she, and I believe, her father before her, was born on the island, and she knows Irish, which I do not.[11]

Early Christian graveslab

Before leaving Hare Island John O'Donovan enquired about the presence of any inscribed stones or interesting artefacts on the island; Mrs Duffy recalled one such stone with an inscription on it which had baffled earlier scholars who had visited the

Early Christian grave slab from Hare Island based on a drawing by George Petrie in Christian Inscriptions in the Irish Language, *ed. Margaret Stokes, (Dublin, 1873).*

island. She had not seen the stone for some time but O'Donovan eventually located it and made a drawing of it. This stone has been missing for many years. However the accuracy of O'Donovan's drawing has been called into question by modern scholars who favour the drawing done by George Petrie in 1822 and published in *Christian inscriptions in the Irish language* which was edited by Margaret Stokes in 1873. The stone was carved in the Clonmacnois tradition and is related to the group of slabs bearing small crosses potent within a square frame. One example of such a slab has been dated to circa 781 A.D. strengthening the claim that there was a long association between the two centres. Indeed, the presence of this stone together with the ruins of a stone church suggests a continuity of the monastic tradition from the establishment of the first foundation by St. Ciaran in the sixth century until the dissolution of the monasteries in the time of Henry VIII. The inscription on the stone, as recorded by Petrie, reads "Or ar Tuathcharan"– modern scholarship has failed to identify the person commemorated by this stone.

Lord Castlemaine: Hare Lodge

In the nineteenth century the island continued to be occupied by the Duffy family who now served a new master in the person of William Handcock, later to become Lord Castlemaine. Handcock, an M.P. for Athlone, attended a public dinner in Dublin in 1799 and his contribution to the evening's entertainment has been well recorded by Sir Jonah Barrington:

Lord Castlemaine's Lodge, Hare Island.

Never was a more cordial, happy assemblage of men of rank, consideration and proven integrity, collected in one chamber, than upon that remarkable occasion. Every man's tried and avowed principles were supposed to be untaintable, and pledged to his own honour and his country's safety; and amongst others, Mr Handcock, member for Athlone, appeared to be conspicuous: he spoke strongly, gave numerous anti-union toasts, vowed his eternal hostility to so infamous a measure, pledged himself to God and man to resist it to extremities, and to finish and record his sentiments, he had composed an anti-union song of many stanzas, which he sung himself with a general chorus, to celebrate the spirit, the cause, and the patriotism of the meeting; this was encored more than once by the company, and he withdrew towards day with the reputation of being in 1799, the most pure, unflinching opponent of the measure he so cordially resisted.[12]

His loyalty to the cause was short-lived. He was approached by the viceroy who, when he couldn't simply bribe him, endeavoured to persuade him that his principles were disloyal, his song was seditious and that his continued opposition might end in treason. Barrington claims that William held out "until title was added to the bribe, his own conscience was not strong enough to resist the charge, the vanity of his family lusted for nobility." William wavered but eventually yielded to the promise of money, power and title. As Barrington summarises it William "made and sang songs against the Union in 1799, at a public dinner of the opposition; and made and sang songs for it in 1800; he got a peerage."[13]

Thus by 1812 he was rewarded for his support for the Union. He was created Baron and took the title Lord Castlemaine. He soon decided to build a new home in keeping with his status. He employed a leading architect, Sir Richard Morrison, to design it. The building, Moydrum Castle, was completed in 1814 in a sham gothic style giving the external appearances of an ancient castle but having all the comforts of a gentleman's residence of the day. It appears that having designed his castle that he also engaged Morrison to design a hunting lodge on Hare Island which was an ideal retreat for him allowing himself the opportunity to engage in fishing, shooting and boating on Lough Ree.

The Moate-born Gaelic scholar, Thomas O'Neill Russell writing in 1897 had this to say about Hare Island:

"Hare Island is the most beautiful island in the lake; seen from the waters or from the mainland it seems a mass of leaves. The trees grow on it so thickly that they dip their branches into the water almost all round it. Lord Castlemaine has a charming rustic cottage on Hare Island, and the pleasure grounds attached to it are laid out with very great taste and skill. It is one of the most beautiful sylvan retreats in Europe".[14]

The architecture on Hare Island is vastly different to that of any other island on Lough Ree. While vestigial remains of one or two earlier houses survive, the main buildings are two two-storey farm-houses located beside Lord Castlemaine's lodge. These are fine houses probably built to accommodate servants or to provide extra hospitality for visiting guests. The quality of these houses is

The Lord's Harbour, Hare Island, early 20th century.

eclipsed by that of the wonderful lodge which, even in its rather poor state today, still readily impresses the visitor. Looking at the ballroom one can easily imagine the great Victorian *soirées* which were held here and which were attended by the lords and ladies and even by royalty.

We know, for example, that his Royal Highness, Prince George of Cambridge, stayed on Hare Island as a guest of Lord Castlemaine in May 1850. He inspected the troops in the garrison, and having spent a short time in the barracks he expressed himself highly pleased with the general efficiency and appearance of the men. On the occasion of his visit he was presented with an address by members of Athlone town commissioners. Besides the usual frills and trimmings this address contained reference to a matter which was giving rise to a certain amount of anxiety in the town. The relevant part of the address read as follows:

We take leave, most respectfully, to convey to your Royal Highness, the anxious wish of the inhabitants of Athlone and neighbourhood that the garrison would be continued headquarters as a military station, which it has been from time immemorial, and that your Royal Highness would be graciously pleased to have restored to the town the advantages of a resident staff, of which it has lately been deprived. Under these circumstances we have to request your Royal Highness's special attention to the superiority of claim which Athlone possesses over Kilkenny, to which latter town a portion of the staff of this garrison has been removed, and that whilst the Dublin, the Cork or Southern, the Limerick, the Kilkenny and the Belfast districts have each a resident general, Athlone, the centre of Ireland, and heretofore the residence of the general in command of the Western District, has been left without one.[15]

When the prince did not respond to the address the town commissioners decided to follow it up by sending a deputation to Hare Island. However, Lord Castlemaine intervened and wrote to the town clerk, William Kelly stating:

His Royal Highness feels that he has nothing whatsoever to say to the military arrangements, with respect to the general and staff being removed from Athlone (those changes altogether emanating from his grace the commander-in-chief). He sees no use in receiving the deputation and begs me to intimate this to the commissioners through you.[16]

Hare Lodge has been described by Mark Bence-Jones as:

An engagingly hybrid early 19th century 'cottage' on an island in Lough Ree, giving the impression of having been concocted out of the "leftover" from several different houses of various styles and periods: an 18th century classical door-case with a pediment on console brackets, Georgian gothic windows, a mullioned bow-window with leaded lights and a regency veranda with slender iron columns under the eaves of the roof.[17]

The following description of the "Lord's Harbour" on Hare Island was penned by L.T.C. Rolt in *Green and Silver* published in 1949:

...with a narrow entrance between massive stone walls, it was a replica in miniature of the harbours in Cornish fishing coves. We ran in and beached beside a black tub of a boat which was obviously used for transporting livestock. From the water, the island had appeared to be completely clothed in dense woodland, but when we landed we discovered that its southern half consisted of meadow land screened by a narrow shelter belt of trees. The sward was of wonderful green richness, and the condition of the young beasts which were at graze confirmed its quality.[18]

On July 3rd, 1921, in retaliation for the burning of three homes in Coosan by the British military, a party of Republicans arrived at Moydrum Castle and ordered Lady Castlemaine and her daughters to dress and leave the castle. They were allowed to take with them some of the family silver before the building was set on fire. With the burning of Moydrum and the uncertain political situation, the Handcocks abandoned their Moydrum estate and departed, leaving Hare Island in the possession of the Duffy family, who in due course became its owners.[19]

The Twentieth Century

Throughout the twentieth century members of the Duffy family have lived on and farmed Hare Island. Today, although he lives on the mainland, the island continues to be farmed and maintained by Noel Duffy. The Duffy family made short-term lettings of Hare Lodge as a summer home to a number of people. Among those to rent the property were Sean MacBride S.C., later a Nobel and Lenin peace prize recipient. Mr McBride and his family spent many a happy summer having Hare Island as a base for their boating activities on Lough Ree. At other times the lodge was occupied by John and Betty Williams and during their occupation of the lodge it also had many famous visitors. Betty Williams is the daughter of Col Harry Rice the author of *Thanks for the memory,* one of the all-time favourite books on the Shannon. Harry Rice, a native of Portarlington, was a medical doctor who had served with the British army in India. Sean MacBride described him as "a remarkably gifted person – he was a good doctor, a mechanic, a sailor, a writer and a good cartographer"[20] and even this description falls short of the full picture.

Among those who visited Hare Island in the company of Harry Rice were the novelist L.A.G. Strong who spent an evening enthralled by his story-telling and was later to use a story related by Rice as the basis for a novel *The Light above the lake* which was published by Methuen in 1958. In his book *Irsches Tegebuch (Irish Journal)* Heinrich Böll, a Nobel prize-winner for literature has a chapter dealing with his visit

Cover of L.A.G. Strong's novel which was inspired by Harry Rice.

to Hare Island. His diary recaptures highlights of visits which he made to Ireland in 1954 and 1955. His reason for visiting Hare Island was to record on colour film a brief cameo of an old islander, one of the Duffys, who was then eighty-eight years old. Böll describes coming ashore to be met by the "old man" who "raised his cap – his hair was white, fluffy and thick – he made our boat fast, we jumped ashore and, smiling at each other, exchanged the "lovely day" – "nice day" – "wonderful day", the highly complicated simplicity of greeting in countries where the weather is always threatened by rain gods, and as soon as we set foot on the little island it seemed as if time closed over our heads like a vortex."[21]

The boatman who brought Böll and his cameraman, George, to Hare Island was none other than Colonel Harry Rice whom Böll describes as being like a combination of Robinson Crusoe and Mephistopheles. For anyone who wants a wonderfully poetic appreciation of one of the islands of Lough Ree the essay "A Small contribution to Occidental Mythology" in Böll's *Irish journal* is an absolute must.

Another visitor to Hare Island was the artist Pauline Bewick along with her friend and fellow artist Lesley McWeeney who is the sister of Cynthia Rice, Harry Rice's second wife. Pauline Bewick remembers being struck by the beauty of the island.

Today the island remains in private ownership. It is a haven for wild-life and a wonderfully natural habitat, with its predominantly oak woodland and exceptionally rich ground flora.

In 1996/97 a feasibility study was undertaken, with the backing of the Heritage Council, to consider the case for the "Hare Island Millennium Athenaeum" - a multi-purpose study centre in the heart of the Irish midlands. It was hoped that it could become "a centre for thought, learning, reflection, meditation, meeting, discussion and the development of individual creativity expressed through the visual arts, science, philosophy, conservation and leisure."[22]

All those who were involved in the project were convinced of the value of such a centre. However, funding did not materialise and the report was shelved. Perhaps at a future date somebody will resurrect this report and invest in this concept, which would be entirely compatible with the conservation and preservation of this unique island.

CHAPTER 25

Inchmore

As its name suggests Inchmore is the largest of all the islands on Lough Ree. It is situated in the parish of Bunown and the Barony of Kilkenny West in County Westmeath. The island consists of some 200 acres. At the time of Griffith's Valuation in 1854 it was held by the Marquis of Westmeath, though we know there were other residents on the island also.

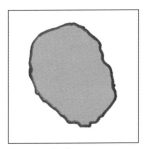

Inchmore

Early History

On high ground at the south end is a ring fort indicating that this island knew human habitation from early times. Throughout Ireland ring forts survived largely due to superstition. They were often called fairy-forts and it was considered unwise to interfere unduly with them; therefore farmers worked around them rather than risk the wrath of the spirit world. In reality these ring forts were protected enclosures for human habitation. During the early Christian period such an enclosure would have contained shelters both for man and beast. The farmers who lived here were strong farmers, possibly the family who founded or supported the local church. The original house, like the fort itself, was circular in shape, with one or two living chambers. As the most likely building material was hazel, which grew locally in abundance, we would expect nothing to survive except the traces of post holes. The circular house had a thatched roof with a smoke-hole above the stone hearth. The sleeping arrangements were platforms of branches and twigs layered with leaves and other vegetable matter. The family occupying this enclosure were self-sufficient, with their own limekiln and a quern-stone for grinding their corn.

Early Monasticism

The monastic ruins on Inchmore consist of one featureless church on the north side. However, despite a dearth of physical evidence surviving today, the early history and tradition relating to Inchmore is of very considerable interest and importance.

The foundation of the monastic settlement is attributed to a fifth century monk, St. Lioban (or Liberius), the son of Lossenus. There is a tradition, which is unsubstantiated by documentation, that by the eighth century this monastery had become an active house of the *céli dé* (or culdees). The *céli dé* brought about an ascetic revival within the Celtic church. For the year 1103 the Four Masters mention the death of "the lector Ua Connmhaigh of the family of Inis Mór." The Ua Connmhaigh name continued to appear among the monastic clergy of the lake islands. (See Saints' Island above)

Canons Regular

Some time before 1170, Inchmore had apparently become a priory of the Canons Regular of St. Augustine. In later times Inishmore was probably dependent on the larger priory at Saints' Island.

From Church to State

In 1567 Sir Henry Sidney, Queen Elizabeth's deputy in Ireland, and the man responsible for building the first stone bridge across the Shannon at Athlone, recommended to her majesty that the Baron of Delvin, a member of the Nugent family of Westmeath, be granted Inchmore on Lough Ree. Elizabeth acceded to Sidney's request and the lands were granted for a period of twenty years. Despite the twenty-year grant the island obviously remained with the family for considerably longer. A further grant recorded in the *Calendar of Papal Documents* relates that in 1635 the Pope permitted the Earl of Westmeath to retain the property during the schism. The papal grant was made on condition that, if the schism should come to an end, the earl would restore the abbeys to whatever orders had previously held them. The Nugent estates were very considerable;

apart from Inchmore they also held the lands of Fore, which had a very large monastic site.

The Marquis of Westmeath

The earls of Westmeath continued to occupy Inchmore over the next two and a half centuries, and some of the best stories concerning the island relate to the Nugent family. One such story is contained in a charming (and scarce) little booklet called *Lough Ree and around it*, written by W.J. Nash and printed for him by Athlone Printing Works in 1949. In it is an anecdote which was passed down to him through his father. He relates it as follows:

> *The Marquis of Westmeath had a summer residence on Inchmore about the middle of the last century. The Marquis, then a very old man, who was in the army when young, used to boast that he had fought Napoleon in Egypt and helped to defeat and capture his army there. He tried to make some of his fellow islanders pay rent to him, but they claimed to be freeholders from time immemorial. One sturdy woman chased him away with a pitchfork when he came to demand rent from her. The islanders remained freeholders. I remember, when we were children and Celia Kinlan an old woman, my father pointed her out to us as the woman who defeated the man who defeated the great Napoleon.[1]*

The Marquis married three times, the third time in 1864 at the age of eighty-one. However, despite his best efforts, he died without male issue and with him died the marquisate and so the islanders of Inchmore remained freeholders.

The Marquis occupied the big house on the island. The house is now in ruins. At the time of Griffith's Valuation the house had a rateable valuation of £6.10.0 per annum whereas many a good family home had a rateable valuation of between 5/- and 15/- per annum. The boundary wall of the old walled garden survives and inside it the remains of an orchard, with some damson and plum trees, still thriving. The house itself was served by Turf House Harbour – which entailed turf for use in the big house being ferried by boat from the Westmeath shore. The boat would then circle the island to allow the unloading of turf out of view of the house and the turf could then be brought to the house through the servants' entrance.

A Very Special School

While the children on the other islands on Lough Ree generally headed to the mainland for their education those on Inchmore and nearby Inchturk were fortunate to have their own school. The first school on the island was grant-aided from 1st January 1905. The teacher, who had trained in Belfast, was Catherine (Kate) McKeon. It was exceptional for a

Child's headline copy-book from the National School on Inchmore, corrected by the teacher on 22 September, 1920.

school to be sanctioned with less than twenty-five pupils, but this school had an average of a dozen scholars only. At first school was held in a room in a vacant house owned by Ralph Smyth, possibly the house vacated by the Marquis of Westmeath. The Smyths, who owned the nearby castle at Portlick, had land on Inchmore also.

The permanent schoolhouse dates from 1927. Due to dwindling populations on Inchmore and the neighbouring islands, this school closed in the 1940s and the pupils and teacher transferred to the mainland. Among those who taught in the national school on Inchmore were: Martha Berry (later Mrs Bergin) who moved to Wexford, Mrs Kathleen Egan of Connaught Street, Athlone and Mrs Brid Gibbons (nee Gavin) of Clonown, who later moved to Cork.

Mrs Kathleen Egan was a popular teacher on the island before she transferred to the national school in Tang. Life as an island schoolteacher was not an easy one. Mrs Egan cycled from Athlone to Killeenmore Point on a Monday morning from where she was transferred by boat to the island. She spent her working week on the island, lodging with the O'Keeffe family, and was transferred back to the mainland on a Friday after school. The O'Keeffe family later moved to Athlone and lived in the vicinity of Fry Place.

The Islanders

From eighteenth century newspapers we learn the names of a few islanders. Miss Bell, the daughter of Robert Bell, died at Inchmore in 1772. In 1776, a Thomas Stanley died on the island, and the same year Edward Cotton married a Miss Stanley on Inchmore.[2] Griffith's Valuation introduces us to the Tiernans, Nolans and Celia Keeffe.

Johnny Harte, born on Inchturk but reared by his grandparents on Inchmore knows a great deal about island life. One of the words which cropped up regularly in his reminiscences was "spraoi", a word used by the islanders to describe a coming together of neighbours to eat, drink and celebrate. The islanders didn't need any great excuse to engage in celebrations: an American wake, the return of a family from abroad, a visitor to the island or the killing of a pig all opened the way for an evening of entertainment. Music, dancing and story-telling would go on well into the night, and the camaraderie and the "craic" were second to none.

The islands could not support large families, so in each generation emigration was a necessity. Most of the

Farm on Inchmore.
Michael Quigley, Brian and Síle Sidey.

Baiting the line.
Joe Quigley and Cliff Archibold.

Brammer's Bucket.
Jim Walsh (half hidden), Inchturk; Pat Slevin, Wineport;
John Walsh, Killeenmore; Joe Igoe and Michael Quigley.

island families had some family members in America. The sense of neighbourliness on the islands was always very strong. In many cases the islanders from one island took marriage partners from a neighbouring island, thus the genealogies of many of the families show such familiar surnames as Tiernan, Quigley, Ganly, Hanly, Walsh and McGee. The killing of a pig on the island was an occasion of joy for all. Not only did the family who owned the pig benefit but all families could expect a share of the bounty. The islanders prided themselves on their self-sufficiency and quite apart from fish each family had hens, ducks, pigs, sheep and perhaps a goat or two. They even grew sufficient potatoes on the islands to sell some in the markets of Athlone.

A Tall Story

There is a story told, perhaps no more than a tall tale, which hints at these islands having been mini-Republics at times. There were two bachelor brothers one of whom borrowed a sum of money from a financial institution in Athlone and forgot to repay it. In due course the dreaded process-server arrived on the island to issue legal proceedings. He sought out the house of the two brothers and was directed as to how to find it. Having made his way he arrived outside the house and was invited in by one of the brothers. When he tried to issue the summons he was ordered to sit at the kitchen table and was made eat the summons complete with the envelope until no trace remained. As he chewed on this tasteless tit-bit the brothers debated with one another what they would do with him if he should ever re-appear. They decided that they would bring him out to Illanfan, a small rocky knoll of less than half an acre in extent, and abandon him there – where they warned he would "never see the eyes of a white man again." As he made his way home he surely glanced at Illanfan and realised the truth of the threat. It is said that just as the brother had forgotten to repay the loan, so too did the process-server forget to return to the island and the original debt was written off.

1901 Census

Name	Relation	Age
John Tiernan	Head	62
Margaret Tiernan	Wife	45
James Tiernan	Son	16
Michael Tiernan	Son	14
John Tiernan	Son	12
Elizabeth Tiernan	Daughter	9
William Quigley	Head	42
James Tiernan	Head	76
Bridgit Tiernan	Wife	73
Thomas Tiernan	Son	42
Margaret Tiernan	Daugh. in law	24
Michael Nolan	Head	82
John Nolan	Son	27
Kate Nolan	Daugh. in law	24
Michael Nolan	Son	24
Nannie Nolan	G.Daughter	3mths.
Matthew Fegan	Head	65
Mary Ann Fegan	Wife	68
John Fegan	Son	36
James Fegan	Son	26
Margaret Fegan	Daughter	20
Bartle Keefe	Head	65
James Keefe	Son	30
Bartle Keefe	Son	28
Ellen Keefe	Daughter	25
Bridget Keefe	Daughter	21
Celia Kinlan	Aunt	76

CHAPTER 26

Inchturk

Inchturk (literally the island of the wild-boar) is in the parish of Noughaval, Poor Law Union of Athlone, and County of Westmeath and consists of 50 acres, 1 rood and 6 perches. Harry Rice in *Thanks for the memory* makes the point that the island was not sufficiently extensive to support a wild-boar but speculates that perhaps one "swam across from the mainland when hunted by

Inchturk

hounds, in ancient times." Rice also makes the interesting observation that the three islands in this part of the lake - Inchmore, Inchturk and Inchbofin - all bear similar names to islands off the Connemara coast[1]. Unlike its neighbouring islands, Inchturk does not have any traces of monastic life or early human settlement. However, as pointed out in the case of Nuns' Island, Micheál Ó Braonáin, the Gaelic poet of the eighteenth century, inherited a tradition of convents of nuns - "dhá theampall" - on this island in medieval times.

At the time of the compilation of the tithe applotment books for the area, in 1829, the island had only one family in residence and the householder was listed as William Ganly. William farmed fifteen acres of first-class land, fifteen acres of second-class land and ten acres of third-class land. The nineteenth century seems to have witnessed a great growth in the island population, and twenty five years later, in Griffith's Valuations, there were four householders listed: William Ganly, Patrick Magee, Patrick Quigley and William Ganly Junior. At the height of its population in the early twentieth century Inchturk had seven or eight lived-in houses. The same family names continued and the list of householders included another family of Ganly as well as the Slevin and Walsh families.

Johnny Harte has recorded the names of several bays and inlets: The Bream-hole (pronounced Brame-hole); The Yackeens, The Rigoges; Connie's Point and Lanarue. There are still some cottages which are habitable but many which have fallen into ruin. As he revisited the island what might have passed as mere derelict cottages were, to him, living relics of childhood. He could recall each family by name and recall the number of children raised in each homestead. These stone-built cottages, with their

Old cattle-boat at Killeenmore, used to transport cattle to and from the island.

thatch long since fallen in, had in his lifetime, buzzed with family life. Looking into a two-roomed ruin he recalled the griddle bread served up by the woman of the house. It was not too difficult to imagine the flock of noisy children gathered at the foreshore to welcome home the fishermen or the early-morning mass-goers leaving from Connie's point, on an empty stomach, for a trip across the lake to the mainland and a long trek to eight o'clock mass in Tubberclare. As they made their way home from Sunday mass the smell of rashers cooking on the island wafted across the lake to meet them. Food never tasted so good.

The death knell for island life on Inchmore and Inchturk was sounded when the Fisheries Board bought out the traditional fishing rights from the islanders.

Evictions

Towards the end of the nineteenth century there were a number of evictions on the island. The islanders had been in dispute with their landlord since 1885 at least. In that year the agent, Ambrose Bole of Ballymahon, visited the islands where he was met by the sheriff's bailiffs. Fr Murray pleaded for the tenants and an amicable settlement was negotiated with the islanders each agreeing to pay what they were able. In 1891-92 they stopped paying again and by the autumn of 1895 police were preparing to carry out evictions. A reporter from *The Westmeath Independent* newspaper wrote a lengthy article which was headed "EVICTION – A Collapse in Inchturk – Police Preparations – Excitement in Athlone – Boats Seized On – The Islanders Prepared." The background to the islander's plight and the reporter's impression of the island are worth quoting:

The island is almost inaccessible. It is in the first instance a tortuous journey from Athlone, but to land requires, at the moment of writing, the manoeuvring of a skilful sailor. The Shannon, disturbed by the weather, is in keeping with the temperament of the inhabitants, whose excitements harmonize with the fury of the swells from the lake which almost threaten inundation. No ruder aspect of life could be presented; suspicion seems inbred in the population. They were in hourly expectation of the eviction party, and the advent of a stranger wakened in them the wildest emotions, so that no small risk was hazarded in landing. One saw a cluster of people down at the water line. They were menacing and demonstrative, but, assured of the fact that this visit was not hostile, were warm and generous. The islanders are miserably poor.

A street is the term applied to what is really a duck-pond running through the extent of five or six houses. They are of the most primitive fashion without any pretension to cleanliness or order. A frame-work of excellent stone is thatched with rushes, and there is plenty of ventilation owing to the absence of doors, and though windows are provided for in the structure, glass has been substituted by rags of various kinds embedded in the aperture. There are no out-offices, and accommodation is provided within the house for such live stock as the inhabitants lay claim to – in this instance a horse, some fowl, and a goat or two. A curiosity are the fish ponds in which are kept during the close season fish for the English markets. Those are indented on various parts of the island, and it is unnecessary to refer to the license of the people – sufficient to say, that at least they have good grounds for their illegalities, in the fact that while fish from northern Europe are placed in the English market two months before Irish fishermen, they have to resort to such practices to be in a position to compete.

In Athlone on Saturday evening the police preparations were of the most active character. The evening trains on the two lines brought in considerable forces from the adjoining districts, and they were stationed in town during the night.

On Sunday they were for the most confined to barracks, but as the occasion of the visit became known the greatest excitement was stirred in the town. This was accentuated by the effort to secure boats. The local policemen were despatched to the various boatmen in the vicinity of the town, but being unable to secure boats, it is stated that a seizure was made in two cases, and by the afternoon all arrangements were completed. The sub-sheriff was to arrive in Athlone by the mail train from Dublin, timed to arrive here at 10.30, and there was a squad of police to meet him. His absence was the first intimation that hostilities were for the time abandoned.

The fact of the evictions as contemplated not taking place on Monday is the first victory for the islanders. A rumour that a settlement had been effected is not the case.

Latest inquiries go to show that there is little probability of a settlement, and that the dispute between landlord and tenants was of longer duration than was hitherto stated. As far back as 1885 they were about to be dispossessed, and on that occasion the agent, Mr Ambrose Bole, Ballymahon, visited the island, where he was met by the sheriff's bailiffs. On that occasion the Rev. Father Murray pleaded for the tenants, and an amicable settlement was made, each paying what they could. Three of the tenants continued to pay to 1891 and 1893 when they stopped paying anything, and it was as a result that the proceedings now pending were instituted. The agent has informed us that to May, 1895, William Ganly, one of the tenants under notice, owed £6, and was asked to pay £1.10s.0d, with £1.10s.0d costs, leaving arrears of £4.10s.0d wiped out. The costs it will be noticed are as much as the rent asked for. In the case of Bridget Ganly there was due £41.18s.6d, and she was asked to pay £6.9s.0d and law costs amounting to £1.12s.6d., and she was forgiven in November, 1887, £17.17s.0d. Against Pat Magee there was due to May, '95, £30 and the landlord was satisfied to settle for £4.0s.0d., with £1.10s.6d costs. Against Edward Quigley, the remaining tenant under notice of eviction, there was due to the same period £29.4s.2d. He paid on account £2, and was asked to pay £2.8s.4d, with costs of £1.8s.6d." 2

At the time of the 1901 census Inchturk had a population of fifty: 17 males and 23 females. There were six inhabited houses on the island. Three had families of Ganly, one McGee, one Walsh and one Quigley. The oldest couple on the island was Patrick and Mary McGee. According to the census form Patrick at 75 years of age was born about 1826 while his wife, Mary, was born around the time that Queen Victoria took the throne in England. In the same house were living the two youngest children on the island: their grandson, Timothy McGee, at a year and a half and an eight month old baby, John Hanly, who was a Hanly of the Black Islands, a family related to the McGees by marriage.

1901 Census

Name	Relation	Age
Mary Ganly	Head	45
Mary A. Ganly	Daughter	28
Kate Ganly	Daughter	26
Bridget Ganly	Head	65
Michael Ganly	Son	35
Elizabeth Ganly	Daugh. in law	22
Ann Ganly	G.Daughter	9 mths
Patrick McGee	Head	75
Mary McGee	Wife	65
James McGee	Son	37
Ann McGee	Daugh. in law	27
Mary McGee	G.Daughter	6
Annmarie McGee	G.Daughter	4
Bridget McGee	G.Daughter	3
Timothy McGee	G.Son	1
John Hanly	G.Son	8 mths

John Ganly	Head	50
Lizzie Ganly	Wife	40
Mary Ganly	Daughter	20
Michael Ganly	Son	18
John Ganly	Son	17
Annie Ganly	Daughter	15
Bridget Ganly	Daughter	13
James Walsh	Head	53
William Walsh	Son	25
John Walsh	Son	20
Mary Walsh	Daughter	18
Norah Walsh	Daughter	16
Maggie Walsh	Daughter	12
Kate Walsh	Daughter	6
Edward Quigley	Head	50
Brigid Quigley	Wife	50
James Quigley	Son	26
Bernard Quigley	Son	20
Patrick Quigley	Son	20
Michael Quigley	Son	18
Mary Quigley	Daughter	16
Brigid Quigley	Daughter	14
Kate Quigley	Daughter	11

Fish-ponds

On Inchturk there is still evidence of the fish-pond, a feature which is to be found on other islands on Lough Ree, as well as by the lakeshore, as for example at Carley's in Portanure, and which was used by the islanders to store fish caught out of season. Where a communal pond was used each family marked their fish by taking a small piece out of a particular fin or from the tail of the fish – in this way each family knew their own fish. While fish were stored in the ponds the greatest threat to their safety was not the water-bailiff but the otter. An otter, which is itself a skilled fisherman would not alone take fish to eat but would continue to kill the fish for fun long after its appetite had been sated. Therefore while there was a good stock of trout in the ponds awaiting the opening of the fishing season, it was usual to mount a guard on the pond and burn bonfires around the perimeter of the pond at night to keep the otter at bay.

Fr Seamus Mulvany PP, Tubberclare, celebrates dawn Mass on Easter Sunday at Portlick on the shores of Lough Ree.

CHAPTER 27

Nuns' Island

Very close to the centre of Lough Ree lies the diminutive Nuns' Island, diminutive that is, in the context of lake islands inhabited at some stage in their history. It contains a mere seven acres. Its name is believed by some to have come from the Poor Clare nuns of Bethlehem, whose convent was plundered in 1642 (see Chapter 9). It is said that they sheltered on this island

Nuns' Island.

prior to escaping into Connacht on the following day. There is even a tradition that two graves on the island are those of the Poor Clare nuns. However, this account does not sit well with recorded events surrounding the attack on the Bethlehem convent. Indeed the suggestion that this island takes its name from the Poor Clares is of comparatively recent origin, and comes from a generation that was rapidly losing touch with the history of the lake and accepting names like King's Island, Hare Island and Quaker Island.

Micheál Ó Braonáin, the eighteenth century poet of the Shannon and Lough Ree, was writing at the onset of this period of national amnesia. His poem makes a unique contribution to the toponomy and nomenclature of the lake. O'Donovan was aware of it, as we know, and translated some of it, but he still had difficulty identifying the islands as most people did not then know that Quaker Island was Inis Clothrann, so great had been the change in the previous

A typical medieval Irish nun.

century. If we can take it that Ó Braonáin was in his fifties, at least, at the time of writing this poem he would, as a child, have heard the *seanchus* and folklore of this locality from the last of the 1600s. The spirit of his writing makes it clear that he was proud of his heritage and eager to conserve it and pass it on. In his poem he gives the name of the island as *"Inse Éan na Caillí Duibhe"*. The Caillí Dubha were the Black Nuns, namely, the Canonesses of St Augustine. The name is replicated at several medieval sites throughout Ireland, notably Templenagalliaghdoo on the shores of Lough Conn in Co. Mayo, in close proximity to Errew, site of a monastery for Augustinian canons in the Middle Ages. Ó Braonáin is absolutely precise in his use of grammar and so the name translates as "the Birds' Island of the Black Nun." He has more to tell us about this island and also Inchturk

> Ar Inis Toirc nach réimiúl timpeall,
> Ina aga i dtrasna bhíodh dhá theampall
> a mbíodh mná rialta, is a lán cinn eile
> I meán Inse Éan na Caillí Duibhe.[1]

which is translated as follows:

> On Inchturk, which is not extensive,
> In its space across there were two churches
> In which there used to be nuns, and many others
> In the middle of Nuns' Island.

These two islands, it would appear, housed the women's foundations on the lake. There are no remains on Inchturk, but Nuns' Island still has the ruins of a partly dilapidated twelfth century church and what appear to be wall footings of other buildings in the vicinity. The foundation is never mentioned in the annals. It has been equally ignored by the Board of Works, past and present, who has conserved most other monuments on the lake, including some that have much fewer surviving features. The Nuns' Island church has a beautiful twelfth century window in the Hiberno-Romanesque style in its east gable. The tooled stones of the embrasure are losing position. Some have already fallen and it would seem that before long the rest must also tumble down. Neither the ancient annals nor the modern state has seemed overly concerned to record the role of women in the Irish church and so this little historic gem from nine hundred years ago is settling down into oblivion.

In 1828, when the tithes list was being compiled, the island was occupied by one Martin Cunniff. He was adjudged liable for one shilling four and a half pence in tithes. Ten years later, O'Donovan visited and found a family - possibly that of Martin Cunniff, he doesn't tell us - residing there. He observed:

"(Nuns' Island) has on it the ruins of a nunnery, now converted into a cabin where resides a poor fisherman. He is obliged to take conacre in the country to feed his family." **2**

In Griffith's Valuation, 1854, it is given as Nim's island. The occupier was one Michael Fenoran living in a house with a rateable valuation of six shillings.

Church ruins, Nuns' Island.

CHAPTER 28

Friars' Island

This island, situated in the inner lakes, on Killinure Lough, is linked to the mainland by a narrow causeway. It takes its name from the Franciscan order, which has had a presence in Athlone since the 1230s. Following the dissolution of the monasteries at the time of the reformation, the outlawed friars of Athlone had a very precarious existence.

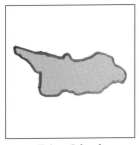

Friars Island.

Eventually a community of friars established itself on Friars' Island under the patronage of the Dillons where they established a permanent convent about 1626. The history of the order in Athlone has been meticulously researched and recorded by the late Fr Fergal Grannell O.F.M. He identifies Fr Anthony McGeoghegan, a native of Westmeath, as one of the first known superiors of the Friars' Island community.

Franciscan Friar as depicted by Archdall in 1786.

Fr Grannell also identifies some of the more famous friars who belonged to this community at one time or another. One was the controversial Franciscan author Raymond Caron (a native of Athlone). He also identifies the Dillon brothers of Killfaughney, Tubberclare, one of whom, Edward, had been appointed as bishop of Achonry in 1641 but he died before his consecration. The second brother, George, had a distinguished career both in

Ireland and France before being "successfully postulated as bishop of Elphin in 1660."[1]

Br Micheal O'Clery

There is a well documented link between the community on Friars' Island and the chief of the Four Masters, Br Micheal O'Clery. The isolation of this island community made it an ideal environment for a scribe to work, and O'Clery benefited from the hospitality of this community on several occasions. It was, apparently, here, in 1630, that the Four Masters worked in collaboration for the first time. Fr Grannell documents three visits by Micheal O'Clery to Friars' Island. During his first visit, in 1628, he transcribed a copy of the Life of St Ruadhan. His second visit was made the following year, at which time he transcribed a Life of St Ciaran, patron of Clonmacnois. His third visit was made in the autumn of 1630. He had been commissioned by Toirleach Mac Cochlain to compile a descriptive list of the monarchs of Ireland and a genealogy of the Irish saints. This work was a major undertaking. The finished product was to be called *Réim Ríoghraidhe na hÉireann agus Seanchas a Naomh.* O'Clery was joined at Friars' Island by three trained annalists: Fearfeasa O'Maolchonaire from County Roscommon, Cuchocriche O'Clery from County Donegal and Cuchocriche O'Duigeannain from County Leitrim – these four scholars have become known to posterity as the Four Masters. Grannell concludes that O'Clery may have stayed here again in 1636. Two fragmentary manuscripts which belonged to the Friars' Island community were given or sold to Sir James Ware in 1639 by the then guardian, Fr Anthony O'Daly, and these are now preserved in the Bodleian Library in Oxford.

The Dillons, patrons of the Franciscan community on Friars' Island, became embroiled in the aftermath of the Ulster Rebellion of 1641. Sir James Dillon had blockaded the bridge of Athlone to protect the Leinster side of Athlone from the armed forces of Viscount Ranelagh (Roger Jones), who was president of Connaught. When Ormond sent reinforcements to Athlone to invade the Dillon territory of Kilkenny West, Sir James was forced to withdraw into

County Longford. Friars' Island was overrun by the English garrison from Athlone and the friars went into hiding. They may have found safe houses in the area, as some of them had strong local connections. However their period of exile was relatively short and within two or three years the order was re-established in Athlone where by 1648 there was a thriving community of eighteen friars living and working in the town.

Causeway at the entrance to Friars' Island.

CHAPTER 29

The Black Islands

The Black Islands is the name given to an attractive archipelago of low-lying islands in the civil parish of Cashel, Co. Longford. The islands are in the barony of Rathcline and the Poor Law Union of Ballymahon. The largest island is King's Island (area circa 17 acres), the other islands include Nut Island (circa 16 acres), Sand Island (circa 4 acres), Long Island (circa 3 acres), Horse Island (circa 2 acres), Red Island (circa 2 acres) and Girls Island which is about a half an acre in extent.

Black Islands.

The Black Islands, although they have no recorded ancient history, are nevertheless a most interesting sociological entity. O'Donovan was most interested in the early history of the islands in Lough Ree although little or nothing is known about the early history of the Black Islands. There are no visible remains of monastic activity nor is anything recorded. A lone cut stone from a church window has been found, built into a boundary wall on King's Island, but this may have been imported with building materials from another location.

The settlement of King's Island

The settlement of King's Island would seem to be a relatively modern development. There is no extant record in the Tithes Applotment Books for County Longford of any occupation of the island, but there is every reason to believe that a community dwelt there at that time. The first record we have is the census returns for 1841, which indicate that the Black Islands had three households with a combined population of twenty-two people: ten male and twelve female. The earliest named inhabitants turn up in Griffith's Valuation of 1854 where Daniel Hanly, Michael Hanly and John O'Hara are recorded. Between them they farmed the seven islands and their landlord was Mr Phipps.

So who were these settlers? Undoubtedly, with names like Hanly and O'Hara, they had migrated to the islands from the mainland. The Hanlys may have been some of those who were dispossessed during the Cromwellian plantation from the territory of Cinel Dofa, a short distance up river from the Black Islands in the area of Slieve Bawn. It is said that the two Hanly families were not related.

Saint Berach's Crozier

The Hanlys of the Black Islands were the hereditary custodians of the "Gearr Beraigh" or the short crozier of St. Berach. St. Berach (or Barry) from whom Tarmonbarry takes its name was a sixth century saint. John O'Donovan in his *Ordnance Survey Letters for County Roscommon* makes many references to the Hanly clan and the crozier. It was eventually handed over to the Royal Irish Academy in the mid-nineteenth century, by Patrick Hanly, an attorney in Athlone, and is now part of the exhibition in the Treasury of the National Museum. As St Barry had used his crozier to kill an "ollphiast" or serpent, the crozier was said to have special powers. It was used by the Hanlys to "kill the worm and the fairies and to cure the blast" according to one of O'Donovan's informants.

Saint Berach

Shortly after Berach was baptised he was put into the care of his uncle, St. Fraoch, who had said "let me have the bringing up of this little one; God will provide for his sustenance."[1] It is said that the young Berach was fed by honey from the lobe of Fraoch's ear. In due course Berach founded his own abbey at Tarmonbarry. As a young wandering monk Berach called in one hot summer day at the hall of Bregha, King of Tara. The building was lined with fifty vats of beer in readiness for an evening of feasting but the king's steward refused the saint as much as a drop to quench his thirst and sent Berach on his way. Soon the king returned from hunting and asked for a draught of ale, but when they went to draw it they found the vats were empty. When the steward told the king about the visitor he had turned away the king sent out his servants to appease the young monk.

When Berach was found he was brought back to Tara where the king prostrated himself before him. The saint made the sign of the cross with his bell and staff over the vats and when the lids were opened the vats were found to be full of quality beer. The king and the young monk became good friends and each year Bregha sent the saint new clothes.

As to the lineage of the saint, Bishop MacNamee claimed that Berach was of the Ui Briuin, but that on his mother's side he was of Conmaicne stock; however it is generally agreed that Berach was in fact an O'Hanly. "After imbibing the rudiments of learning and holiness from his devoted uncle, he became a disciple of St. Daigh of Inis-cain-Degha (now Iniskeen) in County Monaghan. He later studied under St. Kevin at Glendalough before returning to establish his monastery at Kilbarry."[2]

We know from the census returns that there were consistently three houses on the islands from 1841 onwards. In 1841 the population was twenty-two but thirty years later this had dropped to ten, possibly indicating that almost half the population had emigrated. We know that certain family members settled in Providence, Rhode Island. By 1901 the figures had once again risen above twenty.

In recent years the islands are uninhabited, the last two islanders to live on the Black Islands were Paddy Hanly (a direct descendant of Daniel Hanly who was on the island in 1854) and the late Nancy (Babs) Conroy who was descended from Michael Hanly the second Hanly on the island at the time of Griffith's Valuation. Both Paddy Hanly and Nancy (Babs) Conroy left the island in the 1980s to live on the mainland at Lecarrow, Co. Roscommon. The family of O'Hara had died out on the island many years earlier.

The Island Life

The author, Richard Hayward, visited the Black Islands over sixty years ago when he was researching his book *Where the River Shannon flows*. He was struck by the great hospitality of the families. He learned that post was delivered to the island twice a

Group of Black Islanders on "the street" in front of their houses, 1949.

week from Newtowncashel and that the children of the island were educated at the National School on the mainland, in Tipper. The islanders were professional fishermen and farmers who made their livelihood by grazing a few cattle, by fishing for eels on long lines and by netting trout. As with all islanders they were a resourceful breed, they were self-sufficient organic farmers long before this way of life became popular. Mrs. Hanly having given Hayward a meal "fit for a king" pointed out a cottage at the east end of the "street" and indicated that it was once a "wee pub". Hayward was astonished by the need for a pub on such a small island but given the vagaries of the lake and the harsh winters of the nineteenth century it seems that the islanders were taking no risks. This pub or shebeen did not survive within living memory, but obviously, as with so much other lore, Mrs. Hanly had heard about it from an earlier generation of islanders.[3]

The three small cuttings on the shore of King's Island recall a time when each of the families had its own personal landing places. A large flat stone built into a wall as a seat, conjures up images of a matriarch sitting out in the sunshine mending the nets while keeping a watchful eye on the island children.

Untimely Trout

Paddy Hanly has pointed out the dried out remains of a fish-pond. These ponds were used either communally or by individual families to hold trout and other fish which were caught out of season. This gave the islanders a great advantage as they could bring their fish to market in quantities as soon as the season opened. (see also Chapter 25).

There are several reports of fish being sold out of season. One which was reported in *The Westmeath Herald* newspaper of 24th December 1859, concerned a case which came before the Brawney Petty Sessions in Athlone on 20th December. The magistrate in the chair was L. Dundas. Other magistrates present included the Hon. C. Handcock, Mr J. Ross R.M. and W. Potts. Mary Hanly, of the Black Islands was summoned at the instance of John Dalton for having in her possession nineteen trout on the 24th of the previous month, that being the close season. Margaret Jennings, a fish huxter, in whose possession the trout were found by the water-guard, was the chief witness for the prosecution. She appears to have been a somewhat reluctant witness who, rather than having an honest desire to uphold the law, obviously feared that she too could be gaoled for her part in the offence. Her evidence was that the defendant had brought the trout, in a skitting basket, to Mary Duffy's house where they had then changed hands for 4/6d.

Mr. Potts said that the water-guard should have summoned all parties. The plaintiff's attorney said that he would not ask "the whole fine incurred to be inflicted" but instead he asked the fine to be fixed as if Mary had sold only two trout out of season. The outcome was that the defendant was found guilty and fined £1 with 8/6d costs or a month imprisonment. The defendant preferred the alternative and hoped that their "reverences" would allow her to spend Christmas with the children, which privilege we are told was granted and so Mary spent the month of January in gaol![4]

In February 1898 trout to the value of £200 were seized by representatives of the Billingsgate Fish Dealers Association on the grounds that they were taken in the closed season[5]. At an inquiry in Athlone a number of Black Island fishermen made affidavits to the effect that the fish were caught the previous year in the open season and held in ponds from which they were taken at 6 a.m. on the 8th February when the season opened. The trout were destroyed but it seems that no further action was taken. The islanders continued to eke out a living from farming and fishing until the fishing rights on the Shannon were acquired by the Electricity Supply Board thus virtually putting an end to the age old profession of Lough Ree fishermen.

John Keegan Casey "Leo"

The great Fenian poet and patriot, John Keegan Casey (1846-1870) taught at Cleraune national school, Co. Longford, a school which was later superseded by Tipper national school. "Leo" started his teaching career at the age of fifteen at his father's school in Gurteen. He died, aged twenty-four, but not before he had written scores of poems and ballads including "The Rising of the moon." A born romantic, it is said that "Leo" wrote love poems to several young ladies. He may even have fallen in love with Mary Hanly of the Black Islands. Her tragic death evoked from him the beautiful song *A Boating on Lough Ree* which has been revived and recorded in recent years by the well known ballad singer Tim Dennehy.

A Boating on Lough Ree

I'm sad and I am lonely now in this far-off West,
The happy scenes of bygone days at night disturb my rest;
For in this faithful heart of mine, forgotten ne'er can be,
The days I spent with Mary Bawn, a-boating on Lough Ree.

Oh! She was young and beautiful, and gentle as a fawn,
Her eyes – they shone like diamonds bright, or stars at early dawn;
Her smiles she had for everyone, her kisses all for me,
The time I gazed on Mary Bawn, a-boating on Lough Ree.

When she pledged herself to be my bride, how happy then was I,
How fleeting were the joys of life, how swiftly they go by.

But the heaven's light shone in her eyes, she was too good for me,
An angel marked her for his bride and took her from Lough Ree.

I've crossed thro' many a thorny path – my hair's a silvery hue;
Yet her thrilling voice speaks to my heart, in tones I can't subdue:
Her comely form still haunts my mind – her pleasing face I see
The blushing face of Mary Bawn, a-boating on Lough Ree.[6]

Great Boatmen and Women

L.T.C. Rolt states that the Hanlys and O'Hara's had "for generations lived by netting trout and setting eel lines on the lake. On several occasions while we lay at our Athlone moorings we had watched them coming rowing down the river to land their boxes of eels for despatch by rail. As one would expect, they are consummate watermen, both men and women being virtually unchallengeable in pleasure boat events at Athlone Regatta."[7] The traditional craft used by the islanders was the open lake boat with sprit sails. While the islanders belonged to the parish of Cashel they also had a strong affinity with Athlone. They regularly brought their catch to Athlone as described by Rolt. Once they had their business transacted they usually headed to Finnerty's bar and grocery in the Market Square where they stocked up with pro-visions and usually stayed to "wet their whistle." Whenever the men-folk had too much

Boat under sprit-sail leaving the Black Islands in the 1940s.

283

to drink the job of rowing back to the islands was undertaken by the women.

The Black Islands today

The islands today are still farmed by Paddy Hanly. The two Hanly homesteads survive while that of the O'Haras is a roofless ruin. The mirth of children is no longer to be heard here nor is the wise conversation of the adults huddled around the generous hearths. Life on such a remote island holds more disadvantages than advantages to modern people, and bit by bit these islands are returning to nature. However, the story of the Black Islands is an important story of people eking out a living; of the dispossessed finding virgin soil and making a new life for themselves. It is a story of bravery, tragedy and all that is best in communal living. Without a doubt a great deal of this story remains untold but even from the little bit we know we can look at these islanders and say we will never see their likes again.

Dwellinghouses of the last residents of the Black Islands.

1901 Census

Name	Relation	Age
Anne Hanly	Head	45
Mary Hanly	Daughter	20
Pat Hanly	Son	18
Daniel Hanly	Son	15
James Hanly	Son	12
Bernard Hanly	Son	8
William Hanly	Son	3
Thomas Hanly	Head	40
Bridget Hanly	Wife	35
John Hanly	Son	19
Anne Hanly	Daughter	16
Thomas Hanly	Son	14
Eliza Hanly	Daughter	12
William Hanly	Son	10
Kate Hanly	Daughter	5
James Hanly	Son	1
Patrick O'Hara	Head	43
Anne O'Hara	Wife	50
Mary O'Hara	Daughter	21
Maggie O'Hara	Daughter	18
John O'Hara	Son	16
Michael O'Hara	Son	14
Patrick O'Hara	Son	10
Anne Hagerty	Niece	3

CHAPTER 30

Miscellaneous Memories

Down the centuries through good times and bad there has been continuous interaction, referred to above in Chapter 11, between the islanders and those living by the lakeshore. As a tribute to all of the people who live by the shore of Lough Ree and whose ancestors have worked the land and fished the water for generations, we include in this publication the Census Returns of 1901 which is the first available complete listing of people who lived around Lough Ree and on the islands. In its own way it is a most fascinating document. If ages are to be adverted to, many of the people listed would have lived through the night of the "big wind" on the 6th January 1839, through the terrible Famine years of the 1840s, through the Fenian and Land League days of the 1870s, 1880s and 1890s. Not only that but the parents of these people would have been born in the 1700s and folk memory would stretch right back to the battle of the Boyne, the siege of Athlone and even to Cromwell himself. As well as that, a good number included in the list, will have been known personally by many reading through these pages. By including the 1901 Census list, therefore, we feel that we are commemorating both the ancestors and descendants of those listed and we are acknowledging their bravery during the few hundred years leading up to the close of the nineteenth century. Driven from their lands by the usurper and the foreigner we can only marvel at the resilience and the spirit displayed by them.

Intermarriage

With such a historical backdrop, it is no wonder that the generation who now inhabit the townlands surrounding the lake should feel a justifiable pride in their ancestors who have gone before. They walk and work each day in the shadow of a past inhabited by their own people who toiled and travelled on these same landways and waterways from time immemorial. There is enough evidence from the comparatively recent past to suggest that the Lough Ree inhabitants had close and friendly relationships with their neighbours living on the mainland by the lakeshore. This was often strengthened by the bonds of marriage and there are numerous instances of the island people intermarrying with lakeside dwellers. When Pat Dodd from Ballinahinch, Paddy Hanly's grandfather, walked all the way across the ice-covered lake on his wedding day in the winter of 1898, to marry a woman from Carrownavaddy, he was more than likely carrying on a trend that was in existence long before his time. Pat Dodd and his wife had two daughters, one of whom in 1938 married James Hanly, Paddy's father, from the Black Islands.

Kate Carley, Portanure, came from a family that had a tradition of boatbuilding and fishing and when she went as a young bride with Jack Ganly to Inchturk, she became another link reinforcing the strong ties already existing between the islanders and the people living by the lakeshore. She loved the island way of life and together with Jack raised a family of five sons and one daughter. When the exodus from the islands started and Kate went to live with her son on the mainland she is quoted as saying, "I'd rather be 'ithin" referring to her island home on Inchturk. Her nephew, Aidan, who still lives in the family homestead in Portanure, remembers happy hours he spent on the island dropping potatoes and helping out. He recalls that on the island the procedure was a little bit different as the potatoes were dropped first and then the manure was spread over them, rather than the other way round as he would have been accustomed to at home in Portanure. He remembers also Jack Ganly having a lovely well-trained horse that would step into the boat behind him whenever they were going to work on the land on Inchmore, the neighbouring island. His father, Jim Carley, built boats and Aidan remembers after school helping him clinch the nails, while lying under the boat in the wood shavings and holding a buffer against the bottom of the boat. It took about three weeks to build a boat. One big boat built by his father before Aidan's time, for Herbert Mayne, is still lakeworthy and moored at Portanure Lodge.

The Mayne Connection

Brian Mayne, writing a number of years ago about his family's association with the parish of Cashel said:

My father was born in 1879. He and his two elder brothers spent all their summer holidays at Portanure, fishing and shooting. They spent a lot of their time with the O'Haras and the Hanlys from the Black Islands and from them learned a lot of country lore about eel fishing and shooting. The Black islanders were wonderful boatmen and no doubt taught the boys a lot about the lake.

In another part of the same letter he wrote:

In those early days the journey to this part of the country from Dublin was quite complicated. My father remembered travelling by train to Athlone and then taking another train on the Athlone-Roscommon line and getting out at Knockcroghery. There a cart and horse would be waiting to take their luggage down to the lake at the end of Galey Bay. A boat from the Black Islands would be waiting for them in Lord Crofton's harbour and would be rowed or sailed across to Portanure. Lord Crofton had built his harbour as a copy of the one my grandfather had made at Portanure but it has not lasted as well. The boat house was built by Jim Carley in 1927. He had been a friend of my father's from the days of his youth.

Comings and Goings

Josie Warde, Clonterm, who was born and reared on Inchbofin, has memories of her grandfather rowing them out to school in St. Ríoch's N.S. Ballinacliffey. She remembers also seeing Mary Ann Slevin (nee Ganly) rowing from Inchturk past Inchbofin on her way to bring home a boatload of turf from Monascath Bog, near Drumnee.

Peter Brennan from Lismagawley and James Skelly from Derrydarragh both enjoy recounting the good days of the forties, when it was a common occurrence for a boatload of young fellows to row over to Jimmy Furey's near Portrunny and head from there to the Sunday night dance in one or other of the dancing venues at Knockcroghery, Ballymurray or Cullion, all of which were close enough to be reachable on foot from Portrunny. These were the years of the Emergency, when emigration to England and America was almost non-existent and there were crowds of young people in all localities eager to dance and enjoy themselves.

Bill Dooley from Rathmore is another who remembers boat trips across to Saints' Island shore with his friends from Muckenagh, his native place, and from there cycling to dances in the Tom Ashe Hall, Newtowncashel. In the pre-radio and television times of the thirties and forties, when people made their own entertainment, Brigid Rollins from Elfeet, who was born and reared in a footballing house in Carrowbeg, remembers baking extra cakes to cater for the footballers

John Quigley and son Sean - carrying on the tradition.

from across the lake, who would cross by boat on the Sunday, for a match, and afterwards stay on for the dance in the same Tom Ashe Hall that night, at which dance, Brigid recalls with a twinkle in her eye, she would be amply rewarded for all the baking by the number of dances she would get from those gallant travellers from the other side of Lough Ree.

The traffic was not all one way, however, as the following description of a 'Wran Day' (St. Stephen's Day, December 26th) long ago, by Peter Hopkins, Drumnee, and recorded by Declan Gilmore, clearly shows:

"We got a big boat – a cattle boat – all got into her – 'twas organised for a week ahead of that and Mike Dolan and Mike Hopkins – they knew all the roads and walks of Tubberclare and Tang, and we done all the parish a' Tubberclare – and then back for the Pigeons and never stopped until we went into Glasson, and it was dark night then – and to make matters worse it snowed for a few days before Christmas or the Wran Day and started to freeze then and the road was the same as if you were walking upon a wall. We came back to the Pigeons again and drank lots and back to Murrays in Malaghera and Mrs Murray found out that we were going to go back in the boat and sure they weren't able to go anywhere – and she craved in the honour of God for to go home the road no matter how long it took us – but sure we did go home

289

the road and they were all in bed down through Gurteen and along
there and we got into nera house and 'twas a horrid walk from Glasson
back to the Pigeons and from that back to Murrays and then to face the
road again – and the state the road was in. But Jim Dolan gave up at
Payne's gate – he failed there – (we) put him down lying on the side of
the ditch where there was no snow and when we came home his father
was there below in the road and he sez: "Where's Jimeen?" We tould
him where he was. He had an auld white horse. He got out the horse
and got up on him with a bottle of hot tay and he got Jim, and he
almost stiff with frost, without at Payne's quicks. (He) put him on the
horse in front of him, brought him home and he didn't get up for a week
after it."

Kate Shanley, Derrygowna, personifies another island/
mainland connection. Her mother, Mary Hanly from the Black
Islands, married Bernard Skelly from Portanure and Kate has
happy memories of visiting her uncle, Dan Hanly's house on the
island and the warm hospitality dispensed there by his wife, Mary
McCormack from Moydow, and himself. Dan's house was one
where the normal greeting to a stranger or visitor was, "I have a big
trout on the pan for you." She remembers being left back in the boat
to Pollagh and running out the road to her own house in Portanure.

Another story of island/mainland connections is that of Kate
Quigley, formerly Kate Duffy from the townland of Cloontagh in
Killashee parish. The story of how a girl from Cloontagh met a boy
from Inchturk is itself an interesting one and underlines again the
intricacies of the numerous family connections between the islands
and the mainland. Kate Dunne, from Derrahaun was married to Jim
Tiernan from Inchmore. Kate, having been in America, loved dances
and dancing and organised as many as she could, both on Inchmore
and in her original home in Derrahaun. It was at one such dance in
Derrahaun that Kate Duffy first met her husband Mike Quigley, a
native of Inchturk. The romance blossomed into marriage and the
young couple spent six very happy years living on Inchmore before
moving out to the mainland at Ballinacliffy in the early 1960s. Kate
has many happy memories of those years she lived on the island –
of how kind Kate Tiernan was to her and how she helped her in so
many ways; of going in the boat out to midnight Mass in

Tubberclare and having to break the ice in the Nook where they were about to land; of hearing her father-in-law praying aloud in bed at night for the safety of islandmen out in boats. She remembers the work and how fulfilling it was in the peace and quiet of the island. Hens, turkeys and pigs were kept and had to be looked after, while, when the milking was being done, the youngest child would be in the pram at the gate, within sight and within earshot of the sounds of milking. What an idyllic scene that was and how difficult to imagine for people being brought up in the twenty first century. Another image recalled by Kate is of the fish being weighed on the shore at Killeenmore and being bought by a fish-buyer from Omagh called Brammer. The islanders and local people often made the comment, "Brammer's bucket will tell," when the quantity of fish was being discussed. There were two great spring wells on Inchmore so there was never a shortage of pure clear water for household purposes and when the Tilley lamp came it brought extra light to the cosy island homestead. Kate was lonesome leaving the island after her six years there and missed especially Kate Tiernan who was the personification of island hospitality.

Jimmy Furey

One of the great personalities of Lough Ree in the modern era is Jimmy Furey of Mountplunket. Fisherman, boatbuilder, nature lover and raconteur, he knows the lake in all its moods as few others do. He has an endless supply of stories and anecdotes with which to regale the visitor. Born on the shore of the lake in the house in which he still lives, he developed a lifetime affinity with this unique environment. Boats were always a feature of the Furey home whether for purposes of travel, communication or fishing. They played an important part in the economy of the household, especially in the harvest when the turf crop, which had been saved on Clooncagh bog was loaded on to the boat in the Hind River and taken to the landing stage adjacent to the house where it was then unloaded and carried home. The same landing stage welcomed people in boats from the islands and from the mainland, whether they came on business or pleasure, or were three young men who had danced the night away in Cullion Hall and now slept at the fire in Furey's kitchen 'til morning because the lake had become too rough for rowing back to Cashel.

Jimmy's first initiation into boatbuilding was when he spent a week with Jack McArdle of Muckenagh, one of the best boatbuilders on Lough Ree. He maintains that any good carpenter can build a boat but it is the fisherman who is most keenly aware of the finer qualities a boat requires, for he is the one who is alone with his boat facing the elements. Fisherman and boatbuilder combine in Jimmy Furey. He fished eels commercially with Jimmy Hanly and Jack O'Hara of the Black Islands, using the long line and the fish were kept in wooden tanks awaiting marketing. One of his many anecdotes tells of going with Jack O'Hara to Killeenmore with eels. Paddy and Tom Walsh of the Quaker were on the same errand. The Walshs were noted boatmen and when the wind came up they made it back to the Black Islands. O'Hara and Jimmy, however, thought better of it and pulled in to Inchmore. Billy Nolan came down to the shore and brought them up to his house in which were his wife and infant daughter. Micky Ganly had been commissioned to make a cot for the child but Jimmy Furey, anxious not to be imposing on the hospitality of the house while the storm continued, set to work and made the cot. He recalls with a wry smile meeting the same "baby girl" years later when she was raising her own family.

Jimmy was the first of his family to become a boatbuilder. He recalls that Tom Walsh from the Quaker bought the first boat he made in the forties, a great compliment to Jimmy's expertise for the Walshs were good judges of a boat.

Twenty years on, he began to specialise in building the Shannon One Design, described in Chapter 16, and it was with the construction of this boat that most of his life's work was concerned. His boats were high quality and very much in demand. His many Lough Ree clients included the Maynes of Derrydarragh, Graham Goodwin and Eben Hamilton of Barley Harbour. Jimmy talks about the "Dergs," the boatmen from Lough Derg who were big customers. They were also particularly keen competitors. Part of their preparation for a big race involved watching the opposition at a distance and surreptitiously timing the laps with a stopwatch!

Jimmy's vast knowledge of the lake often emerges in casual comments, such as when he refers to Laniush, an island name familiar to the people of Pollagh and Cleraune but now long forgotten by everyone else; or when he mentions that the gravel on the Iskeraulin Shoal was particularly suited for ornamental dashing of dwellinghouse walls, and that people came from far and near to carry it away in boats. He has poignant memories of the fishing closing down and the islanders departing for the mainland. He remembers the day Paddy Walsh said to Jim Tiernan of Inchmore, "You'll never sleep another night on the Gormauns."

Jimmy Furey has reached the autumn of a lifetime devoted to Lough Ree, its waters, its wild life and its boats. He radiates a deep understanding of the beauty and the fragility of this great natural amenity. Like a sunset over Iskeraulin he merges effortlessly with the peace and harmony that have shaped his life, a life that saw him put more back into the lake than he ever took from it.

It is appropriate that the book should end with a commendation of the families listed as living on the islands over a hundred years ago. Their descendants can be numbered in thousands and live now in many different parts of the world. The Sheas, Killians and Connaughtons from Inchenagh; the Brennans from Clawinch; the Donoghues from Rinnany; the Fegans, Nallys, Clarkes, Kellys and Skellys from Saints' Island; the Walshes and Farrells from Inchcleraun; the Heffernans, Skellys and Connells from Inchbofin; the Hanlys and O'Haras from the Black Islands; the Duffys from Hare Island; the Tiernans, Quigleys, Nolans, Fegans and Keefes from Inchmore and the Ganlys, McGees and Walshes from Inchturk all have extended families in which there are people who either lived themselves for part of their lives on one or other of the islands or whose close relations were once island people. They can be rightly proud of their island heritage and as a tribute to all of them the incomplete story of the Killian family from Inchenagh will serve to illustrate how numerous are the descendants of all the aforementioned island families.

When Luke Killian from Inchenagh married Maria Hanly from Ballinaboy just before the Famine they could not have foreseen how their descendants would increase and multiply in the years ahead and how many people from around Lough Ree and much further afield would be able to trace their roots back to the old homestead on Inchenagh.

Luke and Maria were blessed with a family of eight children – Thomas (1846), Michael (1850), Luke (1855), Daniel (1856), John (1858), Mary (1860), Catherine (1863) and Brigid (1866).

Thomas married Winifred Casey and settled in Clonbearla; Michael married Brigid Dunne and settled in Derrygowna; Daniel married Elizabeth Feeney and raised their family in Fermoyle; John married Ann Glennon in Forthill; Mary married James Madden in Elfeet; Catherine married John Skelly, Aughavadden; and Brigid married John Farrell in Portnahinch.

From those unions came another generation. The children of Tom and Winifred Casey in Clonbearla were Patrick (1871), Mary Ann (1873), Winifred (1879), Katie (1881), Elizabeth (1883), Thomas (1885), Teresa (1887), Joseph (1890), Brigid, Margaret and Rose.

The children of Michael and Brigid Dunne in Derrygowna were Mary (1876), Kate (1880), Thomas (1882), John (1883), Luke (1885), Margaret (1887), Michael (1890), Joseph (1892) and Brigid (1894).

To Luke and Teresa Chapman, still living in Inchenagh, were born Luke (1887), John (1889), Mary Ellen (1892), Joseph (1894), Thomas (1896) and William 1897).

Daniel and Elizabeth Feeney in Fermoyle were the parents of Mary (1879), Catherine (1880), Michael (1883), Brigid (1884), Luke (1888) and Elizabeth (1889).

The children of John and Ann Glennon in Forthill were Peter (1884), Mary (1886), Brigid (1887), Ann (1889), Luke (1890), Thomas (1893) and John (1898).

Mary Killian and James Madden had three children, James, Mary and Kate in Elfeet.

Michael, Frank, Dan, James, Joseph, Mary, Bea, Annie, Kate and Lil Skelly were the children of Catherine Killian and John Skelly, Aughavadden.

Brigid Killian and John Farrell in Portnahinch had three children, John, Patrick and Mary.

In the intervening years three more generations of descendants have been born, not only in the Killian line but in all the other island family lines as well, so the total number of people with ties to the different islands is now almost impossible to count.

A final wish and prayer is that their numbers continue to increase and that their loyalty and allegiance to their island roots never wane.

CHAPTER 31

1901 Census of population in townlands around Lough Ree

Name	Relation	Age	Name	Relation	Age
Commons North:			John Finnegan	Son	38
			Daniel Finnegan	Son	25
Bernard Gill	Head	34	Bridget Finnegan	Daughter	23
Margaret Gill	Wife	30	Michael Finnegan	Son	18
Thomas Gill	Son	1 yr			
Michael Gill	Son	–	John Dalton	Head	58
Mary Gill	Sister	36	Anne Dalton	Wife	56
James Maguire	Servant	25	Patrick Dalton: Stableman	Son	27
			John Dalton	Son	21
Patrick Connaughton	Head	65	Joseph Dalton	Son	19
Bridget Connaughton	Wife	60	James Dalton	Son	14
John Connaughton	Brother	60	Thomas Dalton	Son	12
			Lizzie Dalton	Daughter	9
Curreen:			Ellen Dalton	Daughter	6
Mary Jane O'Connell	Head	67	George Geoffroy	Head	54
			Kate Geoffroy	Wife	49
Rathcline:			Maria A. Geoffroy	Daughter	11
			Samuel R. Geoffroy	Son	10
John Rhatigan	Head	57	Francis L. Geoffroy	Son	7
Mary Rhatigan	Wife	44	Maria Geoffroy	Sister	55
Catherine Rhatigan	Sister	64	Jane Smith Sch. teacher	Boarder	23
Patrick Hanley	Servant	19	Teresa Leavy	Servant	20
Thomas Murry: G.keeper	Head	29	Bridget Rooney	Head	47
Anne Murry	Wife	25	Thomas Rooney	Son	27
Elizabeth Murry	Daughter	–	Catherine Rooney	Daughter	24
			Patrick Rooney	Son	22
Richard Belton	Head	56	Mary Rooney	Daughter	16
Mary Belton	Wife	58	Bridget Rooney	Daughter	14
Mary J. Belton	Daughter	27	Annie Rooney	Daughter	12
John Belton	Son	24	Margaret Rooney	Daughter	8
Richard Belton	Son	23			
Patrick Belton	Son	16	Patrick Broderick	Head	62
Catherine Belton	Daughter	9	Mary Broderick	Wife	60
			James Broderick	Son	24
Michael Carroll	Head	76	Catherine Broderick	Daughter	18
Catherine Carroll	Wife	80	John Broderick	Son	14
James Carroll	Son	38			
Elizabeth Carroll	Daugh. in law	28	**Blenavoher:**		
John Farrell	Head	36	Michael Kenny	Head	52
Catherine Farrell	Wife	23	Anne Kenny	Wife	50
Thomas Murry	Head	65	Michael Kenny	Son	21
Bridget Murry	Head	62	Mary Kenny	Daughter	20
			Catherine Kenny	Daughter	18
Catherine Finnegan	Head	60	Nannie Kenny	Daughter	16

Name	Relation	Age
Maggie Kenny	Daughter	11
Jane Kenny	Daughter	9
Frances Kenny	Daughter	7
Patrick Kenny	Head	38
Mary Kenny	Wife	27
Mary Kenny	Daughter	8
Margaret Kenny	Daughter	6
Catherine Kenny	Daughter	4
Bridget Kenny	Daughter	3
Eliza Kenny	Daughter	1
Timothy Shea	Head	42
Margaret Murry	Sis. in law	22
Bridget Shea	Daughter	13
Mary J. Shea	Daughter	12
John Shea	Son	11
Catherine Shea	Daughter	7
Peter Shea	Son	6
Margaret Shea	Daughter	4
Bridget Sweeney	Visitor	19
Patrick Hyland	Head	54
Bridget Hyland	Wife	53
Mary Hyland	Daughter	23
Michael Hyland	Son	21
Patrick Hyland	Son	17
James Hyland	Son	15
Richard Hyland	Son	13
Bridget Hyland	Daughter	10
Willie Hyland	Son	7
John Hanley	Head	57
Bridget Hanley	Wife	47
Mary Hanley	Daughter	21
Patrick Hanley	Son	19
John Hanley	Son	17
Thomas Hanley	Son	16
Michael Hanley	Son	14
Jean Hanley	Daughter	12
James Hanley	Son	9
Charles Martin	Head	33
Margaret Martin	Wife	28
Mary Martin	Daughter	3
Mary Martin	Mother	75
Thomas Grinnen	Head	21
John Grinnen	Brother	17

Name	Relation	Age
Augharanagh:		
Bridget Connor	Head	60
James Connor	Son	32
Bridget Connor	Daughter	25
Michael Hyland	Head	56
Mary Hyland	Wife	30
Michael Hyland	Son	3
John Hyland	Son	2
Patrick Hyland	Son	_
James Connor	Head	70
Mary Connor	Wife	68
Mary A. Connor	Daughter	29
James Connor	Son	28
Aughakeel:		
Daniel Clarke	Head	57
Maria Clarke	Wife	55
Mary Clarke	Daughter	25
John Clarke	Son	23
Patrick Clarke	Son	16
Thomas Clarke	Son	14
Kate A. Clarke	Daughter	12
Cullentra:		
Patrick Fayne	Head	67
Catherine Fayne	Daughter	22
Michael Fayne	Son	19
Anne Fayne	Head	53
Anne Fayne	Daughter	25
Patrick Fayne	Son	21
Winifred Fayne	Daughter	17
John Fayne	Son	15
Luke Kenny	Head	60
Mary Kenny	Wife	50
John Kenny	Son	24
Maria Kenny	Daughter	22
William Kenny	Son	20
Margaret Kenny	Son	18
Luke Kenny	Son	16
Patrick Kenny	Son	13
Michael Kenny	Son	7
Patrick Clarke	Head	55

Name	Relation	Age
Margaret Grealy	Head	55
Mary Grealy	Daughter	24
John Grealy	Son	22
Catherine Grealy	Daughter	21
Thomas Grealy	Son	19
James Grealy	Son	17
Thomas Connaughton	Head	67
Catherine Connaughton	Wife	72
Annie Connaughton	Daughter	38
Ellen Connaughton	Daughter	36
Thomas Connaughton	Son	34
Francis Mulvihill	Head	57
Anne Mulvihill	Wife	42
Bridget Mulvihill	Daughter	11
Catherine Mulvihill	Daughter	10
Anne Mulvihill	Daughter	8
Margaret Mulvihill	Daughter	6
Rose Mulvihill	Daughter	5
Patrick Mulvihill	Son	3
Edward Mulvihill	Son	_
Michael Hopkins	Head	60
Bridget Hopkins	Wife	57
Mary Hopkins	Daughter	25
Patrick Fallon	Head	73
Bridget Fallon	Wife	55
John Fallon	Son	25
Michael Fallon	Son	20
Andrew Fallon	Son	18
Bridget Fallon	Daughter	15
Eliza Fallon	Head	55
John Fallon	Son	34
Patrick Fallon	Son	30
Anne Fallon	Daughter	27
Rebecca Moran	G.Daughter	10
Eliza Moran	G.Daughter	8
John Connaughton	Head	50
Ellen Brennan	Widow/Sis.	52
Michael Brennan	Nephew	17
Mary Brennan	Niece	14
Patrick Ward	Head	35
Mary Ward	Wife	38
Michael Ward	Son	8
Patrick Ward	Son	6
Bridget Ward	Daughter	6

Name	Relation	Age
Mary Ann Ward	Daughter	4
Eliza Ward	Daughter	2

Ballinahinch.

Name	Relation	Age
Frank Fallon	Head	70
Anne Fallon	Wife	60
Maria Fallon	Daughter	28
John Fallon	Son	26
John Dodd	Head	70
Margaret Dodd	Wife	62
James Dodd	Son	31
Maggie Dodd	Daughter	26
Mary Delaney	Head	24
Bridget Delaney	Sister	22
Bridget Bannon	Head	68
James Bannon	Son	40
Thomas Bannon	Son	34
Mary Bannon	Daughter	22
Dan Delaney	Head	60
Margaret Delaney	Wife	50
William Delaney	Son	20
Ned Delaney	Son	18
Mary Delaney	Daughter	15
Eliza Delaney	Daughter	13
Anne Delaney	Daughter	11
Catherine Moughty	Head	50
Bernard Moughty	Son	21
Patrick Moughty	Son	14
Daniel Moughty	Son	12
Thomas Moughty	Son	8
Mary Anne Moughty	Daughter	18
Kate Moughty	Daughter	10
Bridget Casserly	Head	85
Michael Casserly	Son	42
Patrick Casserly	Grand son	14
Michael Casserly	Servant	22
Marianna Ryder W.low	Head	65
John Ryder	Son	43
Marianna Ryder	D.in-law	42
John Ryder	G.Son	13
Sarah Ryder	G.Daughter	7
Annie Rollins K.kenny	Head	41
James Rollins	Son	18

Name	Relation	Age	Name	Relation	Age
John Rollins	Son	14	John Mulvihill	Son	23
Amanda Rollins	Daughter	12	Patrick Mulvihill	Son	21
Frances Rollins	Daughter	9			

Elfeet Burke

Name	Relation	Age	Name	Relation	Age
Mary Jane Ryder	Head	39			
Frances Ryder	Sister	37	Bridget Farrell	Head	50
Eliza Ryder	Sister	35	Willie Farrell	Son	30
Annie Ryder	Sister	33	Maggie Farrell	Daughter	20
			Eliza Farrell	Daughter	18

Cashel

Name	Relation	Age	Name	Relation	Age
			John Rollins	Head	56
William Donnelly	Head	51	Martha Rollins	Wife	61
William Donnelly	Son	19	Eliza Rollins	Daughter	28
Annie Maria Donnelly	Daughter	22	William Rollins	Son	22
Katie Donnelly	Daughter	16			
Catherine Donnelly	Cousin	57	Francis Egan	Head	53
			Bridget Egan	Wife	44
John Bracken Fermanagh	Head	58	Patrick Egan	Son	14
Margaret Bracken	Wife	56	Michael Egan	Son	13
William Bracken	Son	29	Mary Egan	Daughter	11
Margaret Bracken	Daughter	25	Francis Egan	Son	9
Hugh Bracken	Son	22	Anne Egan	Daughter	7
Mary Jane Bracken	Daughter	21	Anne Mulvihill	Aunt	67
Henry Bracken	Son	18			
Alfred Bracken	Son	15	Michael Kelly	Head	75
Wilkin Francis Bracken	Son	13	Catherine Kelly	Wife	72
Rebecca Bracken	Daughter	11	Edward Kelly	Son	26
			Thomas Kelly	Son	34

Lough Farm

Culnagore

Name	Relation	Age	Name	Relation	Age
Michael Connaughton	Head	65			
Anne Connaughton	Wife	64	Patrick Kearney	Head	60
James Connaughton	Son	30	Bridget Kearney	Wife	60
John Connaughton	Son	28	Thomas Kearney	Son	25
Kate Farrell	Niece	5	Mary Kearney	Daughter	20
			Bridget Kearney	Daughter	16
James Hanly	Head	70	Annie Kearney	Daughter	10
Catherine Hanly	Wife	62			
Daniel Hanly	Son	35	**Derrydarragh**		
Jane Hanly	Daughter	21			
			Margaret Coughlan	Head	40
John Cunningham	Head	30	Bridget Coughlan	Sister	36
Bridget Cunningham	Wife	22	Annie Coughlan	Sister	30
Bernard Cunningham	Son	2			
Bridget Cunningham	Daughter	1	Thomas Skelly	Head	80
			Bridget Skelly	Wife	64
William Casserly	Head	54	Peter Skelly	Son	28
Mary Casserly	Wife	55			
Mary Ann Hand	Niece	12	James Farrell	Head	70
			James Hanly	Stepson	40
Patrick Mulvihill	Head	58	Ann Hanly	Stepdaugh.	35
Catherine Mulvihill	Wife	55	James Connaughton	G.son	13

Name	Relation	Age
Patrick Connaughton	G.son	10
Thomas Connaughton	G.son	8
Peter Skelly	Head	64
Bridget Skelly	Wife	60
Edward Skelly	Son	33
Peter Skelly	Son	29
John Connor	Head	80
Patrick Cloonan	Son-in-law	36
Maria Cloonan	Wife	36
Bridget Cloonan	Daughter	8
Mary Cloonan	Daughter	6
John Cloonan	Son	3
Richard Walker R.I.C.	Head	64
Lizzie J.Walker	Cavan Wife	50
George Walker	Son	18
James Skelly	Head	60
Margt. Skelly	Wife	52
Peter Skelly	Brother	70
Margaret Skelly	Sister	66
Peter Skelly	Son	22
John Skelly	Son	15
James Skelly	Son	8
Bridget Skelly	Daughter	12
Vallance Elam G.man	Head	42
Alice Elam(England)	Wife	44
Martha Page	Servant	29
Maria Skelly	Servant	21
Denis Skelly	Head	70
Michael Skelly	Son	24
Kate Skelly	Wife	23
Margaret Skelly	G.Daugh.	3
James Skelly	G.son	_
William Coughlan	Head	60
Ellen Coughlan	Wife	60
Mary Coughlan	Daughter	22
Anne Coughlan	Daughter	20
James Coughlan	Son	18
John Coughlan	Head	40
Margaret Coughlan	Wife	37
Mary Ann Coughlan	Daughter	2

Collum

Name	Relation	Age
Patrick Casserly	Head	66
Honor Casserly	Wife	55

Name	Relation	Age
William Casserly	Son	22
Patrick Casserly	Son	20
Mary Casserly	Daughter	17
Michael Moran(W.Meath)	Head	52
Bridget Moran	Wife	38
Patrick Gilmour	Head	64
James Gilmour	Brother	55
Bridget Gilmour	Wife	47
Maria Gilmour	Daughter	22
Patrick Gilmour	Son	20
William Gilmour	Son	16
James Gilmour	Son	13
William Gilmour	Boarder	40
Patrick Mallon	Head	66
Catherine Mallon	Wife	50
John Kenny	Head	74
Mary Kenny	Wife	70
Patrick Kenny	Son	32
Bridget Kenny	Daughter	28
James Connaughton	Head	40
Anne Connaughton	Sister	38
Catherine Murray	Head	58
Pat Murray	Son	38
Mary Murray	D.in-law	27
John Murray	G.son	5
Pat Dalton	Head	46
Mary Dalton	Niece	17
Pat Cloonan	Head	84
James Cloonan	Son	25
Patrick Skally	Head	78
Mary Skally	Wife	46
Thomas Skally	Son	25
Anne Skally	Daughter	17
Patrick Skally	Son	15

Portanure Bog

Name	Relation	Age
Thomas Coleman	Head	50
Sarah Coleman	Wife	48
Thomas Coleman	Son	4
Patrick Coleman	Son	2

Name	Relation	Age	Name	Relation	Age
Pullagh			Michael Hopkins	Head	55
			Mary Hopkins W.meath	Wife	40
Michael Costello	Head	65	Mary Hopkins	Daughter	8
Margaret Costello	Wife	60	Patrick Hopkins	Son	6
Patrick Costello	Son	30			
Kate Costello	Daughter	25	**Cleraune**		
Peter Kenny	Head	27	Bridget Shea	Head	80
Mary Kenny	Wife	30	Peter Shea	Son	55
			John Shea	Son	53
Laurence Dolan	Head	60	Thomas Shea	Son	50
Eliza Dolan	Wife	50	Annie Shea	Dau-in-law	35
Michael Dolan	Son	26	John Shea	Grandson	9
Peter Dolan	Son	22	Thomas Shea	Grandson	6
Eliza Dolan	Daughter	18	Bridget Shea	G.daughter	4
			Patrick Shea	Grandson	2
Mary Mulvihill	Head	75			
James Mulvihill	Son	40	James Costello	Head	55
Mary Mulvihill	Daugh.in-law	35	Bridget Costello	Wife	50
			James Costello	Son	28
Bridget Mulvihill	Head	60	Mary Costello	Daughter	20
Michael Mulvihill	Son	32	John Costello	Son	18
Eliza Mulvihill	D.in-law	31	Anne Costello	Daughter	16
			Bridget Costello	Daughter	14
Anne Connaughton	Head	60	Bernard Costello	Son	9
Anne Connaughton	Aunt	70			
			Peter Shea, Grocer	Head	60
James Costello	Head	60	Mary Shea	Wife	62
Margaret Costello	Daughter	23			
Patrick Mulvihill	Son-in-law	35	John Healy	Head	67
Maryanne Mulvihill	G.Daugh.	6	Margaret Healy	Wife	57
Kate Mulvihill	G.Daugh.	4	John Healy	Son	30
John Mulvihill	G.son	2	Kate Healy	Daughter	23
Patrick Mulvihill	G.son	1	Patrick Healy	Son	20
James Cloonan	Head	64	Patrick Forde	Head	55
Jane Cloonan	Wife	40	Catherine Forde	Wife	73
Thomas Cloonan	Son	8			
			John Skelly	Head	60
Edward McGowan	Head	35	Eliza Skelly	Wife	55
			John Skelly	Son	23
Margaret Kenny	Head	59			
Mary Kenny	Daughter	26	Catherine Costello	Head	50
			William Costello	Son	24
Thomas Cunningham	Head	56	Margaret Costello	Daughter	23
Mary Cunningham	Wife	60	Bernard Costello	Son	19
Kate Cunningham	Daughter	21			
			Michael Murray	Head	76
Mary Mulvihill	Head	60	Bridget Murray	Wife	76
William Mulvihill	Son	28	Michael Murray	Son	56
			Patrick Murray	Son	45
			Bridget Murray	Dau.in-law	45

Name	Relation	Age	Name	Relation	Age
Annie Murray	G.Daughter	13	John Harrison	Head	50
Margaret Murray	G.Daughter	11	Catherine Harrison	Sister	45
Mary Murray	G.Daughter	9			
John Murray	G.Son	7	William Clarke	Head	64
Bridget Murray	G.Daughter	5	Mary Clarke	Wife	50
Michael Murray	G.Son	2	Bessie Mulvihill	Sr.in-law	50
			John Clarke	Son	17
Patrick Hudson	Head	66	Mary Clarke	Daughter	13
Mary Hudson	Sister	52	William Clarke	Son	11
Michael Hudson	Brother	50			
			John Farrell	Head	40
Peter Mallon	Head	55	Mary Farrell	Sister	37
Mary Mallon	Wife	50	Thomas Smyth	Servant	14
John Mallon	Son	25			
Bridget Mallon	Dau-in-law	30	John Hopkins	Head	81
Patrick Mallon	G.Son	5	Anne Hopkins	Wife	60
Mary Mallon	G.Daughter	3			
			Michael Shea	Head	50
Annie Gill	Head	70	Peter Shea	Brother	48
Mary Gill	Daughter	36			
			John Murray	Head	40
Catherine McCormick	Head	73	Bridget Murray(Brennan)	Wife	25
John McCormick	Son	37			
Patrick McCormick	Son	30	Michael Mulvihill	Head	40
			Annie Mulvihill	Wife	40
William Costello	Head	70	Francis Mulvihill	Son	2
Maria Costello	Wife	52	Patrick Mulvihill	Son	_
William Costello	Servant	24	Bridget Mulvihill	Sister	50
Thomas Clarke	Servant	21			
			Patrick Carley	Head	40
Francis Gill Carpenter	Head	45	Bridget Carley	Wife	45
			John Carley	Son	6
Portanure			Patrick Carley	Son	3
			Catherine Carley	Mother	60
Catherine Mulvihill	Head	63			
Pat Mulvihill	Son	30	John Carley	Head	60
Kate Mulvihill	Daughter	26	Maria Carley	Wife	50
Eliza Mulvihill	Daughter	22			
			John Carley	Head	56
Christy Mulvihill	Head	44	Margaret Carley	Wife	56
Mary Mulvihill	Daughter	17	John Carley	Son	16
Anne Mulvihill	Daughter	15	Kate Carley	Daugh.	15
Bridget Mulvihill	Daughter	13	Patrick Carley	Son	14
Thomas Mulvihill	Son	10	William Carley	Son	12
			Michael Carley	Son	8
James Skelly	Head	65			
Bernard Skelly	Son	28	Bernard Ganly	Head	38
Michael Skelly	Son	26	Mary Ganly	Wife	40
Patrick Skelly	Son	20	James Ganly	Son	9
Bridget Skelly	Daughter	30	Maryanne Ganly	Daugh.	7
Francis Farrell	G.son	2	John Ganly	Son	6
Margaret Costello	Sr.-in-law	50	Eliza Ganly	Daugh.	2

Name	Relation	Age
Thomas Finneran	Head	80
Jane Finneran	Wife	60

Corrool Kenny

Name	Relation	Age
John Smyth	Head	40
Anne Smyth	Sister	42
Patrick Mallon	Nephew	25
Mary Smyth	Head	70
John Smyth	Son	40
Patrick Smyth	Son	35
Mary Smyth	Daughter	34
Mary Smyth	D.in-law	37
John Smyth	G.son	7
James Smyth	G.son	5
Patrick Smyth	G-son	2
John Merrigan	Head	46
Kate Merrigan	Wife	42
Pat Merrigan	Son	19
Maria Merrigan	Daughter	17
Katie Merrigan	Daughter	16
Willie Merrigan	Son	12
John Merrigan	Son	11
Bridget Merrigan	Daughter	8
Patrick Skelly	Head	34
Margaret Skelly	Wife	26
James Skelly	Son	4
Margaret Skelly	Daughter	2
Thomas Skelly	Son	_
Patrick Skelly	Son	67
Daniel Carney	Servant	19
Bridget Kenny	Head	60
John Kenny	Son	43
Pat Kenny	Son	41
Kate Kenny	Daughter	34
Michael Kenny	Boarder	36
John Kelly	Head	58
Margaret Kelly	Wife	40
John McGee	Head	40
James Hanly	Head	87
James Hanly	Son	30
Annie Hanly	Daughter	34
Mary Hanly	Daughter	32
Mary Donlon	G.daugh.	15

Name	Relation	Age
John Kenny	Head	60
Bridget Kenny	Wife	50
Thomas Kenny	Son	21
John Bawle	Head	60
Annie Bawle	Wife	45
Thomas Bawle	Son	25
Maggie Bawle	Daughter	15
John Bawle	Son	12

Corrool Fox

Name	Relation	Age
Thomas Clarke	Head	60
Anne Clarke	Wife	46
Katie Clarke	Daughter	19
Bridget Clarke	Daughter	18
Joseph Clarke	Son	15
Maggie Clarke	Daughter	12
Bridget Lally	G.daughter	_
Michael Flynn	Head	40
Anne Flynn	Wife	44
John Flynn	Son	14
Eliza Flynn	Daughter	13
James Flynn	Son	11
Michael Flanagan	Head	53
Bridget Flanagan	Wife	49
John Flanagan	Son	20
Patrick Flanagan	Son	16
Bernard Flanagan	Son	12
Kate Flanagan	Daughter	11
Bridget Flanagan	Daughter	7
Mary Flanagan	Daughter	5
Patrick Farrell	Head	83
Mary Farrell	Wife	70
James Farrell	Son	37
John Farrell	Son	35
Anne Farrell	Daughter	33
Mary Farrell	Daughter	28
Mary Kelly	G.daugh.	15
Bridget Kelly	G.daugh.	15
Patrick Skally	Head	37
Bridget Mulvihill	Head	72
John Mulvihill	Son	33
Mary Ford	Sister	70
Patrick Clarke	Head	36

Name	Relation	Age	Name	Relation	Age
James Murray	Head	66	Bridget Brennan	Daughter	3
			Mary Brennan	Daughter	2
Patrick Farrell	Head	38	Catherine Brennan	Daughter	1
Bridget Farrell	Sister	40			
			Thomas Murray	Head	63
Michael Fox	Head	55	Anne Murray	Wife	57
John Fox	Brother	52	James Murray	Son	15
			Katie Murray	Daughter	22
John Kennedy	Head	40	Bridget Murray	Daughter	17
Bridget Kennedy	Sister	42			
Margaret Kennedy	Sister	37	John Skally	Head	47
Thomas Kennedy	Brother	35	Edward Skally	Brother	43
			Bridget Skally	Sister	51
Bridget Lally	Head	45	Mary Skally	Niece	17
Mary Lally	Daughter	27			
James Lally	Son	26	Annie Doran	Head	60
Thomas Lally	Son	23	Patrick Doran	Son	27
			James Doran	Son	24
Claris					
			Michael Skally	Head	67
Martin Higgins	Head	64	Annie Skally	Wife	57
Bridget Higgins	Wife	56	Daniel Skally	Son	28
Martin Higgins	Son	30	Kate Skally	Daughter	19
Patrick Higgins	Son	28	Bridget Murray	Boarder	10
James Higgins	Son	16			
Dominick Higgins	Son	13	Eliza Casey	Head	29
Peter Mullany	Head	67	James Casey	Head	73
Patrick Mullany	Son	31			
Rose Mullany	Daughter	33	John Casey	Head	70
			Catherine Casey	Wife	60
Palmer Notley	Head	72	John Casey	Son	30
Annie Notley	Wife	60	Annie Casey	Daughter	26
William P.Notley	Son	36			
Phoebe F. Notley	Dau.in-law	30	**Drumnee**		
Ruby Mabel Notley	G.Daughter	7			
Annie Eleanor Notley	G.Daughter	4	Edward Fegan	Head	55
Mary Gerety	Servant	20	Thomas Fegan	Brother	75
Bridget Fahy	Head	56	Thomas Mallon	Head	70
Thomas Fahy	Son	26	Margaret Mallon	Wife	60
James Fahy	Son	22	Edward Mallon	Son	30
			Joseph Mallon	Son	25
Thomas Lally	Head	71	Patrick Mallon	Son	20
Bridget Lally	Wife	60			
Mary Lally	Daughter	24	Thomas Mallon	Head	42
James Lally	Son	22	Kate Mallon	Wife	30
Thomas Lally	Son	20	Mary K. Mallon	Daughter	8
			Bridget Mallon	Daughter	6
James Brennan	Head	48	Anne Mallon	Daughter	4
Mary Brennan	Wife	32	Lizzie Mallon	Daughter	2
Nannie Brennan	Daughter	4	James Mallon	Brother	40

Name	Relation	Age	Name	Relation	Age
Michael Healy	Head	40	Mary Dolan	Head	50
Mary Healy	Wife	30	Anne Dolan	Sister	40
Thomas Healy	Son	13			
John Healy	Son	10	Laurence Dolan	Head	64
Timothy Healy	Son	7	Mary Dolan	Wife	52
Mary Healy	Daughter	5	James Dolan	Brother	70
Michael Healy	Son	4	Margaret Dolan	Daughter	21
Patrick Healy	Son	2			
James Healy	Son	1mt	Catherine Dolan	Head	70
			John Dolan	Son	29
Peter Hopkins	Head	40	Michael Dolan	Son	28
Bridget Hopkins	Wife	28	Kate Dolan	Daughter	25
Patrick Skelly	Uncle	80	Bridget Dolan	Daughter	28
James Hopkins	Son	5	John Dolan	G.son	2
Marie Hopkins	Daughter	3	Thomas Dolan	G.son	1
Michael Hopkins	Son	1			
			Mary Brennan	Head	58
Patrick Dolan	Head	31	James Brennan	Son	29
Mary Dolan	Wife	31	Catherine Brennan	Daughter	26
Thomas Fallon	Head	55	John Mulvihill	Head	36
Norah Fallon	Wife	49	Michael Mulvihill	Brother	48
Thomas Fallon	Son	27	Mary Mulvihill	Sister	40
Patrick Fallon	Son	24			
Annie Fallon	Daughter	22	Thomas Dolan	Head	50
			Catherine Dolan	Wife	40
James McGowan (Navy)	Head	43	Ellen Dolan	Daughter	15
Maria McGowan	Wife	30	Patrick Dolan	Son	12
Patrick McGowan	Son	2	Thomas Dolan	Son	10
Mary McGowan	Daughter	_	John Dolan	Son	8
			James Dolan	Son	6
Patrick Hopkins	Head	45	Bridget Dolan	Daughter	4
Mary Hopkins	Wife	40			
John Hopkins	Son	16	Peter Hopkins	Head	56
Michael Hopkins	Son	14	Mary Hopkins	Wife	56
Patrick Hopkins	Son	10	John Hopkins	Son	26
Thomas Hopkins	Son	5	Mary Hopkins	Daughter	23
Mary Hopkins	Daughter	12	Ann Hopkins	Daughter	21
Rose Hopkins	Daughter	8			
Bridget Hopkins	Niece	? 82	**Derrynagolia**		
Catherine Hopkins	Servant	49			
			Patrick Forde	Head	55
Catherine Hopkins	Head	80	Mary Forde	Wife	29
John Hopkins	Son	50	Mary Margt.Forde	Daugh.	9
Michael Hopkins	Son	40	Annie Forde	Daugh.	3
Catherine Hopkins	Daughter	45			
Peter Hopkins	Son	36	William Lennon	Head	75
Eliza Hopkins	G.Daugh.	30	Catherine Lennon	Wife	66
James Hopkins	G.son	4	Rose Lennon	Daugh.	32
Mary E. Hopkins	G.Daugh.	3	Bridget Lennon	Daugh.	30
Peter Hopkins	G.son	_	Joseph Ganly	G.son	2
			John Fallon	Servant	30

Name	Relation	Age	Name	Relation	Age
Michael Connaughton	Head	50	**Derrynabuntale**		
Mary Connaughton	Wife	40			
Patrick Connaughton	Son	23	Anne Dimond	Head	48
Michael Connaughton	Son	18	William Dimond	Son	24
Annie Connaughton	Daugh.	14	Arthur Dimond	Son	22
Denis Connaughton	Son	12	Sarah Dimond	Daugh.	21
Bridget Connaughton	Daugh.	10	George Dimond	Son	19
Margt. Connaughton	Daugh.	5	Thomas Dimond	Son	15
Mary Kelly	Mother-in-law	79	William Jordan	Servant	41
Honor Forde	Head	55	Thomas Gerety	Head	75
Mary Forde	Daugh.	10	Margaret Gerety	Wife	70
			Bridget Gerety	Daugh.	45
			William Gerety	Son	35
James Mulry	Head	64			
James Mulry	Son	31	James Hanly	Head	60
Mary Mulry	Daugh.	28			
Bridget Mulry	Daugh.	23	Catherine Lynn	Head	80
			Bernard Lynn	Son	34
Bernard Fox	Head	49	Anne Lynn	Dau.in-law	30
Eliza Fox	Wife	42	Kate Lynn	G.Daugh.	8
Thomas Fox	Son	24	John Lynn	G.son	6
Kate Fox	Daugh.	18	Patrick Lynn	G.son	4
Lizzie Fox	Daugh.	14	Annie Lynn	G.Daugh.	2
Michael Fox	Son	11	Patrick Scully	Servant	23
Annie Fox	Daugh.	9			
Patrick Fox	Son	6	Patrick Fox	Head	40
James Fox	Brother	55	Bridget Fox	Sister	38
			Michael Fox	Brother	36
John Fox	Head	59	James Hanly	Servant	20
Margaret Fox	Wife	40			
Thomas Fox	Son	9	James Kelly (Stonemason)	Head	62
Bernard Fox	Son	7	Mary Kelly	Head	55
Mary Fox	Daugh.	5	Michael Kelly	Son	25
Patrick Fox	Son	3	Patrick Kelly	Son	22
Anne Fox	Daugh.	1	Lizzie Kelly	Daugh.	18
			Annie Kelly	Daugh.	12
Patrick Connaughton	Head	50			
Bridget Connaughton	Wife	35	**Annagh**		
Mary Connaughton	Daugh.	14			
John Connaughton	Son	9	Michael Fox	Head	62
Bridget Connaughton	Daugh.	8	Catherine Fox	Wife	54
Ellen Connaughton	Daugh.	4	Andrew Fox	Son	22
Eliza Connaughton	Daugh.	–	Patrick Fox	Son	20
			Maryanne Fox	Daugh.	16
			James Fox	Son	10
Bernard Mulry	Head	60			
Ellen Mulry	Wife	54	Thomas Fox	Head	48
Mary A. Mulry	Daugh.	25	Anne Fox	Wife	46
Kate Mulry	Daugh.	23	Margt. Fox	Daugh.	4
John Mulry	Son	19	Michael Fox	Son	3
			John Fox	Brother	52

Name	Relation	Age	Name	Relation	Age
Michael Fox	Nephew	23	**Ballinacliffy**		
John Magrath	Servant	64			
			Ann Casey	Head	60
John Lally	Head	67			
Catherine Lally	Wife	70	James Casey	Head	63
Patrick Lally	Son	34	Mary Casey	Wife	40
John Lally	Son	32	Kate Casey	Daugh.	6
Julia Lally	Daugh.	28	John Casey	Son	4
			Mary Casey	Daugh.	1
Bethlehem					
			James Brown	Head	60
Richard Stanley	Head	44	Rose Brown	Wife	40
Alice Stanley	Daugh.	6	Patrick Brown	Son	1
Sidney Stanley	Daugh.	1	Mary Brown	Sister	50
Edmond Stanley	Brother	45			
Margt.Russell	Moth-in-law	67	Catherine McLynn	Head	70
John Reynolds	Servant	25	Catherine McLynn	Daugh.	42
Bridget McGarrell	Servant	13	Charles McLynn	Son	38
Maryanne McGarrell	Servant	17			
			Margaret Connell	Head	40
Bleanaphuttoge			Kate Connell	Niece	25
			John Connell	Nephew	22
William Murtagh	Head	54	Bridget Connell	Daugh.	18
Catherine Murtagh	Wife	42	Patrick Connell	Son	15
Thomas Murtagh	Son	16	William Connell	Son	13
Patrick Murtagh	Son	14	Margt. Connell	Daugh.	14
Andrew Murtagh	Son	10	Elizabeth Connell	Daugh.	10
Catherine Murtagh	Daugh.	5	Maria Connell	Daugh.	8
Bridget Murtagh	Daugh.	2			
			Michael Tracy	Head	50
James Fox	Head	52	John Fox	Head	60
Anne Fox	Wife	38	Mary Fox	Wife	50
Patrick Fox	Son	3	Patrick Fox	Son	30
Maryanne Fox	Daugh.	1	Annie Fox	Daugh.	22
Thomas Fox	Son	_	John Fox	Son	19
Eliz Fox	Sister	25	Michael Fox	Son	17
Michael Dolan	Nephew	18	Catherine Fox	Daugh.	17
			Agnes Fox	Daugh.	13
Ellen Murtagh	Head	58			
John Murtagh	Son	26	Thomas Carty	Head	70
			Mary Carty	Wife	56
Michael Fox	Head	91	Patrick Carty	Son	36
Thomas Fox	Son	48	Francis Carty	Son	34
Patrick Fox	G.son	4	Bridget Carty	Daugh.	28
William Fox	G.son	3	Annie Carty	Daugh.	26
Thomas Fox	G.son	1			
Maryanne Fox	G.Daugh.	_	Margaret Ganly	Head	60
			Mary A. Ganly	Daugh.	35
Francis Dunican	Head	65	Patrick Ganly	Son	34
Ellen Dunican	Sister	52	William Ganly	Son	32
James McDaniele	Traveller	81	Kate A. Ganly	Daugh.	28
Mary Farrell	Visitor	75	Margaret Ganly	Daugh.	26

Name	Relation	Age	Name	Relation	Age
Margaret Reid	Head	72	William Igoe	Head	50
John Reid	Son	54	Margaret Igoe	Wife	40
Bridget Reid	Daugh.-in-law	45	Thomas Igoe	Son	26
Thomas Reid	G.son	11	William Igoe	Son	20
James Reid	G.son	6	Annie Igoe	Daugh.	9
John J. Reid	G.son	4	James Murphy	Head	45
Patrick Reid	G.son	3	Catherine Murphy	Wife	38
Mary Reid	Daugh.	35	William J. Murphy	Son	–
Bernard McLinn	Head	66	Catherine McGee	Head	60
Ellen McLinn	Wife	65	John McGee	Son	30
Michael McLinn	Son	24	Peter McGee	Son	24
			Kate McGee	Daugh.	20
John Kelly	Head	45	Katie Casey	Niece	8
Mary McLinn	Head	41	Edward McGee	Head	63
William McLinn	Son	16	Margaret McGee	Wife	70
Francis McLinn	Son	12			
Joseph McLinn	Son	10	William Murphy	Head	46
Peter McLinn	Son	8	Mary Murphy	Wife	56
Andrew McLinn	Son	6	James Murphy	Son	25
Bernard McLinn	Son	3	William Murphy	Son	17
			Brigid Murphy	Daugh.	12
Muckenagh			Kate Murphy	Daugh.	11
James Reid	Head	45	Daniel Heffernan	Head	62
Thomas Reid	Brother	55	Kate Heffernan	Wife	55
Bridget Reid	Sister	34	Michael Heffernan	Son	16
Thomas P. Reid	Cousin	75			
John Connor	Servant	40	William Murphy	Head	45
James Farrell	Servant	45	Catherine Murphy	Wife	42
			Mary Murphy	Daugh.	11
John McGarrell	Head	77	Patrick Murphy	Son	10
Bridget McGarrell	Daugh.-in-law	37	Bridget Murphy	Daugh.	8
John McGarrell	G.son	17	Kate Murphy	Daugh.	6
James McGarrell	G.son	14	Annie Murphy	Daugh.	4
Kate McGarrell	G.Daugh.	12	James Murphy	Son	2
Patrick McGarrell	G.son	11	John Conlon	Nephew	14
Maggie McGarrell	G.Daugh.	9			
Lizzie McGarrell	G.Daugh.	7	Michael Duck	Head	58
Michael McGarrell	G.son	5	John Duck	Brother	44
Sicille McGarrell	G.Daugh.	–	Ellen Heffernan	Niece	26
Patrick Berry	Head	48	Patrick Duck	Head	46
Ellen Berry	Wife	60	Mary Duck	Wife	40
			James Duck	Son	12
Thomas Igoe	Head	63	Ellen Duck	Daugh.	9
Maggie Igoe	Daugh.	19	Patrick Duck	Son	7
Maggie Igoe	G.Daugh.	–	Anne Duck	Daugh.	5
			Michael Duck	Son	1
Pat Igoe	Head	66			
Bernard Igoe	Son	19			
Mary A. Igoe	Daugh.	17			

Name	Relation	Age	Name	Relation	Age
Mary Heffernan	Head	46	Michael Connorton	Son	11
Edward Heffernan	Son	30	Joseph Connorton	Son	8
Mary Heffernan	Daugh.	28	John Connorton	Son	4
Ann Heffernan	Daugh.	19	Tommy Connorton	Son	2
Michael Connaughton	Nephew	14	Mary Connorton	Niece	1
			Mary E. Connorton	Daugh.	1yr.
James McLynn	Head	73			
			Mary Murphy	Head	50
James McLynn	Head	80	Patrick Murphy	Son	28
John McLynn	Son	38	Mary Murphy	Daugh.	24
Thomas McLynn	Son	40	Kate Murphy	Daugh.	19
Julianne McLynn	Daugh.-in-law	30			
Mary McLynn	G.Daugh.	7	Patrick McCann	Head	40
Kate McLynn	G.Daugh.	5	Anne McCann	Wife	38
Anne McLynn	G.Daugh.	3	William McCann	Son	15
John McLynn	G.son	1			
Agnes McLynn	G.Daugh.	–	John Rushe	Head	30
			Kate Rushe	Wife	30
Mary McLinn	Head	72	Mary Rushe	Daugh.	–.
Thomas McLinn	Son	43			
Ann McLinn	Daugh.	38	John Moran	Head	68
Catherine McLinn	Daugh.	32	Ellen Moran	Wife	60
Thomas Tiernan	Servant	23	John Moran	Son	24
			Margaret Moran	Daugh.	18
James McLynn	Head	35	Kate Moran	Daugh.	16
Michael McLynn	Brother	27			
Mary McLynn	Sister	23	Christy Elliot	Head	54
			Kate Elliot	Wife	46
Ross			Mary Elliot	Daugh.	19
			Francis Elliot	Son	15
Annie Murphy	Head	67	Marcella Elliot	Daugh.	13
Patrick Murphy	Son	25	John Elliot	Son	10
Annie Murphy	Daugh.	27	Lily Elliot	Daugh.	7
Elizabeth Murphy	Daugh.	20			
			Julia Fagan	Head	65
James Coughlin	Head	47	John Fagan	Son	25
Catherine Coughlin	Wife	35	Mary Fagan	Daugh.	30
Mary A. Coughlin	Daugh.	5	Kate Fagan	Daugh.	25
Thomas Coughlin	Son	3			
Bridget Coughlin	Daugh.	1	Thomas Clines	Head	75
			Ann Clines	Wife	63
Patrick Coughlin	Head	35	Michael Clines	Son	21
Killeenmore			Patrick Blagriff	Head	69
			Ann Blagriff	Wife	40
James Connorton	Head	50	James Blagriff	Son	19
Mary Connorton	Wife	40	Kate Blagriff	Daugh.	18
Patrick Connorton	Brother	46	Alice Blagriff	Daugh.	17
Annie Connorton	Daugh.	19			
Maggie Connorton	Daugh.	17	Mary Keegan	Head	45
Francis Connorton	Son	15	Kate Keegan	Daugh.	17
Mary F. Connorton	Daugh.	13	Christopher Keegan	Son	14
			James Keegan	Son	11

Name	Relation	Age	Name	Relation	Age
Portlick			John Keena	Head	50
			Thomas Keena	Son	23
Robert Wolfe Smyth	Head	43	Michael Keena	Son	21
Agnes G. Smyth	Wife	41	Mary Keena	Daugh.	20
Harriet Smyth	Daugh.	8	John Keena	Son	18
Mary Murphy	Servant	34	William Keena	Son	16
Anne Watson	Servant	33	Bridget Keena	Daugh.	13
Kate Madden	Servant	23	Patrick Keena	Son	7
			Kate Keena	Daugh.	5
John Slevin	Head	70			
Ann Slevin	Wife	45	Owen Leavy	Head	70
Thomas Slevin	Son	17	John Leavy	Son	30
Mary K. Slevin	Daugh.	14			
Bridget Sparks	Sr.in-law	30	Thomas Moran	Head	50
			Bridget Moran	Sister	41
Abraham Moore	Head	68	Mary Savage	Niece	25
John Moore	Son	18	William Farrell	Nephew	7
Mary A. Moore	Niece	30			
			John Killion	Head	60
Thomas Thorpe	Head	52	Margaret Killion	Wife	58
Ruth Thorpe	Wife	58	Mary Neil	S.in-law	60
Elizabeth Thorpe	Daugh.	19	Patrick Killion	Son	18
James Thorpe	Son	17	Thomas Killion	Son	15
			John Killion	Son	12
Richard Burns	Head	55	George Killion	Son	10
Jane Burns	Wife	50			
Mary Burns	Daugh.	25	Mary A. Reid	Head	45
William Burns	Son	23	Patrick Reid	Son	18
Richard Burns	Son	22	Francis Reid	Son	17
Andrew Burns	Son	19	John J.Reid	Son	14
Michael Burns	Son	15	Mary Kate Reid	Daugh.	9
Patrick Thorpe	Head	39	Thomas Cunningham	Head	40
Lena Thorpe	Wife	38	Kate Cunningham	Wife	30
Elizabeth Thorpe	Daugh.	7	Mary Cunningham	Daugh.	11
			John Cunningham	Son	9
Killinure Nth.			Bridget Cunningham	Daugh.	7
			Patrick Cunningham	Son	4
Bernard Byrne	Head	64	Julia A. Cunningham	Daugh.	1
Mary Byrne	Sister	60			
			Thomas Casey	Head	43
Andrew Byrne	Head	40	Mary Casey	Wife	33
Ann Byrne	Wife	44	Joseph Casey	Son	11
Pat Byrne	Son	18	William Casey	Son	9
Michael Byrne	Son	16			
James Byrne	Son	11	Patrick Cunningham	Head	64
Thomas Byrne	Son	10			
Mary Byrne	Daugh.	9	William Carthy	Head	60
Margaret Byrne	Daugh.	8	Rose A. Carthy	Wife	42
Anne Byrne	Daugh.	8	Anne Carthy	Daugh.	8
Kate Byrne	Daugh.	6	Margaret Carthy	Daugh.	7
			Catherine Carthy	Daugh.	7

Name	Relation	Age	Name	Relation	Age
Mary Carthy	Daugh.	5	Henry Quigley	Head	38
Patrick Carthy	Son	3	Mary Quigley	Wife	33
Michael Carthy	Son	1	Mary E. Quigley	Daugh.	5
			Peter Quigley	Son	4
Peter Quigley	Head	42	Anne Quigley	Daugh.	4
Margaret Quigley	Wife	45	Joseph Quigley	Son	2
Mary Quigley	Daugh.	12			
John Quigley	Son	10	Bridget Dalton	Head	50
Annie Quigley	Daugh.	9	Katie Dalton	Daugh.	20
Lizzie Quigley	Daugh.	7	Rose Dalton	Daugh.	19
Maggie Quigley	Daugh.	4	Andrew Dalton	Son	15
Thomas Killion	Head	50	Margarita Daniel	Head	68
Sally Killion	Wife	50	Cecelia Daniel	Sister	51
Fergus Farrell	Head	85	Bridget Daniel	Ser.	25
William Farrell	Son	45			
Anne Farrell	Daugh.	47	John Dalton	Head	55
Patrick Finerty	Servant	50			
			William Connell	Head	55
Thomas Farrell	Head	48	Bridget Connell	Wife	50
Anne Farrell	Wife	42	Michael Connell	Son	16
John Farrell	Son	19	Bridget Connell	Daugh.	9
Annie Farrell	Daugh.	16	Thomas Connell	Son	11
Michael Farrell	Son	14			
Thomas Farrell	Son	12	Thomas Early	Head	53
James Farrell	Son	9	Mary Early	Wife	44
Lena Farrell	Daugh.	6	Michael Early	Son	19
Patrick Farrell	Son	3	Peter Early	Son	18
			Thomas Early	Son	17
James Casey	Head	50	Julia Early	Daugh.	12
Jane Casey	Wife	44	Madge Early	Daugh.	9
Mary Casey	Daugh.	15	Anne Early	Daugh.	6
Katie Casey	Daugh.	13			
Ellie Casey	Daugh.	11	John Fagan	Head	41
Janie Casey	Daugh.	9	Julia Nolan	Relative	89
James Casey	Son	7	Michael Murphy	Servant	22
Michael Casey	Son	3			
			Mary Reid	Head	62
Jane Walsh	Head	80	Marcella Reid	Sister	60
James Walsh	Son	45	Mary Melin	Niece	30
			James Higgins	Cousin	23
Edward Dalton	Head	40			
Kate Dalton	Wife	34	Patrick Casey	Head	50
Michael Walton	Son	10	Marcella Casey	Wife	48
Patrick Walton	Son	9	James Casey	Son	15
Maria Walton	Daugh.	7	Christy Casey	Son	14
Annie Walton	Daugh.	5	Mary Casey	Daugh.	12
James Walton	Son	4			
Edward Dalton	Son	3	James Coughlin	Head	64
John Dalton	Son	1	Mary Coughlin	Wife	64
			James Coughlin	Son	25
			William Coughlin	Son	18

Name	Relation	Age
John McCann	Head	58
Ellen McCann	Wife	48
Michael McCann	Son	24
Mary McCann	Daugh.	19
James McCann	Son	18
Annie McCann	Daugh.	16
Bernard McCann	Son	13
William McCann	Son	10
Timothy McCann	Son	8
Thomas McCann	Son	5

Ballinlough

Name	Relation	Age
Thomas Keena	Head	31
Bridget Keena	Wife	32
Patrick Keena	Son	6
Michael Keena	Son	5
Edward Keena	Son	4
Mary Jane Keena	Daugh.	2
Thomas Keena	Son	_

Killinure South

Name	Relation	Age
James Corrigan	Head	41
Julia Corrigan	Wife	39
Mary Corrigan	Daugh.	5
Julia Corrigan	Daugh.	4
Maggie Corrigan	Daugh.	2

Benown

Name	Relation	Age
Robert Kean Brereton	Head	59
Geraldine Brereton	Mother	83
Mary G. Brereton	Sister	54
Adela Brereton	Sister	40
Kate Barker	Visitor	75
Mary Cromwell	Servant	60
Eliza Quigley	Servant	25
Bridget Malone	Servant	21
Patrick Fox (Surgeon)	Head	48
John Hopkins	Head	50
Mary Hopkins		42
Daniel Grennan	Head	70
Kate Grennan	Daugh.	24
Patrick Henson	Head	60
Catherine Henson	Wife	60

Name	Relation	Age
Patrick Breen	Head	29
Bridget Breen	Wife	27
Lily Breen	Daugh.	2
Christopher Boulger	Head	57
Rose Boulger	Wife	48

Portaneena

Name	Relation	Age
Catherine Devine	Head	53
William Devine	Son	23
Michael Murtagh	Head	73
Patrick Murtagh	Son	25
James Murtagh	Son	18
Maggie Murtagh	Daugh.	16
John Murtagh	Son	13
William Moran	Head	53
Margaret Moran	Wife	50
William Moran	Son	21
James Moran	Son	17
John Moran	Son	15
Margaret Moran	Daugh.	12
George Moran	Son	7
Jane Moran	Daugh.	4
Patrick Murray	Head	84
Michael Murray	Son	40
Mary Murray	Daugh.in-law	40
Thomas Murray	G.son	15
John Murray	G.son	13
James Murray	G.son	11
Michael Murray	G.son	9
Bridget Murray	G.daugh.	7
Patrick Murray	G.son	5
Joseph Murray	G.son	2
Thomas Brien	Head	61
Maria Brien	Wife	52
Thomas Brien	Son	37
Sarah Brien	Daugh.	20
Margaret Brien	Daugh.	19

Ballykeeran

Name	Relation	Age
Thomas Rush	Head	40
Kate Rush	Wife	35
Anne Rush	Daugh.	15
John Rush	Son	11
Peter Rush	Son	10
Patrick Rush	Son	7

Name	Relation	Age	Name	Relation	Age
Peter Rush	Head	55	Peter Keenan	Head	53
Eliza Rush	Sister	47	Kate Keenan	Wife	51
			Maggie Keenan	Daugh.	21
John Fitzpatrick	Head	56	Roseanne Keenan	Daugh.	18
Elizabeth Fitzpatrick	Wife	38			
Alice Fitzpatrick	Daugh.	6	Thomas Claffey	Head	80
Mary Fitzpatrick	Daugh.	5			
Elizabeth Fitzpatrick	Daugh.	4	Charles Tiernan	Head	74
Catherine Fitzpatrick	Daugh.	3	Mary Tiernan	Wife	60
John Fitzpatrick	Son	2	Bridget Tiernan	Daugh.	30
Patrick Fitzpatrick	Son	_	John Tiernan	Son	29
Edward Gaffy	Servant	58	Charles Tiernan	Son	25
			Thomas Tiernan	Son	23
James Keenan	Head	30			
Maria Keenan	Sister	30	Ann Hughes	Head	50
			Thomas Hughes	Son	32
Patrick Dockery R.I.C.	Head	52	Michael Hughes	Son	23
Ann Dockery	Wife	49	Kate Hughes	Daugh.	13
Patrick Dockery	Son	20			
Luke Dockery	Son	16	Michael Finneran	Head	56
			Margt. T. Finneran	Wife	44
James Mallon	Head	65			
			Michael Harte	Head	50
Peter Shaughnessy	Head	32	Margt. Harte	Wife	50
Rose Shaughnessy	Sister	30	Bernard Harte	Son	22
			Agnes Harte	Daugh	18
John Shaughnessy	Head	40	Michael Harte	Son	13
Ann Shaughnessy	Wife	40	Margt. Harte	Daugh.	11
Lizzie Shaughnessy	Daugh.	20			
Patrick Shaughnessy	Son	19	James Flynn	Head	38
Mary A. Shaughnessy	Daugh.	19	Margt. C. Flynn	Wife	40
Thomas Shaughnessy	Son	15	Mark Joseph Flynn	Son	7
Agnes Shaughnessy	Daugh.	12	John P.Flynn	Son	6
Kate Shaughnessy	Daugh.	9	Mary Flynn	Daugh.	4
Francis Shaughnessy	Son	6	James Flynn	Son	_.
Daniel Shaughnessy	Son	4			
			Gilbert Murthagh	Head	74
Bernard Gilligan	Head	62	Gilbert Murthagh	Son	19
Jane Gilligan	Wife	62			
Thomas Gilligan	Son		Patrick Breen	Head	76
Mary Jane Gilligan	Daugh.				
			Harriet Kearney	Head	47
Matthew Clark (Tea Merchant) Head		50	William Kearney	Son	25
Lizzie Clark	Wife	48	Bride Kearney	Daugh.	20
			Patrick Kearney	Servant	56
Mary McColgan	Head	60	Thomas Hughes	Servant	50
Margaret Rush	Servant	56			
			Ballykeeran Big		
Elizabeth Flanagan	Head	60			
Thomas Flanagan	Son	28	Mary Murthagh	Head	60
Delia Flanagan	Daugh.	26	John Murthagh	Son	35
Eugene Flanagan	Son	23	Joseph Murthagh	Son	30

Name	Relation	Age	Name	Relation	Age
Thomas Murthagh	Son	29	James Dillon	Head	40
John Neville	Servant	45	Catherine Dillon	Wife	48
Mary Shaughnessy	Servant	45	Michael White (Father-in-law)		88
Catherine Hynes	Head	56	Peter Halligan	Head	50
John Hynes	Son	38	Mary Halligan	Wife	31
Bernard Hynes	Son	36	Margaret Halligan	Daugh.	13
Maggie Hynes	Daugh.	34	Annie Halligan	Daugh.	12
Patrick Hynes	Son	32	Mary Halligan	Daugh.	10
Michael Hynes	Son	30	Bridget Halligan	Daugh.	8
William Hynes	Son	28	Lizzie Halligan	Daugh.	7
Julia Hynes	Daugh	26	Kate Halligan	Daugh.	4
			Hubert P. Halligan	Son	2
Kate Brown	Head	55	William Halligan	Son	_.
Ballykeeran Little			Richard Macken	Head	70
			Ellen Macken	Wife	56
Conor Duffy	Head	36	Richard Macken	Son	27
Mary Duffy	Wife	32	Joseph Macken	Son	21
Bridget Duffy	Sister	20	Mary Macken	Daugh.	17
Henry Kilmurray	Head	57	Catherine Keenan	Head	63
John Kilmurray	Son	21	Patrick Keenan	Son	38
			Bridget Keenan	Daugh.	23
John Hall	Head	41	Elizabeth Keenan	Daugh.	19
Ethel Hall	Wife	27			
Eva Hall	Sister	33	Mary Reilly	Head	36
Clare Hall	Sister	29			
Anne Kilmurray	Servant	23	William Scanlon	Head	46
Claire Kilmurray	Servant	21	Mary Scanlon	Wife	42
			Patrick Scanlon	Son	17
Ann Chivers	Head	50	Catherine Scanlon	Daugh.	17
Ann Molloy	Servant	30	Thomas Scanlon	Son	14
			John Scanlon	Son	10
Margaret Brien	Head	40	Francis Scanlon	Son	7
Mary Brien	Daughter	16	Michael Scanlon	Son	4
James Brien	Son	14	James Kelly	Servant	45
Ann Brien	Daugh.	9			
Henry Brien	Son	5	Patrick Reilly	Head	65
			Catherine Reilly	Wife	50
Coosan			Thomas Reilly	Son	31
			Bridget Reilly	Daugh.	30
Patrick Hughes	Head	79			
Michael Hughes	Son	41	William Ward	Head	51
Kate Hughes	Daugh-in-law	33	Catherine Ward	Wife	60
Patrick Hughes	G.son	7	Margaret Ward	Daugh.	20
Francis Hughes	G.son	6	Thomas Kelly	G.son	14
Gilbert Hughes	G.son	5			
Michael J. Hughes	G.son	4	Michael McCormack	Head	40
Clare Hughes	G.Daugh.	3	Mary McCormack	Wife	39
Alicia Hughes	G.Daugh.	2	Mary McCormack	Daugh.	15
Annie Hughes	G.Daugh.	1	Patrick McCormack	Son	10

Name	Relation	Age	Name	Relation	Age
Michael McCormack	Son	8	Bartle Dillon	Head	34
Christina McCormack	Daugh.	4	Bridget Dillon	Wife	30
			Margt. Dillon	Daugh.	2
Cornelius McCormack	Head	52	Edward Dillon	Son	1mt
Elizabeth McCormack	Wife	45			
Michael McCormack	Son	19	Margaret Malone	Head	57
Patrick McCormack	Son	15	Owen Malone	Son	33
William McCormack	Son	12	Thomas Malone	Son	24
John McCormack	Son	9	Esther Malone	Daugh.	17
Catherine McCormack	Daugh.	8			
Elizabeth McCormack	Daugh.	5	James Dillon	Head	30
Patrick McCormack	Brother	65	Louisa Dillon	Sister	27
Adam Johnston	Head	45	Michael McCormack	Head	28
			Ellen McCormack	Wife	26
Creaghduff South			Sarah Eivers	Head	62
			John Eivers	Son	41
Robert Levinge	Head	50	James Eivers	Son	26
Hester Levinge	Wife	40	Ellen Concannon	Niece	11
Ida Levinge	Daugh.	8			
Walter Levinge	Son	6	John Perry	Head	45
Fanny Anderson	Servant	24	Mary A. Perry	Wife	23
			Mary A. Perry	Daugh.	1
Creaghduff			Bridget Costello	Aunt	70
John Walsh	Head	30	James Costello	Head	65
Eliza Walsh	Wife	52	Margaret Costello	Wife	60
Patrick Norton	Servant	25	Mary Costello	Daugh.	30
			Jane Costello	Daugh.	27
Catherine Reilly	Head	41	Kate Costello	Daugh.	18
Mary Anne Reilly	Daugh.	19	Thomas Costello	Son	25
Patrick Reilly	Son	17	John Costello	Son	23
John Reilly	Son	15			
Michael Reilly	Son	11	Patrick Hynds	Head	60
Bridget Reilly	Daugh.	9	Bridget Hynds	Wife	64
Thomas Reilly	Son	7	James Malone	Nephew	27
William Reilly	Son	5			
Bernard Reilly	Son	2	Edward Blaney	Head	50
			Bridget Blaney	Wife	45
Michael Reilly	Head	55	Bridget Blaney	Daugh.	19
Mary A.Reilly	Daugh.	10	William Blaney	Son	18
Lizzie Reilly	Daugh.	7	Catherine Blaney	Daugh.	17
John J.Reilly	Son	5	Edward Blaney	Son	15
Teresa B. Reilly	Daugh.	2	John Blaney	Son	14
James Reilly	Brother	62	Mary Blaney	Daugh.	9
Eliza McCormack	Boarder	84	Ellen Blaney	Daugh.	8
Ellen Geoghagan		14	Elizabeth Blaney	Daugh.	6
			Sarah Blaney	Daugh	3
Robert Johnson	Head	71	Catherine Blaney	Mother	80
James Johnson	Brother	62			

Name	Relation	Age	Name	Relation	Age
Margaret Geoghegan	Head	41	Peter Connor	Son	4
Henry Geoghegan	Son	21	Thomas Connor	Son	3
Michael Geoghegan	Son	12			
William Geoghegan	Son	9	Thomas Ward	Head	41
			James Ward	Brother	60
Michael Geoghegan	Head	76	Mary Ward	Wife	33
Mary Geoghegan	Wife	74	Elizabeth Ward	Daugh.	6
John Geoghegan	Son	24	Mary Ward	Daugh.	4
			James Hanly	Nephew	6
Meehan			John Scanlon	Head	50
			Catherine Scanlon	Wife	58
Michael Reilly	Head	44	Patrick Scanlon	Son	26
Catherine Reilly	Wife	45	Annie Scanlon	Daugh.	23
Martin Reilly	Son	17			
Catherine Reilly	Daugh.	11	Catherine Connor	Head	75
Patrick Reilly	Son	9	Patrick Connor	Son	42
Ellen Reilly	Daugh.	5	Anne Connor	D.in-law	40
Michael Reilly	Son	3	Francis Connor	G.son	8
			Mary Connor	G.Daugh.	7
Thomas Farrell	Head	72	Catherine Connor	G.Daugh.	5
Patrick Farrell	Son	31	John Connor	G.son	3
			Lizzie Pepper	Servant	13
John Connolly	Head	45			
Catherine Connolly	Wife	35	Martin Golden	Head	44
Margaret Connolly	Daugh.	10	Mary Golden	Wife	43
Michael Connolly	Son	7	Margaret Golden	Daugh.	19
Mary Connolly	Daugh.	5	Ellen Golden	Daugh.	15
Lily Connolly	Daugh.	4	Annie Golden	Daugh.	13
Catherine Connolly	Daugh.	3	Catherine Golden	Daugh.	11
John Boland	Cousin	82	Elizabeth Golden	Daugh.	9
			Patrick Golden	Son	6
William McDonagh	Head	72	Matthew Golden	Son	4
Anne McDonagh	Wife	71	Bridget Golden	Daugh.	1
Michael McDonagh	Son	33			
William McDonagh	Son	30	Martin Mulvihill	Head	50
Anne McDonagh	Daugh.	28	Elizabeth Mulvihill	Wife	43
			Peter Mulvihill	Son	22
Bridget Reynolds	Head	50	Patrick Mulvihill	Son	20
Rosie Reynolds	Daugh.	25	Mary Mulvihill	Daugh.	18
Elizabeth Reynolds	Daugh.	24	Kate Mulvihill	Daugh.	16
Agnes Reynolds	Daugh.	23	Bridget Mulvihill	Daugh.	14
Patrick Reynolds	Son	19	Martin Mulvihill	Son	12
Elsie Reynolds	Daugh.	12	Maggie Mulvihill	Daugh.	10
Bridget Reynolds	Daugh.	9	Annie Mulvihill	Daugh.	7
			Thomas Mulvihill	Son	5
Peter Connor	Head	34	Bernard Mulvihill	Son	1
Thomas Connor	Brother	32	Mary Fallon	Aunt	67
Mary Connor	Wife	33			
Mary Connor	Daugh.	8	Patrick Moran	Head	38
Patrick Connor	Son	6	Mary Moran	Mother	80
John Connor	Son	5	Mary Moran	Wife	32

Name	Relation	Age
Margaret Moran	Head	57
John Moran	Son	31
Margaret Moran	D.in-law	25
Thomas Moran	G.son	1
Edward Farrell	Head	47
Mary Farrell	Wife	47
Michael Farrell	Son	17
James Farrell	Son	13
John Farrell	Son	10
Patrick Farrell	Son	7
Edward Farrell	Son	5
William Farrell	Son	2
Kate Connor	Servant	18
Mary Rourke	Servant	30
Andrew Cunningham	Head	25

Garnafelia

Name	Relation	Age
Robert A. Handcock	Head	36
Ethel V. Handcock	Wife	26
Violet L. Handcock	Daugh.	5
Richard E. Handcock	Son	4
Alice Servis	Sister	33
Anne Eivers	Servant	30
Ellen Myers	Servant	30_

Roscommon Shore

Barrybeg

Name	Relation	Age
Michael Dunning	Head	65
Catherine Dunning	Wife	50
Terence Dunning	Son	28
Thomas Dunning	Son	26
Mary Dunning	Daugh.	19
Pat Henehan	Head	49
Elizabeth Henehan	Wife	45
Marion Henehan	Daugh.	22
Willie Henehan	Son	19
Delia Henehan	Daugh.	17
Patrick Henehan	Son	16
Michael Kennedy	Servant	10
James Martin	Head	70
Margaret Martin	Wife	55
Mary Martin	Daugh.	25
John Martin	Son	24
James Martin	Son	23

Name	Relation	Age
Michael Martin	Head	27
Rose Martin	Wife	27
Elizabeth Martin	Sister	20
James Martin	Son	1
Michael Martin	Son	1m.
Pat Hand	Head	55
Margaret Hand	Wife	35
Bernard Hand	Son	_
Elizabeth Hand	Daugh.	2
Joseph Duffy	Servant	70
Thomas Duignan	Head	37
Bridget Duignan	Wife	35
John Duignan	Son	8
Thomas Duignan	Son	7
Mary K. Duignan	Daugh.	5
Patrick Duignan	Son	3
Margaret Duignan	Daugh.	_
Pat Rigney	Head	68
Catherine Rigney	Wife	60
Margaret Egan	G.daugh.	15
John Carbary	Head	60
John Carbary	Son	19
Catherine Carbary	Daugh.	17
Elizabeth Carbary	Daugh.	10
Thomas Mannion	Head	45
Sarah Mannion	Wife	35
Mary A. Mannion	Daugh.	7
Margaret Mannion	Daugh.	6
Kate Mannion	Daugh.	5
John Mannion	Son	4
Denis Mannion	Son	2_
Thomas Mannion	Son	1_
Michael Hand	Head	50
Mary Hand	Wife	46
Mary Hand	Step-Daugh.	16
Margaret Hand	Daugh.	9
Michael Hand	Son	7
William Mannion	Head	49
Bridget Mannion	Wife	28
Thomas Mannion	Son	4
William Mannion	Son	2
Matthew Mannion	Son	1
Mary Mannion	Niece	16
Margaret Mannion	Niece	14

Name	Relation	Age
James Connor	Head	63
Elizabeth Connor	Wife	60
James Hynes	Head	36
Mary Hynes	Wife	30
Bridget Hynes	Daugh.	5
John Hynes	Son	3
Francis Henaghan	Head	87
Margaret Henaghan	Wife	86
Francis Henaghan	Son	45
Kate Henaghan	D.in-law	34
James Henaghan	G.son	11
Thomas Henaghan	G.son	8
Tresea Henaghan	G.Daugh.	6
Catherine Henaghan	G.Daugh.	5
Margaret Henaghan	G.Daugh.	2
Catherine Henehan	Head	70
James Henehan	Son	30
Lizzie Henehan	G.Daugh.	8
Mary K. Henehan	G.Daugh.	7
William Henehan	G.son	5
Michael Henehan	G.son	4
James Henehan	G.son	2
Thomas Henehan	G.son	1
William Ramsay	Head	52
Ann Ramsay	Wife	43
James Ramsay	Son	16
Mary A. Ramsay	Daugh.	14
Delia Ramsay	Daugh.	13
Patrick Ramsay	Son	11
William Ramsay	Son	9
Margaret Ramsay	Daugh.	7
Bernard Ramsay	Son	5
David Ramsay	Head	38
Ann Ramsay	Wife	34
John Ramsay	Son	11
Rose A. Ramsay	Daugh.	12
Robert Ramsay	Son	9
Thomas Ramsay	Son	4
David Ramsay	Son	1
George Ramsay	Son	7
John Curley	Head	55
Catherine Curley	Wife	50
Patrick Curley	Son	20
Annie Curley	Daugh.	10
James Curley	G.son	7

Name	Relation	Age
Michael Feeley	Head	45
Michael Feeley	Son	16
Margaret Feeley	Daugh.	14
Patrick Feeley	Son	12
John Feeley	Son	10
Mary Feeley	Daugh.	8
Annie Feeley	Daugh.	6
Francis Cunningham	Head	75
Ann Cunningham	Wife	55
Thomas Cunningham	Son	22
Joseph Cunningham	Son	15
Bernard Cunningham	Son	13
Mary Naughton	Head	34
Ellen Doyle	Daugh.	11
John J. Grenham	Son	4
James McDonagh		4
Bridgie Rowen	Head	65
Thomas Rowen	Son	36
John Rowen	Son	34
Pat Head	Head	68
Mary Head	Wife	65
Catherine Morgan	Head	37
John Morgan	Son	15
Mary Morgan	Daugh.	13
William Morgan	Son	11
Michael Morgan	Son	9
Bridget Morgan	Daugh.	7
Eliza Morgan	Daugh.	5
Charles Morgan	Son	3
Michael Duffy	Head	46
Margaret Duffy	Wife	35
Bridgit Duffy	Daugh.	8
Annie Duffy	Daugh.	6
Mary K. Duffy	Daugh.	4
Bernard Duffy	Son	3
Bernard Rafferty	Head	65
Joseph McGovern	Head	75
Rose McGovern	Wife	66
Mary A. McGovern	Daugh.	40
Joseph McGovern	Son	28
Patrick Duignan	Head	60
Brigid Duignan	Wife	60
Thomas Duignan	Son	30

Name	Relation	Age	Name	Relation	Age
Lizzie Duignan	Daugh	23	William Mahon	Head	40
Patrick Duignan	Son	21	Edith Mahon	Wife	38
			Maurice Gunning	Stepson	13
Luke Duignan	Head	69	Vera Gunning	Step Daugh.	12
Luke Duignan	Son	25	Violet Gunning	Ditto	10
James Duignan	Son	21	Dudley Gunning	Stepson	8
			Muriel Gunning	Step Daugh.	5
Patrick Fleming	Head	33	Charles Fox	Visitor	48
			Mary Austin	Servant	28
Catherine Doorley	Head	42			
Patrick Doorley	Son	14	Peter Brown	Head	50
John Doorley	Son	12	Bridget Brown	Wife	46
			Jane Brown	Daugh.	20
Barrymore			Annie Brown	Daugh.	15
			Delia Brown	Daugh.	13
Michael Doyle	Head	60	John Brown	Son	12
John Doyle	Son	30	William Brown	Son	10
Brigid Doyle	D.in-law	30	Peter Brown	Son	8
Mary K. Doyle	Niece	3	Thomas Brown	Son	6
Elizabeth Doyle	Niece	1	Margaret Brown	Daugh.	4
Maria Madden	Head	26	Patrick McCann	Head	50
Mary J. Madden	Daugh.	6	Elizabeth McCann	Wife	45
Elizabeth Madden	Daugh.	5	John McCann	Son	19
Francis Madden	Son	3	Patrick McCann	Son	17
Bridget Madden	Daugh.	1	Agnes McCann	Daugh.	15
Louisa Bond	Head	62	Edward McCann	Head	60
William Hudson	Brother	57	Rose McCann	Wife	61
Michael Gately	Servant	41	James McCann	Son	30
			Mary McCann	Daugh.	26
John Tiernan	Head	46	Catherine McCann	Daugh.	24
Mary Tiernan	Wife	46	Edward McCann	Son	22
Mary Tiernan	Daugh.	25	William Walshe	Boarder	5
Francis Tiernan	Son	18	John Gatley	Boarder	5
William Jennings	Head	30			
Jane Jennings	Wife	24	Thomas Jennings	Head	55
John Jennings	Son	2	Mary Jennings	Wife	45
William Jennings	Son	–	Thomas Jennings	Son	24
			Ellen Jennings	Daugh.	18
John McCann	Head	36	Kate Jennings	Daugh.	15
Mary E. McCann	Wife	28	John Jennings	Son	13
Michael J. McCann	Son	7	Martin Jennings	Son	11
William McCann	Son	5	Bridget Jennings	Daugh.	9
George McCann	Son	3	Thomas McDaniel	–	–
Rose A. McCann	Daugh.	1	Patrick Burke	–	–
Bernard Connaughton	Head	55			
Thomas Connaughton	Son	24			
Kate Connaughton	Daugh.	19			
Andrew Connaughton	Son	18			
John Connaughton	Son	17			

Name	Relation	Age	Name	Relation	Age
Anne Kelly	Head	42	Mary Heavy	Daugh.	11
Bernard Kelly	Son	10	William Heavy	Son	6
Bridget Kelly	Daugh.	8			
Michael Kelly	Son	14	Michael Geehan	Head	54
Tessy Kelly	Daugh.	7	Mary Geehan	Wife	52
			Ellen Geehan	Daugh.	16
John Ivers	Head	53			
Ellen Ivers	Wife	44	Annie Feeley	Head	32
Annie Ivers	Daugh.	26	Annie Feeley	Daugh.	9
John Ivers	Son	18	Margaret Feeley	Daugh.	7
Thomas Ivers	Son	15	Josephine Feeley	Daugh.	2
Francis Ivers	Son	13			
Michael Ivers	Son	11	John Reilly	Head	40
Ellie Ivers	Daugh.	7	Frances Reilly	Wife	36
Bridget Ivers	Daugh	4	John Reilly	Son	1
Margaret Ivers	Daugh.	2	Eugene Reilly	Son	1
			Patrick McConkey	Boarder	8
Edward Ennis	Head	70			
Thomas Ennis	Son	30	John Brien	Head	66
			John Brien	Son	27
Thomas McGuire	Head	72	Maggie Brien	Daugh.	19
Ellen McGuire	Wife	56			
Thomas J. McGuire	Son	22	Patrick Greene	Head	60
James Maguire	Son	20	Delia Greene	Wife	47
Mary Noone	Boarder	5	Mary Greene	Daugh.	18
Bridget McGuire	Boarder	2	John Greene	Son	15
			Thomas Greene	Son	13
Michael Fitzgerald	Head	59	Edward Greene	Son	11
Catherine Fitzgerald	Wife	40	Michael Greene	Son	10
Mary E. Fitzgerald	Daugh.	9			
John B. Fitzgerald	Son	8	Thomas Feeley	Head	37
Michael P. Fitzgerald	Son	6	Annie Feeley	Wife	30
			Michael Feeley	Son	7
Bridget Heavy	Head	56	Thomas Feeley	Son	5
Patrick Heavy	Son	24	Mary Feeley	Daugh.	4
Michael heavy	Son	22	Lilla Feeley	Daugh.	3
Mary A. Heavy	Daugh.	21	Annie Feeley	Daugh.	2
Bridget Heavy	Daugh.	15	Willie Feeley	Son	_
			Kate Byrne	Servant	19
Michael Dempsey	Head	50			
Catherine Dempsey	Wife	50	William Greene	Head	60
Thomas Dempsey	Son	24	Catherine Greene	Wife	50
Ellen Dempsey	Daugh.	20	William Greene	Son	26
James Dempsey	Son	17	Thomas Henehan	Br.in-law	35
Michael Dempsey	Son	15	Patrick Kelly	Servant	22
John Dempsey	Son	11	Martin Curley	Head	60
Luke Dempsey	Son	9	Julia Curley	Wife	44
			John Curley	Son	18
William Heavy	Head	48	Thomas Curley	Son	16
Catherine Heavy	Wife	42	Peter Curley	Son	14
Patrick Heavy	Son	15	Bernard Curley	Son	12
			James Curley	Son	10

Name	Relation	Age	Name	Relation	Age
Mary Curley	Daugh.	8	**Cornaseer**		
William Reilly	Head	33	James Sweeney	Head	74
Bridget Reilly	Wife	34	James Sweeney	Son	29
Michael J. Reilly	Son	2	Bernard Sweeney	Son	27
			Michael Sweeney	Son	25
Edward Feeney	Head	70	Katie Sweeney	Daugh.	25
Kate Feeney	Daugh.	34	Bridget Sweeney	Daugh.	21
Mary A. Feeney	Daugh.	31			
Edward Feeney	Son	24	John Sweeney	Head	37
Peter Feeney	Son	22			
			John Byrne	Head	64
Patrick Murry	Head	32	Honorah Byrne	Wife	57
Brigid Murry	Sister	19	Ellie Byrne	Daugh.	24
William Feeley	Nephew	8	Molly Glynn	Boarder	7
Francis Macken	Head	32	Charles Byrne	Head	70
Julia Macken	Wife	28	Hannah Dillon	Sister	50
Martha Tiernan	Visitor	11	Patrick Dillon	Nephew	16
			James Dillon	Nephew	14
James Tiernan	Head	55			
Margaret Tiernan	Wife	55	Catherine Prendergast	Head	55
William Tiernan	Son	19	John Prendergast	Son	27
Michael Tiernan	Son	15	Bridget Fallon	Niece	32
Kate Tiernan	Daugh.	13			
James Tiernan	Son	9	Bridget Kelly	Head	75
			Margaret Kelly	Sister	55
Thomas Morgan	Head	55			
			Anne Sweeney	Head	50
Patrick Fahy	Head	42	Delia Harrington	Daugh.	18
William Fahy	Brother	50	Patrick Sweeney	Son	19
Mary A. Fahy	Sister	48	Joseph Walshe	Boarder	7
			Charles Deignan	Boarder	7
Patrick Martin	Head	50	Catherine Kelly	Boarder	7
Eliza Martin	Wife	34	John Harrington	Boarder	24
Mary martin	Daugh.	6	Thomas Harrington	S.in-law	29
Kate Martin	Daugh.	4			
Lizzie Martin	Daugh.	3	Margaret Cullen	Head	39
Patrick Martin	Son	1	Molly Cullen	Daugh.	10
Mary Higgins	Servant	12	Margaret Cullen	Daugh.	7
			Frances A. Cullen	Daugh.	3
Michael Finneran	Head	65			
Sarah Finneran	Wife	45	William Moylott	Head	60
Michael Finneran	Son	25	Catherine Moylott	Wife	42
James Finneran	Son	20	Catherine Moylott	Daugh.	21
Mary A. Finneran	Daugh.	18	James Moylott	Son	19
Thomas Finneran	Son	16	Rebecca Moylott	Daugh.	15
William Finneran	Son	14	William J. Moylott	Son	13
Kate Finneran	Daugh.	12	Margaret Moylott	Daugh.	10
Bridget Finneran	Daugh.	9	Bridget Moylott	Daugh.	7
			Mary E. Moylott	Daugh.	3

Name	Relation	Age	Name	Relation	Age
John Donnelly	Head	59	Martin O Beirne	Head	59
Elizabeth Donnelly	Wife	49	Michael Doyle	Servant	34
Brigid Donnelly	Daugh.	20	Mary Higgins	Servant	48
Margaret Donnelly	Daugh.	18			
Michael Donnelly	Son	16	John Donnelly	Head	42
Ellie Donnelly	Daugh.	14	Mary Donnelly	Wife	38
William Donnelly	Son	10	Andrew Clogher	Uncle	68
Joseph F. Donnelly	Son	6			
Teresa Donnelly	Daugh.	4	Patrick Doyle	Head	68
Elizabeth Donnelly	G.daugh.	_			
			John Mannion	Head	40
Michael Donnelly	Head	38	Sarah Mannion	Wife	36
Bridget Donnelly	Wife	36	Mary K. Mannion	Daugh.	7
Bridget Donnelly	Daugh.	6			

Moyvannan

Name	Relation	Age	Name	Relation	Age
Michael Meely	Head	50	John Finneran	Head	60
Bridget Meely	Wife	48	Bessie Finneran	Wife	50
John Meely	Son	19	Bridget Finneran	Daugh.	18
Rose Meely	Daugh.	17	John Finneran	Son	16
Margaret Meely	Daugh.	13	Margaret Finneran	Daugh.	11
Annie Meely	Daugh.	11	Patrick Finneran	Son	10
Dannie Meely	Son	7	Michael Sinnet	Boarder	40
			Terence Callery	Boarder	20
Bridget Meely	Head	80			
			Sarah Gormley	Head	60
Mary Gallagher	Head	55	Elizabeth Dunne	Boarder	28
John Gallagher	Son	32	Margaret Goldin	Lodger	70
Edward Gallager	Son	24			
Mary A. McLoughlin	Boarder	12	Luke Green	Head	58
Sarah McLoughlin	Boarder	11	Mary Green	Daugh.	15
			Patrick Green	Son	13
Margaret Curley	Head	70	Bridget Green	Daugh.	11
Sarah Greene	Servant	16			
James Nolan	Servant	50	Edward Leonard	Head	61
			Mary Leonard	Daugh.	30
William Beades	Head	49	John Leonard	Son	28
Maria Beades	Wife	50	James Leonard	Son	26
John Heavy	Servant	22	Batty Leonard	Son	20
Catherine Molloy	Head	72	James Lyons	Head	64
Paul Conniffe	Nephew	55	Bridget Lyons	Wife	58
Bridget McDonagh	Boarder	9	Kate Lyons	Daugh.	24
			Mary Lyons	Daugh.	17
Catherine Rafferty	Head	61			
Louisa Rafferty	Daugh.	19	Thomas Murray	Head	47
Alice Rafferty	Daugh.	19	Mary Murray	Wife	44
Thomas Martin	G.son	2	Mary F. Murray	Daugh.	15
			William Gilleran	Servant	28
John Daly	Head	76	Delia McGuffin	Servant	19
Ellen Daly	Wife	55			

Name	Relation	Age	Name	Relation	Age
James Shine	Head	50	Patrick Leonard	Head	66
Anne Shine	Wife	50	Bridget Leonard	Wife	50
Thomas Shine	Son	29	John Leonard	Son	20
Rose Shine	Daugh.	22	Jessie Leonard	Daugh.	15
Richard Smith	Head	50	Martin Leonard	Head	65
Lizzie Smith	Wife	43	Anne Leonard	Wife	60
Bridie Pickering	Aunt	55	James Leonard	Son	20
			William Leonard	Son	18

Carrowmurragh

Name	Relation	Age	Name	Relation	Age
			Patrick Leonard	Head	80
Patrick J. Leonard	Head	83	Anne Leonard	Wife	70
Elizabeth Leonard	Wife	58	Patrick Leonard	Son	36
John Leonard	G.son	2	Marcus Leonard	Son	26
John Kerrigan	Head	82	John Morris	Head	68
Bridget Kerrigan	Wife	63	Mary Morris	Wife	59
John Kerrigan	Son	35	Patrick Morris	Son	25
Pat Kerrigan	Son	25	Hugh Morris	Son	22
			Margaret Morris	Daugh.	27
Sarah Kerrigan	Head	55			
James Kerrigan	Son	32	Margaret Kenny	Head	70
Laurence Kerrigan	Son	30	Michael Kenny	Son	32
John Kerrigan	Son	23			
Michael Kerrigan	Son	19	Patrick Nolan	Head	25
Patrick Kerrigan	Son	17	Kate Nolan	Wife	31
Brigid Kerrigan	Daugh.	25	Michael Nolan	Son	2
Laurence was a stonecutter.			Mary J. Nolan	Daugh.	_
James Doyle	Head	67	Marcus A. Levinge	Head	83
			Clara Alice Levinge	Wife	55
Mary Farrell	Head	50	Emily Gilbert	Niece	33
John Farrell	Son	29	Helen Gilbert	G.niece	7
Patrick Farrell	Son	27	Percy Gilbert	G.nephew	1
James Farrell	Son	18	Bridget Smyth	Servant	23
Maggie Farrell	Daugh.	16	Margaret Woodhams	Servant	25
Delia Quigley	Niece	5	Charles McCarthy	Coachman	20
William Brennan	Head	50	Brigid Burke	Head	60
Mary K.Kelly	Visitor	12	Ann Burke	Niece	34
Thomas Feeley	Head	42	Edward Connell	Head	34
Rose Feeley	Wife	29	Ellen Connell	Wife	29
Mary K. Feeley	Daugh.	4			
Annie Feeley	Daugh.	3	Charles Beirne	Head	32
Rose Feeley	Daugh.	1	Mary Beirne	Wife	30
			Francis Beirne	Son	7
Rose Leonard	Head	50	Thomas Beirne	Son	4
James Feeley	Son	25			
Joseph Kennedy	Head	38	Mary A. Short	Head	45
Daniel Burns	Nephew	12	Patrick Short	Son	31
			Christine Boyd	Niece	18

Name	Relation	Age	Name	Relation	Age
John Daly	Head	50	Ellen Kenny	Daugh.	26
Ann Daly	Wife	60	William Kenny	Son	17
Mary Geoghagan	Sister	75	Thomas Kenny	Son	16
James Gordon	Head	65	Richard Kenny	Son	14
Deborah Gordon	Wife	75	John J. Kenny	G.son	2
Mary Regan	Head	60	Michael Rourke	Head	42
			Mary Rourke	Sister	39
Patrick O Brien	Head	70			
Joseph Troy	Lodger	17	John Rourke	Head	45
			Bridget Rourke	Wife	30
Thomas O Brien	Head	55	Mary Rourke	Daugh.	_
Mary A. O Brien	Wife	45			
Patrick O Brien	Son	20	Bridget Rourke	Head	66
Richard O Brien	Son	18	Bridget Rourke	Daugh.	23
John O Brien	Son	16	James Rourke	Son	27
Thomas O Brien	Son	13	James Mee	Servant	18
Winifred O Brien	Daugh.	5			
			Owen Gormley	Head	50
Catherine Kenehan	Head	33	Mary Gormley	Wife	44
			William Gormley	Son	20
Mariah Shine	Head	92	Sarah Gormley	Daugh.	18
			Bridget Gormley	Daugh.	16
John Gilligan	Head	55	John Gormley	Son	14
Mary Gilligan	Wife	46	Owen Gormley	Son	11
Michael Gilligan	Son	17	Ellen Gormley	Daugh.	10
Bridget Gilligan	Daugh.	17	Margaret Gormley	Daugh.	9
Kate Gilligan	Daugh.	13	Rose Gormley	Daugh.	7
			Rebecca Gormley	Daugh.	6
William Quinn	Head	40	Annie Gormley	Daugh.	5
Mary Quinn	Daugh.	16	Elizabeth Gormley	Daugh.	4
Margaret Quinn	Daugh.	14	Patrick Gormley	Son	
Patrick Quinn	Son	8			
Thomas Quinn	Son	6	Margaret Wiggins	Wife	28
			William G. Wiggins	Son	5
Owen Gormley	Head	34			
			Carnagh East		
Martin Quinn	Head	55			
Brigid Quinn	Wife	66	James Conry	Head	77
Thomas Quinn	Son	33			
Patrick Quinn	Son	28	Annie Levinge	Head	40
			Joan Ellis[Singapore]	Boarder	7
Honorah Kenny	Head	43	Dorothea Ellis[Ditto]	Boarder	7
Patrick Kenny	Son	25	William Duncan	Servant	24
Mary A. Kenny	Daugh.	22	Mary Reilly	Servant	18
James Kenny	Son	20			
Ellen Kenny	Daugh.	15	Daniel Higgins	Head	52
John Kenny	Son	13	Mary Higgins	Wife	50
Catherine Kenny	Daugh.	7	Patrick Higgins	Son	21
			Mary A. Higgins	Daugh.	19
John Kenny	Head	65	Daniel Higgins	Son	17
Mary Kenny	Wife	55	Thomas Higgins	Son	13

Name	Relation	Age	Name	Relation	Age
Joseph Hawkins	Head	80	Patrick Dowling	Head	23
			Mary A. Dowling	Sister	19
Patrick Gannon	Head	58	Margaret Dowling	Sister	13
Ellen Gannon	Wife	58	James Dowling	Brother	11
Thomas Gannon	Son	22	Michael Dowling	Brother	7
			George Dowling	Brother	4
James O Connor	Head	32			
John O Connor	Brother	44	Patrick Connerton	Head	65
Eliz. O Connor [Teacher]	Sister	40	Mary Connerton	Wife	59
Ellen O Connor	Sister	37	Rose Connerton	Daugh.	22
			Fanny Connerton	Daugh.	20
Thomas Keogh	Head	62	Delia Connerton	Daugh.	18
Alice Keogh	Wife	60			
Annie Higgins	Boarder	6	Thomas Connaughton	Head	67
			Marg. Connaughton	Daugh.	34
Anne Hannon	Head	71	Marg. Connaughton	G.Daugh.	15
Thomas Hannon	Son	45			
Anne Hannon	Daugh.	29	Michael Cuddy	Head	68
Ellie Hannon	Daugh.	26	Catherine Cuddy	Wife	60
			John Cuddy	Son	17
Patrick Fallon	Head	55	Kate Cuddy	Daugh.	14
Mary Fallon	Sister	70			
			Mary Gleavy	Head	64
John Egan	Head	60			
Mary Egan	Wife	55	**Carrowphadeen**		
Patrick Egan	Son	17			
Thomas Egan	Son	12	William Martin	Head	40
			Annagusta Martin	Wife	37
William Murphy	Head	40	Francis Martin	Son	13
Mariah Murphy	Wife	34	Kathleen Martin	Daugh.	12
James Murphy	Son	13	Mary Martin	Daugh.	10
Hubert Murphy	Son	11	Margaret Martin	Daugh.	9
Michael Murphy	Son	9	Elizabeth Martin	Daugh.	9
Mary A. Murphy	Daugh.	7	Joseph Martin	Son	8
William Murphy	Son	5	William Martin	Son	6
Thomas Murphy	Son	3	Annie Martin	Daugh.	4
John Murphy	Son	1	Batty Martin	Son	2
			Elizabeth Ward	Servant	17
Michael Doran	Head	70	John Murry	Servant	40
Elizabeth Doran	Wife	40			
			Colman McGuire	Head	40
Daniel Quigley	Head	70	Maria McGuire	Wife	42
Mary Quigley	Wife	40	Thomas Maguire	Son	17
Owen Quigley	Son	24	Francis McGuire	Son	15
Thomas Carroll	Head	66	Mary A. McGuire	Daugh.	12
Kate Carroll	Wife	46	Kate McGuire	Daugh.	10
Patrick Carroll	Son	27	Gretta McGuire	Daugh.	7
Dan Carroll	Son	20	Patrick McGuire	Son	5
Mary A. Carroll	Daugh.	16	Joseph McGuire	Son	2
James Carroll	Son	12			
Bee Carroll	Daugh.	8	Patrick Feeley	Head	72
			Mary Feeley	Wife	60

Name	Relation	Age	Name	Relation	Age
Thomas Feeley	Son	29	Patrick Donnelly	Son	28
Winifred Feeley	Daugh.	27	Dominick Donnelly	Son	22
Katie Feeley	Daugh.	23	Ellen Donnelly	Daugh.	21
Patrick McGuire	Servant	14	Lizzie Donnelly	Daugh.	18
Thomas Perrse	Head	57	Thomas Costello	Head	60
Catherine Perrse	Sister	46	Mary Costello	Wife	50
Patrick Perrse	Nephew	27	Edward Costello	Son	20
Brigid Perrse	Niece	17	Kate Costello	Daugh.	24
Patrick Brennan	Head	41			
Eliza Brennan	Wife	28	**Warren**		
Catherine Brennan	Mother	65			
Mary C. Brennan	Daugh.	5	Thomas Luneen	Head	46
Thomas Brennan	Son	4	Margaret Luneen	Wife	45
Francis Brennan	Son	2	Patrick Luneen	Son	17
Brigid Brennan	Daugh.	_	Thomas Luneen	Son	16
			Mary Luneen	Daugh.	14
Sarah Ward	Head	64	Annie Luneen	Daugh.	11
Kate Ward	Daugh.	29	Maggie Luneen	Daugh.	9
			Freddie Luneen	Son	7
Timothy Dolan	Head	60	Catherine Luneen	Daugh.	5
Brigid Dolan	Wife	60	Lizzie Luneen	Daugh.	3
John McGann	Lodger	70	Elizabeth Grady	Niece	3
Thomas McGuire	Head	16	**Rinnagan**		
Brigid McGuire	Sister	18			
			Peter Fallon	Head	60
Michael McGann	Head	40	Maria Fallon	Wife	52
			Dorothy Fallon	Daugh.	21
Mary Doonighan	Head	55	Eliza Fallon	Daugh.	20
Anne Doonighan	Daugh.	20	William Fallon	Son	19
			John Fallon	Son	18
Maria Feeley	Head	50	Teresa Fallon	Daugh.	16
Thomas Feeley	Son	19	Peter Fallon	Son	15
Mary Feeley	Daugh.	21	Matilda Fallon	Daugh.	13
			Margaret Fallon	Daugh.	11
			Bernard Fallon	G.nephew	6
Carrownure					
			Catherine Grady	Head	70
Hugh G. Constable	Head	32	Patrick Grady	Son	29
Elinor May Constable	Wife	28			
Ella Constable	Daugh.	7	Peter Duffily	Head	75
John H. Constable	Son	5			
Lyndon Bomford	Br.in-law	30	John Seery	Head	59
Margaret Radcliffe	Visitor	23	Owen Seery	Brother	56
Elizabeth Tevelin	Servant	17	Mary Seery	Sister	48
Ellen Smyth	Servant	23			
John Smyth	Servant	22	James Grady	Head	60
			Bridget Grady	Wife	50
Dominick Donnelly	Head	65	Mary A. Grady	Daugh.	18
Winifred Donnelly	Wife	60	Thomas Grady	Son	16

Name	Relation	Age	Name	Relation	Age
James Grady	Son	8	Michael Duffily	Head	21
Anne Grady	Daugh.	7	Ellen Duffily	Sister	18
			James Duffily	Brother	16
Patrick Kenny	Head	27	Celia Duffily	Sister	13
Catherine Kenny	Wife	25	Teresa Duffily	Sister	10
Winifred Donnelly	Head	60	Patrick Duffily	Head	25
			Margaret Duffily	Sister	27
Catherine Brennan	Head	38			
Mary Brennan	Daugh.	16	Alex Gunning	Head	60
Michael Brennan	Son	14	L.E.Gunning	Wife	40
Bridget Brennan	Daugh.	11	Alex A. Gunning	Son	25
			Fred G. Cady	Visitor	28
Catherine Ganley	Head	62	Daisy M. Cady	Visitor	27
James Ganley	Son	25	Lily G. Cady	Visitor	23
Rebecca Ganley	Daugh.	22	Teresa Connaughton	Servant	36
Bridget Seery	Mother	91			
			Patrick Looby	Head	70
Patrick Grady	Head	40	Thomas Looby	Nephew	55
Ellen Grady	Wife	34	Mary A. Looby	Niece	45
Mary Grady	Daugh.	13			
Lena Grady	Daugh.	8	Patrick Duffily	Head	55
Margaret Grady	Daugh.	6	Margaret Duffily	Daugh.	25
Thomas Grady	Son	4			
James Grady	Son	1	Patrick Kelly	Head	63
			Mary Kelly	Wife	60
Thomas Ganley	Head	60			
Thomas Ganley	Son	26	Bridget Fallon	Head	70
Teresa Ganley	Daugh.	22			
			Mary Carroll	Head	61
James Grady	Head	53	Patrick Grady	S.in-law	26
Mary Grady	Wife	16	Kate Grady	Daugh.	25
Margaret Egan	Visitor	70			
			Catherine Fitzgerald	Head	76
Catherine Donnelly	Head	65			
			Patrick Egan	Head	32
James Grady	Head	24	Margaret Egan	Sister	34
Michael Grady	Brother	22			
Mary A. Grady	Sister	19	Patrick Grady	Head	55
Margaret Grady	Sister	16	Sarah Grady	Wife	50
			Ellen Grady	Daugh.	16
Patrick Hanley	Head	75	Teresa Grady	Daugh.	14
Richard Hanley	Son	29	Patrick Grady	Son	9
Elizabeth Hanley	Daugh.	26			
John P. Hanley	G.son	7	**Carrownamaddy**		
Michael Duffily	Head	29	Bernard Mahon	Head	51
Kate Duffily	Wife	26	Maria Mahon	Wife	38
Annie Duffily	Sister	24	John Hayes	Br.in-law	55
Hannah Ward	Visitor	20			
			Dorothy Hayes	Head	80
			Kate Hayes	Daugh.	30

Name	Relation	Age	Name	Relation	Age
John Brady	Head	81	Jane Casserly	Daugh.	17
Bridget Brady	Wife	61	Michael F. Casserly	Son	15
John Brady	Son	35			
Sarah Brady	Daugh.	19	Thomas Curley	Head	60
Mary Kelly	M. in-law	82	Matthew Curley	Brother	45
			Margaret Curley	Sister	42
Bridget Somers	Head	48			
Katie Somers	Daugh.	22	Bernard Glennon	Head	52
Nannie Somers	Daugh.	14	Bridget Glennon	Wife	50
John Somers	Son	10	Margaret Glennon	Daugh.	20
James Andrew Somers	Son	7	Bernard Glennon	Son	14
William Glennon	Servant	28	Ellen Glennon	Daugh.	13
Patrick Donnelly	Servant	24			
			John Luneen	Head	45
Thomas Rogers(Shepherd)	Head	40	Mary Luneen	Wife	39
Mary Rogers	Wife	30	Sarah C. Luneen	Daugh.	8
Mary A. Rogers	Daugh.	8	Mary A. Luneen	Daugh.	4
Dominic Rogers	Son	7			
Bridget Rogers	Daugh.	3	**Kilmore**		
Thomas Rogers	Son	1			
Martin Donnelly	Servant	16	Bridget Luneen	Head	68
			Thomas Luneen	Son	40
Mountplunkett			Mary Luneen	D.in-law	25
			John Grady	G.son	11
Allan Cameron	Head	59	Maria Luneen	G.daugh.	3
Zina Cameron	Wife	34	James Luneen	G.son	1
Mary Byrnes	Servant	16			
John Black	Boarder	34	Luke Rooney	Head	85
James Sheridan	Boarder	26	Thomas Rooney	Son	38
David Coutts	Boarder	15			
			Patrick Seery	Head	80
Thomas Glennon	Head	47	Patrick Seery	Son	38
Bridget Glennon	Wife	39	Julia Seery	D.in-law	40
Bernard Glennon	Son	16	Thomas Seery	G.son	12
Patrick Glennon	Son	14	Patrick Seery	G.son	10
Michael Glennon	Son	12	Michael Seery	G.son	8
Mary Glennon	Daugh.	10	Mary Seery	G.daugh.	4
Bridget Glennon	Daugh.	8	Margaret Seery	G.daugh.	3
Thomas Glennon	Son	6			
John Glennon	Son	3	Catherine McLoughlin	Head	65
			Mary McLoughlin	Daugh.	34
Margaret Kelly	Head	55	Francis McLoughlin	Son	28
Mary Kelly	Daugh.	30			
Dan Kelly	Son	28	Michael Mullally	Head	55
Patrick Kelly	Son	26	Margaret Mullally	Wife	60
Bridget Kelly	Daugh.	22	Margaret Mullally	Daugh.	22
Thomas Kelly	Son	21	Michael Mullally	Son	21
Luke Kelly	Son	18	Patrick Mullally	Son	20
			Francis Mullally	Son	19
James Casserly	Head	60			
Catherine Casserly	Wife	56	Bernard Glennon	Head	55
Ellen Casserly	Daugh.	19	Agnes Glennon	Wife	45

Name	Relation	Age	Name	Relation	Age
Robert Glennon	Son	20	**Galey**		
Mary Glennon	Daugh.	18			
Agnes Glennon	Daugh.	15	Robert Payne	Head	35
Thomas H. Glennon	Son	12	Bessie Payne	Sister	33
Frederick Glennon	Son	10	Mary Casserly	Servant	25
Patrick Mullally	Head	35	Patrick O Roarke	Head	45
			Delia O Roarke	Wife	33
Martin Glennon	Head	54	Michael O Roarke	Br.	50
Catherine Glennon	Wife	45			
Patrick Glennon	Son	22	Patrick Garrick	Head	82
Mary A. Glennon	Daugh.	19	Mary Garrick	Wife	70
Elizabeth Glennon	Daugh.	17	Michael Garrick	Son	36
Catherine Glennon	Daugh.	15	John Garrick	Son	30
Clare Glennon	Daugh.	13	Margaret Garrick	Daugh.	28
Martin Glennon	Son	11	Maria Garrick	Daugh.	26
Agnes Glennon	Daugh.	9	Mable Taylor	G.Niece	3
Teresa Glennon	Daugh.	6	Fanny Taylor	G.Niece	2
Thomas Kelly	Head	75	Anne Dillon	Head	50
			Thomas Dillon	Son	33
Mary Curley	Head	40	Matthew Dillon	Son	25
Carowndrisha			Thomas Egan	Head	30
			Kate Egan	Wife	24
Robert Bentley	Head	54	Kate McNama	M.in-law	50
John Bentley	Brother	52	Bridget M. McNama	Sr.in-law	10
Edward Bentley	Brother	38	Thomas J. Egan	Son	1
Michael Roarke	Head	77	James McCarroll	Head	33
John Roarke	Son	25	Rose McCarroll	Wife	28
John Dillon	Head	60	Thomas Perdue	Head	60
Margaret Dillon	Wife	52	Mary Perdue	Wife	50
John Dillon	Son	24			
James Dillon	Son	19	**Longnamuck**		
Joseph Dillon	Son	10			
			Michael Garrick	Head	71
Maria Feeney	Head	50	Mary A. Garrick	Daugh.	39
Katie Sharkey N.T.	Boarder	24	Michael Garrick	Son	33
			Teresa Garrick	Daugh.	26
John Coyle	Head	48	Bridget Garrick	Daugh.	24
Winnie Coyle	Wife	36			
Mary Coyle	Daugh.	13	Daniel Martin	Head	87
James Coyle	Son	11	Daniel Martin	Son	31
Michael Coyle	Son	9	Mary A. Martin	D.in-law	28
Patrick Coyle	Son	7	Patrick Martin	G.son	1
Thomas Coyle	Son	5			
Lizzie Coyle	Daugh.	2	Michael P. Harding	Head	40
			Mary Emily Harding	Wife	31
Thomas Curley	Head	70	Sarah Quigley	Servant	30
Rose A. Curley	Daugh.	24	Thomas Reilly	Servant	33

Name	Relation	Age
Cruit		
Thomas Farrell	Head	78
Mary Killian	Daugh.	45
James Killian	S.in-law	45
Thomas Killian	G.son	20
Luke Killian	G.son	18
Annie Killian	G.Daugh.	17
John Killian	G.son	15
Lackan		
Ann Kavanagh	Head	70
Mary Kavanagh	Daugh.	40
Brigid Moran	Head	50
Thomas Ganley	Son	24
Patrick Moran	Son	16
James Brennan	Head	53
Kate English	Niece	20
Michael Brennan	Head	52
John Tully	Nephew	18
John Siggins	Head	45
Ann Siggins	Wife	40
George Siggins	Son	19
Ann Siggins	Daugh.	17
Mary E. Siggins	Daugh.	7
Patrick Mullooly	Head	45
Ann Mullooly	Sister	47
Michael Conry	Head	60
Catherine Conry	Wife	60
Bridget Conry	Daugh.	30
Patrick Cunningham	Head	70
Margaret Cunningham	Wife	60
Dan Cunningham	Head	70
Kate Cunningham	Sister	66
George Dixon	Head	80
Mary Dixon	Wife	78
Edward Dixon	Son	40
Mary A. Dixon	Daugh.	36
Charles Kelly	Head	62
Margaret Kelly	Head	80

Name	Relation	Age
Bridget Kelly	Sister	78
Catherine Kelly	Sister	74
Ellen Dolan	Head	45
Mary Norman	Head	64
George Norman	Son	35
Portrunny		
James Breheny	Head	74
John Breheny	Son	34
Bridget Breheny	D.in-law	33
James Breheny	G.son	7
John Breheny	G.son	5
Mary Breheny	G.Daugh.	3
Patrick Breheny	G.son	2
Delia Breheny	G.Daugh.	–
Mary Taffe	Servant	
Thomas Murray	Head	32
Cooltona		
Michael Tiernan	Head	70
Margaret Tiernan	Wife	50
James Tiernan	Son	24
Mary Hanly	Head	62
Patrick Hanly	Son	28
Ellen Hanly	Daugh.	26
Bryan Finneran	Head	70
Mary Finneran	Wife	66
Patrick Dolan	Head	76
Bridget Dolan	Wife	57
James Dolan	Son	26
Christina Dolan	Daugh.	24
Bernard Dolan	Son	20
Luke Cline	Head	30
Anne Cline	Wife	40
Catherine Fayne	Head	54
Patrick Fayne	Son	28
Owen Fayne	Son	24
Winifred Fayne	Daugh.	20
Andrew Fayne	Son	18
Peter Fayne	Son	16
Mary K. Fayne	Daugh.	14

Name	Relation	Age	Name	Relation	Age
Sarah Hanly	Head	38	Thomas Geraghty	Head	38
Bernard Hanly	Son	17	Lizzie Geraghty	Wife	31
Luke Hanly	Son	15	John Geraghty	Son	6
			Mary K. Geraghty	Daugh.	5
Fearagh			Gretta Geraghty	Daugh.	4
			Lizzie Geraghty	Daugh.	2
John Feeney	Head	56	Michael Geraghty	Son	_
Ann Feeney	Wife	38			
Mary Feeney	Daugh.	12	James Fallon	Head	60
Edward Feeney	Son	11			
Ellie Feeney	Daugh.	10	Anne Murray	Head	61
Annie Feeney	Daugh.	9	James Murray	Son	24
John Feeney	Son	7	Lizzie Murray	Daugh.	19
Lizzie Feeney	Daugh.	4			
			John Casey	Head	60
Thomas Gannon	Head	62	John Casey	Son	19
Bridget Gannon	Wife	60			
John Gannon	Son	18	Michael McDonnell	Head	68
			Brigid McDonnell	Wife	60
Patrick Gannon	Head	65	Patrick McDonnell	Son	24
Bridget Gannon	Wife	63	Michael McDonnell	Son	18
Edward Gannon	Son	25	John McDonnell	Son	14
Patrick Lyster	Head	90	John Daly	Head	70
Maria Lyster	Wife	63	Mary Daly	Wife	65
Patrick Lyster	Son	30			
			Patrick Connor	Head	52
Mary Lyster	Head	68	Kate Connor	Wife	41
John Lyster	Son	40	Mary A. Connor	Daugh.	8
Michael Lyster	Son	37	Anne Connor	Mother	76
			Joseph Gannon	Nephew	19
Patrick Fallon	Head	54			
Anne Fallon	Wife	50	Bridget Naughton	Head	90
Thomas Fallon	Son	18	Patrick Naughton	Son	38
Ellen Fallon	Daugh.	14	Margaret Naughton	D.in-law	38
Mary A. Fallon	Daugh.	10	Mary A. Naughton	G.Daugh.	14
Brigid Fallon	Daugh.	8	Ellen Naughton	G.Daugh.	12
			Margaret Naughton	G.Daugh.	10
Margaret Kelly	Head	50	Michael Naughton	G. Son	8
Sarah Kelly	Daugh.	19	John Naughton	G.Son	6
John Kelly	Son	16	Thomas Naughton	G.Son	4
			Patrick Naughton	G.Son	2
Brigid Egan	Head	35			
Edward Egan	Son	15	Thomas Connor	Head	60
John Egan	Son	10	Annie Connor	Wife	50
			Kate Connor	Daugh.	20
Michael Kelly	Head	70	Thomas Connor	Son	18
Catherine Kelly	Wife	56	John Connor	Son	15
Michael Kelly	Son	29	Teresa Connor	Daugh.	12
Patrick Kelly	Son	20			
Bernard Kelly	Son	18	Ann Gillespie	Head	70
			Andrew Gillespie	Son	25

Name	Relation	Age
Ann Naughton	Head	50
Michael Naughton	Son	25
Thomas Naughton	Son	23
James Naughton	Son	21
Winifred Naughton	Daugh.	16
Peter Feeney	Head	33
Kate Feeney	Wife	28
Ann Feeney	Daugh.	8
Mary Feeney	Daugh.	7
Patrick Feeney	Son	6
Bridget Feeney	Daugh.	4
Peter Feeney	Son	–
Patrick Feeney	Head	70
Catherine Feeney	Wife	60
Thomas Feeney	Son	23
Edward Feeney	Son	21
Michael Feeney	Son	19
John Feeney	Son	17
Patrick Feeney	Son	15
Michael Brennan	Head	50
Bridget Brennan	Wife	40
Michael Brennan	Son	18
Ellen Brennan	Daugh.	16
Maria Brennan	Daugh.	15
Thomas Feeney	Head	60
Margaret Feeney	Wife	45
Edward Feeney	Son	21
Mary Feeney	Daugh.	18
John Feeney	Son	17
Thomas Feeney	Son	15
Ellen Feeney	Daugh.	13
James Feeney	Son	11
Margaret Feeney	Daugh.	9
Michael Feeney	Son	7
William Feeney	Son	5
Kate Feeney	Daugh.	3
Margaret Davis	Head	41
Patrick Davis	Son	9
Thomas A. Wilson	Head	50
Josephine Wilson	Wife	40

Rinnany Island

Name	Relation	Age
Michael Donohoe	Head	28
Annie Donohoe	Wife	30

Name	Relation	Age
Mary A. Brennan	Step-daugh.	12
Patrick Donohoe	Son	–

Clooneskert

Name	Relation	Age
Michael Murphy	Head	58
Mary Murphy	Daugh.	26
Patrick Finneran	Head	70
Mary Finneran	Wife	62
Sarah Finneran	Daugh.	28
Francis Finneran	Son	16

Cloonmore

Name	Relation	Age
John McDermott	Head	60
Anne McDermott	Wife	54
John McDermott	Son	21
Maggie McDermott	Daugh.	16
Michael McDermott	Son	16
Charles McDermott	Son	14
Patrick McDermott	Son	12
Ellie McDermott	Daugh.	10
Delia A. McDermott	Daugh.	8
Lisa Brehony	Head	84
Michael Brehony	Son	60
Henry Killion	Head	69
Mary Killion	Wife	43
Kate Killion	Daugh.	22
Martin Killion	Son	21
Ellen Killion	Daugh.	18
Bernard Killion	Son	16
Maggie Killion	Daugh.	14
Peter Killion	Son	10
John Fayne	Head	60
Celia Fayne	Wife	35
Alice Fayne	Daugh.	13
Thomas Fayne	Son	12
John Fayne	Son	10
Mary Fayne	Daugh.	8
Patrick Fayne	Son	7
Michael Fayne	Son	5
Winnie Fayne	Daugh.	4
Lizzie Fayne	Daugh.	2
Owen Fayne	Son	–
Winifred Fayne	Sister	52
Patrick McDermott	Head	70
Mary McDermott	Wife	60

Name	Relation	Age	Name	Relation	Age
Larry McDermott	Son	30	**Cloonlarge**		
Patrick McDermott	Son	22			
Bridget McDermott	Daugh.	19	Bridget Cunnane	Head	48
			Kate Cunnane	Daugh.	20
Patrick Fuery	Head	60	Thomas Cunnane	Son	13
Maggie Fuery	Wife	50			
John Fuery	Son	20	James Kelly	Head	64
Katie Fuery	Daugh.	16	Bridget Kelly	Wife	60
Patrick Fuery	Son	14	Winifred Kelly	Daugh.	30
			Thomas Kelly	Son	23
Bridget Brennan	Head	57	Peter Kelly	Son	22
Owen Brennan	Son	19	Ann Kelly	Daugh.	20
Sarah Brennan	Daugh.	17			
John Brennan	Son	15	James Kelly	Head	64
			Annie Kelly	Wife	52
Michael Tracey	Head	46	Patrick Kelly	Son	21
Bridget Tracey	Wife	57	Peter Kelly	Son	18
Maggie Tracey	Daugh.	21	George Kelly	Son	16
Patrick Tracey	Son	15	Thomas Kelly	Son	14
			Annie Kelly	Daugh.	10
Daniel Killion	Head	67			
Anne Killion	Wife	60	Kate Devanny	Head	50
John Devanny	S.in-law	26	Joseph Devanny	Son	28
Mary Devanny	Daugh.	27	Brigid Devanny	Daugh.	25
Kate A. Devanny	G.daugh.	_	Daniel Devanny	Son	20
			Thomas Devanny	Son	18
Ann Treacy	Head	50	Mary Devanny	Daugh.	11
Patrick Treacy	Son	17			
Michael Treacy	Son	14	Martin Devanny	Head	72
Ellen Treacy	Sr.in-law	55	Ellen Devanny	Wife	54
Martin Treacy	Br.in-law	40	Martin Devanny	Son	23
			Mary Devanny	Daugh.	20
Annaghmore					
			Clooneigh		
Eliza Lally	Head	80			
James Lally	Son	42	Thomas Hanly	Head	70
Anne Lally	Daugh.in-law	39	Joseph Hanly	Son	35
Thomas Lally	Son	12	Mary A. Hanly	D.in-law	26
Bartholamew Lally	Son	5	Peter Hanly	G.son	2
Patrick Lally	Son	3	Kate Hanly	G.Daugh.	_
Mary E. Lally	Daugh.	2			
			Ann Kilcline	Head	60
Henry McDermott	Head	65	Patrick Kilcline	Son	33
Anne McDermott	Wife	55	Maria Kilcline	Daugh.	24
Kate McDermott	Daugh.	24			
Ellen McDermott	Daugh.	23	Michael Martin	Head	60
Patrick McDermott	Son	21	Hannah Martin	Daugh.	20
Michael McDermott	Son	20	Ellen Martin	Daugh.	26
			Thomas Martin	Son	24
			Michael Martin	Son	18
			Hannah Martin	Sister	56

Name	Relation	Age	Name	Relation	Age
Anne Hanly	Head	59	**Gallagh**		
Kate Hanly	Daugh.	31			
James Hanly	Son	29	Michael Barlow	Head	65
William Hanly	Son	26	Ellen Barlow	Wife	42
Teresa Hanly	Daugh.	23	James Barlow	Son	16
Annie Hanly	Daugh.	19	Mary Barlow	Daugh.	18
Sarah Breheny	G.Daugh.	9	Thomas Barlow	Son	14
			Anne Barlow	Daugh.	12
			Patrick Barlow	Son	10
Portnahinch			John Barlow	Son	7
			Sarah Barlow	Daugh.	6
Patrick Connell	Head	55	Celia Barlow	Daugh.	4
Maria Connell	Wife	35	Joseph Barlow	Son	1
James Igoe	Head	58	James Scally	Head	53
Katherine Igoe	Wife	55	Kate Scally	Wife	40
Mary Igoe	Daugh.	19	Mary Scally	Daugh.	13
James Igoe	Son	17	John Scally	Son	11
John Igoe	Son	14	Bridget Scally	Daugh.	9
			Annie Scally	Daugh.	7
Thomas Scally	Head	60	Patrick Scally	Son	5
Mary Scally	Wife	45	Margaret Scally	Daugh.	3
Catherine Scally	Sister	58	Kate Scally	Daugh.	1
Nannie Scally	Daugh.	19			
Margaret Scally	Daugh.	16	Ann Nolan	Head	70
John Scally	Son	11	Bridget Scally	Sister	54
Tom Scally	Son	6	Ann Scally	Head	70
			John Scally	Son	25
James Conry	Head	52	Peter Farrell	Servant	21
Catherine Conry	Wife	40			
Patrick Conry	Son	19	Peter Scally	Head	32
Bridget Conry	Daugh.	15	Kate Scally	Wife	20
Peter Conry	Son	12	Kate Connor	Head	81
Anne Conry	Daugh.	9	Thomas Connor	Son	60
James Conry	Son	8	Ellen Connor	D.in-law	40
Rose Conry	Daugh.	5	John Connor	G.son	13
Joseph Shiel	Head	60	**Gardenstown**		
Catherine Shiel	Wife	50			
Joseph Shiel	Son	26	Patrick Farrell	Head	40
Ellen Shiel	Daugh.	15	Kate Farrell	Wife	36
Kate Shiel	Daugh.	13	Francis Farrell	Son	10
			Peter Farrell	Son	8
John Farrell	Head	45	Patrick Farrell	Son	6
Bridget Farrell	Wife	34	Michael Farrell	Son	4
James Farrell	Son	10	Bridget K. Farrell	Daugh.	2
John Farrell	Son	9	John Farrell	Son	1
Luke Farrell	Son	1	Thomas Conmey	Servant	41
Mary Farrell	Daugh.	7			
Katie Farrell	Daugh.	5	Bridget Clyne	Head	97
Rose Farrell	Daugh.	3			
Mary Madden	Niece	17			

Name	Relation	Age	Name	Relation	Age
Michael Casserly	Head	73	Bridget Hanley	Head	75
Thomas Skelly	Nephew	20	Michael Hanley	Son	40
			Ellen Hanley	Daugh.	34
Thomas Casserly	Head	37	Margaret Hanley	Daugh.	20
Ellie Casserly	Sister	27			
Joseph Gavigan	Relative	11	John Dowling	Head	72
			Joseph Dowling	Son	30
Margaret Carroll	Head	70	Ellen Kenny	Daugh.	40
James Carroll	Son	30	Thomas Kenny	Son-in-law	36
Mary Carroll	D.in-law	25	Kate Kenny	G.Daugh.	3
Catherine Oates	Head	60	Michael Dooner	Head	55
Mary A. Oates	Daugh.	20	Ellen Dooner	Wife	53
Luke Oates	Son	24	Bridget Dooner	Daugh.	22
James Oates	Son	18	James Dooner	Son	20
			Margaret Dooner	Daugh.	18
Shanballymore			Michael Dooner	Son	16
James Fox	Head	67	Michael Coen	Head	53
Ellen Fox	Wife	50	Catherine Coen	Wife	50
John Fox	Son	27	Annie Coen	Daugh.	26
Rose Fox	Daugh.	21	Katie Coen	Daugh.	23
Kate Fox	Daugh.	15	Thomas Coen	Son	20
Patrick Fox	Son	14	Mary Brennan		60
Thomas Gill	Head	70	Bernard Gill	Head	62
Michael Gill	Son	41	Bridget Gill	Wife	58
			Patrick Gill	Son	36
Kilnacloghey			Jane Gill	Daugh.	30
			Peter Gill	Son	32
Simon Regan	Head	25			
John Curran	Servant	50	Peter Hopkins	Head	62
			Luke Hopkins	Brother	48
Cloonadra			Anne Hopkins	Sister	40
			Bridget Hopkins	Niece	19
Bernard Kilcline	Head	40			
Winifred Kilcline	Wife	36	Martin Gill	Head	35
Patrick Kilcline	Son	18	Ellen Gill	Sister	34
John Kilcline	Son	16			
Luke Kilcline	Son	12	Thomas Brennan	Head	41
James Kilcline	Son	10	Maria Brennan	Wife	36
Mary M. Kilcline	Daugh.	8	Thomas Brennan	Son	14
			Maria Brennan	Daugh.	12
Martin Fallon	Head	36	Kate Brennan	Daugh	10
Mary Fallon	Wife	35	Margaret Brennan	Daugh.	9
Sara M. Fallon	Daugh.	12	Patrick Brennan	Son	8
Bridget K. Fallon	Daugh.	10	Michael Brennan	Son	7
Martin Fallon	Son	8	Ann Brennan	Daugh.	5
Stephen Fallon	Son	6	John Brennan	Son	3
Patrick J. Fallon	Son	4	Ellen Brennan	Daugh.	_
John James Fallon	Son	_			

Name	Relation	Age	Name	Relation	Age
Thomas Irwin	Head	40	John Gavigan	Head	65
Ellen Irwin	Sister	38	Kate Gavigan	Daugh.	20
Mary K. Noone	Niece	9			
John T. Noone	Nephew	7	Catherine Hughes	Head	70
Joseph Hanley	Servant	31	Sarah Connolly	Niece	12
James Hopkins	Head	54	Thomas Cox	Head	36
Kate Hopkins	Daugh.	21	Mary A. Cox	Daugh.	7
			Maggie Jane Cox	Daugh.	5
Michael Brennan	Head	55	Kate Cox	Daugh.	2
Bridget Brennan	Wife	53	Alicia Cox	Sister	22
Ellen Brennan	Daugh.	25			
Patrick Brennan	Son	21	Peter Davis	Head	46
John J. Brennan	Son	18	Bridget Davis	Wife	36
Martin Brennan	Son	15	Frances Davis	Daugh.	12
Michael Brennan	Son	13	Mary Alice Davis	Daugh.	11
			Bridget Davis	Daugh.	9
			Ann Davis	Daugh.	6
Culliaghy			Margaret Davis	Daugh.	4
			Teresa Davis	Daugh.	2
Eliza Garrick (Dressmaker)	Head	62	Patrick Scally	Visitor	66
Maggie Garrick	Daugh.	24			
Kate Garrick	Daugh.	22	Luke Connaughton	Head	80
Hubert Nertney	Head	50	Anne Murphy	Head	46
Ellen Nertney	Wife	40	Mary Murphy	Daugh.	15
James Nertney	Son	18	James Murphy	Son	13
Mary A. Nertney	Daugh.	16	Michael Murphy	Son	11
Patrick Nertney	Son	14	John Murphy	Son	8
Hubert Nertney	Son	12	Bridget Murphy	Daugh.	5
Thomas Nertney	Son	10			
			Ballyleague		
Patrick Rhatigan	Head	48			
Thomas Rhatigan	Son	13	Patrick Farrell	Head	29
Mary Rhatigan	Daugh.	10	Annie Farrell	Wife	28
			Mary Gwendoline Farrell	Daugh.	4
Thomas Garrick	Head	38	Olive Farrell	Daugh.	2
Jane Garrick	Wife	37	Gerard Farrell	Son	_
			Bridget Kelly	Servant	23
			Thomas Skelly	Servant	26
Ballyclare					
			John Rorke	Head	61
Richard Hughes	Head	68	Bridget Rorke	Sister	48
Margaret Hughes	Wife	65	Mary O Keefe	Niece	25
Patrick Hughes	Son	37			
Richard Hughes	Son	25	Maria Browne	Head	37
Ellen Hughes	Daugh.	23	Matthew Browne	Son	14
			Peter Browne	Son	13
Patrick Quinn	Head	59	John Browne	Son	11
Mary Quinn	Wife	58	Mary Browne	Daugh.	8
James Quinn	Son	19	Edward Browne	Son	7
Bridget Quinn	Daugh.	17			

Name	Relation	Age	Name	Relation	Age
James Nerney	Head	46	Michael Martin	Head	57
Mary Nerney	Wife	44	Thomas Martin	Brother	50
Annie Nerney	Daugh.	8	Catherine Martin	Sister	46
Mary Ellen Nerney	Daugh.	7			
Winnie Murphy	Servant	18	Ellen Curran	Head	70
			Francis Curran	Son	33
Luke Farrell (Pub.)	Head	32	Mary Curran	Daugh.	30
Margaret Farrell	Wife	25			
Patrick Ed.	Son	_	Bartholomew Coleman	Head	60
Bridget McCormack	Servant	20	Bernard Coleman (Tailor)	Son	29
			Peter Coleman	Son	20
Michael Petitt (Pub.)	Head	37	Bridget Coleman	Daugh.	17
Tessie Petitt	Wife	40			
Mary K. Petitt	Daugh.	4	Kate Fallon	Head	36
Emma Petitt	Daugh.	2	Thomas Fallon	Son	22
Michael Petitt	Son	_	Jane Fallon	Daugh.	21
Jane Keary	Servant	14	Kate Fallon	Daugh.	18
Mary Kelly	Sis.-in-law	32	Mary A. Fallon	Daugh.	16
Bridget Casserly	Head	22	Constable John Lawlor	Head	41
			Ellen Mary Lawlor	Wife	40
Sarah Gaharan	Head	65	Thomas W. Lawlor	Son	11
James Gaharan	Step-son	47	Mary Jane Lawlor	Daugh.	9
Maria Gaharan	Daugh.	45	John James Lawlor	Son	8
Margaret Gaharan	Daugh.	43	Joseph Lawlor	Son	5
Annie Gaharan	Daugh.	40			
Laurence Gaharan	Son	37	Patrick Brennan	Head	43
			Kate Brennan	Wife	41
John Hyland N.T.	Head	46	John Brennan	Son	8
Richard Hyland	Brother	44	Patrick Brennan	Son	6
Eliza Brennan	Niece	17	Eliza Kate Brennan	Daugh.	2
Ellen Daly	Head	70	Edward Murray	Head	60
Patrick Daly	Son	25	Margaret Murray	Wife	50
			Thomas Murray	Son	15
Anne Martin	Head	68	James Murray	Son	13
Kate Martin	Daugh.	38	Margaret Murray	Daugh.	9
Ellen Martin	Daugh.	27			
			Andrew Carthy	Head	69
Patrick Farrell	Head	61	Maria Carthy	Wife	60
Kate Farrell	Daugh.	15			
			Thomas Murphy	Head	50
Francis Hanley	Head	50	Ann Murphy	Wife	49
Kate Hanley	Wife	35	John Murphy	Son	19
Lizzie Hanley	Daugh.	18			
Francis Hanley	Son	16	Bridget Curran	Head	77
Peter Hanley	Son	14	Patrick Curran	Son	35
John Hanley	Son	10			
			John Tiernan	Head	82
Thomas Larkin	Head	38	Margaret Tiernan	Wife	65
Sarah Larkin	Wife	30	John Tiernan	Son	33

Name	Relation	Age	Name	Relation	Age
Martin Gill	Head	30	Maggie Fallon	Daugh.	11
			Joseph Fallon	Son	10
Rev John Curley	Head	41	Winifred Fallon	Daugh.	9
Betty D'Alton	Niece	20	Dominick Fallon	Son	7
Dan Lawlor	Servant	22	Bridget Fallon	Daugh.	5
			Lucy Kate Fallon	Daugh.	2
Nicholas Garahan	Head	46			
Bridget Garahan	Wife	40	John Feeney	Head	81
Mary K. Garahan	Daugh.	10	Bridget Feeney	Daugh.	30
James J. Garahan	Son	9	John Feeney	Son	28
Bridget Garahan	Daugh.	7			
Francis Garahan	Son	6	Anne Molloy	Head	62
William J. Garahan	Son	4	Patrick Molloy	Son	22
Nicholas Garahan	Son	1			
			Patrick Murphy	Head	60
John Hoar	Head	76	Winifred Murphy	Wife	50
Margaret Hoar	Wife	65	Patrick Murphy	Son	23
Michael Hoar	Son	35	Joseph Murphy	Son	15
			Lizzie Murphy	Daugh	12
Dominick Fallon	Head	56			
Winifred Fallon	Wife	43	Ann Dennigan	Head	62
Mary Fallon	Daugh.	21	Bridget Farrell	Boarder	53
James Fallon	Son	18	Michael Farrell	Boarder	17
Patrick Fallon	Son	16			
Susan Fallon	Daugh.	15	Mary Farrell	Head	60
Peter Fallon	Son	14	Peter Farrell	Son	28
Hanna Fallon	Daugh.	13	John Farrell	Son	24

Chapter 1: **Beginnings**

[1] Banim, Mary. *Here and there through Ireland.* (Dublin, 1892) pp 334-335.
[2] Iskeraulin: the traditional name of the shoal off Inchcleraun sometimes interpreted as eiscir álainn.
[3] Ó Corráin, Donncha. *Ireland before the Normans* (Dublin, 1972) pp 68-69.
[4] Clans on the eastern shore of Lough Ree in medieval times.
[5] *Annals of Four Masters sub anno* A.D. 1155.
[6] Portaneena: Port an fhíona: harbour of the wine, also known by the English name Wineport.
[7] Crawford, Henry S. 'Lough Ree and its islands' in *JRSAI,* Vol 17, 1907, p323
[8] Hayward, Richard. *Where the River Shannon flows.* (London, 1940) pp.166-67.
[9] O'Curry, Eugene. *On the manners and customs of the ancient Irish.* (Dublin, 1873).
[10] Biggar, Francis Joseph. 'Inis Chlothran (Inchcleraun) Lough Ree: its history and antiquities' in *JSRAI,* 30, 1900. *Proceedings of the R.I.A.* November 1899. p.69.

Chapter 2: **Christianity**

[1] Corkery, John. *Cluain Chiaráin: the city of Ciaran* (Longford, *1979) pp 25-26*
[2] Bieler, Ludwig (ed). *The Irish penitentials.* (Dublin, 1963) p.93.

Chapter 3: **Vikings**

[1] Jones, Gwynn. *A History of the Vikings.* (Oxford. 1984) pp2-3.
[2] Moore, Thomas 'Let Erin remember the days of old' in *Moore's Irish melodies* (London: The London Printing and Publishing Company, n.d., c1879)
[3] *Annals of Clonmacnois sub anno* A.D. 830.
[4] *Annals of Ulster sub anno* A.D. 922
[5] Brawney in Co Westmeath on the southern shores of Lough Ree.
[6] Smyth, Alfred P. *Scandinavian York and Dublin.*Vol.2. (New Jersey/ Dublin. 1979) pp. 250-251.
[7] *Annals of Inisfallen sub anno* A.D. 988.
[8] Ath Liag: present day Lanesborough/Ballyleague.
[9] *Annals of Inisfallen sub anno* A.D. 993.
[10] *Cogadh Gaedhel re Gallaibh.* Ed. James Henthorn Todd. London 1867. "Plein Pattoici. This place is now *Bleanaphuttoge a townland in the barony of Kilkenny West, County of Westmeath on the shore of Lough Ree. Ord Map, Sheet 15."*
[11] *Annals of Inisfallen sub anno A.D. 1006.*
[12] Jones, Gwynn. *op cit*

Chapter 4:   Post-Viking Era

[1] The workshop of Roscommon monastery was located at Clooncraff in the parish of Kilteevan.

[2] Giolla-na-Naomh O Duind, who died on the 18 December 1160, was chief bard to the king of Leinster.

[3] O'Reilly, Edward. 'A Chronological account of nearly four hundred Irish writers…' in *Transactions of the Iberno-Celtic Society* for 1820, vol 1, pt 1. (Dublin: A O'Neil for the society,1820) p.lxxxv-lxxxvi.

[4] *Ibid*

[5] The poems Are: 'A chogaidg chaoin Chaibre Chruaidh' Ms 3/C/12; 'Airgialla a hEmain Macha' Ms 23/P/2; 'Aoibhinn, sin, a Eire ard' Ms 23/M/18; 'Cruacha Chonnacht raith co rath' Ms F/vi/2; 'Coced Laigen ne lecht riog' Ms 23/A/40 and 'Eire iarthar talman torthigh' Ms D/ii/1.

[6] *Annals of Four Masters sub anno* A.D. 1082.

[7] Watt, John. *The Church in Medieval Ireland.* (Dublin 1972). p.6.

[8] Mc Namee, James J. *History of the diocese of Ardagh.(Dublin 1954). p.176.

[9] *Annals of the Four Masters sub anno* A..D.1156

Chapter 5:   The Normans

[1] *Four Masters sub anno* A.D. 1172

[2] *Ibid*

[3] *Annals of Loch Cé sub anno* A.D. 1177

[4] *Four Masters sub anno* A.D.1174

[5] *Ibid sub anno* A.D. 1180.

[6] *Annals of Loch Cé sub anno* A.D. 1181.

[7] *Four Masters sub anno* A.D. 1186. Bregh Maine was then part of the kingdom of Teathbha.

[8] Ibid sub anno A.D. 1189.

[9] *Ibid sub anno A.D. 1190.*

[10] *Ibid sub anno A.D. 1199*

[11] *Ibid sub anno A.D. 1210*

[12] *Annals of Loch Cé sub anno* A.D. 1221

[13] *Four Masters* sub anno AD 1220

[14] *Ibid sub anno A.D. 1225*

[15] *Ibid sub anno A.D.1227.*

[16] *Annals of Ulster sub anno* A.D. 1230.

[17] *Annals of Loch Cé sub anno* A.D. 1236.

[18] *Annals of Clonmacnois sub anno* A.D. 1236.

[19] *Calendar of documents relating to Ireland. 1252-1284.* There are the ruins of a windmill with a masonry tower still visible on Rindoon, which may be occupying the same site as the original mill.

[20] *Four Masters sub anno A.D. 1244*. Curreen Connachtach is the most northerly point of Lough Ree on its western shore at Ballyleague while Cluain-tuaiscirt was a monastery of Canons Regular situated about a mile upstream on the west bank of the river Shannon.

[21] Thomas, Avril. *The Walled towns of Ireland*. Vol II, (Dublin, 2006), pp 185-186.

Chapter 6: Gaelicisation

[1] *Four Masters* sub anno A.D. 1256.

[2] *Ibid. sub anno A.D. 1272.*

[3] *Annals of Clonmacnois sub anno A.D. 1299.*

[4] *Annals of Clonmacnoise* sub anno 1351.

[5] O'Sullivan, Catherine Marie. *Hospitality in medieval Ireland 900-1500.* (Dublin: Four Courts Press, 2004).

[6] Based on Eleanor Knott's English translation of the poem.

[7] O'Donovan, John. *The tribes and customs of Hy-Many* (Dublin: 1843) p104.

[8] Ó Dálaigh, Gofraidh Fionn 'Filidh Eireann go haointeach: William O Ceallaigh's Christmas feast to the poets of Ireland, AD 1351. Ed. and trans by Eleanor Knott. In *Eriu*, v (1911) p60.

[9] *Ibid* p64-65.

[10] Carney, James (ed) *Topographical poems by Seán Mór Ó Dubhagáin and Giolla-na-Naomh Ó Huidhrín* (Dublin: 1943) p22.

[11] O'Donovan, John *The Topographical poems of John O'Dubhagain and Giolla na Naomh O'Huidhrin* (Dublin, 1862) p63

[12] O'Donovan's footnote reads: "Corca-Sheachlann, or Corca-Achlann, a territory in the east of the county of Roscommon, comprising the parishes of Bumlin, Kiltruscan and Cloonfinlough, and the western part of the parish of Lissonuffy. See *Annals of the Four Masters*, A.D. 1256, p.458, note 1. The Clann-Branain, or MacBranans of this territory are descended from the noble Druid, Ona, who granted Imleach-Ona, now Elphin, to St. Patrick. See *Annals of the Four Masters*, A.D. 1256, p.358, note 1. The O'Maoilmhichils, or Mulvihils of this territory would appear to have lost their rank as chieftains at an early period, as only one notice of the family occurs in the Annals of the Four Masters, scil. at the year 1189. The MacBrannans still possess a small estate at Bellmont in the original territory".

[13] O'Donovan's note reads: "Cinel-Dobhtha, now called Doohy-Hanly, from its chiel O'Hanly, senior of the Cinel-Dobhtha family. This territory extended along the river Shannon, from Carandoe Bridge to Drumdaff in the south of the parish of Kilgefin, and was divided from the Corca-Achlann by the ridge of the mountain of Slieve Baune. It comprises the parishes of Kilglass, Termonbarry, Cloontuskert, and the eastern half of the parish of Lissonuffy. See *Annals of Four Masters*, A.D. 1210, pp 169-170 note*".

[14] *Annals of Ulster sub anno A.D. 1368*
[15] *Four Masters sub anno A.D. 1447*
[16] See Dr S.F.O'Cianain. ' The Meares of Annalie' In. *Journal of the Ardagh and Clonmacnois Antiquarian Society* Vol. 1 No.4 pp.68-69
[17] *Four Masters sub anno A.D. 1376.*
[18] *Four Masters sub anno A.D. 1455*
[19] *Ibid sub anno A.D. 1462.*
[20] *Ibid sub anno A.D. 1464.*
[21] *Ibid sub anno A.D. 1472.*
[22] *Ibid sub anno A.D. 1475.*

Chapter 7: Darker Days

[1] *Four Masters sub anno A.D. 1542.*
[2] *Ibid sub anno A.D. 1547*
[3] *Ibid sub anno A.D. 1552.*
[4] *Ibid sub anno A.D. 1557*

Chapter 8: The Reformation

[1] *Four Masters sub anno* A.D. 1537
[2] *Extents of Irish monastic possessions, 1540-1541, from manuscripts in the Public Record office, London.* Ed.Newport B. White (Dublin 1942). Annale or Annaly, the territory of the O Farrell clan.
[3] *34, Henry VIII, 1543.*
[4] *Fiants of Elizabeth No 1511(1229).1567 A.D.*
[5] *Ibid:* 3641 (2867). 1571
[6] *Visitatio Regalis 1615.* RC 15/4 National Archives.

Chapter 9: Confiscations around the lake

[1] O Brien, Gearóid. *St. Mary's Parish Athlone: a history.* (Longford,1989). p.107.
[2] *Annals of Loch Cé sub anno A.D. 1251*
[3] Claffey, John A. 'Medieval Rindoon'. In *O.A.S. Jn,* ii, no. 5, p.13.
[4] *Fiants of Elizabeth.* 1483(1246)26 January, ix. sub anno 1567 A.D. Note: The Taghtample referred to is the house of the Knights Templars in Co Sligo.
[5] *Analecta Hibernica No 1.* Dublin 1930. p.139. Note: It is of interest that a memo on the first leaf of this manuscript shows that local chief McCarroon mortgaged his family estate to Dom Jacobus Dillon, Prior of Gillekania [Kilkenny].
[6] *Four Masters sub anno A.D. 742.*
[7] *Ibid sub anno A.D. 979.*
[8] *Ibid sub anno A.D. 1052.*

9 *Ibid sub anno A.D. 1266.*
10 O'Donovan, John. *Ordnance Survey Letters, Co. Roscommon.* p.77
11 Taheny, Luke O.P. *The Dominicans of Roscommon.* (Dublin 1990) p6.
12 *Ibid. p14.*
13 Piers, Sir Henry. A chorographical description of the county of Westmeath. Written A.D.1682. In Charles Vallencey (ed), *Collectanea de rebus Hibernicis*, i, (Dublin 1770). pp. 1-126.
14 Woods, James. *Annals of Westmeath, ancient and modern.* (Dublin, 1907) p
15 Murtagh, Harman. *Athlone, history and settlement to 1800.* (Athlone, 2000). p. 96,
16 *Ibid .pp.118-19.*
17 Conlon, Patrick 'Bethlehem of Westmeath' In *O.A.S. Jn.*,ii, no.7 p.190-94.
18 Kirby, John. 'Our Lady of Clonfert' In. *The Word.* Ed. Vincent Twomey, S.V.D. May 2005. p 16.

Chapter 10: Cromwell and the Plantation

1 *Ireland under the Commonwealth being a selection of documents relating to the government of Ireland, 1651-59*, Ed. Robert Dunlop. (Manchester, 1913.) p.86.
2 *Ibid p137.*
3 *Ibid pp143-44.*
The articles of agreement between the Hon. Commissary-General Reynolds and Captain Fergus O'Farrell, Governor of the fort of Ballileague for the surrendering thereof, being Feb. 24, 1651.

1. That the fort be surrendered to the Commissary-General or whom he shall appoint tomorrow by ten of the o'clock in the morning, being the 25th of this inst. Feb.

2. That the goods there belonging to Capt. Farrell he, or whom he appoints, be permitted to carry them away within the space of ten days, during which time himself and two servants are to remain in the said fort.

3. That he shall be received into protection and live in the Island of Loughbanon and have the liberty of 12 musketeers to defend himself and family from idle persons, provided he gives security and that they shall not act anything prejudicial to the State of England.

4. That the said Capt. Farrell be permitted to march out of the said fort with all his soldiers, with their arms, bag and baggage to return within 24 hours, all his firearms, about the number of 30 to the officer now commanding the fort by order from the Commissary-General and to have allowed him three parts of a barrel of powder with a proportion of ball and match out of the said fort. (Signed) Fergus Farrell. Articles of Capitulation of Cities, Towns and Garrisons on behalf of the Commonwealth. (Public Record Office, Dublin).

Note: The fort of Ballileague (Ballyleague) was located on the east bank of the River Shannon to the rear of the present St. Mary's Hall. It was the castle built by Geoffrey Meares in 1228.

[4] Grose, Daniel. *The Antiquities of Ireland.A supplement to Francis Grose.* Ed. Roger Stalley (Dublin, 1991). p.178

[5] Dowdall, Nicholas. *In Journal Ardagh and Clonmacnoise Antiquarian Society,.* Vol 1 No 3. From Phillips Ms 6682.

[6] Story, George. *A true and impartial history of the most material occurrences in the kingdom of Ireland.* (London, 1693), quoted by Padraic O'Farrell in *'Shannon through her literature'* (Dublin, 1983) p52

[7] *Ibid,* p53.

Chapter 11: **Independence on the wane**

[1] *Analecta Hibernica..* No 25, 1967. pp. 198-201
[2] *Moran Ms. N.L.I. Vol. 4. sub anno 1742.*
[3] *Ibid Vol.1 sub anno 1743*
[4] *Ibid Vol.1 sub anno 1747*
[5] *Ibid Vol.1 sub anon 1751*
[6] Ibid Vol.1 sub anno 1761
[7] *Ibid Vol.1 sub anno 1768*
[8] *Faulkner's Dublin Journal.* 6 January 1784.
[9] *Freeman's Journal.* 25 May 1793
[10] *Moran Ms. Vol. sub anno 1819.*
[11] *Ibid, vol 2, sub anno 1800*
[12] *Vide* O Háinle,Cathal. *Éigse Lár na hÉireann.* (Má Nuad 1975). Also Seosaimhín Ní Mhuirí. 'Seán O Neachtain agus Brian O Fearghail, two poets of the classical age' In. *Journal of the Old Athlone Society* Vol. 2 No 7 2003 p.195.
[13] Ó Braonáin, Micheál. *Príomhshruth Éireann,* trans. by Art Ó Maolfabhail. (Luimneach 1994).
[14] Corkery, Daniel. *The Hidden Ireland.* (Dublin 1924). p.101

Chapter 12: **Social tensions around the lake**

[1] *Moran Mss. N.L.I. Vol. 2, sub anno 1819*
[2] *Ibid sub anno 1811*
[3] *State of the country papers. Co. Longford. 1718/15*
[4] *Moran Mss. Vol. 2, sub anno 1814*
[5] *Ibid*
[6] *Ibid*
[7] *Faulkner's Dublin Journal* 22 March 1824.
[8] *Moran Mss. Vol. 2, sub anno 1822.*
[9] *Ibid sub anno 1831.*
[10] *Outrage Papers. Co. Longford. 1834.*

[11] *Ibid 1835*
[12] *Moran Mss. Vol.2. sub anno 1845*
[13] *Ibid*
[14] *Ibid*
[15] *Ibid sub anno 1844*
[16] *Ibid sub anno 1845.*

Chapter 13: The changing environment on Lough Ree

[1] Weld, Isaac. *Statistical survey of the county of Roscommon,drawn up under the direction of the Royal Dublin Society.* (Dublin, 1832). p151-2.
[2] *Ibid.* p153.

Chapter 14: The Great Famine

[1] Keegan, John. *A young Irishman's diary (1836-1847).* (March, 1928) pp114-15.
[2] *Freeman's Journal.* 10 January 1843
[3] Cahill, Sean and Casey, Jimmy. *"Tell me Shawn O'Farrell": the life and work of John Keegan Casey 1846-1870.* (Longford, 2002). p.370. "The Green flag in France" was serialised in *The Shamrock* between April and October 1868.

Chapter 15: The Land Question and Emerging Nationalism

[1] *Moran Ms. N.L.I.* Vol. 3 sub anno 1882.
[2] *Ibid* Vol. 4 *sub anno* 1887.
[3] *Ibid* Vol. 4 sub anno 1896.
[4] *Ibid* Vol. 4 sub anno 1897.
[5] *Ibid Vol. 4 sub anno 1887.*
[6] *Ibid* Vol. 4 sub anno 1890
[7] *Ibid*
[8] Poet, writer, linguist. Born 1905. Grandson of Dr. Sigerson Piatt. Attended Pearse's school, Scoil Éanna. Wrote *Stair na Gaeilge, Dánta ó'n Oirthear* and made many translations from other languages
[9] Piatt, Donn Sigerson. *Irisleabhar Feis Naomh Mel, 1944. Leathanach* 15

Chapter 16: Pastime and Pleasure

[1] Wakeman, W.F.. *Three days on the Shannon from Limerick to Lough Key.* (Dublin 1852).p39.
[2] *The Freeman's Journal.* 28 August 1862.
[3] *Moran Ms.* Vol 3. *sub anno* 1886.
[4] *Ibid sub anno* 1887.
[5] *Westmeath Independent. 25 April 1914.*

[6] Lecarrow Canal, first opened in 1842, had become blocked with weeds and silt. It was reopened by Roscommon Co. Council at the behest of Harry Rice and the I.W.A.I. in 1966.

[7] Banim, Mary. *Here and there through Ireland.* (Dublin 1891).p335.

Chapter 17: Flora and Fauna

[1] *Lough Ree: lake of kings, king of lakes* (Athlone, nd, c1989) p85.

[2] McCracken, Eileen. *The Irish woods since Tudor times* (Newton Abbot, 1971) p44.

[3] Weld, Isaac. *A Statistical survey of the county of Roscommon.* (Dublin 1832).p147.

[4] Brennan, Ned. Poet, *"The Wood of St John's".* Typescript in the Aidan Heavey Public Library, Athlone.

[5] Maher, Helen. *Roscommon authors* (Roscommon, 1978) p17.

[6] Rice, Harry. *Thanks for the Memory.* (Athlone, 1952.) p39.

[7] *Lough Ree, lake of kings,* p82-84

[8] *Hare Island millennium athenaeum* (Athlone, 1997)

[9] *IWeBs Survey,* 1997-98

[10] *Lough Ree: lake of kings,* p86.

[11] The Shell guide to the Shannon (Dublin, 1989)

[12] O'Brien, Gearoid (ed) *Athlone tourist trail,* 2nd ed. (Athlone, 1995) p2.

[13] Rickards, Barrie and Ray Webb. *Fishing for big ten*ch (London, 1976). p112-14.

[14] *Lough Ree: lake of kings,* p86.

[15] *Lough Ree: lake of kings,* p18.

Chapter 18: Inchenagh

[1] *Four Masters sub anno* A.D. 898

[2] *Martyrology of Donegal* (Féilire of Aengus). 1630 decimo kal. Augusti

[3] *Analecta Hibernica,* 1967, Vol. 25, pp 198-201.

[4] Tommy Murray acknowledges:
   1. His father's account of the incident. He died in the last hour of 1989 in his ninety fourth year.
   2. His uncle Joe's story of his mother's involvement in the nursing of the injured. Joe Farrell celebrated his eightieth birthday recently and is still involved in buying, breeding and grooming horses at Lisnacusha, Co. Longford.
   3. The key elements of the story were checked against the account written by Micheál O'Callaghan in his excellent outline of the part played by the Volunteers of Co. Roscommon in the fight for Independence - *For Ireland and Freedom.* 1964.
   4. An article by Bill Mulligan published in *The Roscommon Association Yearbook*.1986.

5. An article by John Casey. Stories of Inchenagh in *Pathways to the Past*. (Rathcline. 1985). Editors. Sean Cahill and Jimmy Casey.
6. Conversations with members of the Shea and Connaughton families, formerly from Inchenagh island who now live on the hill of Rathcline overlooking the island, and with Patrick Shea, Carrowroe, Roscommon, son of the late Jimmy Shea, Blenavoher.
7. Conversations with Sean Gannon, son of Jimmy Gannon, and Seamus Farrell, nephew of John Scally.
8. Conversation with Danny Farrell, Elfeet, Newtowncashel and formerly of Inchcleraun (Quaker Island).
9. Kathleen Hegarty Thorne *They put the flag a-flying* (Eugene, Oregon, 2005) pp95-96.

Chapter 19:   Clawinch

1 *Fiants. 26 September ix Elizabeth*
2 Fiants. 12 August xxxii Elizabeth
3 Family tradition also tells us that around the year 1770, the time the Delameres left Cashel another member of the family, Anne Delamere married Lewis Rhatigan of Kilnacarrow, Lanesborough. He was the son of William Rhatigan and Rachel Lewis whose romance was commemorated in song down through the years. It is said that after her marriage Anne rode pillion saddle to her new home in Kilnacarrow! The Rhatigan family who had come from Killashee had extensive lands in Kilnacarrow. Rachel Lewis was the daughter of a Quaker, William Lewis, who had a brewery on the Shannon banks at Lanesborough. His ale had a particularly attractive flavour believed to have come from certain wild berries found on the local bogs.
Note 2: Inscription on headstone in Lanesboro Cemetery: "Sacred to the memory of William Ratigan, late of Kilnacarra, departed this life 10th March 1818 aged 92 years also his consort Rachel Ratigan alias Lewis who departed this life on the 4th Nov 1830 aged 98 years and their granddaughter Catherine Ratigan who departed this life on the 10 Feb 1830 aged 21 years. This monument was erected by the affectionate son of the former, parent of the latter, Lewis Ratigan as a filial and paternal tribute. Also the said Lewis Rattigan died on the 31st May 1834 aged 78 years. This supplement is added by his affectionate wife, Ann Rattigan, alias Dillamer". May they rest in peace.
4 Davis family records (unpublished Longford County Library).

Chapter 20:   Rinnany

1 Bridie Donoghue 'My life on the island' In *Evening Echoes: a selection of writings by members of Co Roscommon Active Age Groups*. [Ed.Tommy Murray] (Roscommom. 2000). pp 75-7.

Chapter 21: **Saints' Island**

1 Ó Braonáin, Micheál. Príomhshruth Éireann. (Luimneach. 1994). p.35.
2 *Register of Tristernagh. The Register of the priory of the Blessed Virgin Mary at Tristernagh was transcribed and edited from the manuscript in the cathedral library Armagh by M.V. Clarke .(Dublin 1941).*
3 *Lateran Regesta.* Vol XLIV. Sub anno 1397.
4 *Annals of Saints' Island. Fragment 3 of Miscellaneous Annals.* 1405 Subsection 22.(Dernagolia in the parish of Shrule and Dermeana in the parish of Cashel)
5 McNamee, James. *History of the diocese of Ardagh.* (Dublin. 1954). p.181.
6 *Lateran Regesta* Martini V, an. 8. lib. 109, f.38 sub anno 1442.
7 *Lateran Regesta.* Vol CCCCLXXXIX - sub anno 1442.
8 *Four Masters. Sub anno* A.D. 1464
9 Ware, Sir James 1594-1666, was born in Dublin and was a great collector of valuable historical material on Gaelic Ireland. He published a number of treatises in Latin on Irish literary and ecclesiastical antiquities as well as editions of Campion's *"History of Ireland"* and Spenser's *"View of the state of Ireland".* His son, Robert Ware translated and re-published his works, which gained wide circulation*"The whole works of Sir James Ware"* was published in three volumes in Dublin (1739-1764) by Walter Harris, husband of his granddaughter, hence Ware-Harris.
10 McNamee. *op cit p.180.*
11 *Annals of Saints' Island. Fragment 3 of Miscellaneous Annals.* 1405 Subsection 22. Richard Rawlinson. 1680-1755, son of Sir Thomas Rawlinson, Lord Mayor of London. Richard was a noted antiquarian and a collector of books and manuscripts. At his death he bequeathed 5205 rare manuscripts to the Bodleian Library Oxford.
12 Ó hInnse, Séamus. *Miscellaneous Irish annals (A.D. 1114-1437).* (Dublin, 1947). p.xvi.
13 McNamee. op cit p.181.
14 Grose, Daniel. *The Antiquities of Ireland.* R. Stalley. Ed. (Dublin, 1991). p.85.
15 *Ibid*
16 Corrahacapickeen. Pat Costello of Pollagh had this placename from his childhood. He died in 1993, aged 87 years.
17 Moran Mss. N.L.I. Vol. 4 sub anno 1889..
18 Ó Braonáin, Micheál. *op cit, p35*
19 Grose, Daniel. *op cit, p84.*
20 Farrell, James P. *History of the County Longford. (Longford 1891) p331.*
21 Letter preserved in Redemptorist Archive. Courtesy Fr Louis Eustace C.S.S.R. Dundalk.

Chapter 22: Inchcleraun

1 Condren, Mary. *The Serpent and the Goddess. (New York. 1989) p.70.*
2 O'Donovan, John. *Ordnance Survey Letters, Co. Longford,* 1837. p.75
3 *Ibid*
4 Biggar, Francis 'Inis Chlothrann (Inis Cleraun), lough Ree: its history and antiquities' In *J.R.S.A.I.,* Vol 30, 1900. p.70. Biggar was a member of a well known Belfast nationalist family, associated with Isaac Butt and the Home Rule movement.
5 Mac Niocaill, Gearoid *Ireland before the Vikings. (Dublin, 1972) p 27.*
6 Corkery, John. *Cluain Chiarain: the city of Ciaran.* (Longford 1979). p22.
7 Monastery of Faughalstown, Co. Westmeath. Rory Masterson. Some lesser-known ecclesiastical sites in Fore, Co Westmeath. In *Ríocht na Midhe.* Gwynn and Hadcock. *Medieval Religious Houses of Ireland.* (London, 1970) p.384.
8 *Annals of Four Masters. sub anno* A.D. 780.
9 *Annals of Ulster sub anno* A.D. 870.
10 Ó Corráin, Donncha. *Ireland before the Normans.* (Dublin, 1972) p79.
11 *Annals of Inisfallen sub anno* 922 A.D.
12 *Annals of Four Masters sub anno* A.D. 987.
13 *Annals of Clonmacnoise sub anno* A.D. 1087.
14 *Annals of Four Masters sub anno* A.D. 1136.
15 *Ibid sub anno* A.D. 1141.
16 *Ibid sub anno* A.D. 1160.
17 *Ibid sub anno* A.D. 1167
18 *Ibid sub anno* A.D.1168
19 *Ibid sub anno* A.D. 1170.
20 *Ibid sub anno* A.D. 1174
21 *Ibid sub anno* A.D. 1189
22 *Annals of Loch Cé sub anno* A.D. 1193.
23 *Ibid 1143*
24 *Ibid sub anno* A.D. 1220.
25 *Annals of Four Masters sub anno* A.D. 1232
26 *Ibid sub anno* A.D. 1244
27 *Lateran Registers sub anno* 1424 O hUbagan et al
28 Casey, Jimmy and Sean Cahill, Eds. *Rathcline: pathways to the past* (Lanesborough,. 1995) *p.75*
29 Leask, H.G. *Irish churches and monastic buildings.i,* (Dundalk, 1987) p52.
30 Biggar, Francis J. *op cit.p72.*
31 O'Donovan. *Ordnance survey letters, Co. Roscommon Letters.* 9 July 1837.
32 Biggar, Francis J. *op cit. p72.*
33 *Fiants of Elizabeth 1590*
34 Weld, Isaac. *Statistical survey of Co. Roscommon.* (Dublin, 1832). p461.
35 Acknowledgement to Albert Siggins, Castlecoote for his invaluable help and for making available his considerable research on the Quaker settlement here and also to Tommy Murray, Roscommon.

Chapter 23:   Inchbofin

[1] Concannon, Maureen *The Sacred Whore* (Cork, 2004). p.17.
[2] Joyce, P.W. *A Social history of ancient Ireland* (Dublin, 1903) p619.
[3] Condren, Mary. *The Serpent and the Goddess* (New York, 1989). p 26.
[4] O Donovan, V. *Christianity rediscovered.* (New York 1982). pp.20, 155.
[5] MacGivney, Joseph. *Placenames of Co. Longford.* (Dublin, 1908) p138
[6] *Annals of Four Masters sub anno* A.D. 750.
[7] *Ibid sub anno* A.D. 809.
[8] *Ibid sub anno* A.D. 916.
[9] Crawford, Henry S. 'The churches and monasteries of Inis Bó Finne, Co. Westmeath'. In *J.R.S.A.I.*, Vol 47, 1917. p142.
[10] Crawford identified ten slabs or fragments which he described in great detail. All but one have survived to the present day. Some which were damaged or broken have been re-assembled by the staff of *Dúchas*.

Chapter 24:   Hare Island (Inis Aingin)

[1] O'Donovan, John. *Ordnance survey letters, Co. Westmeath.*
[2] O'Hanlon, John. *Lives of the Irish saints* (Dublin, 1875-1903), p. 216
[3] *Ibid* p. 218
[4] *Ibid* p. 219
[5] *Ibid*
[6] *Annals of Four Masters sub anno* A.D. 894.
[7] *Annals of Clonmacnois sub anno* A.D.1087
[8] Graham-Campbell, J.A. 'A Viking age gold hoard from Ireland' In *The Antiquaries Journal,* Vol 54, Pt 2, 1975. pp269-72.
[9] A sum equal to approx. 1000 guineas
[10] Graham-Campbell, J.A. 'A Viking age gold hoard from Ireland'
[11] O'Donovan, John. *Ordnance Survey letters,* Westmeath.
[12] Barrington, Jonah. *The rise and fall of the Irish nation.* (Dublin, James Duffy, nd, c1833) p.268
[13] *Ibid* p269.
[14] Russell, T.O. *Beauties and antiquities of Ireland* (London, Kegan Paul, Trench Trubner, 1897) pp 50-51.
[15] Moran Mss. N.L.I.
[16] *Ibid*
[17] Bence-Jones, Mark. *Burke's guide to country houses, volume 1: Ireland.* (London: Burke's Peerage, 1978).
[18] Rolt, L.T.C.. *Green and Silver* (London, 1949) p.27
[19] Sheehan, Jeremiah. *South Westmeath farm and folk.* (Dublin, 1978).
[20] McBride, Sean. "The battle to protect the Inland Waterways." In Michael Martin (ed) *Inland Waterways Association of Ireland, Athlone, Silver Jubilee 1954-1979* (Athlone, I.W.A.I., 1979) pp. 55-61.
[21] Böll. Heinrich. *Irish journal*
[22] *Hare Island Millennium Athenaeum.* (Athlone, 1997)

Chapter 25: Inchmore

[1] Nash, W.J. *Lough Ree and around it.* (Athlone 1949).p3.
[2] *Moran Ms. N.L.I. Vol.1 sub anno A.D. 1776.*

Chapter 26: Inchturk

[1] Rice, H.J. *Thanks for the memory* (Athlone, 1952) p55.
[2] *The Westmeath Independent.*

Chapter 27: Nuns' Island

[1] Ó Braonáin, Mícheál. *Príomhshruth Éireann* (Luimneach) 1994.
[2] Ó Donovan, John. *Ordnance Survey Letters Co. Roscommon* 1837.

Chapter 28: Friars' Island

[1] Grannell, Fergal. *The Franciscans in Athlone* (Athlone, 1978) p36.

Chapter 29: Black Islands

[1] Mc Namee, James J. *History of the diocese of Ardagh.* (Dublin 1954). p 111.
[2] *Ibid.*
[3] Hayward, Richard. *Where the River Shannon flows* (London, 1940)
[4] *Westmeath Herald,* 24 December 1859
[5] Billingsgate: the famous London wholesale fish market. It had occupied an important site close to London Bridge for almost 1,000 years, from the 9th century until it relocated in 1982.
[6] Cahill, Sean and Jimmy Casey. *"Tell me Shawn O'Farrell": the life and work of John Keegan Casey 1846-1870* (Longford, 2002) pp. 107,123.
[7] Rolt, L.T.C. *Green and Silver.* (London. 1949). pp.193-4.

Bibliography:

Manuscript Material

Moran Mss = A collection of materials copied from various printed sources (mainly National newspapers) relating to the history of Athlone and surrounding area compiled by Malachy J. Moran. National Library of Ireland, Mss 1543-47, 4 vols + index.
1901 Census of Ireland.

Journals

Irish Biogeographical Society Bulletin (Athlone Field Meeting) No 1, 1976.
Irish Naturalist
Journal of the Old Athlone Society
Journal of the Ardagh and Clonmacnoise Antiquarian Society
Journal of the Roscommon Historical and Archaeological Society
Journal of the Royal Society of Antiquaries of Ireland
Teathbha: Journal of Longford Historical Society.

Printed sources

Annals of Clonmacnoise, being annals of Ireland from the earliest period to A.D. 1408, translated into English, A.D. 1627 by Conall Mageoghegan, Ed. Denis Murphy (Dublin: R.S.A.I., 1896).
Annals of the Four Masters = Annals of the kingdom of Ireland by the Four Masters from the earliest period to the year 1616, Ed. John O'Donovan, 7 vols, (Dublin, Hodges & Smith, 1851).
Annals of Lough Cé: a chronicle of Irish affairs 1014-1690, Ed. W.M. Hennessy, 2 vols, (London: Longman & Trubner, 1871).
Annals of Inisfallen, Ed. Sean MacAirt (Dublin: Dublin Institute for Advanced Studies, 1951).
Annals of Ulster, otherwise annals Senait, annals of Senat: a chronicle of Irish affairs 431-1131, 1155-1541, Ed. W.M. Hennessy and B MacCarthy, 4 vols, (Dublin: H.M.S.O. / Alex Thom, 1887-1901)
Archdall, Mervyn. *Monasticon Hibernicum: or a history of the abbies, priories or other religious houses in Ireland,* 2 vols, (Dublin, Luke White, 1786).

Banim, Mary. *Here and there through Ireland, Part II* (Dublin, The Freeman's Journal, 1892).
Barrington, Jonah. *The Rise and fall of the Irish nation* (Dublin, James Duffy, nd, c. 1833).
Beirne, Francis (ed). *The Diocese of Elphin: people, places and pilgrimage* (Dublin: The Columba Press, 2000).
Bence-Jones, Mark. *Burke's guide to country houses, volume 1: Ireland* (London: Burke's Peerage, 1978).

Birds in central Ireland, mid-Shannon bird report. Ed. Stephen Heery. 1st, 2nd and 3rd reports. (Dublin: BirdWatch Ireland, 1996-2005),

Böll, Heinrich. *Irish journal: a traveller's portrait of Ireland.* Translated from the German by Leila Vennewitz (London: Secker & Warburg, 1983).

Böll, Heinrich. *Irisches tagebuch* (Koln / Berlin: Keipenheuer & Witsch, 1957).

Bradshaw, Brendan and Dáire Keogh, eds. *Christianity in Ireland: revisiting the story* (Dublin, Columba Press, 2002).

Bulfin, William. *Rambles in Eireann* (Dublin: Gill, 1907).

Cahill, Sean & Jimmy Casey. *"Tell me Shawn O'Farrell" The life and works of John Keegan Casey 1846-1870.* (Longford: The John Keegan Casey Society, 2002).

Calendar of documents relating to Ireland, 1171-1307. 5 vols. (London: H.M.S.O. 1875-86).

Campbell, Patrick. *My life and easy times* (London: Anthony Blond, 1967).

Casey, Jimmy & Sean Cahill Eds. *Rathcline: pathways to the past.* (Lanesborough, Rathcline Heritage Society, 1995).

Chinery, Michael. *Collins guide to butterflies: a photographic guide to the butterflies of Britain and Europe.* (London: HarperCollins, 1998).

Clare, Rev. Wallace (ed). *A Young Irishman's diary (1836-47) being extracts from the early journal of John Keegan of Moate* (March: printed for the author, 1928).

Condren, Mary. *The Serpent and the Goddess* (San Francisco: Harper & Row, 1989).

Concannon, Mrs Thomas [Helena]. *The Poor Clares in Ireland, 1629-1929* (Dublin: Gill, 1929).

Concannon, Maureen. *The Sacred Whore: Sheela Goddess of the Celts* (Cork: Collins, 2004).

Corkery, Daniel. *The Hidden Ireland* (Dublin: M.H. Gill & Son, 1924).

Corkery, John. *Cluain Chiarain: the city of Ciaran* (Longford: printed by Turner's Printing Co. Ltd., 1979).

Cox, Liam. *Placenames of Westmeath, the baronies of Clonlonan and Kilkenny West.* (Moate, Moate Historical Society, 1994).

Delany, Ruth. *Ireland's inland waterways* (Belfast, Appletree, 1986).

Delany, Ruth. *By Shannon shores* (Dublin: Gill and Macmillan, 1987).

Dempsey, Eric and Michael O'Clery. *The complete guide to Ireland's birds.* 2nd ed. (Dublin: Gill and Macmillan, 2002).

Dinsdale, Tim. *The Leviathans* (London: Routledge & Kegan Paul, 1966).

Donovan, Vincent J. *Christianity rediscovered* (New York, Orbis Books, 1982).

Dunlop, R. *Ireland under the commonwealth 1651-59* (Manchester: Manchester University Press, 1913).

English, N.W. *First decade of "The Inland Waterways Association of Ireland"* (Athlone: I.W.A.I., 1965).

English, N.W. *Lough Ree Yacht Club 1770-1970* (Athlone, L.R.Y.C., 1970).

Fabius G. Th. J. and Maas, P.R.M. *Vegetation and soils of the Lough Ree area, Shannon basin, Ireland,* Typescript. Utrecht: Doctoraal verslag Inst. V. Syst. Plankt. Utrecht, 1968.

Farrell, James P. *History of the county Longford* (Dublin: Dollard, 1891).

Flanagan, P.J. and Toner, P.F. *A preliminary survey of Irish lakes.* (Dublin: An Foras Forbatha, 1975).

Goodbody, L.M. and Ruth Delany. *The Shannon One Design class 1922-1999.* (Dublin, privately printed, 2000).

Grannell, Fergal O.F.M. *The Franciscans in Athlone* (Athlone: The Franciscan Friary, 1978).

Griffith, Richard. *The valuation of tenements .... counties the various volumes for the baronies in Westmeath, Roscommon & Longford.*

Grose, Daniel. *The Antiquities of Ireland, a supplement to Francis Grose,* Ed. Roger Stalley (Dublin: Irish Architectural Archives, 1991).

Gwynn, Aubrey and Hadcock, Neville. *Medieval religious houses: Ireland* (London: Longman, 1970).

Hare Island millennium athenaeum, unpublished feasibility study (Athlone, 1997).

Harvey, R. *The Shannon and its lakes* (Dublin: Hodges Figgis & Co., 1896).

Hayward, Richard. *Where the River Shannon flows* (London: Harrap, 1940).

Heery, Stephen. *The Shannon floodlands – a natural history of the River Shannon* (Kinvara: Tír Eolas, 1993).

Hessel, P. and Rubers, W.V. *Flora, vegetatie en bodem in het stroongebied van de Shannon, met name in de omgeving van Lough Ree.* Typescript. Utrecht: Doctoraal verslag Inst. V. Syst. Plankt, Utrecht. 1971.

Hickie, David. *Nature in Westmeath: a wildlife and habitat guide* (Mullingar: Westmeath County Council, 2005).

Hughes, Kathleen. *The Church in early Irish society* (London: Methuen, 1966).

The Irish fiants of the Tudor soverigns during the reigns of Henry VIII, Edward VI, Philip & Mary, and Elizabeth I. 4 vols. (Dublin: Edmund Burke Publisher, 1994).

The Irish penitentials. Ed Ludwig Bieler. (Dublin: Dublin Institute for Advanced Studies, 1963).

Jones, Gwyn. *A history of the Vikings second edition* (Oxford: OUP, 1984).

Joyce, P.W. *A Social history of Ancient Ireland.* (Dublin: Phoenix Publishing Co., 1903).

Klein, Johannes. *An Irish landscape: a study of natural and semi-natural vegetations in the Lough Ree area of the Shannon basis* (Utrecht: Rijksuniversiteir te Utrecht, 1975).

Leask, Harold. *Irish churches and monastic buildings,* 3 vols, (Dundalk: Dundalgan Press, 1955-60).

Legg, Marie Louise (ed.) *The census of Elphin 1749* (Dublin, Irish Manuscripts Commission, 2004).

Levinge, R. *A sportsman's guide to the Shannon* (Athlone, Athlone Printing Works, nd).

Lough Derg and Lough Ree catchment monitoring and management system. Final report. Kirk McClure Morton in Association with Brady Shipman Martin, April 2001.

Lough Ree lake of kings king of lakes (Athlone: Athlone Chamber of Commerce & Industry Ltd., nd, c.1997).

Lyons, John C. *The book of surveys and distribution of the estates in the county of Westmeath forfeited in the year 1641.* (Mullingar, Ledeston, 1852).

McCracken, Eileen. *The Irish woods since Tudor times* (Newton Abbot: David & Charles, 1971).

McGivney, Joseph. *The Placenames of county Longford* (Dublin: J. Duffy, 1908).

McNamee, James. *History of the diocese of Ardagh* (Dublin: Browne & Nolan, 1954).

MacNiocaill, Gearoid. *Ireland before the Vikings.* (Dublin, Gill & Macmillan, 1972).

Maher, Helen. *Roscommon authors.* (Roscommon, Roscommon County Library, 1978).

Martin, Michael (ed). *Inland Waterways Association of Ireland, Silver Jubilee 1954-79* (Athlone: IWAI, 1979).

Mills, Stephen. *Nature in its place: the habitats of Ireland.* (London: Bodley Head, c1998).

Miscellaneous Irish annals, A.D. 1114-1437, Ed. Seamus O hInnse, (Dublin, Dublin Institute for Advanced Studies,1947)

Monahan, John. *Records relating to the dioceses of Ardagh and Clonmacnoise* (Dublin: Gill, 1886).

Murtagh, Harman. *Athlone: history and settlement to 1800* (Athlone: Old Athlone Society, 2000).

Murtagh, Harman (ed). *Irish midland studies: essays in commemoration of N.W. English* (Athlone, Old Athlone Society, 1980).

Murtagh, Harman. *No 6, Athlone in Irish historic towns atlas,* i, (Dublin: R.I.A., 1996).

Nash, W.J. *Loughree and around it* (Athlone, printed for the author, 1949).

Ó Braonáin, Micheál. *Príomhsruth Éireann* (translated and edited by Art Ó Maolfabhail) (Luimneach: Bardas Luimnigh, 1994).

O'Brien, Gearoid. *St. Mary's parish Athlone: a history* (Longford: St. Mel's Diocesan Trust, 1989).

Ó Conchúir, M.F. *Gealladh Báistí* (Baile Átha Cliath, Foilseacháin Náisiúnta Teoranta 1974).

Ó Corráin, Donncha. *Ireland before the Normans* (Dublin: Gill and Macmillan, 1972).

O'Curry, Eugene. *On the manners and customs of the ancient Irish, 2 vols.* (Dublin: Williams, 1873).

O'Donovan, John. *Letters containing information relative to the antiquities of the county of Longford, collected during the progress of the Ordnance Survey in 1837.* Typescript (Bray: Reproduced under the direction of Rev. Michael O'Flanagan, 1926).

O'Donovan, John. *Letters containing information relative to the antiquities of the county of Roscommon, collected during the progress of the Ordnance Survey in 1837, 2 vols,* Typescript (Bray: Reproduced under the direction of Rev. Michael O'Flanagan, 1926).

O'Donovan, John. *Letters containing information relative to the antiquities of the county of Westmeath, collected during the progress of the Ordnance Survey in 1837*, two vols in one,. Typescript (Bray: Reproduced under the direction of Rev. Michael O'Flanagan, 1926).

O'Donovan, John. *The Tribes and customs of Hy-Many, commonly called O'Kelly's Country* (Dublin, Irish Archaeological Society, 1843)

O'Farrell, Padraic. *Shannon through her literature* (Dublin / Cork: Mercier Press, 1983).

Ó hÁinle, Cathal. *Éigse lár na hÉireann 1500-1750* (Má Nuad: An Sagart, 1975).

O'Hanlon, John. *The Lives of Irish saints*, 10 vols. (Dublin, 1875-1903).

O'Sullivan, Catherine Marie. *Hospitality in medieval Ireland 900-1500.* (Dublin: Four Courts Press, 2004).

Piers, Sir Henry. 'A chorographical description of the county of Westmeath, written AD 1682'. In Charles Vallancey (ed) *Collectanea de rebus Hibernicis, I,* (Dublin, 1770) pp1-126.

Rice, H.J. *Thanks for the memory* (Athlone, Athlone Printing Works, 1952).

Rickards, Barrie and Ray Webb. *Fishing for big tench.* (London, Rod and Gun Publications, 1976).

Rolt, L.T.C. *Green and Silver* (London: Allen & Unwin, 1949).

Russell, T.O. *The beauties and antiquities of Ireland.* (London: Kegan Paul, Trench Trubner & Co Ltd, 1897)

Sharkey, P.A. *The Heart of Ireland* (Boyle: M.J. Ward, nd, c1927).

Sheehan, Jeremiah. *Westmeath: as others saw it.* (Moate, the author, 1982).

Sheehan, Jeremiah. *South Westmeath farm and folk* (Dublin: The Blackwater Press, 1978).

Shell guide to the Shannon. Ed Ruth Delany. (Dublin: Gill and Macmillan, 1989).

Silver River: a celebration of 25 years of the Shannon Boat Rally (Dublin: IWAI, 1985).

Simington, Robert C. (ed). *Books of survey and distribution: being abstracts of various surveys and instruments of title, volume I: county of Roscommon* (Dublin: Stationery Office, 1949).

Smyth, Alfred P. *Scandinavian York and Dublin Vol 2* (New Jersey: Humanities Press, 1979).

Stokes, G.T. *Athlone, the Shannon and Lough Ree* (Dublin, Hodges, 1897).

Story, George. *A true and impartial history of the most material occurrences in the kingdom of Ireland during the last two years* (London: 1691).

Story, George. *A continuation of the impartial history of the wars of Ireland.* (London: 1693)

Taheny, Luke OP. *The Dominicans of Roscommon* [edited by Hugh Fenning] (Dublin:Saint Mary's Priory, Tallaght, nd, c1990)

Thomas, Avril. *The Walled towns of Ireland, 2 vols* (Dublin: Irish Academic Press, 2006).

Thorne, Kathleen Hegarty. *They put the flag a-flyin': the Roscommon Volunteers 1916-1923.* (Eugene, Oregon: Generation Organization, 2005).

Todd, James Henthorn. *Cogadh Gaedhel re Gallaibh - The War of the Gaedhil with the Gaill* (London, Longmans, Green, Reader, and Dyer, 1867).

Wakeman, W.F. *Three days on the Shannon from Limerick to Lough Key* (Dublin: Hodges and Smith, 1852).

Walsh, Paul. *The Placenames of Westmeath* (Dublin, Dublin Institute of Advanced Studies, 1957).

Watt, John. *The Church in medieval Ireland* (Dublin: Gill and MacMillan, 1972).

Webb, D.A. et al. *An Irish flora*. 7th revised ed. (Dundalk: Dundalgan Press (W. Tempest) Ltd, 1996).

Weld, Isaac. *The statistical survey of the county of Roscommon drawn up under the direction of the Royal Dublin Society* (Dublin: R Graisberry, 1832).

White, N.B. (ed): *Extents of Irish monastic possessions 1540-1541 from manuscripts in the Public Record Office*, London (Dublin: Stationery Office, 1943).

Woods, Cedric C. *Freshwater life in Ireland*. (Dublin: Irish University Press, 1974).

Woods, James: *The Annals of Westmeath, ancient and modern* (Dublin: Sealy, Bryers & Walker, 1907).

Index

Barrington, Richard M. 143
Barrington, Sir John 250
Barrybeg *1901 List* 316
Barrymore *1901 List* 317
Bates, Florence 181
Battle of Hastings 50
Beam Island 6
Beechwood 165
Bell, Miss 260
Bell, Robert 260
Bence-Jones, Mark 252
Benown *1901 List* 311
Berry, Martha 259
Bethlehem *1901 List* 305
Bethlehem 88,91,93,271
Bewick, Pauline 254
Big Freeze 189
Biggar, Francis J. 18,206,225
Birch, Robert 162
Black Death 67
Black Islands *1901 List* 285
Black Islands 5,121,69,131,277,279,
    281,283, 284,287,288,290,292,293
Black Sea 27,28
Blackbrink Bay 120
Blackfeet 112
Bleanaphuttoge *1901 List* 305
Bléan-Gaille 48
Blenavoher 130,160,167,168,170
Blenavoher *1901 List* 295
Bóand 233
Board of Works 4,272
Bodleian Library 196,275
Bole, Ambrose 265
Böll, Heinrich 254
Bolton, W.J. 136
Bond, William 203
Bonenadden 85
Book of Armagh 40
Book of Lismore 241
Book of Navan 241
Boston Pilot 145
Bowman, J.J. 157
Boyle 10,140,216
Brabazon, William 73,226

Bracknagh 189
Brammer, Mr 291
Brammer's Bucket 261
Brawny 12,240,281
Breach of the Boats 44
Breaghmaini 7,12,33,52,215
Bream-hole 264
Breensford River 2
Brehon Laws 20,61
Breifne 39,50,52
Brennan, Jeffrey Michael 181
Brennan, Luke 181
Brennan, Mary Ann 183
Brennan, Ned 145
Brennan, P. 288
Brennan, Pat 189
Brennan, Patrick 181,182
Brennan, Seamus 182
Brennan, Thomas 181
Brennan, Vincent 181
Brian 38
Brian Boru 38,40,47
Brick Island 127,137
Bridges, James 196
Britain 26,29,33,37
Brittany 32
Broderick 133
Brodir 41
Brodir of Man 40
Brown, Fr. 113
Browne, Archbishop 226
Browne, Michael 127
Browne, Sr. Catherine 94
Bunown 256
Burke, John 75
Burke, Joseph 133
Burke, Ulick 75
Caenchomrac 160
Caille Focladha 161,209
Caillí Dubha 272
Cairbre Crom 243
Caladh na hAnghaile 12,70,75,98
Calraidhe 12
Calry 193
Camach 215

Cameron, D. 136
Campbell, Rev Mr 225
Campbell, W.J.V 225
Canterbury 44
Caol Uisce 60
Cappabrack 112
Carbry Island 6,135,146,247
Carey, Fr 126
Carley, Aidan 287
Carley, Jim 287, 288
Carley, Kate 287
Carmelites 85
Carnagh East *1901 List* 323
Caron, Raymond 274
Carowndrisha *1901 List* 327
Carrabeg 231,289
Carrick Hill 126
Carrowmurragh *1901 List* 321
Carrownamaddy *1901 List* 326
Carrownavaddy 287
Carrownure *1901 List* 325
Carrownure 3
Carrownure Bay 2
Carrowphadeen *1901 List* 324
Casey, Caitriona 177
Casey, John 168
Casey, John Keegan 124,282
Casey, Winifred 294
Cashel *1901 List* 297
Cashel 2,3,37,55,65,75,111,113,121,
137, 174,191,217,277,288,291
Cashel House 174
Cashel Lodge203,204
Caspian Sea 28,37
Castleblakeney 64
Castlecoote
Castlerea 10,125
Cathal Crovderg 53,54,55,59
Cavan 1,2
Ceallach 44
Cearbhall 33
Céli Dé 24,257
Celtic Monastery 20
Celtic Rituals 16
Central Plain 1

Chapel Lane 83
Chapman, Teresa 294
Charlemagne 22,27
Charlie's Island 156
Church Island 231
Churchpark 229
Cinél Dofa 10,278
Cinnétig 37
Cistercians 45
Claffey, John A.84
Clairvaux 45
Clan Colmáin 12,35
Clare 37
Claris 174
Claris *1901 List* 302
Clarke, Anne 201
Clarke, Edward 198
Clarke, Mary 201
Clarke, William 201
Clawinch *1901 List* 182
Clawinch 5,98,104,162,174,182,
183,187,188,293
Cleraune *1901 List* 300
Cleraune 293
Cleraune N.S 282
Clonard 19,208,240
Clonbearla 294
Clondra 117
Clones 208
Clonfert 30,53
Clonmacnois 7,19,22,24,30,31,32,33,
42,53,73, 86,161,208,240,243,248,
275
Clonmore 172
Clonown 259
Clonsellan 86,87
Clontarf 40,43,213
Clonterm 288
Clontuskert 162
Cloonadra *1901 List* 334
Cloonan, James 127
Clooncagh Bog 291
Clooncraff 86,87,165,181
Clooneigh *1901 List* 332
Clooneigh Bay 5,35,160

Clooneigh River 2
Clooneskert *1901 List* 331
Cloonlarge *1901 List* 332
Cloonmore 168
Cloonmore *1901 List* 331
Cloontagh 290
Cloontogher 105
Cloontuskert 165,169
Cloontymullen 165,169
Clothra 206
Cluain-Tuaiscirt 58
Coen, F. 136
Colgu 22
Colla 33
Collins, Michael 136
Collum 127
Collum *1901 List* 299
Coman 86
Commons Nth. *1901 List* 295
Conlon, Patrick O.F.M.93
Conmaicne 12,33
Connaught 10,30,34,35,38,40,47
Connaughtons 172
Connell, Bryan 238
Connell, John 4
Connemara 264
Connie's Point 264
Connla's Well 15,16
Connor, John 168
Connor, Johnny 166
Connorstown 91
Conroy, Nancy 131,279
Cooltona *1901 List* 329
Coosan 144,241,253
Coosan *1901 List* 313
Coosan Lough 2
Coosan Point 6,115,146,240
Coote, Sir Charles 245
Corco-Baiscin 242
Corgarve 229
Cork 30
Corkery, John 22,209
Cormacan 238
Cornahinch 226
Cornaseer *1901 List* 320

Corool Fox *1901 List* 302
Corool Kenny *1901 List* 301
Corrahacapikeen 198
Corraphortanarla 226
Cotton, Edward 260
Crawford, Henry S. 235
Creaghduff 137,144
Creaghduff *1901 List* 314
Creaghduff South *1901 List* 313
Creggan 3
Creggan Lough 2
Crescent Ballroom 140
Cribby Islands 6
Crofton, Edward 105,106,111,228,229
Croftons 104
Croke, Archbishop 128
Cromwell 82,96
Cromwell, Lord 226
Cromwellian Plantation 10
Cross of Cong 42,87
Cross of the Scriptures 32
Cruit *1901 List* 328
Cruit 206
Cuchulainn 206
Cuilcagh Mountains1
Cuircne 12, 44,70
Culdees 24
Cullentra 182
Cullentra *1901 List* 296
Culliaghy *1901 List* 334
Cullion 288
Cullion Hall 291
Culnagore 146
Culnagore *1901 List* 298
Cumann na mBan 167
Cunniff, Martin 273
Curley 133
Curoi 210
Curreen *1901 List* 295
Curreen 1,58
Cusacks 162
Cut 1
Daingen-Uí-Chuinn 55
Dal gCais 37,39
Dalton, John 281

Daltons 69
Darerca 232,240
Daroge 3
Davis, Matt 168
Davitt, Michael 128
Dawson, John 105
Dawsons 104
De Burgh, William 57
De Cogan, Milo 51
De Courcy, John 54
De Grey, John 73
De Lacy, Hugh 52,54
De Lacy, Walter 55
De Marisco, Geoffrey 56
De Nangle, Gilbert 215
De Nangles(Costelloes) 215
De Ufford, Robert 58
Dealbhna 44
Delamere, Anne 181
Delamere, Brigid 181
Delamere, Elizabeth 181
Delamere, Jeffrey 181
Delamere, John 174,181
Delamere, John Thomas 181
Delamere, Martin 181
Delamere, Mary 181
Delamere, Patrick 181
Delamere, Sir John 60
Delamere, William 174
Delamers 67,104
Delaney, Ruth 139,140
Delaney, Vincent 139,140
Delvin, Baron of 257
Dennehy, Tim 282
Dermot Stone 207,225
Dernagolia 3
Derrahaun 290
Derrydarragh *1901 List* 298
Derrydarragh 3,288
Derrygowna 181,290,294
Derrynabuntale *1901 List* 305
Derrynagolia *1901 List* 304
Devanny, John 186
Dillon, Cecily 93
Dillon, Edward 274

Dillon, Eleanor 93
Dillon, George 274
Dillon, Gerald 122
Dillon, James 72, 86
Dillon, Mother Cecily 89
Dillon, Rev Thomas 85
Dillon, Robert 85
Dillon, Sir James 89,92,93,245,275
Dillon, Theobald 93
Dillon,Edward Roe 73
Dillons 12,104,162
Dodd, Pat 287
Doire Meinci 192
Doire na gCailleach 192
Dolan, Jim 290
Dolan, Mary 112
Dolan, Mike 289
Dominican Priory 67
Donal Dubh 13,14
Donegal 275
Donimoney 86
Donlon, Catherine 181
Donlon, John 181
Donlon, Nurse 167
Donnan 242,243
Donoghue family 167
Donoghue, Bridie 183
Donoghue, Michael 183,186
Donoghue, Pat 186
Dooley, Bill 288
Dooley, John 122
Doonis 2
Dowdall, Nicholas 100
Doyle, Thomas 112
Drogheda 94
Drum 108
Drumnee *1901 List* 303
Drumnee 288,289
Drumraney 85,112
Dubhgall 41
Dublin 30,32,34,40,42,47,50,51
Duffy, Kate 290
Duffy, Mary 281
Duffy, Mrs 247,248
Duffy, Noel 253

Gaelic League 128,129
Galbraith, Susan 239
Galey *1901 List* 328
Galey 62,65
Galey Bay 133,288
Galey Castle 63
Gallagh 165
Gallagh *1901 List* 333
Gallagher, Tommy 140
Galway 89,95,204
Ganly, Willie 127
Ganly, Bridget 267
Ganly, Jack 287
Ganly, Micky 292
Ganly, William 264,267
Gannon, Jimmy 166,167
Gannon, Tom 124
Gardenstown *1901 List* 333
Garmley, Rose 88
Garnafelia *1901 List* 315
Gavigan, John 114
Gearóid Mór 71
Gearr Beraigh 16,278
Geraghty, Edward 113
Germany 37
Gibbons, Bríd 259
Giles, Morgan 136
Gillachrist Mac Carghamhna 7
Gilleran, Kathleen 181
Gilligan, Canon Michael 203
Gilmore, Declan 289
Girls Island 277
Glasson 128,290
Glasson Team 129
Gleann Máma 39
Glendalough 279
Glennon, Ann 294
Glennon, Pat 186
Glennon, Sr Kathleen 187
Godfrith 33,37
Goldsmith, Oliver 102
Goodbody, L.M. 139
Goodwin, Graham 292
Gormauns, The 4,292
Gormflaith 41

Gosling, Michael 122
Gothfrithsson 34,36
Graham-Campbell, J.A. 244
Grand Canal 117
Grannell, Fr Fergal 274
Gravelines 93
Greenland 28
Grianán Maedbha 206,223
Grose, Daniel 98,196,238
Gurteen 124,282,290
Gwynn and Hadcock 244
Halloween 18
Halton, Pat 149,150,153,179
Hamilton, Eben 292
Handcock, C.281
Handcock, Major 136
Handcock, Robert 105
Handcock, William 249
Handcocks 104
Hanly, Dan 290
Hanly, Daniel 127,277
Hanly, James 287
Hanly, Jimmy 292
Hanly, John 268
Hanly, Maria 293
Hanly, Mary 281,290
Hanly, Michael 277
Hanly, P. 140
Hanly, Paddy 131,279,284,287
Hare Island 6,36,146,240,241,244,
   245,247250,252,254,271,293,
Hare Lodge 252,253
Harte, Johnny 260,264
Hatfield, Ridgely 245
Hayward, Richard 13,279
Headen, John 123
Headen, Larry 123
Hegarty Thorne, Kathleen 166,168
Hennessy, Ann 149, 153, 154,178,180
Henry of Anjou 50
Henry VII 71
Henry VIII 76
Hessel and Rubers 143
Heveran, Pat 238
Hidden Ireland 102

Hind River 3,87,228,291
Hoare, Joseph 203
Hodson Bay 6,146,137
Hodson, Oliver 110
Hodsons 104
Hogan, M.J. 136
Hogan, Tom 140
Hoord, Captain 101
Hopkins, Mike 289
Hopkins, Peter 289
Horan, Tess 181
Horohoe, Michael 114
Horse Island 277
Hugh de Lacy 50
Iceland 27,29,33
Igoe, Joe 261
Illanfan 262
Imhar Mac Carghamhna 7
Inch 104,162
Inchbofin *1901 List* 239
Inchbofin 4,5,17,18,22,30,32,
47,48,98,125,214,234,237,
264,288,293
Inchcleraun 5,18,19,32,46,52,53,
78,80,98,104,161,162,168,169,
183,187,191,205,206,209,210,
214,215,217,219,227,229,293
Inchcleraun *1901 List* 231
Inchenagh *1901 List* 163
Inchenagh 3,5,35,37,52,98,104,
130,131,160,161,163,166,168,
169,170,172,188,293
Inchmore 4,5,35,37,69,98,121,
131,241,256,257,259,260,264,
265,290,292,293
Inchmore *1901 List* 263
Inchturk 5,37,98,127,131,180,259,264,
265,272,273,287,288,290,293
Inchturk *1901 List* 268, 269
Inis Aingin (see also Hare Island)
6,32,36,98,191,208,214,243
Inis Mhic Ualaing 234
Inismurray 18,30,237
Inner Lakes 2
Inny 2,12,67,75,97,147

Inse, Island 4
Iona 26,29
Ireland 29
Iskeraulin Shoal 293
Islandbridge 33
Isle of Man 15
Italy 46
Jamestown 97
Jennings, Margaret 281
Jervis St Hospital 167
Johnston, St George 230
Jones, Frances 181
Jones, Roger 275
Jones, Sir Theophilus 97
Jordan, John 114
Justiciar Macmorish 57
Jutes 26
Keaveney, Hugh 113
Keefe, Celia 260
Keegan, John 121
Keenan, J.D. 126
Kellet, Simon 113
Kelly, D.H. 64
Kelly, Dr C. 167
Kelly, James 112
Kelly, John 168
Kelly, Johnny 166,167
Kelly, Mr P. 133
Kelly, William 252
Kenagh 9
Keneavy, Patrick 137
Kenny family 182
Kenny, Kathleen 168
Kenny, Kieran 140
Kenny, Miss 168
Kerney, John 123
Kerry 30,235
Kilbarry 279
Kilbeggan 192
Kilclare 52
Kilcline, Luke 186
Kildare 162,232
Kilkenny 235
Kilkenny West 2,12,85,88,91,128,
193,245,256,275

Meehan *1901 List* 314
Meehan Wood 146
Meelick 74
Mellifont 45
Middle East 37
Midhe 12,30,32,37,38
Miscellaneous Annals 195
Moate 12,121,250
Mochua 23
Moffett, James 111
Molloy, P.C. 140
Monascath Bog 288
Moran 133
Moran MS. 198
Moran, Fr. 140
Moran, James 206,230
Moran, John 230
Morrison, Sir Richard 250
Mote Park 105,228,229
Mount Prospect 184
Mount Temple 69
Mountjoy 125
Mountplunket 291
Mountplunkett *1901 List* 326
Moydow 290
Moydrum Castle 147,245,250,253
Moyvannan *1901 List* 321
Muckenagh 108,137,288,292
Muckenagh *1901 List* 306,307
Muckinish 212
Muintir Anghaile 214
Muintir Mael tSionna 12
Muintir Thadhgain 7
Muintir Tlamain 7
Muintir-Maelshinna 7
Muldoon, Brian 174
Mulligan, Bill 166
Mullingar 75
Mulvany, Fr Seamus 270
Mulvihill 133
Mulvihill, Thomas 201
Munster 32,37,47,213
Murchad 40
Murray, Jim 165
Murray, Mrs 290

Murray, Rev Fr 265
Murray, Thomas 127
Murray, Tommy 165
Murtagh, Harman 92
Muslim 28
Naghton, Mr 247
Nally, Catherine 201
Nash, W.J.258
Naughton, Christopher 182
Nazareth 93
Newcomens 162
Newell, John 140
Newtowncashel 166,199,280,289
Niall Glundubh 33
Niall the Great 12
Nolan, Billie 292
Norman Invaders 10
Normandy 33,49
Normans 12,49
Norsemen 27
North Africa 46
North Sea 28
Northumberland 27
Northumbria 29
Noughaval 12,69,85,126,264
Nugents 104,162
Nuns' island 6,69,89,95,264,271,273
Nut Island 277
O'Beirnes 10
O'Braoins 12
Ó Braonáin, Mícheál
   108,109,163,264,271
O'Breen, Brian 69,193
O'Brien, Muircheartach 47
O'Brien, Murtagh 214
O'Brien, Turlough 44,47
O'Byrne, Tyrlagh 238
O'Callaghan, J. 140
O'Callaghan, Michael 166, 167
O'Carroll Family 162
O'Carroll, Dr Fred 227
O'Carroll, John 227
O'Carroll, Rory 51,215
O'Cleirigh, Cuchocriche 275
O'Clery, Michael 81,94,195,196,275

Rundel and Bridge 244
Rutherford, Mr 114
Saints Island *1901 List* 201, 202
Saints Island 5,23,78,80,98,99,104,
    162,191, 200,204,257,277,289,293
Sand Island 277
Sandys, Major 121
Sankey, Henry 99,201
Sargasso Sea 155
Saxons 26,33
Scally, John 165,168,169,201
Scally, Pat 201,238
Scally, Widow 201
Scandinavia 27
Scattery Island 16,241
Scotland 36
Shanballymore *1901 List* 333
Shanley, Kate 290
Shannon 1,10,12,15,30,32,33,37,42,51
Shannon Harbour 117
Shannon One Design 292
Shannon Pot 1
Shaskeens 112
Shea, Dan 130
Shea, Jimmy 167
Shea, Patrick 130,170
Sheas 172
Shelbourne Hotel 139
Shenglass 112
Shetlands 29
Shine, Sid 140
Sidney, Sir Henry 75,257
Siggins, Albert 229
Siggins, William 229
Sigtrygg Silkbeard 41
Sigurd 41
Sigurd the Stout 40
Sinann 15
Sitric 33
Skally, Patt 113
Skelly, Bernard 290
Skelly, James 288
Skelly, John 294
Slevin Family 264
Slevin, Mary Ann 288

Slevin, Pat 261
Slí an Aifrinn 83
Slieve Aughty 38
Slieve Bawn 1,2,4,10,114,278
Sligo 18,30,83
Smithwick, Capt. 133
Smyth, Alfred P. 34
Smyth, Ralph 259
Smyths 104
Society of Friends 228
Somers, Rev M.203
St Aidan 27,29
St Augustine 46,235
St Barry 16
St Berach 278
St Brigid 232
St Canice 85
St Ciaran 6,7,19,23,86,191,199,203,
    208,240,242,243,248,275
St Colum 208
St Colmcille 26
St Columbanus 27
St Dermot's Well 230
St Diarmaid 16,19,207,210
St Enda 208,240
St Fechin's Church 235
St Finian 19,208,240
St George, Arthur 245
St John's 2,84,108
St John's Point 30
St John's Wood 5,144,145,147
St Kevin 278
St Lioban 257
St Patrick 19,44
St Ríoch 288
St Ruadhan 16,275
St Senan 16,241
St Sinneach 209
St Tighernach 208
Stanley, Thomas 260
Statutes of Kilkenny 67
Stirabout Harbour 113
Stokes, Margaret 248
Stoyte, John 105
Strokestown 10,35,167,246

Strong, L.A.G. 254
Strongbow 52
Stuart, James 80
Stubbs, Captain 123
Sulcóid 38
Swift, Dean 102
Taffe, William 84
Tain 205
Táin Bó Cuailne 13
Tallaght 24
Tamar Mac Ailche 33
Tang 259,289
Tang River 2
Tans 165
Tara 19
Tarmon 16
Tarmonbarry1
Tashinny 209
Teabhtha 12,50
Teach Molaise 18
Teampall Dhiarmada 217,219, 223,225
Teampall Mhuire 221
Teampall Mór 219,221,225
Teampall na Marbh 222
Teampall na mBan 224
Teffia 193
Temple Island 134,135
Temple, Robert H. 134
Templenesgart 78
Tenelick 99
Terryglass 38,208
The Clogas 223
The Faes 75
The Moor 217
The Nook 291
The Pigeons 289
Thomas, Avril 59
Three Jolly Pigeons 127
Threshers 111
Tiernan, Jim 290,292
Tiernan, Kate 290,291
Tipper N.S. 280,282
Tobar Ríoch 230
Toichiuch 243

Tolka 40
Tom Ashe Hall 289
Tonagh 2
Tordelhach 40
Tormey, W.A. 140
Tracy, Margaret 181
Trim 76
Tristernagh, Register of 192
Tuath nElla 33
Tuatha de Danann 15
Tubberclare 93,105,265,274,289, 290,291
Tuite, Richard 54,60
Tuite, Sir Edward 89,93
Tuites 69
Turf House Harbour 258
Turgesius 30,31,32,35,56,212
Turrough 106
Tyrells 69
Ua Braein, Diarmaid 215
Ua Braein, Tipraide 216
Ua Ceithearnaigh, Cinaeth 214
Ua Connmhaigh 257
Ua Duind, Giolla na Naomh 43,214
Uí Máine 10,60
Uisneach 38
Ullard Church 235
Ulster 40
Vallancey, Charles 244
Vikings 13,23,26,30,32,34,40,42,213
Vinnian 23
Viscount Ranelagh 275
Visitatio Regalis 80
Volunteers 165
Vowell, Richard P. 143
Wakeman, W.F. 132
Walderstown 112
Wales 50
Walsh Family 264
Walsh, Jim 261
Walsh, John 261
Walsh, Kate 230
Walsh, Michael 230
Walsh, Paddy 292
Walsh, Thomas 230,292